Drawing the Global Colour Line

In 1900 W. E. B. DuBois prophesied that the colour line would be the key problem of the twentieth-century and he later identified one of its major dynamics: the new religion of whiteness that was sweeping the world. Whereas most historians have confined their studies of race-relations to a national framework, this book offers a pioneering study of the transnational circulation of people and ideas, racial knowledge and technologies that underpinned the construction of self-styled white men's countries from South Africa to North America and Australasia. Marilyn Lake and Henry Reynolds show how in the late nineteenth century and early twentieth century these countries worked in solidarity to exclude those they defined as not-white, actions that provoked a long international struggle for racial equality. Their findings make clear the centrality of struggles around mobility and sovereignty to modern formulations of both race and human rights.

MARILYN LAKE holds a Personal Chair in the School of Historical and European Studies, LaTrobe University, Melbourne. Her publications include *Getting Equal: The History of Australian Feminism* (1999), *Faith: Faith Bandler, Gentle Activist* (2002) and, as co-editor, *Connected Worlds: History in Transnational Perspective* (2006).

HENRY REYNOLDS holds a Personal Chair in History and Aboriginal Studies at the University of Tasmania. His previous publications include *The Other Side of the Frontier* (1981), *Why Weren't We Told?* (2000) and *The Law of the Land* (2003).

T0371455

Critical Perspectives on Empire

Editors

Professor Catherine Hall
University College London

Professor Mrinalini Sinha
Pennsylvania State University

Professor Kathleen Wilson
State University of New York, Stony Brook

Critical Perspectives on Empire is a major new series of ambitious, cross-disciplinary works in the emerging field of critical imperial studies. Books in the series will explore the connections, exchanges and mediations at the heart of national and global histories, the contributions of local as well as metropolitan knowledge, and the flows of people, ideas and identities facilitated by colonial contact. To that end, the series will not only offer a space for outstanding scholars working at the intersection of several disciplines to bring to wider attention the impact of their work; it will also take a leading role in reconfiguring contemporary historical and critical knowledge, of the past and of ourselves.

Drawing the Global Colour Line

White Men's Countries and the International Challenge of Racial Equality

Marilyn Lake

La Trobe University, Melbourne

and

Henry Reynolds

University of Tasmania

CAMBRIDGE
UNIVERSITY PRESS

CAMBRIDGE UNIVERSITY PRESS
Cambridge, New York, Melbourne, Madrid, Cape Town,
Singapore, São Paulo, Delhi, Mexico City

Cambridge University Press
The Edinburgh Building, Cambridge CB2 8RU, UK

Published in the United States of America by Cambridge University Press, New York

www.cambridge.org
Information on this title: www.cambridge.org/9780521707527

First published 2008
Third printing 2011

A catalogue record for this publication is available from the British Library

ISBN 978-0-521-88118-0 Hardback
ISBN 978-0-521-70752-7 Paperback

For our children:

Katherine and Jessica

and

John, Anna and Rebecca

Contents

Acknowledgments

This book has built on the scholarship of many historians, over many years, in many countries, whose published work we have acknowledged, as much as practicable, in the text and endnotes. We are grateful, too, for the helpful reports from the readers and editors at Cambridge University Press and Melbourne University Press and for the painstaking work of our literary agent, Lyn Tranter.

This book has been many years in the making and we thank each other for commitment, forbearance, good humour and dedication to what turned out to be a very much larger project than first imagined. We also wish to thank more particularly research assistants, colleagues, family and friends, funding authorities, and the staff of archives and libraries.

Marilyn Lake

I would like to give special acknowledgment to the work of my research assistants – Natasha Campo, Nikki Henningham, Tim Jones, Jemima Mowbray and Amanda Rasmussen – whose imagination and conscientiousness have made such an important contribution to the extensive research on which this book is based. I would also like to thank La Trobe University and the Australian Research Council, whose generous funding made possible the employment of research assistance and my own research trips throughout Australia and to Singapore, the United States and the United Kingdom. Just as important was the opportunity to write full-time provided by the award of a five-year Australian Professorial Fellowship.

Archivists and librarians have been invariably helpful and often in advance of my visits: I wish to note in particular the assistance of the staff at the Bancroft Library at the University of California, Berkeley; the US National Archives at College Park; Harvard University Archives; the Houghton and Law Libraries at Harvard University; the New York Public Library; the Bodleian Library at Oxford University; the UK National Archives; the National Archives at Singapore; the National

Library of Australia; the University of Tasmania Archives; and the State Libraries of New South Wales and Victoria.

I am also deeply grateful for the responsiveness and suggestions of audiences of early drafts of particular chapters presented at the Australian National University, Columbia University, Harvard University, the University of Maryland, the Institute for Historical Research at the University of London, La Trobe University, the University of Queensland and the University of Sydney, and at conferences of the American Historical Association, the Australian Historical Association, the International Congress of Historical Sciences, the European Social Sciences History Association and the World History Association. For conversation, comment and advice, about different chapters and related themes, and in many cases for their generous hospitality, I thank David Armitage, Evelyn Brooks Higginbotham, Nancy Cott, Ann Curthoys, Graeme Davison, Desley Deacon, John Fitzgerald, Laura Frader, David Goodman, Catherine Hall, Stuart Hall, John Hirst, Jon Hyslop, Akira Iriye, Alice Kessler-Harris, Stuart Macintyre, Adam McKeown, Sonya Michel, Amanda Rasmussen, Bill Schwarz, Mrinalini Sinha and Henry Yu.

Finally, but foremost, I thank my husband Sam, whose company at Harvard, in New York and in San Francisco, added so much to the enjoyment of the research and whose early gift of a first edition copy of Charles Pearson's *National Life and Character: A Forecast* was foundational in many ways to the conception of the project. His work as an engaged intellectual has made possible my own. Our girls, Kath and Jess, have, as always, been my inspiration.

Henry Reynolds

While writing and researching this book I was supported by an Australian Research Council Professorial Research Fellowship and a Senior Writer's Fellowship granted by the Literature Board of The Australia Council. I also received the support of the Faculty of Arts and the School of History and Classics at the University of Tasmania. Elizabeth Foxcroft provided valuable help in preparing my contribution to the final manuscript.

With such wide-ranging research I owe thanks to the staff of many institutions including the National Library of Australia; the Public Library of New South Wales; the Tasmanian Parliamentary Library; the British Library and the UK National Archives; the Bodleian Library and Rhodes House in Oxford; the libraries of the United Nations, the League of Nations and the International Labor Organization in Geneva; and the New York Public Library.

As ever, I give my thanks to Margaret and our family for being great supporters of my intellectual and political projects.

Introduction

In 1910, in an article published in a New York journal, the *Independent*, called 'The Souls of White Folk', W. E. B. DuBois, the distinguished black American historian and activist, wrote about his perception of a sudden change of consciousness sweeping the world: 'the world, in a sudden emotional conversion, has discovered that it is white, and, by that token, wonderful'. Suddenly, white folks had become 'painfully conscious of their whiteness', 'the paleness of their bodily skins . . . fraught with tremendous and eternal significance'.[1]

At the meeting of the Pan-African Congress, in London, in 1900, DuBois had memorably declared that the problem of the twentieth century was the 'problem of the color line', an observation that he elaborated in the path-breaking collection of essays called *The Souls of Black Folk*, published in 1903. In the best-known essay, first printed in *Atlantic Monthly* as 'Strivings of the Negro People', DuBois famously defined the condition of the African-American in terms of 'his two-ness – an American, a Negro: two souls, two thoughts, two unreconciled strivings'.[2] White America, he insisted, had a black history of injustice, struggle and unmet longing: 'The history of the American Negro is the history of this strife – this longing to attain self-conscious manhood, to merge his double self into a better and truer self.'[3]

The Souls of Black Folk has been described by an American historian, David Blight, as 'an extended meditation on racial prejudice, political leadership, the economic oppression of black labourers in the South, and the development of African American culture both before and after emancipation'.[4] Historians of the United States now rightly recognise

---

[1] W. E. B. DuBois, 'The Souls of White Folk', *Independent* (18 August 1910) p.339; this essay was re-published in a revised form in W. E. B. DuBois, *Darkwater, Voices from within the Veil* (New York, Harcourt, Brace and Howe, 1920).

[2] David Levering Lewis, *W. E. B. DuBois: Biography of a Race 1868–1919* (New York, Henry Holt, 1994) vol.1, pp.279–382.

[3] *Ibid.* p.281.

[4] David Blight, *Race and Reunion: The Civil War in American Memory* (Cambridge, Belknap, 2001), p.251.

1

this to be a work of key significance in their national history, but DuBois was also, already, keenly aware of the global dimension of the colour line, which he had defined, in 1900, as 'the relation of the darker to the lighter races of men in Asia and Africa, in America and the islands of the sea'.[5] By 1910, it was also clear to DuBois that the problem of the colour line was the problem of what he called 'whiteness', which had recently acquired the force of a charismatic religion: 'Wave upon wave, each with increasing virulence, is dashing this new religion of whiteness on the shores of our time.'[6]

DuBois saw in this tidal wave of whiteness a new, modern, phenomenon. To be sure, colour consciousness had been present in earlier ages, but 'the discovery of personal whiteness among the world's peoples is a very modern thing – a nineteenth and twentieth century matter, indeed'. Whiteness provided a mode of subjective identification that crossed national borders and shaped global politics. 'What is whiteness', DuBois wondered, 'that one should so desire it?' Whiteness, he realised, was fundamentally proprietorial: 'Whiteness is the ownership of the earth forever and ever, Amen.'[7]

This book argues, following DuBois, that the assertion of whiteness was born in the apprehension of imminent loss. Seeking a reason for white folks' sudden stridency, DuBois noted that around the world, colonised and coloured peoples were everywhere in revolt: 'Do we sense somnolent writhings in black Africa, or angry groans in India, or triumphant "Banzais" in Japan? "To your tents, O Israel!" these nations are not white. Build warships and heft the "Big Stick".'[8]

It was the United States president, Theodore Roosevelt, who had advocated the diplomacy of speaking softly and carrying a big stick in response to the triumphant Japanese, whose spectacular naval victory over Russia, in 1905, had deeply dismayed white men, but galvanised colonised peoples everywhere, from Africa, to Asia, to the Americas. In a bid to intimidate Japan, Roosevelt had despatched the United States fleet on a tour of the Pacific Ocean. Its rapturous reception by Australians, in Sydney and Melbourne, was reported in a long article in the New York *Independent*, the same journal that would publish 'The Souls of White Folk'. 'It is delightful to us to say', an Australian journalist, W. R. Charlton, told his New York readers, 'whether it be delusion, half-truth or the truth-absolute – that the Americans are our kinsmen, blood of our blood, bone of our bone, and one with us in our ideals of the brotherhood of man.'[9] We can probably assume that DuBois, by then living in

---

[5] Lewis, *W. E. B. DuBois*, p.283.   [6] DuBois, 'The Souls of White Folk', p.339.
[7] *Ibid*. p.339.   [8] *Ibid*. p.340.
[9] W. R. Charlton, 'The Australian Welcome to the Fleet', *Independent* (8 October 1908) p.815.

New York, was one of Charlton's readers. Perhaps he also read reports of the press luncheon in Sydney, where Rear Admiral Sperry had greeted his gratified hosts as a 'white man to white men, and may I add, very white men'.[10]

This book charts the spread of 'whiteness' as a transnational form of racial identification, that was, as DuBois noticed, at once global in its power and personal in its meaning, the basis of geo-political alliances and a subjective sense of self. The emergence of self-styled 'white men's countries' represented whiteness in defensive, but defiant, mode, a response to the rising power of what Charles Pearson, a Liberal politician in the colonial parliament of Victoria, had named, in *National Life and Character: A Forecast*, 'the black and yellow races'.[11] Pearson's prophecy challenged imperial complacency, but as one of his London reviewers noted, Pearson wrote from a different vantage point in the world:

> The reader can indeed discern that Mr Pearson's point of view is not London or Paris, but Melbourne. He regards the march of affairs from the Australian point of view, and next to Australia what he seems to see most clearly is the growth of Chinese power and of the native populations of Africa. In this forecast, in fact, Europe loses altogether the precedence it has always enjoyed. It appears here as not only the smallest, but as the least important continent.[12]

In his arresting commentary on changing world forces, Pearson was indeed, to use Dipesh Chakrabarty's phrase, 'provincialising Europe'.[13]

Pearson's apprehension of a postcolonial world in which white men would be 'elbowed and hustled, and perhaps even thrust aside' by peoples whom they looked down upon as servile, set alarm bells ringing around the globe. In his own alarmist tract, *The Rising Tide of Color*, published nearly two decades later, an American, Lothrop Stoddard, paid tribute to Pearson's book as 'epoch-making' and hailed the 'lusty young Anglo-Saxon communities bordering the Pacific – Australia, New Zealand, British Columbia, and our own "coast" as pace-setters in declaring themselves "All White"'. Nor were their policies separate developments. 'Nothing was more striking', Stoddard noted, 'than the instinctive and instantaneous solidarity which binds together Australians and Afrikanders, Californians and Canadians, into a "sacred Union" at the mere whisper of Asiatic immigration'.[14] Stoddard was lobbying for what would become the Johnson Act of 1924, which has usually been

[10] *Age* (27 August 1908).
[11] Charles Pearson, *National Life and Character: A Forecast* (London, Macmillan, 1893).
[12] *Athenaeum* (4 March 1893).
[13] Dipesh Chakrabarty, *Provincialising Europe: Postcolonial Thought and Historical Difference* (Princeton, Princeton University Press, 2000).
[14] Lothrop Stoddard, *The Rising Tide of Color: Against White World Supremacy* (New York, Charles Scribner's Sons, 1923) p.281.

understood within the framework of US national history, but is better illuminated when placed in the larger frame of the transnational solidarities of which Stoddard himself wrote.

In recent scholarship, 'whiteness studies' have emerged as a productive new field of historical enquiry, but most investigations have conceptualised their subject within a national frame of analysis, identifying local dynamics at work within histories deemed distinctive or even exceptional.[15] Studies that now acknowledge the necessity for a global context still confine their own analyses within a national interpretative frame and that has been especially the case with United States scholarship.[16] But, as DuBois and contemporaries on the other side of the colour line saw clearly, the emergence of the 'new religion' of whiteness was a transnational phenomenon and all the more powerful for that, inspiring in turn the formation of international movements of resistance, such as the pan-African and pan-Asian alliances that threatened to bring about the very challenge to their world dominion that white men feared.[17]

In *Drawing the Global Colour Line*, we trace the transnational circulation of emotions and ideas, people and publications, racial knowledge and technologies that animated white men's countries and their strategies of exclusion, deportation and segregation, in particular, the deployment of those state-based instruments of surveillance, the census, the passport and the literacy test. The project of whiteness was thus a paradoxical politics, at once transnational in its inspiration and identifications but nationalist in its methods and goals. The imagined community of white men was transnational in its reach, but nationalist in its outcomes, bolstering regimes of border protection and national sovereignty. A project that took shape in international conversations about inter-racial encounters increased isolationism. Thus one somewhat dismayed observer was moved to describe the Commonwealth of Australia as a 'Hermit Democracy', cutting itself off from all international intercourse.[18]

---

[15] On 'whiteness' see, for example, Ruth Frankenberg, *White Women, Race Matters: The Social Construction of Whiteness* (Minneapolis, University of Minnesota Press, 1993); David Roideger, *The Wages of Whiteness: Race and the Making of the American Working Class* (London, Verso, 1991); Matthew Frye Jacobson, *Whiteness of a Different Color: European Immigrants and the Alchemy of Race* (Cambridge, Harvard University Press, 1999); Aileen Moreton-Robinson, *Talkin' Up to the White Woman: Indigenous Women and Feminism* (St Lucia, University of Queensland Press, 2000). On the influence of external ideas on national formations see, for example, Russell McGregor, *Imagined Destinies: Aboriginal Australians and the Doomed Race Theory, 1880–1939* (Melbourne, Melbourne University Press, 1989).

[16] See, for example, Mae N. Ngai, *Impossible Subjects: Illegal Aliens and the Making of Modern America* (Princeton, Princeton University Press, 2004).

[17] Viator, 'Asia Contra Mundum', *Fortnightly Review* (1 February 1908) p.200.

[18] 'Australian Ideals', *The Times* (5 September 1908), Deakin papers 1540/15/2567 National Library of Australia (NLA).

In drawing the global colour line, immigration restriction became a version of racial segregation on an international scale, as Lothrop Stoddard memorably stated. Not surprisingly, the education or literacy test, first used to disenfranchise black voters in Mississippi in 1890, also became the basis of United States immigration restriction laws, promoted by Anglo-Saxonists such as Henry Cabot Lodge and the members of the Boston-based Immigration Restriction League, legislation which served in turn as a model for Natal and the other British Dominions. The republican origins of the literacy test as an instrument of racial exclusion were significant. In dividing the world into white and not-white it helped render the imperial non-racial status of British subjects increasingly irrelevant and provided a direct challenge to the imperial assertion that the Empire recognised no distinction on the basis of colour or race, that all subjects were alike subjects of the Crown. This book is also, then, about the British betrayal of the idea of imperial citizenship.

Histories of immigration policy, like studies of whiteness, have usually been told as self-contained national stories, their dynamics located in distinctive local reactions against particular groups of foreign immigrants – whether Chinese, Indian, Islanders, Japanese, Jews or southern Europeans. Some historical studies have, to be sure, identified parallel developments in Australasia, British Columbia and New Zealand and on the west coast of the United States.[19] Usually, however, their stories have remained parallel, rather than dynamically inter-connected and thus mutually formative. What most histories have tended to miss is what DuBois could see clearly, that is, the significance of racial identifications to the constitution of modern political subjectivities and ways of being in the world, in a process that shaped white men's sense of collective belonging to a larger community, joined together by what Theodore Roosevelt always liked to call 'fellow feeling'.[20]

In his influential book, *Imagined Communities*, Benedict Anderson defined nations as 'imagined communities' in the sense that they were composed of individuals who, though they might never meet face to face, came to identify with their compatriots and believed themselves to hold certain values, myths and outlooks in common. At the core of this process of identification was the cultural and historical imagination, its key

---

[19] See, for example, Charles Price, *The Great White Walls Are Built: Restrictive Immigration to North America and Australasia, 1836–1888* (Canberra, ANU Press, 1974); Robert A. Huttenback, *Racism and Empire: White Settlers and Coloured Immigrants in the British Self-Governing Colonies 1830–1910* (Ithaca, Cornell University Press, 1976); Andrew Markus, *Fear and Hatred: Purifying Australia and California 1850–1901* (Sydney, Hale and Iremonger, 1979).

[20] See Theodore Roosevelt, 'Fellow Feeling as a Political Factor', in Theodore Roosevelt, *The Strenuous Life: Essays and Addresses* (London, Grant Richards, 1902) pp.71–87.

instruments the novel and newspaper. Anderson stressed the affective, as well as the imaginary, dimension of national identification, which he imagined, significantly, as 'fraternal'.[21] Paradoxically, one outcome of Anderson's argument has been to naturalise the nation as *the* imagined community of modern times, an effect that has obscured the ascendancy of transnational racial identifications and their potency in shaping both personal identity and global politics. This book seeks to elucidate the dynamics and effects of a transnational project that sought, in effect, dominance over four continents, an ambition that led one commentator to warn that the new solidarity of white men would drive Chinese and Indians into an unprecedented pan-Asiatic alliance, led by Japan, that would ultimately see the eclipse of Western civilisation.[22]

The idea of the 'white man's country' emerged in the context of nineteenth-century imperialisms and the great modern migrations that saw some 50 million Chinese, the same number of Europeans and about 30 million Indians migrate to new homes around the world. A large proportion of these voyagers went to South Africa, the Americas and Australasia, to lands taken by force from their Indigenous inhabitants, who were systematically displaced or destroyed. Migration rested on and required Aboriginal dispossession.

White men claimed a special right to lands in the 'temperate zone', claims made against their Indigenous inhabitants and all those peoples they would designate as 'not-white', including Afghans, Chinese, Indians, Japanese, Sryrians and Pacific Islanders. Though recently established, white men's countries sought legitimacy through locating themselves in the long tradition of Anglo-Saxon race history that dated back to the mythic glories of Hengist and Horsa. They shared an English-speaking culture and newly ascendant democratic politics, priding themselves, as Anglo-Saxons, on a distinctive capacity, indeed a genius, for self-government. It was their commitment to democratic equality that made racial homogeneity seem imperative. In the tradition of J. S. Mill, they argued that democracy could only survive in the absence of distinctions of caste and colour.

White men's countries rested on the premise that multiracial democracy was an impossibility: this was the key history lesson learnt from the great tragedy of Radical Reconstruction in the United States, propounded by numerous writers including the British Liberal politician and historian, James Bryce, whose *American Commonwealth* was taken up as

---

[21] Benedict Anderson, *Imagined Communities: Reflections on the Origins and Spread of Nationalism* (revised edition, London, Verso, 1991).
[22] Viator, 'Asia Contra Mundum', p.200.

a 'Bible' by white nation-builders in Australia and South Africa.[23] Bryce also wrote about the countries of Latin America, which were ineligible for membership of the white men's club: their Spanish or Portuguese ancestry, their mixed-coloured populations and political instability were regarded as regrettable, but related, disqualifications, regardless of their own aspirations.

White men's countries emerged in the radical challenge posed by democracy and trade unionism to hereditary aristocratic privilege. This was an age when 'glorious manhood asserts its elevation', in the words of New South Wales republican poet, Daniel Deniehy, when pride of manhood found expression in pride of race to enshrine the white man as the model democrat. In the New World encounters of diverse peoples, the masculine democracies of North America and Australasia defined their identity and rights in racial terms: the right of Anglo-Saxons to self-government and the commitment of white workers to high wages and conditions, against those they saw as undermining their new-found status, whether they be aristocrats or 'coolies'. In their social and political experiments in equality – and with 'state socialism' in Australasia – they were utopian in their modernist vision.

When glorious manhood asserted its elevation, white men monopolised the status of manhood itself. Coolies, Islanders, Asiatics and Blacks were cast as not simply deficient as workers, colonists and citizens, but also as men. They were docile, servile, dependent, unfree. Hence, the struggles of coloured and colonised men to achieve recognition, or restitution, of their manhood as well as national independence. For example, Indian nationalists, such as Lajpat Rai, frequently charged that British rule was 'sapping our manhood ... polluting the very foundations of our manhood', while DuBois told the Universal Races Congress, in 1911, that 'the present Negro problem of America' was 'whether at last the Negro will gain full recognition as a man'.[24]

Chinese and Japanese campaigns for an end to racial discrimination were, on the other hand, more likely to invoke the equality of nations enshrined in international law. When Lowe Kong Meng, Cheok Hong Cheong and Louis Ah Mouy, the authors of *The Chinese Question in Australia*, cited the 'illustrious Vattel' and other authorities on the equality of

[23] James Bryce, *The American Commonwealth* (New York, Macmillan, 1888).

[24] *Nationalities and Subject Races Conference Report* (London, King and Son, 1910) pp.27–8; W. E. B. DuBois, 'The Negro Race in the United States of America', in G. Spiller (ed.), *Inter-Racial Problems* (London, King and Son, 1911) p.364. See also Mrinalini Sinha, *Colonial Masculinity: The 'Manly Englishman' and the 'Effeminate Bengali' in the Late Nineteenth Century* (Manchester and New York, Manchester University Press, 1995); Radhika Mongia, 'Gender and the Historiography of Gandhian Satyagraha in South Africa', *Gender and History* (vol.18, 1, April 2006).

sovereign nations and their obligations of reciprocity under international law, local Australian democrats responded by insisting on their sovereign right to self-government, to say who could or couldn't join their political community.[25] Against the sovereignty of nations, or emperors, white men invoked the status of the elevated sovereign masculine subject.[26] International treaties, guaranteeing freedom of movement, were attacked precisely for detracting from the sovereignty of autonomous self-governing men.

Immigration restriction became the quintessential expression of the masculine sovereignty of 'self-governing communities', a popular formulation that worked to collapse the distinction between independent republics and British colonies, thereby recasting the meaning of sovereignty itself. 'It should be stated', the San Francisco *Daily Evening Bulletin* advised its readers, 'that the six separate Australian colonies, though nominally under British rule, are practically, each of them, separate republics, electing their own legislatures by universal suffrage, levying and expending their own revenues, and each one of them separately making their own laws'. In aristocratic societies, such as China, treaties might be maintained against popular wishes, advised the editor, but not so in Australia or America, where 'the power of the people' was supreme.[27]

In Australia, Alfred Deakin constantly intoned the mantra of Victorian and later, Australian self-government against Colonial Office interference and presumption. In 1908, he provocatively praised Theodore Roosevelt's leadership in discharging his responsibilities 'to the lasting benefit of your fellow citizens of the United States and of all self-governing people, especially this new Commonwealth of Australia', the national name chosen precisely for its American republican resonances.[28] The figure of the 'white man', in whose name white men's countries were forged, was produced in a convergence of imperial and republican discourse that found political expression in the late nineteenth century in talk of an Anglo-American alliance. Previous studies have charted racial discourse across the British Empire or drawn attention to the links between the anti-Chinese policies of California and the Australian colonies, but few have analysed the inter-relationship of British and American racial regimes in

---

[25] Lowe Kong Meng, Cheok Hong Cheong and Louis Ah Mouy, *The Chinese Question in Australia 1878–79* (Melbourne, F. F. Bailliere, 1879) p.28.

[26] See James L. Hevia, *English Lessons: The Pedagogy of Imperialism in Nineteenth-Century China* (Durham, Duke University Press, 2004) p.103.

[27] *Daily Evening Bulletin* (10 April, 29 July 1878).

[28] Deakin to Roosevelt, Deakin papers, NLA, MS 1540/15/3909). For the American associations of 'Commonwealth', see Marilyn Lake '"The Brightness of Eyes and Quiet Assurance Which Seem to Say American", Alfred Deakin's Identification with Republican Manhood', *Australian Historical Studies*, 129 (April 2007).

the same analytical frame.[29] Yet, crucially, the idea of the 'white man's country' crossed and collapsed the imperial/republican divide, drawing on the discursive resources of both traditions to enshrine the dichotomy of white and not-white. The British Empire drew a distinction between ruling and ruled races; republican ideology drew a distinction between races fit and not fit for self-government. United States naturalisation law rested on the dichotomy of white and not-white.

In the figure of the white man, the imperialist became a democrat and the democrat an imperialist. The Australian prime minister, Alfred Deakin, commended the statement of the New Zealand prime minister, Richard Seddon, about the British Empire:

> though united in the whole, [the Empire] is, nevertheless, divided broadly in to two parts, one occupied wholly or mainly by a white ruling race, the other principally occupied by coloured races who are ruled. Australia and New Zealand are determined to keep their place in the first class.[30]

When writing about the necessity of American rule in the Philippines in *The Strenuous Life*, Theodore Roosevelt pointed to the composition of the population: 'half-caste and native Christians, warlike Moslems, and wild pagans. Many of their people are utterly unfit for self-government, and show no signs of becoming fit. Others may in time become fit, but at present can only take part in self-government under a wise supervision, at once firm and beneficent.'[31]

One indicator of the global ascendancy of the politics of whiteness was its ability to recast the previous multiplicity of nations, races and religions – Aryan, Caucasian, Chinese, Hindus, Kanakas, Islanders, Malays, Blacks, Lascars, Moslems, Japanese – in binary terms as 'white' or 'not-white'. English-speaking countries were pace-setters in this regard. Thus, in 1902, the French government wrote to the British Foreign Office to enquire whether the Japanese should be categorised as white or not-white.[32] Japan considered their categorisation as not-white a grievous injury: 'The Japanese belong to an Empire whose standard of civilization is so much higher than that of Kanakas, Negroes, Pacific Islanders, Indians or other Eastern peoples, that to refer to them in the same terms cannot but be regarded in the light of a reproach, which is hardly warranted by the fact of the shade of the national complexion', wrote the

---

[29] For a recent exception see Paul A. Kramer, *The Blood of Government: Race, Empire, the United States and the Philippines* (Chapel Hill, University of North Carolina Press, 2006).
[30] *Morning Post* (28 May 1906), in J. A. LaNauze (ed.), *Federated Australia: Selections from Letters to the Morning Post 1900-1910* (Melbourne, Melbourne University Press, 1968).
[31] Roosevelt, *The Strenuous Life*, p.9.
[32] Foreign Office to Colonial Office, Enclosure, M. Cambon to Lansdowne, 24 September 1902. CO 885/8/1.

Japanese consul in Sydney to the Australian government in 1901.[33] Again, as DuBois noted, the effect of the dichotomy of white and not-white was to say that not-white was 'nothing'.[34]

Recent postcolonial scholarship has established the importance of viewing metropolitan and colonial formations within the same analytical frame. In our study, the binary of metropole and colony – like Europe itself – loses its analytical primacy, as we trace the circulation of knowledges and the production of identities in formative encounters in New World communities bordering the Indian and Pacific oceans, in relations between Asian powers and white men's governments, between Indian and South African imperial subjects, in Durban and London, between an American philosopher and an Australian political leader in the Blue Mountains in New South Wales, between republican citizens and British colonists in Vancouver, Seattle and Washington. Our book explores the influence of key thinkers and political leaders, such as Charles Pearson, James Bryce, Lowe Kong Meng, Theodore Roosevelt, W. E. B. DuBois, M. K. Gandhi, Tokutomi Soho, W. M. Hughes and Jan Smuts. We look at the discursive frameworks that shaped race thinking and justified racial exclusion, as well as the diverse ways in which the peoples thus excluded argued the injustice of what one Chinese diplomat at the Universal Races Congress in 1911 called the 'White Policy'.

White racism was attacked on different grounds, from different vantage points, with critics drawing on different discursive resources. They variously quoted international law, cited the equality of imperial subjects, the principle of racial equality, the rights of man(hood) and the idea of non-discrimination. They organised international conferences, such as the Universal Races Congress, formed pan-African and pan-Asian movements and called for international covenants on racial equality and human rights. Importantly, international campaigns for racial equality and human rights often began as a response to the barriers to mobility and other racial discriminations enacted by New World democracies in the nineteenth century. In charting these demands our book suggests a new genealogy of human rights. It also points to the importance of the diasporic experience of Chinese and Indian colonists, patriots in exile such as Gandhi and Sun Yat Sen, in shaping nationalist agendas.

Nineteenth-century commentators were preoccupied with the implications and consequences of the unprecedented encounters of diverse peoples, made possible by new steam-powered transport technologies that,

---

[33] Eitaki to Prime Minister Edmund Barton, 3 May 1901, CO 418/10, UK National Archives.
[34] DuBois, 'The Souls of White Folk', p.339.

in James Bryce's words, had the effect of 'making the world small'.[35] In his influential Romanes lecture, published in 1902, Bryce argued that the far closer and more widespread contact of peoples in modern times, 'in particular of the more advanced and civilized races with the more backward', was so fraught with danger 'that it may be deemed to mark a crisis in the history of the world, which will profoundly affect the destiny of mankind'.[36] Writing from the other side of the colour line, DuBois shared this sense of urgency. In 1910, he joined other members of the newly established National Association for the Advancement of Colored People, to found a magazine they named *Crisis*. 'It takes its name', declared the first editorial, 'from the fact that it is a critical time in the history of the advancement of man.'[37] This book explains that sense of historical crisis and the political struggles that defined, or attempted to erase, the global colour line.

One outcome of the political mobilisation of white men was the increasing dissension within the British Empire between self-governing white Dominions and the imperial subjects of India, a conflict that ultimately forced British political leaders, threatened by the prospect of the United States assuming leadership of a new white men's alliance, to 'come out', as it were, as 'white'. By 1919, at the Paris Peace conference, the leaders of the British delegation, the arisocratic A. J. Balfour and Lord Robert Cecil, followed their fellow white men – the alliance of the United States, Australia, South Africa, New Zealand and Canada – in defeating Japan's bid to have a racial equality clause included in the Covenant of the League of Nations. In support of their position, Balfour declared that he did not believe in the eighteenth-century proposition that 'all men are created equal': 'He believed it was true in a certain sense that all men of a particular nation were created equal, but not that a man in Central Africa was created equal to a European.'[38]

Following the Second World War, in which Japan vanquished the British fortress at Singapore and sent bombing raids over Hawaii and Australia, the conferences called to establish the United Nations and draw up a Universal Declaration of Human Rights, chose to frame their conception of human rights, not in terms of the equality of nations or races, as Japan had proposed twenty years earlier, but in the French and

[35] James Bryce, 'The Relations of History and Geography', *Contemporary Review* (Jan–Jun 1886) p.442.
[36] James Bryce, *The Relations of the Advanced and the Backward Races of Mankind*, Romanes lectures (Oxford, Clarendon Press, 1902) pp.6–7.
[37] Editorial, 'The Crisis: A Record of the Darker Races', *Crisis* (vol.1, 1910).
[38] Quoted in David Hunter Miller, *The Drafting of the Covenant*, cited in David Armitage, *The Declaration of Independence: A Global History* (Cambridge, Harvard University Press, 2007) p.276.

American traditions of the rights of individuals and the principle of non-discrimination, enunciated in 1929 by the Institut de Droit International. Still, two decades would pass before the erstwhile white men's countries moved, in response to concerted domestic and international pressure, to abolish racially discriminatory immigration policies and outlaw racial segregation within their borders. As the recent experience of asylum seekers and refugees attests, this process is not yet complete.

Old fears now return in new forms. James Bryce's anxiety about the 'world made small', about the consequences of mobility and the unprecedented encounters of different peoples, re-awakens. The United States plans to build a fence along its Mexican border, Australia imprisons asylum seekers on offshore islands and riots engulf French cities that are home to thousands of Muslim immigrants from Africa. As Europe is drawn into the New World so multiculturalism loses its appeal in countries with immigrant minorities; everywhere there is renewed talk about national values, social cohesion and the necessity of border protection. In Iraq, the United States, Britain and Australia fight together in a 'coalition of the willing' that recapitulates the Anglo-Saxon solidarity of earlier times with devastating consequences. This book charts the emergence of the transnational community of white men in the globalised world of the late nineteenth century.

Part 1

Modern mobilities

1 The coming man: Chinese migration to the goldfields

Lowe Kong Meng arrives in Melbourne to find prosperity and prejudice

In 1853, Lowe Kong Meng, a young Chinese merchant and master of his own ship, arrived in the port of Melbourne, in the British colony of Victoria, carrying cargo from Mauritius. Gold had been discovered in the colony just two years earlier and the rush to be rich had begun. Immigrants poured in from around the world. The area around Melbourne was the traditional country of the Kulin people, but British settlers arriving across Bass Strait in 1835, proceeded, on the basis of a dubious treaty with the traditional owners, to occupy the land along the Yarra River and the rich pastoral country that lay beyond.

Within a couple of decades, local Indigenous communities were overwhelmed by the disease, dispossession and violence that accompanied colonial settlement. Survivors living near Melbourne were forced to reside on the swampland on the outskirts of the bustling new city. The logic of settler colonialism invariably meant displacement, if not extermination, of Indigenous peoples.[1] British colonists assumed a right of entitlement secured by the imperial relations of racial domination.

Melbourne residents had celebrated their separation from New South Wales with the passage of the Australian Colonies Government Act in 1850; with extensive rolling pastures and fertile agricultural land the colony's future looked assured. Then the discovery of vast new mineral wealth attracted hundreds of thousands of fortune-seekers, including merchants and traders, like Lowe Kong Meng, who were keen to provide goods and services to the rapidly expanding market. In just three years, between 1850 and 1853, the Victorian population quadrupled, shipping increased sevenfold and the value of imports twentyfold.[2]

---

[1] See Patrick Wolfe, 'Settler Colonialism and the Elimination of the Native', *Journal of Genocide Research* 8(4) (2006) pp.387–409.
[2] L. G. Churchward, *Australia and America: An Alternative History* (Sydney, Alternative Publishing Cooperative, 1979) p.52.

The United States joined Great Britain as a major source of imports and immigrants. In the year Lowe Kong Meng sailed into the port of Melbourne, 143 American ships anchored in Hobson's Bay and 40 per cent of imports came from the United States. American merchants, including George Francis Train, formerly a Boston shipping agent, helped revive the ailing Chamber of Commerce. Melbourne, he declared, 'though situated so far out of the way, cannot fail to be a great city'.[3]

Lowe Kong Meng also saw great commercial opportunities in this southern outpost, and for Chinese merchants, Australia was not so far out of the way. Though only twenty two years of age, Lowe Kong Meng was already a successful businessman, trading between Mauritius and Calcutta (Kolkata) in the Indian Ocean and Singapore and Canton (Guangzhou) in the South China Sea. After a brief tour of inspection of the goldfields, he departed for India, returning the following year with fresh merchandise, with which he set up shop. Kong Meng & Co. sold tea and other provisions from a building in Little Bourke Street, in the heart of Melbourne's Chinatown. Like several thousand other Chinese who arrived in the Australian colonies that year, Lowe Kong Meng came and went freely; no-one asked for papers or passport or proof of naturalisation.

Born in the Straits Settlements to Lowe A Quee, a merchant, and his wife, Chew Tay, Lowe Kong Meng was a British subject whose forbears, like the majority of Chinese who would seek gold in Victoria, came from the Sze Yap district near the port of Canton, long a centre of Arab, Malay, Siamese and European shipping and trade. Educated in Penang and Mauritius, Lowe Kong Meng was well read in world literature and could speak English and French fluently. A loyal son of the Sze Yap district, he was also a man of the world and an exponent of what he would call 'cosmopolitan friendship and sympathy'.[4] His sympathies only stretched so far, however. Family legend had it that on one occasion, when accosted on the goldfields by a ruffian, who addressed him in pidgin, he explained that he would be very pleased to converse in French, Chinese or English, but that he did not understand his assailant's peculiar lingo.[5]

Many languages, dialects and accents could be heard among the 'colourful medley of polyglot nationalities' that mingled on the

---

[3] G. Francis Train, *An American Merchant in Europe, Asia and Australasia*, quoted in Norman Harper (ed.) *Australia and the United States* (Melbourne, Nelson, 1971) p.22.
[4] Lowe Kong Meng, Cheok Hong Cheong and Louis Ah Mouy, *The Chinese Question in Australia 1878–79* (Melbourne, F. F. Bailliere, 1879) p.30.
[5] Isaac Selby, *The Old Pioneer's Memorial History of Melbourne: From the Discovery of Port Phillip Down to the World War* (Melbourne, Old Pioneer Memorial Fund, 1924) p.147.

Victorian goldfields in the 1850s.[6] Hundreds of thousands of people arrived from all over the world. By the end of the decade, the population of the colony had increased fivefold. Most newcomers sailed from Europe, the majority from Britain and Ireland, but there were also large numbers of Germans at the diggings and smaller groups of French and Italians, including Carboni Raffaello, whose book, *The Eureka Stockade*, provided one of the most lively accounts of goldfields politics.[7] The Swiss miners concentrated at Daylesford, while Scandinavians supported their own club and newspaper at Ballarat. Several thousand goldseekers also crossed the Pacific from California, where gold had been discovered in 1849. Many Australian prospectors lured to the Californian goldfields now returned. These were mobile, multicultural and largely masculine communities.

The Victorian goldfields, like those on the west coast of the United States, New South Wales and, later, Queensland, also attracted thousands of Chinese fortune-seekers keen to share in the bonanza. By 1852, according to the United States census, there were 25,000 Chinese miners in California, and, as in the case of Victoria, nearly all came from Guangdong Province.[8] During 1852 and 1853, a few hundred arrived in Victoria, then the number quickly increased, with around 10,000 Chinese landing in Melbourne in 1854. Most of those who left Canton for Victoria in the early 1850s were farmers and traders, mostly literate and with some money of their own.[9] Others made use of the so-called credit-ticket system whereby Chinese bankers and merchants lent money for fares that had to be repaid. The 'Gold Mountain' of California and the 'New Gold Mountain' of Australia promised sudden fortunes.

Victoria looks to California, but leads the way in immigration restriction

In both Victoria and California there had been protests in the late 1840s against the attempted landing of convicts, a presumed source of moral contamination. The sudden arrival of large numbers of Chinese prompted discussions of a different kind of threat, the danger posed by aliens or foreigners. A tax on alien miners was introduced by the

---

[6] Geoffrey Serle, *The Golden Age: A History of the Colony of Victoria 1851–1861* (Melbourne, Melbourne University Press, 1977) p.75.
[7] Carboni Raffaello, *The Eureka Stockade* (Melbourne, Melbourne University Press, [1855] 1969).
[8] Elmer Clarence Sandmeyer, *The Anti-Chinese Movement in California* (Urbana, University of Illinois Press, 1973, first published 1939), p.12.
[9] Lowe Kong Meng, Minutes of Evidence, *Report of the Select Committee on Chinese Immigration* (Legislative Council, *Victorian Parliamentary Papers* (*VPP*), 1857) p.10.

Californian legislature in 1850, disallowed the following year, and introduced again in 1852, the same year in which a landing tax was introduced, payable by the ship's master for each alien passenger.[10]

American miners also took direct action against the Chinese, forming numerous vigilante committees to drive the alien race away by force.[11] Possessed by 'a presumptuous spirit of monopoly', American miners were intent on clearing 'the entire mining region of Celestials' as one San Francisco newspaper noted.[12] As yields declined, Chinese labourers increasingly congregated in San Francisco, where they found success in the laundry and restaurant business. Anti-Chinese agitation began to centre on complaints of cheap labour, low wages and unfair competition.[13] Industrial employment as well as gold were claimed as the exclusive preserve of white men.

Agitation against the Chinese in Australia was frequently inspired by the example of California.[14] A significant proportion of the miners on the Victorian fields had come directly from the lawless districts of the Pacific Slope and they often carried their preference for direct action with them. The Americans were better armed than the majority of the diggers and more ready to use their guns to defend their property and interests. In Bendigo, in 1854, where 2,000 Chinese were digging among a group of 15,000 miners, agitators suggested that a mass action take place on American Independence Day: 'a general and unanimous uprising should take place in the various gullies of Bendigo the 4th July next ensuing, for the purpose of driving the Chinese population off the Bendigo goldfields'.[15] Cooler heads prevailed and the demonstration was postponed, but hostility simmered. In Ballarat, the American propensity for guns was evident in the formation of the Independent Californian Rangers Rifle Brigade, about 200 strong, which was involved in organising military drill prior to the miners' revolt over licence fees, that culminated in the battle at the Eureka Stockade at the end of 1854.

On the Californian and Victorian goldfields, European miners criticised the Chinese because of their alien customs, clannishness, pagan

[10] Sandmeyer, *The Anti-Chinese Movement*, pp.41–2.
[11] Andrew Markus, *Fear and Hatred Purifying Australia and California 1850–1901* (Sydney, Hale and Iremonger, 1979) p.4.
[12] *Ibid.* pp.3–4.
[13] Charles Price, *The Great White Walls are Built: Restrictive Immigration to North America and Australasia, 1836–1888* (Canberra, Australian National University Press, 1974) p.62; Sandmeyer, *The Anti-Chinese Movement*, ch.2.
[14] For pioneering studies of comparisons and connections between Australian and American responses to Chinese on the goldfields, see Price, *The Great White Walls are Built* and Markus, *Fear and Hatred*.
[15] Serle, *The Golden Age*, pp.322–3.

rituals, lack of women, labour competition and fast increasing numbers.[16] Increasingly, their objections were couched in the language of race and colour. In a significant move, in 1854, the Californian government introduced a new tax on alien miners, that in exempting those eligible for naturalisation, effectively classified and targetted the Chinese as non-white.[17] (Under the United States law of 1790, naturalisation was restricted to 'free white persons'.) Invoking the same binary logic of white and not-white, the Californian Supreme Court ruled that Chinese could not give evidence against a white man, because the legislation providing that 'no Black, or Mulatto person, or Indian, shall be allowed to give evidence' also applied to the Chinese, being of the same 'Mongolian type' as Indians.[18] In categorising blacks, Indians and Chinese as not-white, the Californians were also defining themselves, not just as Americans, but as 'white men', invoking a sense of self with which miners in the Australian colonies quickly identified.

At the end of 1854, in Victoria, following the Eureka uprising in which several miners and soldiers were killed, the Victorian government appointed a Commission of Enquiry to investigate the turbulent conditions of the goldfields. It emphasised the part played by foreign elements in fomenting the rebellion: 'The foreigners formed a larger proportion among the disaffected than among the miners generally. It seems certain that some of their number acted a very prominent part in regard particularly to the drilling with firearms – a lawless form of demonstration'. The main 'foreigners' the Commission had in mind here were Irish, Americans and Germans, but another group also came to the Commission's attention: 'large numbers of a pagan and inferior race'. By that time, the Chinese comprised about one-sixth of all gold-diggers, but the reported statement by one of their number that 'all' his fellow countrymen were coming to Australia pointed to 'an unpleasant possibility of the future', warned the Commission. A 'comparative handful of colonists' would be 'buried in a countless throng of Chinamen'.[19] The radical newspaper, the *Age*, similarly alarmist, suggested that colonists faced an 'invading army'.[20]

---

[16] See, for example, Anon, *The Chinese Question Analyzed; with a Full Statement of Facts: By One Who Knows* (Melbourne, Steam Press, Fairfax and Co., 1857).

[17] Price, *The Great White Walls are Built*, p.63.

[18] *Ibid.*; Sandmeyer, *The Anti-Chinese Movement*, p.45; Charles J. McClain and Laurence Wu McClain, 'The Chinese Contribution to the Development of American Law', in Sucheng Chan (ed.) *Entry Denied: Exclusion and the Chinese Community in America, 1882–1943* (Philadelphia, Temple University Press, 1991) p.4.

[19] Legislative Council, Commission to enquire into the conditions of the goldfields of Victoria (Official Reports and Documents, *VPP*, 1855) p.6.

[20] Markus, *Fear and Hatred*, p.23.

The Commission of Enquiry deplored the 'degrading customs' and 'vicious tendencies' of the Chinese, including their 'custom of acting in concert' and their tendency to 'cling strictly together as such a race is apt to do in the midst of its superiors'. Ironically, new regulations required all Chinese diggers to reside together in specially designated camps, thus confirming critics' accusations that they failed to assimilate into the broader community. The Commission recommended a Californian-type tax to 'check and diminish this influx', but the Victorian government also introduced the first form of 'immigration restriction', utilising, at the suggestion of the Colonial Office, the British Passengers Act, that limited the number of passengers for health and safety reasons to one passenger for every two tons of ship's burthen. In 'An Act to make provision for certain Immigrants' in 1855, the number of 'immigrants' permitted to land was restricted to one for every ten tons of ship's burthen and 'immigrant' was defined as 'any male adult native of China or its dependencies or any islands in the Chinese Seas or any person born of Chinese parents'. The lawlessness of the goldfields focussed attention on the dangers of difference and dissidence. In acting to exclude Chinese men from the colony, Victorian legislators were also affirming that the ideal colonist was European, civilised and a family man.

With the passage of the first Immigration Restriction Act in 1855, the Victorian government was also challenging prevailing British and international doctrines of freedom of movement and reciprocity of treaty rights. When the Victorian governor advised the Colonial Office that the law didn't violate the Treaty of Nanking of 1842, because it neither prohibited Chinese from landing nor denied them full protection and liberty, British officials agreed, noting that the inflow was formidable enough to justify the measure.[21] Meanwhile, in California, efforts to implement similar immigration restrictions were frustrated when the Supreme Court ruled that legislation to restrict or prohibit Chinese immigration was unconstitutional, because it encroached on federal jurisdiction over foreign commerce and immigration.

In Victoria, the Immigration Restriction Act, though not disallowed, proved ineffective, because ships' masters evaded the law by detouring to the neighbouring colony of South Australia, where Chinese passengers were off-loaded just over the border, thence to complete their long journey to the goldfields on foot. Many died on the arduous walk, but with thousands of Chinese fortune-seekers still arriving in Victoria, their

---

[21] Price, *The Great White Walls are Built*, pp.69–70; for a suggestion of British complicity, see Robert A. Huttenback, *Racism and Empire: White Settlers and Colored Immigrants in the British Self-Governing Colonies 1830–1910* (Ithaca, Cornell University Press, 1976) pp.61–2.

population on the goldfields continued to grow. When South Australia also passed restrictive legislation in 1857, Chinese gold-diggers travelled to Victoria via New South Wales and by the end of the decade their number in the southern colony had reached 45,000.[22]

Agitation against the Chinese continued. In 1857, for example, a public meeting at Geelong 'numbering not less than one thousand persons' sent a petition demanding the parliament 'check any further increase of the Chinese race in Victoria'; the Local Court at Castlemaine presented a Memorial against the 'Chinese influx' while miners at a goldfield named 'Jim Crow' near Ballarat collected 345 signatures in favour of Chinese exclusion.[23] Not all protest was so constitutional. In the same year, at Ararat in western Victoria, where Chinese overlanding from South Australia had discovered one of the richest alluvial leads in the colony, their tents and stores were burned by European competitors and they were forced to abandon their new ground.

Two months later, again on American Independence Day, a small group of white miners on the Buckland River determined to evict more than two thousand Chinese from the river valley in north eastern Victoria. With acts of 'brutal violence and base robbery', they drove the Chinese eight miles down the valley, leaving three dead from drowning and others injured. According to a local newspaper:

Eye-witnesses told of ruffianly behaviour, unmanly violence and unbounded rapacity. One said he had seen Chinamen knocked down and trampled on; another said he could have walked dry shod across the river on the piles of bedding with which its surface was covered and its current interrupted just before the Lower Flat.[24]

European miners once again asserted their presumed proprietorial rights to the land and its wondrous store of precious minerals.

Lowe Kong Meng had invested in and worked the Majorca goldmine, soon after his return to Victoria in 1854, but as he told the Select Committee into Chinese Immigration in 1857, his treatment at the hands of other miners was 'very bad'.[25] He suffered further misfortune when the Europeans burned the Chinese tents at Ararat, where he had stores, and he lost three to four hundred pounds. When the Select Committee asked him about the arson and violence at Ararat, suggesting that robbery must

---

[22] Estimates varied. See William Young, 'Report on the Condition of the Chinese Population in Victoria', *VPP* (56/1868) p.50; see also Geoffrey A. Oddie, 'The Chinese in Victoria, 1870–1890', M.A. thesis (School of History, University of Melbourne, 1959) p.9.
[23] Petitions, 15 July and 12 August 1857, *VPP* (1856–7).
[24] *Ovens and Murray Advertiser* (8 July 1857), quoted in Serle, *The Golden Age*, p.326.
[25] Lowe Kong Meng, Minutes of Evidence, p.12.

also occur in China, he replied: 'This is not robbery ... They burnt all the tents to try and keep away the Chinese from that place'.[26]

Like many of his fellow countrymen settled into the Melbourne community, Lowe Kong Meng was a merchant turned migrant. By 1857, there were about forty Chinese merchants working in the city, mostly importing provisions – rice, tea and sugar – from China to sell to their compatriots as they headed to the goldfields. Most Chinese migrants left their wives and families at home and sent money back, hoping to commute at regular intervals. Their plans to return to China and come back again – 'to live both here and there' – took freedom of movement for granted.[27] If they stayed for ten years or so in the new country, they might bring their families to live with them, but in Victoria, by 1857, the Chinese diggers were too frightened to contemplate such a move. 'I do not think they would bring their families to settle here under any circumstances now', Lowe Kong Meng told the Select Committee.[28]

Writing later about the complaint that Chinese men weren't true colonists because they didn't bring their wives and families with them, Lowe Kong Meng, with co-authors Cheok Hong Cheong and Louis Ah Mouy, asked: 'Can it be wondered at?' Reports of the scandalous treatment of Chinese miners on the Buckland River had gone back to China. How could it be imagined, they asked:

when the news of this atrocity went home to China, any woman of average self-respect would expose herself to be chased through the country by a band of infuriated ruffians, and to see her children burnt to death, perhaps, in her husband's flaming tent? Treated as pariahs and outcasts by the people of this great, 'free' country, the Chinamen in Victoria have hitherto had but scanty encouragement to invite their wives to accompany or to follow them. Subject to be insulted and assaulted by the 'larrikins' of Australia, what Chinaman could be so destitute of consideration for the weaker sex as to render them liable to the same ignominious and contumelious treatment?[29]

In 1860, Lowe Kong Meng married a European woman, Mary Ann, the daughter of William Prussia from Tasmania, and they would eventually raise twelve Australian children. In 1863, in recognition of his service to the local Chinese community, the Chinese Emperor awarded Lowe Kong Meng the title of mandarin of the blue button, civil order. With fellow countryman Louis Ah Mouy, he was also a founding director and major

[26] *Ibid.*
[27] C. Y. Choi, 'Chinese Migration and Settlement in Australia with Special Reference to the Chinese in Melbourne', Ph.D. thesis (Australian National University, 1971) pp.40–1; on Chinese mobility see Adam McKeown, *Chinese Migration Networks and Cultural Change: Peru, Chicago, Hawaii, 1900–1936* (Chicago, University of Chicago, 2001).
[28] Lowe Kong Meng, Minutes of Evidence, p.11.
[29] Lowe Kong Meng *et al.*, *The Chinese Question in Australia*, p.19.

shareholder of the Commercial Bank of Australia. Both men were leading advocates for their community and encouraged their fellow countrymen to join them in their new land.[30]

Freedom of movement: international treaties and transnational solidarities

The long nineteenth century was the great age of global mobility. According to Patrick Manning, the period between 1850 and 1930 was the most intensive period of migration in human history.[31] The burgeoning fortunes made possible by economic liberalism fostered remarkable freedom of movement, while the advent of steam ships and railways made travel cheaper and faster. Millions of people left Europe, China and India and travelled to North and South America, South East Asia, the East Indies, the West Indies, Australasia and the Pacific. Adventurous and ambitious, cowed or courageous, people travelled in pursuit of work, to make a new life, to provide fresh opportunities to their families or simply to satisfy their curiosity about foreign lands.

Modernity meant mobility. In the United States, future president Theodore Roosevelt's paean to nineteenth century progress focussed on the liberation afforded by modern travel. 'The ordinary man of adventurous tastes and a desire to get all out of life that can be gotten', he wrote, 'is beyond measure better off than were his forefathers of one, two, or three centuries back. He can travel round the world; he can dwell in any country he wishes; he can explore strange regions.'[32] Although the freedom to 'dwell in any country' was, as this book shows, a privilege increasingly reserved for whites, more than 50 million Chinese embarked for new lands in these decades, an equal number of Europeans and about 30 million Indians.[33]

With the abolition of slavery during the first half of the nineteenth century, new sources of cheap labour were needed for colonial plantations, mines and industry. Millions of Indians were recruited as contract labourers to work in British colonies in the Caribbean, South East Asia, South Africa and the Pacific, becoming effectively the global working class of the British Empire. But Indians also travelled individually, for education, to pursue their profession, to do business and to see the world.

---

[30] Madeline Yuan-yin Hsu, *Dreaming of Gold, Dreaming of Home: Transnationalism and Migration between the United States and South China, 1882–1943* (Stanford, Stanford University Press, 2000).

[31] Patrick Manning, *Migration in World History* (New York, Routledge, 2005) p.149.

[32] Theodore Roosevelt, 'National Life and Character' in Theodore Roosevelt, *American Ideals and Other Essays Social and Political* (New York, Publisher, 1897) pp.274–5.

[33] Manning, *Migration in World History*, p.149.

Millions of Chinese were also recruited to work in the British, Dutch and Spanish Empires. Although the Chinese Emperor formally prohibited the emigration of his subjects to barbarian lands, China had been forced to engage in trade and treaties with Western powers following the first Opium War in 1840–42.[34] Under the terms of the Treaty of Nanking, Britain opened five Treaty Ports – Amoy, Canton, Fuzhou, Ningbo and Shanghai – and Hong Kong became a Crown colony. In allowing the British to 'hire any kind of Chinese person who may move about in the performance of their work or craft without the slightest obstruction of Chinese officials', the Treaty effectively imposed freedom of movement.[35]

In their pamphlet *The Chinese Question in Australia*, written in 1879 to defend Chinese rights of migration and settlement, Lowe Kong Meng, Cheok Hong Cheong and Louis Ah Mouy referred to the significance of British imperial intervention. It was the British who had forced their way into China in pursuit of trade in opium and tea and who said, in effect: 'We must come in, and you shall come out. We will not suffer you to shut yourselves up from the rest of the world.'[36] It was the British who had incited the Chinese to engage with the world and who invited them to travel and work in their colonies.

From the 1840s, Chinese merchants had themselves invested in plantations, tin mines and trade in South East Asia and recruited contract workers from home. From 1847, the Spanish began transporting labourers from the ports of Macau and Amoy to Cuba and Peru. During the next three decades, shiploads of so-called Chinese 'coolies' were sent across the seas to labour in Singapore, the Straits Settlements, the Americas, Hawaii and the West Indies, but contract labour was complemented by the credit ticket system and other modes of voluntary emigration, notably to Australasia and North America.

In the case of migration to settler societies, emigrants usually left overcrowded countries with a low standard of living for places where labour was scarce and resources abundant, lands where settlement was often made possible by the ongoing and taken for granted dispossession of Indigenous peoples. In their account of Chinese migration to Australia, Lowe Kong Meng, Cheok Hong Cheong and Louis Ah Mouy explained

---

[34] Yen Ching-Hwang, *Coolies and Mandarins: China's Protection of Overseas Chinese during the Late Ch'ing Period (1851–1911)* (Singapore, Singapore University Press, 1985) ch.1.

[35] Michael Godley, 'China's Policy Towards Migrants, 1842–1949', in Christine Inglis *et al.* (eds.) *Asians in Australia: The Dynamics of Migration and Settlement* (Singapore, Institute of Southeast Asian Studies, 1992) p.3. On the role of humiliation in British imperial domination of China, see James L. Hevia, *English Lessons: The Pedagogy of Imperialism in Nineteenth-Century China* (Durham/Hong Kong, Duke University Press/Hong Kong University Press, 2003) pp.74–118.

[36] Lowe Kong Meng *et al.*, *The Chinese Question in Australia*, p.4.

the decision in terms of the logic of taking up empty lands in their own region of the world. When they had heard that:

> there was a great continent nearly half as large again as China, and containing only a few hundreds of thousands of civilized people thinly scattered around the coast; that it was rich in precious metals and very fertile; and that it was only a few weeks' sail from our own country, numbers of Chinese immigrants set out for this land of promise.[37]

In China, they advised, with a population of more than 400 million, many men, women and children died each year from starvation. Australia comprised an area of close to 3 million square miles, but its population was small: 'no more than 2,100,000 white people, and a few thousand blacks'. In the 'face of those facts', they asked their fellow colonists:

> Would you seek to debar us from participating in the abundance with which a bountiful Providence – or, as our Master Confucius says, the most great and sovereign God – rewards the industrious and the prudent in this country? Did man create it, or did God?

Whoever had created Australia, white men were certain that 'this land of promise' belonged to them. It seemed fortuitous that the original inhabitants appeared destined to fade away before the superior forces of civilisation and progress.

In fact, the Aboriginal population had been decimated by the rapidity of dispossession in Victoria, where a lack of natural barriers meant that settlers moved onto Aboriginal lands 'as fast as any expansion in the history of European colonisation'.[38] By the end of the goldrush decade, the Aboriginal population had fallen to less than two thousand people, the survivors mostly living on reserves or missions. In Melbourne, one Chinese resident observed sorrowfully that: 'eight out of every ten of the Yarra Yarra tribe, the late possessors of the soil on which the great City of Melbourne is built . . . are dead'.[39] Alarmed by the possibility of teeming hordes coming from China, some Europeans feared that they, in turn, might be overwhelmed.

In this age of economic liberalism, international treaties provided the framework in which reciprocal rights of freedom of commerce and movement were claimed by the British, other Europeans, the United States and also by the Chinese.[40] In 1860, the Convention of Peking (Beijing)

---

[37] *Ibid.* p.5.
[38] Richard Broome, *Aboriginal Victorians: A History Since 1800* (Sydney, Allen and Unwin, 2005) p.97.
[39] Anon, *Brother Shem or the Wrongs of the Chinese* (Melbourne, Goodhugh and Hough, 1857) p.9.
[40] On the imperial context of international treaties, see Antony Anghie, *Imperialism, Sovereignty and International Law* (Cambridge, Cambridge University Press, 2005).

contracted between the British and Chinese governments extended rights of freedom of movement and guarantees of protection for persons and property in each other's Empires. British pressure on Australian colonists to adhere to the new treaty provisions led the colonies to repeal their initial discriminatory legislation, with Victoria complying in 1865 and New South Wales in 1867.

In 1868, the Burlingame Treaty between the United States and China went even further than the British treaties in recognising freedom of movement and migration as universal rights: 'the inherent and inalienable right of man to change his home and allegiance and also the mutual advantage of the free migration and emigration of their citizens and subjects respectively from one country to the other for purposes of curiosity, of trade or as permanent residents'.[41] In California, however, few citizens could see the mutual advantage of free migration and the ensuing campaign of opposition to the Treaty was relentless.

The struggle over free migration highlighted the contradictions inherent in political liberalism. Individual liberty and freedom of movement were heralded as universal rights, but only Europeans could exercise them.[42] The conflict also highlighted competing and changing understandings of sovereign rights. The Chinese cited the 'illustrious Vattel' to invoke their sovereign rights as a nation bound by treaty under international law. As John Fitzgerald has pointed out, to Chinese readers Emmerich de Vattel and other authorities on international law guaranteed the equality of nations and provided a framework in which they would demand equality of treatment.[43] Californians and Australians, by contrast, utilised a republican discourse on the rights of the sovereign male subject to insist on their democratic right to determine who could join their self-governing communities.

As the San Francisco *Daily Evening Bulletin* explained to its readers, of all those parts of the world where the Chinese had gained a footing, 'the Australian colonies most resemble California'. Thus, the experience of Australia 'becomes valuable to us':

---

[41] Sandmeyer, *The Anti-Chinese Movement*, pp.78–9.

[42] Uday Singh Mehta, *Liberalism and Empire: A Study in Nineteenth-Century British Liberal Thought* (Chicago, University of Chicago Press, 1999); Ann Curthoys, 'Liberalism and Exclusionism: A Prehistory of the White Australia Policy', in Laksiri Jayasuriya, David Walker and Jan Gothard (eds.) *Legacies of White Australia: Race, Culture and Nation* (Crawley, University of Western Australia Press, 2003).

[43] John Fitzgerald, 'Introduction', in Sechin Y. S. Chien and John Fitzgerald (eds.) *The Dignity of Nations: Equality, Competition and Honor in East Asian Nationalism* (Hong Kong, Hong Kong University Press, 2006); Emmerich de Vattel, *The Law of Nations or Principles of the Law of Nature, Applied to the Conduct and Affairs of Nations and Sovereigns: From the French of Monsieur de Vattel* (Philadelphia, Johnson and Co., [Leyden, 1758] 1883).

Though nominally under British rule, the six separate Australian colonies are practically, each of them, separate republics, electing their own legislatures by universal suffrage, levying and expending their own revenues and each one of them separately making their own laws subject only to the veto of the British authorities, when such laws are opposed to British treaties with other nations.

Importantly, however, whereas 'in aristocratic forms of Government [such as in China] treaties may be maintained against popular wishes', in democracies, 'the power of the people is supreme and cannot be reduced or signed away in whole or in part'.[44]

Anti-Chinese campaigners in California and Australia also drew on the supporting discourse of Anglo-Saxonism to argue that the capacity for self-government was the preserve of the Anglo-Saxon race.[45] The Chinese, characterised collectively as contracted coolies and servile labour, were said to lack the manly independence and self-possession necessary to participate as individuals in a representative democracy. 'The Chinaman is by tradition and education a monarchist', declared the *Daily Evening Bulletin*, 'regarding aristocracy as the only reasonable form of government; and he thrives best under its sway ... For the elective franchise he is entirely unfit, not would he care for the privilege of exercising it if thrust upon him'.[46] When anti-Chinese activists thus campaigned against the Chinese as colonists, citizens and workers, they also impugned their manhood. 'Rice-eating men', declared Australians and Californians in chorus, had neither the rights nor responsibilities of masculine 'beef-eating' men.

International doctrines of freedom of movement thus collided with the ascendant democratic power of white manhood. In an age when 'glorious manhood asserts its elevation', in the words of republican Australian poet Daniel Deniehy, Chinese labour, represented as docile and servile, was cast as a profound threat to the new-found status of the independent, upright, working man, a figure increasingly coded as 'white'.[47] The elevation of manhood in the democracies on the Pacific Coast was thus forged in the molten mix of global migration, class politics and a discourse on racial difference. International doctrines of freedom of movement and the treaties that guaranteed it provoked strong resistance from self-styled 'white men's countries', a proprietorial formulation used successively against Indigenous peoples, Chinese, Indians and ultimately all those labelled as Asiatics.[48]

---

[44] *Daily Evening Bulletin*, 10 April, 29 July 1878.
[45] Matthew Frye Jacobson, *Whiteness of a Different Color: European Immigrants and the Alchemy of Race* (Cambridge, Harvard University Press, 1998) pp.26–31.
[46] *Daily Evening Bulletin*, 26 September 1878.
[47] Daniel Deniehy, quoted in *Sydney Morning Herald*, 16 August 1853.
[48] Price, *The Great White Walls are Built*, p.62.

Nineteenth-century migration created new identities and new ways of being in the world. Opponents of Chinese migration forged a sense of transnational community, identifying as white men under siege, men whose sovereign right of self-government was threatened, not just by the Chinese, but by distant metropolitan centres of power. California was frustrated by the constitutional power of the United States federal government located in Washington and the 14th Amendment that required states to guarantee to all persons 'equal protection' of their laws. Victoria and the other Australian colonies were constrained by the imperial power of the British government centred in London. Newspapers and politicians on both sides of the Pacific Ocean seeking to make common cause repeatedly stressed the 'Similarity between Californian and Colonial Experience'.[49]

In California, Congressman Horace Davis, the owner of the Golden Gate Flour Mills and a noted radical in politics, kept a scrapbook of newspaper cuttings about Australian developments and referred to colonial laws as a guide to what could be achieved to restrict Chinese immigration to his own country, where local legislators were frustrated not only by their lack of constitutional power, but also the readiness and success of local Chinese in taking legal action to challenge discriminatory laws and ordinances.[50]

Davis' contribution to Congressional debate on the Chinese question was notable for his assiduous research into the global dimensions of Chinese migration, which enabled him to refer at length to Singapore, Siam (Thailand), Manila, Cochin China (Vietnam), Java and Australia. One admiring correspondent commended the impact of his global perspective:

Congressman Davis appears to have made a considerable impression upon the House by his speech on the Chinese question, and his success is due to the fact that he struck out a new line of argument, based upon independent research. Instead of repeating the familiar denunciations of the Chinese in America, which have ceased to appeal to Eastern audiences, he undertook to show how the same kind of immigration has affected other countries, and he succeeded in demonstrating that it has everywhere, and under all circumstances, been productive of evil.[51]

It was the 'Example and Experience of Australia', however, 'so nearly parallel to us' in history and culture, that provided, in its capitation taxes and

[49] Markus, *Fear and Hatred*, pp.64–6.
[50] Horace Davis scrapbooks, 89/151 (Bancroft Library, University of California, Berkeley); McClain and McClain, 'The Chinese Contribution', p.7.
[51] Horace Davis scrapbooks, vol.2, p.44.

tonnage restrictions recently introduced in new legislation in Queensland, an example of a solution to the Chinese question.[52]

In Washington, following ongoing demands from California that the Burlinghame Treaty be revoked, a Congressional Joint Special Committee was appointed in 1876 to investigate 'the character, extent, and effect of Chinese immigration to this country' and to examine at first hand the situation on the west coast. There were 129 witnesses, including lawyers, manufacturers, working men and women, policemen and public officials and spokesmen for the Six Companies, district-based organisations that represented the interests of Chinese residents. No subject received more coverage than the effect of Chinese labour on 'white labor'. Despite much evidence of the irreproachable conduct of the Chinese and their contribution to economic development, the Committee found that:

> there was danger of the white population in California becoming outnumbered by the Chinese; that they came here under contract, in other words as coolies or a servile class; that they were subject to the jurisdiction of organized companies ... that Chinese cheap labor deprived white labor of employment, lowered wages, and kept white immigrants from coming to the state.[53]

Its findings were widely publicised in Australia as well as in the United States and multiple copies placed on the shelves of parliamentary and public libraries. The *Sydney Morning Herald* suggested that British governments could learn from American experience: the Chinese problem was 'being worked out in the United States, and the experience gained there should not be thrown away either upon the Home or the Colonial authorities'.[54]

Newspaper accounts of the Congressional Committee Report provided the framework in which new Australian developments, such as the sudden arrival of thousands of Chinese on the Palmer River goldfields in Queensland and their entry into urban crafts such as furniture making in Melbourne, were understood. Reports of a worsening Chinese problem in California were important in fuelling Australian anxieties, even as the actual number of Chinese people living in Victoria and New South Wales declined. Andrew Markus has shown that of thirteen *Sydney Morning Herald* articles on the Chinese Question between 1875 and 1877, ten of them referred specifically to the experience of California or the United States more generally.[55] Australian newspapers employed their own correspondents in San Francisco and regularly received American files and personal

---

[52] Horace Davis Scrapbooks, 'The Chinese Question: Argument of Congressman on the Subject', Newspaper cutting, vol.2.
[53] Cited in Price, *The Great White Walls are Built*, p.129.
[54] Markus, *Fear and Hatred*, p.81.   [55] *Ibid.* pp.80–1.

accounts from travellers taking the popular San Francisco–Sydney shipping route.[56]

The evils of San Francisco's Chinatown, depicted so graphically by witnesses to the Congressional Committee, became a common point of reference in Australia as well as in the United States and were cited in the debates on the new Queensland legislation, in 1877, to warn of the dire consequences of the recent Chinese influx of gold-diggers. Californian politicians and newspapers referred in turn to the Queensland legislation to urge the introduction of anti-Chinese laws in defiance of United States Treaty obligations.

In 1877, the Queensland government had introduced both an entry tax and immigration restriction on the Chinese, measures which, despite British treaty commitments, received royal assent. Californians were quick to seize on this initiative as a precedent and to question the power of international treaties to detract from citizens' sovereign democratic rights:

> To hold that a nation cannot modify a treaty until it gets the consent of the other party is to admit that it had parted with a portion of its sovereignty. In our case the missing portion is located at Peking ... The British, with their heavy lumbering monarchical form of government, it would also seem, can solve an unexpected difficulty much more speedily and satisfactorily than we can.[57]

Beef-eating men versus rice-eating men

In the late 1870s, in both California and the Australian colonies, anti-Chinese agitation was given fresh vigour by newly powerful labour movements. Organised working men, armed with manhood suffrage, were determined to exercise their new-found electoral power, much to the disquiet of those, including Chinese community leaders, who were appalled at politicians seeking popularity by pandering to popular prejudice. In California, the short-lived Workingmen's Party, founded in 1877 and led by Denis Kearney, won one-third of the vote with the slogan: 'The Chinese Must Go'. 'We make no secret of our intentions', declared their Manifesto:

> We make none. Before you and before the world we declare that the Chinaman must leave our shores. We declare that white men, and women, and boys, and girls, cannot live as the people of the great republic should and compete with the single Chinese Coolie in the labor market.[58]

Anti-Chinese sentiment dominated the State's Constitutional Convention held in 1878 and it issued not just from organised workers. 'This

---

[56] *Ibid*. p.80.   [57] *Daily Evening Bulletin*, 26 August 1879.
[58] Sandmeyer, *The Anti-Chinese Movement*, p.65.

State should be a State for white men, without any respect to the treaty, or misinterpretation of any treaty', said a farmer from El Dorado County.

The State has the right of self-preservation. It is the same right that a man of family has to protect his house and home … We want no other race here. The future of this republic demands that it shall be a white man's government, and that all other races shall be excluded.[59]

As a result of this mobilisation, the state's Second Constitution, ratified in 1879, included an article prohibiting any corporation employing 'directly or indirectly, in any capacity, any Chinese or Mongolian' and prohibiting the employment of Chinese 'on any state, county, municipal, or other public work, except in punishment for crime'. The Constitution also excluded Chinese from the citizenship rights of owning land and voting.[60] All these provisions would be challenged in the courts.

In the Australian colonies, trade union protest over the employment of Chinese labour erupted in the Seamen's Strike of 1878, called in response to moves by the Australasian Steam Navigation Company to follow the Hong Kong Eastern Australian Mail Steamship Company in replacing European seamen by Chinese on its run to Fiji and New Caledonia at half the cost. The Seamen's Union, covering workers in Victoria, New South Wales and Queensland, received widespread support from the trade union movement, radical politicians and political reform groups in the capital cities and extensive coverage in Californian newspapers.[61] 'Foreign cheap labor seems to be the question of vital importance wherever the Chinese plant themselves', noted the Star.[62]

In 1879, the Intercolonial Trade Union Congress unanimously condemned any further importation of Chinese labour and called for the introduction of a heavy poll tax on those already resident in Australia. In Victoria, an Anti-Chinese League demanded 'the restriction, or if found necessary, the complete prohibition of immigration of Chinese to this colony'.[63] In demanding the exclusion of Chinese workers, the labour movement increasingly defined the white working man as a figure defined by his 'civilized' standard of living. The difference between the Chinese worker and the white worker, said one supporter in the Victorian parliament, sounding an international theme, was the difference

[59] Ibid. p.70.
[60] Matthew Frye Jacobson, Barbarian Virtues: The United States Encounters Foreign Peoples at Home and Abroad 1876–1917 (New York, Hill and Wang, 2000) p.79; Sandmeyer, The Anti-Chinese Movement, pp.67–72.
[61] Ann Curthoys, 'Conflict and Consensus', in Ann Curthoys and Andrew Markus (eds.) Who Are Our Enemies? Racism and the Working Class in Australia (Sydney, Hale and Iremonger, 1978).
[62] Star, 1 January 1879.   [63] Price, The Great White Walls are Built, pp.163–4.

between 'a rice-eating man and a beef-eating man'. 'People who can subsist on a handful of rice and content themselves with the barest shelter are formidable opponents of European labor', said a colleague.[64] Moreover, the 'unfairness of the competition is added to by the intense industry of these Asiatics. They stand in as little need of rest and recreation, apparently, as they do of a generous diet or wholesome housing and they consequently offer their services for wages upon which European workmen could not subsist'.[65]

In both Australia and the United States, working class identities were constituted in a discourse of racial difference that defined the white worker as the bearer of civilisation and its responsibilties. The Chinese responded to these claims about their lack of civilised standards by continually pointing to the impressive achievements of their own civilisation, distinguished by its antiquity, high learning and technological invention.

In *The Chinese Question in Australia*, written in response to the industrial crisis, Lowe Kong Meng, Louis Ah Mouy and Cheong Cheok Hong pointed to the credentials of the Chinese as workers and colonists. They were experienced seamen, yet they faced trade union opposition to their employment on steamships; they were the major suppliers of fresh vegetables and fish, thus contributing to better standards of health in the colonies, yet they were regularly confronted with 'severe rebuffs, angry vituperation and threats of personal violence' as they hawked their wares. They had proven to be law-abiding settlers, yet unlike French or Germans or Italians or Swedes, they were daily vilified.

Lowe Kong Meng and his colleagues recognised that in the Australian colonies, as in California, the most vociferous opposition to Chinese immigrants issued from organised labour, from white workers fearful that cheap competition would increase unemployment and drive down their standard of living. They wrote:

Chinamen are told – 'You must not work in Australian ships or in Australian factories: you must not earn a livelihood by hawking or by handicrafts in these colonies. You must leave off cultivating gardens, and fabricating furniture, and following the industrial employments you have adopted; and you must either starve, beg, steal, or vanish'.[66]

But why were only the Chinese to be excluded? They were after all highly civilised, certainly not an inferior people:

[64] *Victorian Parliamentary Debates*, Legislative Assembly (10 November 1881), p.699.
[65] *Age*, 17 April 1888.
[66] Lowe Kong Meng et al. (eds.) *The Chinese Question*, p.4.

No one can say so who knows anything of our history, our language, our literature, our government, or our public and private life. China had reached a very high standard of civilization when Britain was peopled by savages. The art of printing, the use of gunpowder, and the mariner's compass were known to us centuries before they were re-invented by Europeans.[67]

In their own country, literacy was widespread and most people educated. In Australia, all Chinese were stigmatised as 'ignorant pagans' and 'filthy barbarians' by persons who were themselves ignorant. Most Australians had never been to China, knew nothing of its long history or its moral, intellectual, and social life, and yet formed hasty judgments against its people from a very slight acquaintance with a few immigrants. 'In Australia', they said, 'the vilest epithets are bestowed upon our countrymen by speakers on platforms, who know nothing whatever about China or its people'. Persecuted Chinese had long expressed astonishment at politicians' ignorance of Chinese civilisation and at the fact that law-making was based on such ignorance.[68]

In proposing solutions to the racial conflict in Victoria, the three community leaders took a cue, like their critics, from developments across the Pacific. They were familiar with the Congressional Committee and stressed that despite the prejudices of Californians, the actual evidence before the Committee 'proved incontestably that [the Chinese] had been of immense service to the country . . . In the farm, the factory, the kitchen, the workshop, and the laundry, they have proved invaluable'. Nevertheless, anti-Chinese agitation had assumed formidable proportions there and required the six Chinese Companies to issue an address to the American public. The authors drew attention to this address and 'the excellent sentiments entertained by our compatriots in America', who recommended that if the United States was intent on preventing Chinese from immigrating, the country should repeal the Burlingame Treaty, openly and honourably. If not, Americans must honour the principles of equality and reciprocity enunciated in international law. In the event, the United States government renegotiated the Treaty to allow for legislation to prevent the immigration of Chinese labourers.

The main claim of *The Chinese Question in Australia* was that the Chinese had a 'perfect right to settle in any part of the British Empire' on the basis of the reciprocal rights accorded the British and Chinese by the Peking Covention of 1860. In support of this 'right', they quoted Vattel on 'the law of nations': 'as the engagements of a treaty impose, on the one

---

[67] *Ibid.* pp.9–10.   [68] See, for example, Anon., *Brother Shem*, pp.6–9.

hand, a perfect obligation, they produce, on the other, a perfect right. The breach of a treaty is therefore a violation of the perfect right of the party with whom we have contracted; and this is an act of injustice against him'. Chinese community leaders protested at the demeaning and discriminatory treatment they suffered at the hands of 'these British dependencies' and demanded their rights as members of the Chinese Empire in the name of international law and the comity of nations. As John Fitzgerald has pointed out, numerous Chinese colonists in Australia also sent petitions worded in these terms to the Chinese Foreign Ministry in Beijing.[69] In response to these appeals to international law, Australians invoked with increasing stridency their masculine rights as sovereign subjects and self-governing communities.

In the United States, recent developments in Australia attracted renewed attention with the publication and wide circulation of an article by John Wisker in the British magazine *Fortnightly Review*, which was reprinted or reported with commentary in *Nation, Harper's*, the *Chicago Tribune* and a range of Californian newspapers. Wisker was one of a number of literary men advised by doctors to go to the colonies for the sake of his health. A British Chess champion, sports journalist and novelist, he was found to be suffering from tuberculosis in 1877 and encouraged to migrate to Australia.

On his arrival, he found a continent preoccupied with the question of 'the coloured man': 'the stock subject of the newspapers, the regular topic at public meetings and theme of numerous parliamentary debate'.[70] There were diverse types of coloured men posing different sorts of challenges – Aborigines, Pacific Islanders and Asians – but as 'an object of public interest and public dread' the Chinaman had no equal. 'This ubiquitous, all-suffering, all-capable individual – the future possessor of the world in his own opinion – has invaded Australia in thousands'.

Although, in fact, the number of Chinese resident in Victoria and New South Wales had rapidly declined since the 1860s, in part as a result of earlier discriminatory legislation and persecution, Wisker reported that four thousand of 'the obnoxious race' still lived in Sydney. But it was in the northern colony of Queensland where the Chinese were now most numerous. Of the 17,903 gold miners in Queensland, 13,269 were Chinese and 'the white men considered themselves robbed of their property'. The article outlined the discriminatory Acts recently passed by the

---

[69] John Fitzgerald, 'Advance Australia Fairly: Australian Voices at Federation', in Sophie Couchman, John Fitzgerald and Paul McGregor (eds.) *After the Rush. Regulation, Participation and Chinese Communities in Australia 1860–1940. Special Issue of Otherland Literary Journal* (December 2004).

[70] John Wisker, 'The Coloured Man in Australia', *Fortnightly Review* (1 July 1879) p.82.

Queensland government. 'Whether this repressive legislative is in accordance with the spirit of British treaties with China is a question for the Colonial Secretary at home, but 'certain it is that the desire of the vast majority of Queenslanders is rapidly being realised'. Wisker also provided an account of the seamen's strike and its national racial significance: 'It was a strike against the yellow man. Thus it acquired a sacred character; it became an Australian movement, securing universal sympathy, and what was more to the purpose, substantial support'.

Wisker made clear his own sympathy with the colonial attitude – white men were usually converted once in the colonies for the issue was one of 'self-preservation' – and his article was taken up enthusiastically by Americans lobbying for the renegotiation of the Burlingame Treaty and the introduction of immigration restriction. In 1879, a Restriction Bill was passed by the Congress, but vetoed by President Hayes who declared: 'I cannot but regard the summary disturbance of our existing treaties with China more inconvenient to much wider and more permanent interests of this country'. The Californian *Daily Examiner* regretted that the Administration was so ready with its veto 'in the interest of the Chinese and against the white labouring interests of California as well as the whole country'.[71]

Racial exclusion and Chinese protest

In 1881, the Victorian parliament introduced a new Chinese Influx Restriction Bill – imposing a £10 entry tax, a tonnage restriction of one Chinese migrant to every 100 tons of shipping, and a requirement that Chinese departing temporarily be required to obtain a certificate to prove their identity on their return. Members of parliament frequently justified the new measures with reference to the troubles in San Francisco, as documented in the Congressional report, a copy of which, they advised, could be found in the Parliamentary Library.[72] The last United States census showed a population of 105,000 Chinese in California and they had 'seriously interfered with labour and also threaten[ed] some political disturbance'.[73]

The Victorian government also included a clause in the new Bill to disenfranchise Chinese voters. Until then, ratepayers' rolls were used as the basis for enrolment to vote in Victorian parliamentary elections. Supporters of disenfranchisement invoked racial difference as a political

---

[71] *Daily Examiner*, 14 February 1879.
[72] *VPD*, Legislative Council (30 November 1881) p.932; Price, *The Great White Walls are Built*, p.171.
[73] *VPD* Legislative Council (30 November 1881) pp.931–2.

disqualification: the Chinese were racially unfit for political rights for they knew nothing of Caucasian civilisation and they lacked the capacity for independence, being controlled by headmen. There was also strong opposition to the Bill, however, with liberal critics citing the constitutional right of all (male) colonists in a self-governing community to shape the laws by which they were governed. It was cowardly and unmanly, they said, to oppress the weak in this way: the Chinese were a small minority and were being treated like negroes in the southern states of the United States.[74] But as in the southern American states, an increasing number of white men considered that their manhood rested on the exercise of racial domination. Anything else spelt humiliation.

By the 1880s, one of the most common arguments used to justify further restrictions on the Chinese was the recently recorded fact of China's vast population of 400 million people – 'the largest population of any country in the world', 'a third of the population of the globe' – a fact that the Chinese themselves had helped publicise. Charles Pearson, a recently elected Liberal member for Castlemaine in the Victorian Legislative Assembly – and a man with a penchant for facts – was especially eloquent in warning of the prospect of the 'white population' being 'swamped' by the Chinese tidal wave:

The population of China was nearly 400,000,000, and the mere natural increase of that population in a single year would be sufficient to swamp the whole white population of the colony. Australia was now perfectly well known to the Chinese; communication between the two countries was thoroughly established; and, in the event of famine or war arising in China, Chinamen might come here at any time in hordes. He had read the Bill with great satisfaction, and he considered it reflected great credit upon the Government.[75]

Pearson was himself a relative newcomer to Victoria. A former Fellow of Oriel College and professor of history at King's College, he, like chess champion Wisker, had migrated to the colonies in part for health reasons, first arriving in South Australia to take up a wheat farm in 1864, just eleven years after Lowe Kong Meng had sailed into Port Phillip Bay.

In 1868, following his return to England, Pearson had travelled to the United States and it was there that a disturbing thought occurred to him: the frontier was closing and the country was fast filling up. Land in the temperate zone was limited: white men might soon be denied the chance to emigrate. He published his thoughts on 'The Land Question in the United States' in *Contemporary Review*, elaborating an argument that in some ways anticipated Frederick Jackson Turner's famous 'frontier thesis'

[74] *VPD* Legislative Assembly (4 October, 10 November 1881) pp.698,701.
[75] *VPD* Legislative Assembly (4 October 1881) p.220.

of 1893. Whereas Turner was interested in the implications of the closing frontier for American national character and history, Pearson was concerned about the place of the white man in the larger world. Noting both the flow of Chinese into California and the British tendency to treat the world as an outlet for its surplus population, Pearson warned that white men might soon be 'cramped for land'. 'The Land Question' would form the basis of the first chapter of his disturbing work of prophecy, *National Life and Character: A Forecast*, published by Macmillan in London and New York in 1893.

One of the most worrying elements of Pearson's forecast was his prediction of China's 'inevitable position as one of the great powers of the world'.[76] Impressed by Chinese expansion and the growing intervention of the Chinese Empire in international relations, he warned that the balance of world forces was changing. He became convinced that the Chinese people, along with other 'yellow races' would soon be 'represented by fleets in the European seas, invited to international conferences and welcomed as allies in the quarrels of the civilized world'.[77] In 1887, Pearson witnessed at first hand the status accorded China as a power when two Imperial Commissioners, General Wong Yung Ho and U Tsing, arrived in Melbourne to investigate 'the social relations of Chinese subjects residing in British colonies' and the prompt response to their demand that the British government bring the colonies into line.

The Chinese government had, in fact, been relatively tardy in moving to protect their subjects overseas, but reports of the ill-treatment of Chinese settlers in the British and Spanish Empires had finally prompted its officials to establish a series of consulates, first in Singapore in 1875, followed by Yokohama and San Francisco in 1878, Havana in 1879 and New York in 1883.[78] The announcement in 1886 of a visit by the Chinese Commissioners to South East Asia and the Australian colonies was seen as a significant event by all sides of the Chinese Question in Australia.[79] Chinese community leaders welcomed the opportunity to report to the Commissioners on the discrimination and humiliation suffered by their fellow countrymen in these 'dependencies of the British Crown' and to call for redress.

They forwarded a petition, signed by forty-four Chinese Australians to the Commissioners at their quarters at the Oriental Hotel, enumerating

---

[76] Charles H. Pearson, *National Life and Character: A Forecast* (London, Macmillan, 1893) p.49.
[77] Pearson, *National Life and Character*, pp.84–5.
[78] Godley, 'China's Policy Towards Migrants', p.8; Yen Ching-Hwang, *Coolies and Mandarins*, pp.144, 213.
[79] Correspondence, *Chinese Immigration*, VPP (1888) vol.1, p.4.

the 'penalties and disabilities inflicted on [their] nation by the law of the land'. What was urgently required, they said, was the redress of 'international wrong'. They named three main grievances: first, the £10 poll tax, the imposition of which departed from 'all the principles of international right and equity'. Second, there was the injustice of the demand that they pay the tax again should they leave the colony and attempt to return. The only alternatives were that they 'expatriate themselves by choosing to become naturalized British subjects' or they obtain 'tickets of leave'. Otherwise, when they travelled to another colony and attempted to return they would be seized like contraband goods and detained until they could 'pay the duty levied upon us'. 'Imagine what an outcry would be raised against Chinese perfidy if a Briton were thus treated in China, yet such is precisely the treatment meted out to us by these dependencies of the British crown, in direct violation of all international law and usage, and in contravention of the Treaty engagements entered into by the Governments of the two Empires'. Their third grievance centred on the abuse and assaults directed at tea and vegetable vendors by cowardly youth incited to violence by the very same laws and law-makers. For these larrikin offenders they recommended the introduction of corporal punishment: 'the use of the lash'. '[We] trust that Your Excellencies will lend the weight of your official influence to bring it about'.[80]

On their return to China, the Commissioners reported on the extent of discrimination in Australia and elsewhere and recommended the establishment of a network of consulate offices and a naval force to back up Chinese insistence on the fair treatment of their people abroad.[81] The Board of Foreign Affairs instructed the Chinese Minister in London to take up the matter of increasing discrimination, particularly with regard to poll taxes and the possible violation of Sino–British Conventions. The Chinese Minister, Lew-Ta-Jen wrote to the British Prime Minister, the Marquis of Salisbury, drawing his attention to the existence of 'exceptional and exceptionable laws' in the colonies which were surely 'at variance with Treaty obligations and International Usage'. 'In the Crown Colonies', the Minister observed, 'it has not been found necessary to treat Chinese subjects differently from the subjects of other Powers, and it is difficult to understand why it should be otherwise in those Colonies on whom a certain amount of self-government has been conferred'.[82]

---

[80] Petition to Wong Yung Ho and U. Tsing from Lowe Kong Meng *et al.* Enclosure, Chinese Imperial Commissioners to Governor of Victoria, 13 June 1887, *Chinese Immigration*, *VPP* (1888) pp.6–7.

[81] Myra Willard, *History of the White Australia Policy to 1920* (first edition, Manchester University Press, 1923; reprint New York, Augustus M. Kelley, 1968), pp.74–6.

[82] Lew-Ta-Jen to the Marquis of Salisbury, 12 December 1887 Enclosure, *Chinese Immigration, VPP*, p.15; see also Godley, 'China's Policy Towards Migrants', p.9.

The Secretary of State for the Colonies called upon the colonial governments to explain: to 'report on any exceptional legislation affecting Chinese subjects . . . showing the objects for which such legislation was adopted'.[83] In response, the Premiers re-iterated their intention to bring an end to Chinese immigration. Discussions ensued as to whether this could be best achieved through the British re-negotiating the Treaty, following the recent United States example, or by colonial governments introducing their own laws.[84] Some colonists objected to Britain acting on their behalf, because such a course of action implied a 'surrender of the right of self-government', a surrender of their manhood.[85]

In comparing their situation with that of the United States ('the principle has been asserted by the Chinese Exclusion Acts that a community is justified in refusing admittance'), Australian colonists invoked a republican discourse on self-government, even while forced to acknowledge their dependence on the Empire for their ultimate defence.[86] The Australians were also forced to acknowledge that only the British government could enter into treaties with foreign powers, but 'treaty or no treaty we are legally entitled to exclude any contribution to our population which we object to, and that we intend to exercise that right by excluding the Chinese'.[87] The colonial Premiers agreed to determine the method of exclusion at a special conference called for June 1888 in Sydney.

In the midst of preparations for the conference, two ships, the *Afghan* and *Burumbeet*, arrived in Melbourne, the former carrying 268 Chinese passengers and the latter a smaller number trans-shipped from Sydney, all of whom were immediately identified as harbingers of a larger Chinese invasion.[88] In fact, many of the men on board were returning home after short filial visits to China.[89] Wang Gay, for example, had lived in Victoria for thirteen years, working for ten years as a market gardener in Malvern, in close proximity to the residence of Lowe Kong Meng. Ah Hung had worked as a miner in Ballarat for eight years, Sing Diu was a market gardener in Richmond, while Gee Singhad worked for eight years as a

---

[83] H. T. Holland to Governor of Victoria, 23 January 1888. *Chinese Immigration, VPP,* 1888, p.14.

[84] Premier of Victoria to Premiers of the Australian Colonies (22 March 1888) p.15; Henry Parkes to Premier of Victoria (30 March 1888), *Chinese Immigration, VPP.* The terms of the Treaty between the United States and China were printed in full in the *Argus,* 7 May 1888.

[85] *Age,* 2 April 1888; on the Sydney meetings see Willard, *History of the White Australia Policy,* pp.80–1.

[86] *Age,* 5 April 1888.   [87] *Ibid.* 17 April 1888.

[88] For an account of the 'sudden and almost inexplicable' panic that ensued in New South Wales when the *Afghan* arrived in Sydney, see Willard, *History of the White Australia Policy,* pp.84–5.

[89] *Age,* 5 May 1888.

labourer. The *Argus* newspaper made much of the case of Sandy Williams, or Sun San Lung: 'the Chinaman whose wife and family came down from Castlemaine to meet him, but who was not allowed to land from the *Afghan*'. He had first arrived in Victoria twenty-five years before.[90] The passengers asked Lowe Kong Meng as a kind of unofficial consul in Australia to negotiate with the authorities so that they could land, but the government was determined, as the *Age* newspaper put it, invoking the American cry, that 'the Chinese must go'.[91]

Lowe Kong Meng must have reflected on how much had changed since he had first stepped ashore in Melbourne without let or hindrance thirty-five years before. Now, even passengers carrying British naturalisation papers and the small number eligible to come ashore on the payment of the poll tax were prohibited from landing by the executive decision of government – an act characterised by political opponents as 'arbitrary and high-handed', and by Cheok Hong Cheong as a 'coup d'etat'.[92]

Word of this sudden turn of events soon reached Lew-Ta-Jen in London, who promptly expressed his outrage about the 'irregular proceeding of the colonial authorities' to the British Prime Minister. He reminded the Prime Minister that although he didn't recognise the validity of colonial laws unless they were in accordance 'with the Treaties and Laws of Nations', surely colonial governments could be expected to obey 'Statutes that they themselves had enacted'. 'Whether, then, the action of the Australian Executive in refusing to allow the immigrants to be landed be considered from a conventional, or international, or a statutory standpoint, it would appear to be equally unjustifiable, and this all the more because the immigrants having been embarked at Hong Kong, a British colony, the authorities not only assented to their shipment but sanctioned it'.[93]

The validity of the government's actions was tested in a legal challenge issued in the name of one of the Chinese passengers by solicitors Cleverdon and Westley. In *Chung Teong Toy v. Musgrove*, the Supreme Court of Victoria in a majority decision rejected the government's argument that it had a sovereign right to exclude aliens from its territory as an act of state. The majority argued that the Victorian government's authority was 'limited'. Under its Constitution Act, the colony of Victoria 'enjoyed a perfect scheme of local government, limited to its internal relations'.[94]

[90] *Argus*, 7, 8 May 1888.   [91] *Age*, 4 May 1888.

[92] William Ross, Convener of the Public Questions Committee, Presbyterian Church of Victoria, to Premier Gillies, 16 May 1888; Cheok Hong Cheong to Victorian Premier, 1 June 1888, *Chinese Immigration, VPP*, 1888, vol.1, p.48.

[93] Lew-Ta-Jen to the Marquis of Salisbury, 16 May 1888, *Chinese Immigration, VPP*, pp.48–9.

[94] *Chung Teong Toy v. Musgrove, Victorian Law Reports*, vol.14, 1888, pp.439–40.

Colonial leaders preferred, however, to speak not of 'local', but of 'self-government', which they would later invoke to argue their sovereign right to racial homogeneity. In the event, in an ironic twist, the Supreme Court decision was overturned on appeal to the Privy Council in London, which held that 'an alien has no legal right enforceable by action to enter British territory' and that 'all the prerogative necessary for the protection of the people had passed with self-government, to the Representatives of the Crown, on the advice of responsible Ministers'.[95]

Race homogeneity as the basis of healthy national life

In early June 1888, another ship sailed into Melbourne in the wake of the storm caused by the arrival of the *Afghan* and *Burrumbeet*. The *Freeman* had sailed all the way from Boston and it carried a rather more welcome visitor, a young Harvard philosopher, Josiah Royce, whose doctor had recommended a long sea voyage to recover from mental exhaustion. He carried with him a letter of introduction from Richard Hodgson, a friend of the philosopher, William James, addressed to Alfred Deakin, with whom Hodgson had attended Melbourne Grammar School in the 1860s. Deakin was the youthful Chief Secretary in the Victorian government and a protégé of Pearson from university days. He would play a major part in the recent political crisis precipitated by the arrival of the *Afghan*.

When Royce arrived, Deakin was preparing to travel to Sydney for the inter-colonial conference on immigration restriction and he invited Royce to join him on the train journey. Deakin had visited the United States just three years before, on an official mission to investigate irrigation in California, when he took the opportunity to travel east to Massachusetts, making a pilgrimage to the grave of Emerson in Concord and touring the sites of the revolution in and around Boston. Deakin was a great admirer of American republican manhood and welcomed Royce with enthusiasm. The two subsequently spent an intense week together in the Blue Mountains, walking and talking, about politics and government, metaphysics and religion, conversations that lay the basis for a passionate friendship that would last for more than twenty years. Deakin told Royce that his was 'the best trained and best informed mind in metaphysics and kindred topics' that he had ever encountered.[96] Royce returned the compliment: 'Few memories stand out more clearly and encouragingly,

---

[95] Appeal from a judgment of the Supreme Court of Victoria, Musgrove and Chun Teeong Toy [*sic*], Privy Council *Law Reports*, 1891, pp.282–3.
[96] Deakin to Royce, 30 June 1888, Deakin papers, 1540/1/49, National Library of Australia (NLA).

and more pleasingly, in my life, than our meeting in 1888, our days together in the wonderland of your mountains, our talks, and your kindness and the gracious cheer of all your hospitality'.[97]

They talked, inevitably, of the Chinese question. Royce, who grew up on the Californian goldfields and attended university at Berkeley, was at pains to condemn race prejudice of a vulgar sort: 'Has not the American agitation against the Chinese been on the whole rather disgraceful to our intelligence? Are not the best of us even now ashamed of it?' But when nation-building was the issue – as in the case of Australia – then there were 'far more significant' considerations to take into account. 'We in this country', Royce reflected in an article in *Atlantic Monthly* written shortly after his return to the United States, 'have suffered and will yet suffer far too deeply from the presence in our midst of a few million very docile and well meaning Negroes to be in a position to doubt the dangers of founding a great nation in a new country upon a basis of race heterogeneity'.[98] Royce pointed to the lessons to be learnt from American experience:

Race homogeneity is the basis of healthy national life; and even the mixture of the European stocks themselves, although it is inevitable, involves, as here in America, evils enough on the way. It would be suicidal for Australians to encourage such free intercourse with China as would give them, in fifty years from the present time, when their white population will number perhaps fifteen millions, a Chinese population of say five millions or more.

The issue was so important, he concluded, that it would probably precipitate political separation from Britain.

Royce's account of Australian feeling on this issue drew heavily on his conversations with Deakin, whose nationalism had become more determined following his clash with the British Prime Minister just the year before at the first Colonial Conference in London. Australia and Britain had different interests in Asia and the Pacific, Royce reported. 'We conclude, then, that no base prejudice, but the highest political wisdom, calls Great Britain and Australia along pathways that must further and further diverge'. He looked forward to Australia's 'happy destiny' as an independent nation, when Americans and Australians might greet each other as 'sister republics' across the Pacific.[99]

Following the Conference on Chinese Immigration in Sydney, in 1888, the colonial governments resolved to introduce uniform legislation,

---

[97] Royce to Deakin, 18 April 1908, Deakin papers, 1540/1/1964, NLA.
[98] Josiah Royce, 'Reflections after a Wandering Life in Australasia', *Atlantic Monthly* (June 1889) p.825.
[99] Royce, 'Reflections after a Wandering Life', p.826.

drafted by Deakin, that would effectively ban Chinese from entering Australia, regardless of whether they were British subjects. This was a new departure, but as Victorian Premier Duncan Gillies explained: 'naturalized British subjects are still Chinese and therefore are as objectionable as if they were to come from the centre of China'.[100] The Bill was introduced into the Victorian parliament in December. In deference to the Chinese Minister in London, the poll tax would be dropped, but severe penalties would apply to Chinese arriving overland from other colonies. In defending the rights of Chinese residents already in Victoria to travel from one colony to another, William Shiels, one of Charles Pearson's students, but a liberal of the old school, made a last passionate plea for recognition of 'one of the dearest rights of citizens – the perfect liberty of locomotion'.[101]

In a final protest, the Chinese Committee in Victoria drew up a forty-three-page 'Remonstrance to the Parliament and the People of Victoria' signed by nine Committee members and their Chairman, Cheok Hong Cheong, in which they attempted, once more, to reverse the prevailing racial discourse on civilisation. The new Victorian legislation was 'barbarous' they said, 'a relapse so distinct as to fix an indelible stain on the Australian name'. In a six-page attachment, they elaborated on 'Chinese Civilization and Attainments' pointing to their tradition of government by the wise and talented, the wide diffusion of education, their extensive literature and inventive genius. But the Remonstrance also registered that the issue was not really civilisation, but colour. The Chinaman, they lamented, was denied 'common human rights' because he differed from the European in 'the color of his skin'.[102] How could this be when Christianity taught that all nations were of one blood?

A time may come

But perhaps the time for forbearance was past. Perhaps the Chinese should consider retaliation or revenge. Didn't Australians realise, warned the Chinese Committee, the foolishness of giving offence to a nation that was surely destined for greatness: 'Our own land has no equal on earth for fertility and resources which by and by will cause her to weigh heavy in the scale of nations'. Evil treatment would bear bitter fruit and wounds would fester. 'A time may come', they warned, 'nay, probably will come sooner than is supposed, when the presence and power of China as a great nation will be felt in these seas, and it lies with you to say, as wise men

---

[100] *VPD*, Legislative Assembly, 6 December 1888, p.2,357.   [101] *Ibid.* p.2,369.
[102] Cheok Hong Cheong, *Chinese Remonstrance to the Parliament and People of Victoria* (Melbourne, Wm Marshall & Co., 1888), p.6.

or otherwise, if this be for good or evil'.[103] 'A time may come' encoded a warning that Charles Pearson would make his own in *National Life and Character* just five years later.

Among the signatories of the Chinese Remonstrance, one name was conspicuously absent. Lowe Kong Meng had died suddenly in 1888 at the age of sixty-seven. In his portrait of Melbourne's leading Chinese merchant in *Australian Representative Men*, published that year to mark the centenary of Australian settlement, T. W. H. Leavitt had written of him as thoughtful and humane, a cultured and honest man, in short, a gentleman.[104] Leavitt urged his readers to take the opportunity to get to know Chinese colonists on an individual and collective basis, because with their energy, industry and undoubted capacity, their future was unbounded: 'the time is at hand when the Chinaman will seek settlement in every civilised land, and will become a part of the population of every populous city'. Indeed, wrote Leavitt, the Chinaman 'might well be designated "the coming man", not for one country, or some one particular part of the earth, but for the whole world'.[105]

This was also the view of Charles Pearson, Liberal politician and journalist, and a leading supporter of immigration restriction. He agreed with Leavitt's assessment of the significance of Chinese migration, but thinking about population movements in world historical terms had concluded that there were even larger issues at stake. In the recent Chinese diplomatic intervention, and in the messages sent by Chinese leaders in Melbourne, he saw the first phase of a global power struggle between those he called the 'higher and lower races'. Pearson was always careful to point out, however, that these were relative terms, signifying not innate difference, but relative historical advancement. The Chinese petitioners were right. The time would surely come, Pearson concluded, when China would emerge as a great power.

As a historian, Pearson was attuned to large historical transformations. In his analysis of changing world forces, he joined the 'Chinese Question' with the 'negro problem', recently publicised by his younger friend from Oriel days, James Bryce, in his magisterial survey *The American Commonwealth*, first published in 1888, and in his article on the 'negro problem' in *North American Review* in 1891. Pearson had also read and reviewed a new book on Haiti and was persuaded that the advent of 'the

[103] *Ibid.*, p.15.
[104] T. W. H. Leavitt, *Australian Representative Men* (Melbourne, Wells and Leavitt, 1887).
[105] *Ibid.*

Black Republic' pointed the way to the future.[106] Anglo-Saxon triumphalism and complacent assumptions about the never-ending expansion of Greater Britain were seriously misguided. Besides, democratic progress also had its costs, now becoming evident in the spread of 'state socialism' following the advent of manhood suffrage in the colonies. As a Liberal politician, advocate of a progressive land tax, Minister of Public Instruction and committed feminist, Pearson was a radical reformer, but he worried about the enervating effects of 'state socialism' even as he helped to implement its ambitious program.

On a more subjective level, the frail, proud, refined Englishman worried about the effects of changing world forces on the white man's personal sense of self. Would his pride of race guarantee his primacy of place in the world, or was he destined for racial decline and wretched humiliation, elbowed aside by the ascendant 'black and yellow races'?

[106] Charles Pearson, 'The Black Republic', in H. A. Strong (ed.), *Reviews and Critical Essays* (London, Methuen, 1896).

Part 2

Discursive frameworks

2　*The American Commonwealth* and the 'negro problem'

James Bryce publishes a work of biblical authority

James Bryce's three volume survey of United States political and social institutions, *The American Commonwealth*, first published in 1888, revised in 1889 and re-issued in an expanded third edition in 1893–5, was 'a study of an experiment in the rule of the multitude, tried on a scale unprecedently vast, and the results of which everyone is concerned to watch'.[1] *The American Commonwealth* also played a key role in educating English-speaking peoples around the world about what he called the 'negro problem', which he defined as the unfortunate legacy of Radical Reconstruction, the ill-fated experiment in multi-racial democracy that followed the Civil War. In later writings, Bryce continually returned to the lessons of this episode in history, pointing to 'the risks a democracy runs when the suffrage is granted to a large mass of half-civilized men'.[2]

During the revolutionary project of Radical Reconstruction, between 1865 and 1877, the freed Negro, Bryce declared in an interpretation that would soon become orthodoxy, had proven himself completely unfit for the responsibilities of democratic citizenship. 'Emancipation found them utterly ignorant; and the grant of the suffrage found them as unfit for political rights as any population could be'.[3] In his book and related articles and lectures, Bryce became a key interpreter of southern white thinking for English-speaking peoples in Britain, North America, South Africa and Australasia.

The American Commonwealth rapidly acquired the status of a classic and Bryce became 'the accepted authority on American race relations', as John Cell has noted in his study of the origins of the modern

---

[1] James Bryce, *The American Commonwealth*, 3 vols. (London and New York, Macmillan, 1888) Introduction.
[2] James Bryce, *The Relations of the Advanced and the Backward Races of Mankind* (London, Clarendon Press, 1902) p.38.
[3] Bryce, *The American Commonwealth*, p.92.

doctrine of segregation in the American South and South Africa.[4] In the United States, Frederick Howe recalled that in university circles *The American Commonwealth* was treated as 'a work of Biblical authority. When he visited our seminar on politics, professors and students accepted his opinions as above and beyond question'.[5] In Australia, too, colonial leaders meeting in the 1890s to frame a constitution for their new Commonwealth, adopted Bryce's book as their 'Bible'. 'It was quoted or referred to more than any other single work', wrote J. A. La Nauze in his *The Making of the Australian Constitution*, 'never criticised, it was regarded with the same awe, mingled with reverence, as the Bible would have been in an assembly of churchmen'.[6] For thirty years, reported the English *Review of Reviews* in 1907, Bryce had been 'recognised by all Britons as the best authority in this country on the American Commonwealth, and his book bearing that name has long since become a classic in every American library'.[7]

Born into a Scottish Presbyterian family, Bryce was a reforming liberal by conviction and an Anglo-Saxonist by training, tutored at Trinity College by E. A. Freeman, a leading Anglo-Saxonist historian and admirer of the United States. In 1864, at the age of twenty-six, Bryce published his prize-winning essay on the *Holy Roman Empire*, which, as Freeman noted 'by a single youthful effort, placed himself on a level with men who had given their lives to historical study'.[8] His survey of Aryan development, tracing the classical inheritance bestowed on the Teutonic branch of the race as it advanced in power and influence showed clearly 'the seminal influence of his mentor in faithfully reflecting Freeman's central belief in the continuity of history'.[9]

E. A. Freeman: university mentor and historian of race

Historians of the mid-century, as Reginald Horsman has noted, were 'particularly susceptible to racial explanations of the course of

[4] John W. Cell, *The Highest Stage of White Supremacy: The Origins of Segregation in South Africa and the American South* (Cambridge, Cambridge University Press, 1982) pp.22–23.
[5] Hugh Tulloch, *James Bryce's American Commonwealth: The Anglo-American Background* (Woodbridge, Boydell Press, 1988) p.10.
[6] J. A. La Nauze, *The Making of the Australian Constitution* (Melbourne, Melbourne University Press, 1972), pp.18–19; John Hirst, *The Sentimental Nation: the Making of the Australian Commonwealth* (Melbourne, Oxford University Press, 2000) p.167; Helen Irving, *To Constitute a Nation: a Cultural History of Australia's Constitution* (Melbourne, Cambridge University Press, 1997); Matthew N. C. Harvey, 'James Bryce, *The American Commonwealth* and the Australian Constitution', *The Australian Law Journal* vol.76 (2002).
[7] *Review of Reviews*, 1 March 1907.
[8] Tulloch, *James Bryce's American Commonwealth*, p.14.   [9] *Ibid.* p.39.

history'.[10] There was a new emphasis in English writings on the genius of Anglo-Saxon political institutions and their Teutonic heritage. Anglo-Saxons, according to Thomas Carlyle and Thomas Arnold, were destined to conquer and occupy the world. If the small western rim of Europe became 'over-peopled', said Carlyle, 'does not everywhere else a whole vacant Earth . . . call to us, Come and till me, come and reap me!'[11]

But was the earth outside Europe really vacant and might not climate prove to be an obstacle to Anglo-Saxon expansion? In *The Races of Men*, published in 1850, Robert Knox popularised the idea of climatic determinism: Anglo-Saxons could only live in temperate zones, while the Negro flourished in the tropics. The erstwhile colony of San Domingue had already become black and Europeans would soon be driven out of the West Indies.[12]

Freeman, the pre-eminent English historian of race, went to Oxford as a student in 1841, a time when, as Horsman notes, 'the ingredients for the new racial interpretation of Anglo-Saxon destiny were all present'.[13] Freeman applied the comparative method to chart the racial progress of the Teutonic branch of the Aryan race and its continuity through European and American history. By the end of the 1840s, Freeman was writing of 'Teutonic greatness' and, comparing seeds planted in the 'German forest or on . . . Scandinavian rock' with the legacy of Greece and Rome, was able to declare confidently in favour of the former.[14]

In his square, sturdy frame, red hair and ruddy complexion, his plain habits of life and straightforwardness in deed and word, it was said that Freeman embodied the Teutonic type. Others regarded him as a bully.[15] Now almost completely forgotten, Freeman's 'extravagant Saxonism' – as Charles Pearson termed it – presented in numerous public lectures and books, had a major impact on historical thinkers and political leaders of the late nineteenth century, especially in the young countries of the United States and Australia, where English-speaking peoples were keen to identify with their long 'race history'.[16]

In the United States, Henry Baxter Adams, Theodore Roosevelt, Henry Cabot Lodge and Alfred Mahan were among Freeman's ardent

---

[10] Reginald Horsman, *Race and Manifest Destiny: The Origins of American Racial Anglo-Saxonism* (Cambridge, Harvard University Press, 1981) p.24.

[11] Quoted in Catherine Hall, *Civilising Subjects: Metropole and Colony in the English Imagination 1830–1867* (Cambridge, Polity, 2002) p.30.

[12] *Ibid.* p.49.   [13] Horsman, *Race and Manifest Destiny*, p.75.   [14] *Ibid.*

[15] C. J. W. Parker, 'The Failure of Liberal Racialism: the Racial Ideas of E. A. Freeman', *The Historical Journal* 24, 4 (1981) p.825.

[16] Charles Henry Pearson, 'The Story of My Life', in William Stebbing (ed.) *Charles Henry Pearson: Memorials by Himself, His Wife and His Friends* (London, Longmans, Green and Co., 1900) p.92.

disciples. In Australia, liberal politicians Andrew Inglis Clark, Isaac Isaacs and Alfred Deakin were followers. A. M. Topp, a journalist and, like Deakin, a member of the Eclectics Society, commended Freeman in the *Melbourne Review* as an 'intellectual force among Englishmen of the present generation': 'It is hardly too much to say that, among the historical writers of the century, Mr Freeman, on the whole, occupies the highest place. Certainly, among English historians there can be no question of this'.[17]

An admirer of Charles Darwin, Freeman claimed that 'history [was] a science which recorded the data of racial progress just as natural science tracked the laws of natural evolution':

From its very beginnings the racial seed predetermined those peculiarly Teutonic characteristics – an innate capacity for orderly self-government – which identified the common origins of that race whatever its consequent diversity in either time or place. The Aryan, be he Greek, Roman or Teuton, could no more escape the burden of ineluctable progress than a sunflower seed could escape its destiny as a sunflower.[18]

In his classic text *The Growth of the English Constitution*, Freeman explained that the English constitution was originally Teutonic, borrowed from 'our forefathers in their old land of Northern Germany before they made their way into the Isle of Britain'.

And that constitution, in all its essential points, they brought with them into their new homes, and there, transplanted to a new soil, it grew and flourished, and brought forth fruit richer and more lasting than it brought forth in the land of its earlier birth . . .

The continued national life of the people, notwithstanding foreign conquests and internal revolutions, has remained unbroken for fourteen hundred years.[19]

History was the story of Anglo-Saxon triumph and its lessons were 'matters closely connected with our present political being'.[20] In 1863, Freeman wrote to tell Bryce that 'Fed. Govt. Vol. 1 was to be out this week . . . Macmillan speaks with horror of its size and it will be fat, but hardly fatter than some volumes of Grote, Macaulay, Palgrave, Buckle, and Alison . . . I began Vol.11 yesterday'.[21] These works on federal government would become, like Bryce's own *American Commonwealth*, key

---

[17] A. M. Topp, 'Review of E. A. Freeman's *Historical Geography of Europe*', *Melbourne Review* vol.VI (Jan–Oct 1881) p.392.
[18] Tulloch, *James Bryce's American Commonwealth*, p.40.
[19] E. A. Freeman, *The Growth of the English Constitution from the Earliest Times* (London, Macmillan, first published 1872, reprinted 1898) p.18.
[20] Freeman, *The Growth of the English Constitution*, Preface to first edition, p.ix.
[21] Freeman to Bryce, 5 December 1863, Bryce papers, Bodleian Library.

reference works for the Australian 'federal fathers' meeting in conference and convention in the 1890s to draw up a constitution for the Commonwealth of Australia.

The cause of the North: looking to America

When Bryce was elected to a Fellowship at Oriel College, in 1862, he joined a group of liberals caught up by the cause of the American Civil War, the crucial political struggle of the age as they saw it: 'a turning point, for good or evil, of the course of human affairs for an indefinite duration'.[22] 'There was no place in England', Bryce later recalled, 'where the various fortunes of that tremendous struggle were followed with more interest than in Oxford and Cambridge, and none in which so large a proportion of the educated class sympathised with the cause of the North. Mr Goldwin Smith led the section which took that view, and which included three quarters of the best talent in Oxford'.[23]

It was at Oxford that Bryce met fellow radical and dissenter, Charles Pearson, eight years his senior and renowned as a brilliant debater:

He had left a great reputation in Oxford as one of the most brilliant men of an unusually brilliant generation, that of the early fifties; and this reputation rested on his speeches at the Union ... The strongest impression he made upon us younger men was that of a mind extraordinarily well stored with knowledge and possessed of a remarkable gift of generalising.[24]

Committed to political, educational and religious reform, Pearson and Bryce shared Goldwin Smith's unbounded enthusiasm for the democracy of the United States.

A brilliant journalist and powerful presence, Smith assumed leadership of the liberal cause at Oxford and beyond. Appointed to the Regius Chair in History in 1858, he was a proselytiser rather than researcher, 'anxious for vehement effort and for immediate change'.[25] In 1863, he wrote to his friend, the Dante scholar and high-minded man of letters, Charles Eliot Norton, in Cambridge, Massachusetts, to reassure him that the North did have some friends in England, even though: 'the aristocracy are against you almost to a man. The great capitalists are against you ... The clergy of the Establishment are against you, as a Commonwealth founded in liberty of Conscience. The rich are mostly against you ... A good many

[22] Tulloch, *James Bryce's American Commonwealth*, p.4.   [23] *Ibid.* p.20.
[24] James Bryce, 'His Friends', in Stebbing (ed.) *Memorials*, p.167.
[25] Arnold Haultain, 'Why Goldwin Smith Came to America', *North American Review* 198 (1913) p.692.

of the middle classes are against you, because they ape the aristocracy.'[26] The mass of the intelligent working classes, on the other hand, he felt sure, supported the North. Attitudes towards the United States it seemed were strongly shaped by class. Appalled at the upper classes' 'malignant exaltation over the misfortunes of the American Republic', Goldwin Smith declared himself an 'American citizen in sympathy'.[27]

Several leading English liberals visited the United States during the war.[28] In 1864, Smith prepared to sail to Boston to present lectures and research a book on American political institutions. In the United States lay the 'hopes of man'. 'With all loyalty to the land of my birth', he wrote to Norton on the eve of his departure, 'the heart of a political student cannot fail to be, in some measure, with the nation which in spite of all the calamities which beset and all which (it is to be feared) still await it, bears more than any other, in the bark of its fortunes the political (and, as I believe, the religious) hopes of man'.[29] His lectures were received with enthusiasm and he began to be feted as a celebrity. Two years later, following the death of his father, Smith decided to migrate, accepting a two-year appointment to a lectureship in history at Cornell. Later, he visited family in Canada, where he met his future wife and built a new rural home.

Goldwin Smith, James Bryce and Charles Pearson were passionate democrats in a country whose political structure rested on aristocratic and plutocratic privilege. It was the fervour of their commitment to democracy and equality that led them all to identify with the New World democracies and to espouse the cause of racial homogeneity, which they saw as a prerequisite for democracy. With the final triumph of the North in the Civil War, which had cost more than 600,000 lives, Smith wrote to Norton in April 1865, to rejoice in 'this crowning victory of our cause'. Emancipation was 'an event which will fairly belong to humanity at large'. Yet, he worried: 'The Negro question will, I fear, be a great difficulty. You cannot have a pariah caste without fatally derogating from the splendid principles of your Republic. On the other hand from the difference of color and the physical repugnance, amalgamation seems unlikely'.[30]

Three months later, Smith wrote again about the 'negro question': 'it is such a difficulty as perhaps has seldom occurred in politics before'.[31] And in October 1865, he asked: 'How can there be real political equality

[26] Goldwin Smith to Charles Eliot Norton, 7 November 1863, Norton papers, bMS Am1088, Houghton Library, Harvard University.
[27] *Ibid.* 24 May 1864.
[28] Christopher Harvie, *The Lights of Liberalism: University Liberals and the Challenge of Democracy 1860–86* (London, Allen Lane, 1976) pp.108–111.
[29] Smith to Norton, 22 July 1864, Norton papers.
[30] *Ibid.* 17 April 1865.   [31] *Ibid.* 20 July 1865.

without social fusion? And how can there be social fusion while the difference of color and the physical antipathy remain? I cannot help thinking that Negro emigration on a large scale will form the best way out of the wood'.[32] News of 'catastrophe' in Jamaica added to his despair.[33] The twin triumphs of Governor Edward Eyre and plutocracy, wrote Goldwin Smith, would surely make him an American citizen. Smith was a member of the Jamaica Committee formed to prosecute the colonial Governor for illegal acts. Upper class support for Eyre, as for the South in the Civil War, fuelled his disenchantment with England.

As convinced democrats, Bryce, Smith and Pearson all contributed to the 1867 volume *Essays on Reform,* in support of the English Reform Bill of that year. Bryce wrote a general essay on 'The Historical Aspect of Democracy'. Pearson commended 'The Working of Australian Institutions' based on manhood suffrage, introduced in Victoria and New South Wales during the previous decade: 'whatever theorists may say, the [secret] ballot works simply and effectively in Australia ... there is no bribery at elections, and as the voting is by papers there is no treating and no intimidation'.[34] Smith contributed an essay on 'The Experience of the American Commonwealth' in which he enthused that 'Equality has created in America a nation great both in peace and war'. The success of equality, he argued, depended on the availability of land. If America had an outlet to the West, so England had an outlet in her colonies and if she would only 'be kind to her own kith and kin, in America itself'. Smith also commended the republican ideal exemplified by the 'commonwealth': 'There, instead of individual greatness, you have the greatness of a nation; instead of a king and his subjects, you have a community; instead of loyalty, patriotism and attachment to the common good'.[35]

Goldwin Smith migrated to the United States in 1866. Pearson followed with a visit two years later and met many of the same people who had welcomed Smith, and he, too, formed a warm friendship with Norton. 'My ten days in Boston', he later wrote,' will always remain in my memory as among the pleasantest incidents of my life'. The company there could not be surpassed anywhere in the world: 'Ticknor, Longfellow, Agassiz, Lowell, Wendell Holmes, Charles Norton, Wendell Phillips,

[32] *Ibid.* 1 October 1865.
[33] *Ibid.* 16 December 1865. On Jamaica see Catherine Hall, Keith McClelland and Jane Rendall, *Defining the Victorian Nation Class, Race, Gender and the Reform Act of 1867* (Cambridge, Cambridge University Press, 2000), pp.192–233.
[34] Charles Pearson, 'On the Working of Australian Institutions', [no editor] *Essays on Reform* (London, Macmillan, 1867) p.197.
[35] Goldwin Smith, 'The Experience of the American Commonwealth', [no editor] *Essays on Reform*, pp.218–37.

56   Discursive frameworks

Bowen Fields and Shattock were among the ordinary society of Boston and Cambridge; and Emerson was a frequent visitor'.[36] While in the United States, perhaps with Smith's argument about the significance of land to democratic equality in mind, Pearson enquired into the facts of 'The Land Question'. His conclusion that westward expansion had proceeded more quickly than people had realised and that the frontier was closing challenged Smith's assumption of the unending possibilities of European settlement.

'I talked to everyone I could find': Bryce researches the United States

In 1870, Bryce followed Goldwin Smith and Pearson to the United States, accompanied by his friend A. V. Dicey, who had also written for *Essays on Reform*, with a contribution on 'The Balance of Classes'. They, too, were impressed by American friendship and the democratic informality of social life. Bryce began to plan a book about American democracy, in particular its political institutions, and made it his business to talk to as many potential informants as possible. Following Smith's example, and as a tribute to its republican principles, he would call his study 'The American Commonwealth'.

He returned on a second trip in 1881, when he visited Johns Hopkins University, crossing paths with Freeman, who had been invited there by his American disciple, Herbert Baxter Adams, the founding Director of Research in Advanced Institutional History, who liked to emphasise that 'the whole tenor of our researches ... is to show the continuity of English institutions in America'.[37] Freeman was in the United States to visit his son in Virginia, but he was entranced by New England, 'where the constitution of old Archaia is born again'. His philological researches bristled, Tulloch has noted, with the pursuit of etymological origins that might conclusively prove Anglo-Saxon continuities.[38]

Freeman delighted in his sense of feeling 'at home' in the United States. 'My chief feeling is the strangeness at the lack of strangeness', he wrote to a friend. 'I go hither and thither in Europe and see really strange things; then I make a much longer journey [across the Atlantic] only to be at home again at the end of it'. But he was alarmed at the political power

---

[36] Stebbing, *Memorials*, p.131.
[37] Tulloch, *James Bryce's American Commonwealth*, p.42; see too E. A. Freeman to Edith Thompson, 4 December 1881, in W. R. W. Stephens, *The Life and Letters of Edward A. Freeman* vol.2 (London, Macmillan, 1895) p.240.
[38] Tulloch, *James Bryce's American Commonwealth*, p. 41; and see E. A. Freeman, *Lectures to American Audiences* (London, Macmillan, 1882).

of blacks in this multi-racial democracy. He felt at home, but there was a 'queer' difference:

The really queer thing is the niggers who swarm here; my Aryan prejudices go against them, specially when they rebuke one and order one about. And the women and children are yet stranger than the men. Are you sure they are men? I find it hard to feel that they are men acting seriously: tis . . . easier to believe that they are big monkeys dressed up for a game.[39]

And he continued his racist diatribes in a letter to the Rev. N. Pinder:

I think I get on mightily with all folk here save railway folk, who are simply brutal, and often black to boot. But the freed nigger seems to have a fancy generally for making us feel our Aryan inferiority – I am sure 'twas a mistake . . . making them citizens. I feel a creep when I think that one of these great black apes may (in theory) be President.

Freeman also saw some Indians ('less repulsive than niggers, but dumpy figures with dull faces') and noted the demand on the west coast for Chinese exclusion: 'only the natural instinct of any decent nation to get rid of filthy strangers'.[40]

Bryce listened to similar views from John W. Burgess, a southerner and, like so many of his contemporaries, a German-trained Anglo-Saxonist. In 1886, Burgess founded the *Political Science Quarterly*, which Bryce would disseminate in England. In 1890, he published *Political Science and Comparative Constitutional Law*, which hailed the nation-state as the highest expression of Teutonic political genius.[41] Nation-states required ethnical homogeneity, a common language and homogeneous institutions to maintain national unity. A nation might therefore 'righteously deport the ethnically hostile element in order to shield the vitals of the state from the forces of dissolution and in order to create the necessary room for a population sufficient in numbers, in loyalty and capacity to administer the Empire and protect it against foreign powers'. It was obligatory, then, for the state to protect its nationality from 'the deleterious influences of foreign immigration'. It was the highest duty of the state to 'preserve, strengthen, and develop its national character'.[42]

Bryce travelled again to the United States in 1883–4, spending time with the poets and publishers of the east coast, including Ralph Waldo Emerson, Oliver Wendell Holmes Sr., Henry Wadsworth Longfellow and James Russell Lowell, as he recorded in his diary:

[39] Freeman to Professor Dawkins, in W. R. W. Stephens (ed.), *The Life and Letters of Edward A. Freeman* (London, Macmillan, 1895), vol.2, p.234.
[40] Stephens, *The Life and Letters of Edward A. Freeman*, p.254.
[41] John W. Burgess, *Political Science and Comparative Constitutional Law* vol.1 (Boston, Gunn and Co., 1890) p.38.
[42] Burgess, *Political Science*, pp.42–4.

I go to see Lowell at the far end of Cambridge, where he inhabits remote mansions in spacious grounds – an ideal place all doors . . . large cool rooms full of books and pictures. Lowell very cordial and pleasant – he is not specially poetical looking, nor perhaps very striking, tho his brow is full & well formed and there is a great look of firmness and intensity about him . . . He still feels bitter about England's conduct & thinks the feeling in the States generally is bitter – no wonder.[43]

Bryce would make the goal of reconciliation between Britain and the United States a lifetime pursuit that culminated in his appointment as Ambassador to Washington between 1907 and 1913.

Seeking to get a sense of 'public opinion' Bryce talked to a wide range of people across the country, on the east and west coasts and in the south. His interlocutors remembered an eager curiosity about their part of the world, an interest in everything American. He later reflected on his method of enquiry, counting himself a good listener. He wrote *The American Commonwealth* 'out of conversations to which I listened. I talked to everyone I could find in the United States, not only to statesmen in the halls of Congress, not only at dinner parties, but on the decks of steamers, in smoking cars, to drivers of waggons on the Western prairies, to ward politicians and city bosses'.[44]

He travelled to the Pacific coast where 'public opinion' expressed itself as 'popular hatred of the Chinese'.[45] He made extensive enquiries into the formation of Denis Kearney's Working Men's Party, with its slogan that 'The Chinese Must Go'. Bryce made a point of deploring the excesses of hoodlums in San Francisco but, as in the South, he found the actions of white men understandable and legitimate: 'The movement which gave birth to the new Constitution was a legitimate political movement. It was crude in its aims, and tainted with demagogism in its methods. But it was evoked by real evils; and it sought however ignorantly, the public good'.[46] He attached a copy of the 1879 Californian Constitution, with its explicit discriminations against Chinese, as an Appendix to *The American Commonwealth*.

During his visits, Bryce formed close friendships with several Americans, including arch-enemies E. L. Godkin, the Irish-born New York editor of the *Nation*, and Theodore Roosevelt, whom Bryce first met in 1886 when the American travelled to Europe for his marriage to his second wife, Edith Carow. As a leading Liberal MP, Bryce was Roosevelt's

---

[43] James Bryce diary, USA, 1883–84, MSS 334–40, Bodleian Library.
[44] Quoted in Tulloch, *James Bryce's American Commonwealth*, p.58.
[45] Bryce papers, Notes for American Commonwealth, MS 334–341, Bodleian Library; and Bryce, *American Commonwealth*, third edition, p.434.
[46] Bryce, *American Commonwealth*, third edition, p.447.

personal guide on a tour of Westminster.[47] Elected to the House of Commons as member for Tower Hamlets in the East End in 1880, and then for South Aberdeen in 1885, Bryce served in the Gladstone Ministry, which was defeated on Home Rule. Though a successful politician, Bryce, who had also been appointed Regius Professor of Civil Law at Oxford in 1870, always retained something of the scholar about him. It was said that he was too much the professor to be widely popular. He lectured rather than spoke, but it was a mode of communication that only served to enhance his status as an academic authority.[48]

Bryce asked Roosevelt to check the galley proofs of *The American Commonwealth*, while Roosevelt returned the compliment by inviting Bryce to visit him when next in Washington, so he could meet more real men actually involved in politics, in contrast to 'those political and literary hermaphrodites the mugwumps' – men such as Godkin of the *Nation*.[49] Roosevelt complimented Bryce on his book, commending 'the singular success with which you have combined a perfectly friendly spirit to America with an exact truthfulness both of statement and comment'. He compared Bryce's achievement with Alexis De Tocqueville's *Democracy in America*, but on second thoughts, considered the comparison unfair, because Bryce's book was more insightful and sympathetic to democracy – he 'pricked certain hoary bubbles; notably the "tyranny of the majority" theory'.[50] Roosevelt rightly saw in Bryce a warm friend of America.

Trained by Freeman to look for racial continuity and the unity of history, Bryce became more interested in historical change, especially the effects of the unprecedented racial encounters of the New World. As John Stone has remarked, his cross-cultural perspective enabled him to realise 'the vital significance of race relations and racism as forces moulding the parameters of twentieth century society'.[51] Freeman's world was European, not global or even imperial. 'In thus tracing the historical geography of Europe, we have made the round of the world', Freeman wrote in *Historical Geography of Europe*. 'But we have never lost sight of Europe; we have never lost sight of Rome. Wherever we have gone, we have carried Europe with us.'[52] Freeman's Teutonic preconceptions and prejudices

[47] Theodore Roosevelt to Corinne Roosevelt Robinson, 6 March 1887; Elting E. Morison (ed.), *The Letters of Theodore Roosevelt* (Cambridge, Harvard University Press, 1951), vol.1, p.125.
[48] *Review of Reviews*, 1 March 1907.
[49] Roosevelt to Lodge, *Letters*, 15 February 1887, p.122.
[50] Roosevelt to Bryce, *Letters*, 6 January 1888, p.135.
[51] John Stone, 'James Bryce and the Comparative Sociology of Race Relations', *Race* XIII, 3 (1972) p.325.
[52] Topp, 'Freeman's *Historical Geography*', p.397.

constrained his historical enquiry; the important events of his world were the battles of Marathon and Hastings, the fall of Rome and the unification of Germany, rather than the fate of Governor Eyre, or the Indian Mutiny or the partition of Africa.[53] As a voyager in the New World, Bryce, like Pearson, was more interested in charting mobility and change and he became fascinated by the implications of the great global migrations. He published his first essay on this theme – 'History and Geography' – in 1886, in *Contemporary Review*, the same journal in which Pearson had noted that white men were becoming 'cramped for land'.

The world made small

In 'History and Geography', Bryce repeated Pearson's observation that temperate lands were filling up, but he was most interested in the new forms of racial contact being produced by modern migrations. Whereas in medieval times, people's place of residence and capacity for travel were constrained by nature, now, with scientific discovery and technological innovation, people could migrate where and how they pleased and, most importantly, labour could be carried from one continent to another. Thus were different races brought into close proximity in historically unprece-dented encounters. 'Think of the great migration of the Irish to America, of the great migration of the Chinese to Western America and the isles of the Pacific', he wrote. 'In Hawaii the Chinese now begin to form the bulk of the labouring population; and they are kept with difficulty from occu-pying Australia. The enormous Negro population of North and South America is due to the slave trade. We have in our own times begun to import Indian coolies into the West India islands ... Such transfers of population would be impossible but for the extreme cheapness of trans-port due to recent scientific discovery'. Indeed, Bryce concluded, 'one of the great achievements of science has been in making the world small, and the fortunes of every race and state are now or may at any moment become involved with those of any other'.[54]

As the relations of people and countries grew 'closer and more deli-cate' so new complex and difficult political and social problems arose. Bryce speculated further on the outcome of these different encounters in another essay on conquest and colonisation, where, true to Freeman, he noted 'the persistence of racial character in the New World' and the ten-dency of the more vigorous races to absorb the weaker. Negroes, however,

---

[53] Parker, 'The Failure of Liberal Racialism', p.827.
[54] James Bryce, 'The Relations of History and Geography', *Contemporary Review* vol.XLIX, (Jan–Jun 1886) pp.442–3.

seemed to be an exception: 'along the southern coasts of North America, in the West India Islands, and in some districts of Brazil, the Negroes form the largest part of the population . . . they increase rapidly in South Carolina and the Gulf States of the Union'. Yet they remained apart. Some had suggested 'their re-migration to Africa', but there was no reason to think that this would take place to any extent. Yet how could the two races continue to co-exist in a democratic republic?[55]

The relations of American blacks to whites was a subject Bryce researched in detail for *The American Commonwealth*, establishing a file for his research notes and thoughts in progress under the heading 'The Negro Problem' in 1885.[56] He travelled to the United States on a further research trip in 1890, to complete work for a new edition of the book and an article, 'Thoughts on the Negro Problem', for *North American Review*. The late 1880s saw a major revival of deportationist thinking and Bryce joined the debate on whether black Americans – 'an alien element, unabsorbed and unabsorbable' – should be expelled from the country. But as uneasy as whites were in South Carolina and Mississippi, he noted, most realised they could not do without black workers in a climate in which the white race was defeated by 'heat and malaria'.[57]

The debate on deportation was also noticed in Australia, where one newspaper editorial on the 'race problem' concluded: 'Whether the white man and the negro can live in harmony under conditions of equality may be doubted'. 'The latest solution of the race problem', advised the Melbourne *Age*, 'has been propounded by Mr Butler and Senator Morgan. They would remove the Blacks to Africa, which was provided for the negro as certainly as the Garden of Eden was prepared for Adam and Eve'. Senator Morgan declared that 'on the banks of the Congo the American negroes could found a republic which would be the glory of the age'. But, queried the editor of the *Age*, if the negroes should be 'returned' to their natural home in Africa, why should not Europeans be returned to Europe? Why did the white man have rights to settle in new lands, but other races not? That was precisely the question Lowe Kong Meng and his co-authors had posed in *The Chinese Question in Australia* just a few years before.

---

[55] James Bryce, 'Geography as a Basis of History', *Contemporary Review* vol.LXII (Jul–Dec 1892) pp.136–47.

[56] James Bryce, Notes for *American Commonwealth*, 'The Negro Problem' (May–Jun 1885) Bryce papers MSS 334–341, Bodleian Library.

[57] James Bryce, 'Thoughts on the Negro Problem', *North American Review* (December 1891) p.652; on deportationist thinking more generally, see George M. Frederickson, *The Black Image in the White Mind: The Debate on Afro-American Character and Destiny, 1817–1914* (New York, Harper and Row, 1971) pp.263–6.

Two races so differently advanced

In his article for *North American Review*, Bryce based his assessment that blacks were unfit for political rights in the discourses of 'history' and 'science'. 'History and science tell us', he wrote, 'that social and moral advancement is an extremely slow process, because it issues from a change in the physical as well as mental nature of a race'. Since the Negro was well behind the white man in evolutionary development, many thousands of years must pass before he would reach 'the pinnacle of modern wisdom and knowledge upon which the Caucasian stands today'.[58] In any case, black enfranchisement had met with extreme resistance. Given that the white man would never accept Negro rule – 'to him it [was] a simple question of self-preservation' – reasonable means had to be found to restrict the suffrage by some educational or pecuniary qualification (although Bryce noted that 'American sentiment dislikes a property qualification'), which would exclude many or most of the Negroes, not as Negroes, but because they are ignorant or poor'.[59]

Prevented by the 14th and 15th Amendments from disenfranchising voters on the basis of colour or race, the Mississippi Constitutional Convention led the way in recommending the device of a literacy test, that specified that a person 'should be able to sign his name and read any section of the Constitution, or be able to understand the same when read to him, or to give a reasonable interpretation thereof' to be registered as a voter. The Supreme Court of Mississippi explained its rationale:

Within the field of permissible action under the limitations proposed by the Federal Constitution, the Convention swept the field of expedients to obstruct the exercise of suffrage by the Negro race. By reasons of its previous condition of servitude and dependency, this race had acquired or accentuated certain peculiarities of habit, temperament, and of character, which clearly distinguished it as a race from the whites.[60]

Although not ostensibly discriminatory, the educational test permitted race distinctions in several ways, as Gilbert Stephenson observed in his study of *Race Distinctions in American Law*:

In the first place, registration officers may give a difficult passage of the Constitution to a Negro, and a very easy passage to a white person, or vice versa. He may permit a halting reading by one and require fluent reading by the other. He may

---

[58] Bryce, 'Thoughts on the Negro Problem', p.643; see too I. A. Newby, *Jim Crow's Defence: Anti-Negro Thought in America 1900–1930* (Baton Rouge, Louisiana State University Press, 1965) p.174.
[59] Bryce, *American Commonwealth*, third edition, p.511.
[60] Gilbert Thomas Stephenson, *Race Distinctions in American Law* (New York and London, Appleton and Co., 1910) p.295.

let illegible scratching on paper suffice for the signature of one and require of the other a legible handwriting. But race discriminations in such cases rest with the officers; they do not have their basis in the law itself.[61]

Other southern states followed suit: South Carolina in 1895, Louisiana in 1898, North Carolina in 1900, Alabama in 1901, Virginia in 1901 and Georgia in 1908.

The suggestion of a literacy test to effect racial discrimination would also prove useful to white men in the British Empire seeking to negate the racial equality promised to British subjects. In 1892, J. X. Merriman, the Liberal leader in the Cape Colony, wrote, when visiting London, to enquire of Bryce how the test worked: 'I have just been reading your article in the *North American Review* on the position of the Negro in the United States'. Merriman pointed out that the race problem was much greater in South Africa, where whites were everywhere in a minority. 'The best solution of the difficulties will probably be found in the same remedy that you suggest for the Southern States – viz by an educational test . . . My object in troubling you is to ask you where I can find out how the plan works.'[62]

Bryce invited Merriman to visit him and the two became friends. Their conversations confirmed for Bryce the usefulness of a comparative study of race relations between the United States and South Africa and the desirability of a new research trip. 'I should be very glad if I could impress upon you the importance and interest of the South African problem', Merriman wrote to Bryce, 'which does not consist – as those who have devoted a superficial attention to it seem to think – in a sort of faction fight between English or Dutch or in the development of more mines, but in the silent struggle that is going on between black and white along the whole line'.[63]

In the revised 1893–5 edition of *American Commonwealth*, Bryce advised that the example of the Mississippi literacy test had been taken up in the Cape: 'the advantages of such a method were obvious and suggested its adoption in a British Colony . . . where the presence of a large coloured population has raised a problem not dissimilar' to that in the United States. A footnote elaborated: 'In Cape Colony, the Franchise and Ballot Act of 1892 raises the property qualification for the suffrage and provides that no person shall be registered as an elector unless he is able to sign his name and write his address and occupation'. These provisions,

[61] Stephenson, *Race Distinctions*, pp.303–4.
[62] Merriman to Bryce, 22 February 1892, in Phyllis Lewsen (ed.) *Selections from the Correspondence of John X. Merriman 1890–1898* (Cape Town, Van Riebeeck Society, 1963) pp.93–4.
[63] *Ibid.* 25 February 1892, p.96.

he commented, 'disqualify the great bulk of the native coloured people'.[64] In *Equal Subjects, Unequal Rights* Julie Evans and her co-authors comment that the legislation targeted the tribal Africans of the Transkei – derogatorily called 'blanket Kaffirs'. In the debate on the legislation, Cecil Rhodes commented that the Cape had previously allowed too many Africans to vote; now they must exclude those with tribal tenure.[65]

Bryce's interest in the race relations of the New World deepened. In new chapters for the revised edition of *American Commonwealth* – 'The South Since the War' and 'Present and the Future of the Negro' – his assessment became more bleak and his sympathy with white southerners more explicit. The negro was a child and a primitive: 'His intelligence is rather quick than solid, and though not wanting in a sort of shrewdness, he shows the childishness as well as lack of self-control which belongs to primitive peoples'.[66] He also returned to the proposal for 'retransportation', but there were two 'fatal objections' to the plan: 'One is that they will not go; the other is that the whites cannot afford to let them go'. Blacks were needed in the South for their labour in the fields, the streets, the mines and tobacco factories, but how should they be treated as citizens?[67] Bryce echoed liberal imperial opinion that blacks should be accorded equal civil rights, but that their lack of advancement rendered them ineligible for political rights.

Seeking to explain southern white opinion to British readers, Bryce explained black incapacity in historical evolutionary terms. In the United States, the observer was confronted with 'a singular juxtaposition of the most primitive and the most recent, the most rudimentary and the most highly developed types of culture':

Not greater is the interval which separates the chipped flints of the Stone Age from the Maxim gun of to-day. A body of savages is violently carried across the ocean and set to work as slaves on the plantations of masters who are three or four thousand years in advance of them in mental capacity and moral force.

The great mass of their descendants, wrote Bryce, remain in their notions and their habits much what their ancestors were in the forests of the Niger or the Congo.

The radical experiment of political equality during the years of Radical Reconstruction, Bryce insisted, had been a terrible mistake. Suddenly, even more suddenly than they were torn from Africa, Negroes

[64] Bryce, *American Commonwealth*, third edition, pp.511–12.
[65] Julie Evans, Patricia Grimshaw, David Philips and Shurlee Swain, *Unequal Subjects, Unequal Rights. Indigenous Peoples in British Settler Colonies, 1830–1910* (Manchester, Manchester University Press, 2003) p.167.
[66] Bryce, *American Commonwealth*, third edition, p.496.   [67] *Ibid.* p.515.

found themselves, not only freed, but full citizens and active members of the most popular government the world has seen, treated as fit to bear an equal part in ruling, not only themselves, but also their recent masters. Bryce emphasised the revolutionary nature of these developments by drawing a comparison with the contemporary state of political rights in England: 'Rights which the agricultural labourers of England did not obtain till 1885 were in 1867 thrust upon these children of nature, whose highest form of pleasure had hitherto been to caper to the strains of a banjo'.[68]

In his chapter on 'The South Since the War', Bryce provided an historical summary of the reforms introduced by Radical Reconstruction and the passage of the 14th and 15th Amendments that guaranteed equal voting rights regardless of race. He stressed the foolishness of Northern insistence on freed blacks' rights to equality in voting and political representation and resultant white fears of negro domination. Furthermore, childlike blacks, 'children of nature', who in South Carolina and Mississippi comprised the majority of electors, were at the mercy of unscrupulous white carpet-baggers and other adventurers, who through 'frauds of every kind' gained control of the Negro vote and political office.[69]

As Hugh Tulloch has observed, Bryce's account 'classically stated the Gilded Age orthodoxy which was developed more fully in the historical works of such friends as C. F. Adams, James Ford Rhodes, Woodrow Wilson, John W. Burgess and W. A. Dunning' – an orthodoxy that would not be seriously questioned until the publication of W. E. B. DuBois' *Black Reconstruction in America 1860–80* in 1935.[70] Bryce's summary that 'such a Saturnalia of robbery and jobbery has seldom been seen in any civilised country and certainly never before under the forms of free self-government' would, as Tulloch wrote, be 'oft-quoted'.[71]

Bryce noted the combination of force and fraud that had re-instated white power by the late 1870s and white men's determination to resist 'Negro domination': 'the whites, being again in the saddle, meant to stay there'.[72] He regretted the pernicious effects of electoral corruption on the processes and reputation of democratic government and the deterioration of national character resulting from widespread violence. The practice of lynching accustomed southerners to cruelty and fostered a spirit of lawlessness, 'which tells for evil on every branch of government

[68] *Ibid.* pp. 494–5.   [69] *Ibid.* p. 476.
[70] W. E. B. DuBois, *Black Reconstruction in America: An Essay Toward a History of the Part Which Black Folks Played in the Attempt to Reconstruct Democracy in America, 1860–1880* (New York, Atheneum, [1935] 1969); see also Eric Foner, *Reconstruction: America's Unfinished Revolution, 1863–1877* (New York, Harper and Row, 1988).
[71] Tulloch, *James Bryce's American Commonwealth*, p.196.
[72] Bryce, *American Commonwealth*, third edition, p.484.

and public life'.[73] Blacks, meanwhile, could hope for no improvement in their position. 'No prospect was open to them', wrote Bryce, 'whatever wealth or culture they may acquire, of finding an entrance into white society, and they are made to feel in a thousand ways that they belong to a caste condemned to perpetual inferiority'.[74]

The close proximity of 'two races so differently advanced' had proven disastrous to public life, yet there was no obvious solution to this problem. Blacks comprised the majority of the population in three states. The 'negro question' was 'the capital question in national as well as State politics'. Yet there was no possibility of domestic integration or social intermixture. Whereas familiarity and intimacy were no threat to racial hierarchies under slavery, 'race repulsion' had intensified since emancipation so that segregation had become the rule and in many places the law:

> In many States the law requires the railroad and even the horse-car companies to provide separate cars . . . In most parts of the South a person of colour cannot enter a public refreshment-room used by the whites except as the servant of a white; and one may see the most respectable and, possibly, even educated coloured woman, perhaps almost white, forced into the coloured car among rough Negroes, while the black nurse in charge of a white child is admitted to the white car. The two races are everywhere taught in distinct schools and colleges, though in one or two places Negroes have been allowed to study in the medical or law courses. They worship in different churches.[75]

Bryce also pointed out that intermarriage was 'in every State, forbidden by law'. Under 'so complete a system of separation' there was no prospect of the development of a spirit of fellow feeling and public security essential to the working of a democracy and civil society.[76] And yet Bryce could see no alternative to segregation.

American race relations, he concluded, faced two challenges, one political and one social:

> How is the determination of the whites to rule to be reconciled with the possession by the Negroes of equal rights to suffrage? How can the social severance or antagonism of the two races – by whichever term we are to describe it – the haughty assertion of superiority by the whites and the suppressed resentment of the more advanced among the coloured people, be prevented from ripening into a settled distrust and hostility which may affect the peace and prosperity of the South for centuries to come?[77]

Although many white illiterate electors in Mississippi were also disqualified by the literacy test, Bryce noted the flexibility provided by giving decision-making power to state officials. Registering officials could

---

[73] *Ibid.* p.507.   [74] *Ibid.*   [75] *Ibid.* p.505.   [76] *Ibid.* p.507.   [77] *Ibid.* p.509.

admit whites who, though illiterate, were able to give a 'reasonable interpretation' of any section of the Constitution. 'Such whites have, one is
told, been able to satisfy the officials far more generally than have the
negroes'.[78] Bryce was clearly impressed by the utility of an educational
test in effecting racial exclusion, but without appearing to do so: 'It casts
no slur upon the negro race as a race, and does not wear the aspect of a
retrogression from the generosity with which the suffrage was bestowed. It
conforms to a principle reasonable in itself, and already adopted by some
Northern States'.[79] Connecticut and Massachusetts had introduced literacy tests for voting in the 1850s.

Bryce posed as a dispassionate academic observer of the south and he
cautioned fellow Britishers against hasty condemnation of white Southerners. As a British statesman, who was aware of race relations in the
Indian Dominions and of how 'not a few of his countrymen behave to
the ancient and cultivated races of the East whom they have conquered',
he felt that his countrymen were not entitled to sit in judgment. With his
interest in the global history of racial encounters, Bryce preferred to draw
attention to the larger transnational significance of the 'negro question'.
The problem was 'a new one in history', he declared, 'for the relations of
the ruling and subject races of Europe and Asia supply no parallel to it'.[80]
The problem was 'one of the great secular problems of the world, presented here under a force of peculiar difficulty'. There was no solution
in sight as 'the present differences between the African and the European are the product of thousands of years, during which one race was
advancing in the temperate, and the other remaining stationary in the
torrid zone, so centuries may pass before their relations as neighbours
and fellow-citizens have been duly adjusted'.[81]

Reviews of *American Commonwealth* sometimes complained of Bryce's
inconclusiveness, although in England the *Manchester Guardian* was re-
assured that he seemed less pessimistic than Pearson.[82] But whereas Pearson was primarily concerned with the change in 'world forces' and the rise
of China as a great power, Bryce's focus was on the management of race
relations within nation-states already multi-racial in composition. The
Critic reproduced Bryce's scathing assessment of Radical Reconstruction and noted approvingly his recommendation of segregation: 'In the
unchanged character of the dominant race, free from foreign admixture,
Mr Bryce sees the best hope for the future of the Southern people'.[83]

Bryce's old friend, A. V. Dicey, with whom he had first travelled to
the United States, emphasised the need to recognise the practical limits

---

[78] *Ibid.* p.512.   [79] *Ibid.* p.513.   [80] *Ibid.* p.514.   [81] *Ibid.* p.520.
[82] *Manchester Guardian*, 12 February 1895, Bryce papers, MSS 288, Bodleian Library.
[83] *Critic* (1 June 1895). Bryce papers MSS 288, Bodelian Library.

of the theoretical doctrine of equality: 'the doctrine that all men in a civilized country are fit to perform the duties and entitled to enjoy the full rights of citizens, if true at all, is applicable only to countries and races which have reached a certain stage of civilization . . . In every land which is inhabited or ruled by the English race, ordinary men are awakening to the knowledge that they are liable to be pressed upon by classes and races which are certainly unlike, and as Englishmen assume, are inferior to the man of English descent'.[84]

Some American liberals were dismayed, however, at Bryce's endorsement of segregation. Wendell Phillips Garrison wrote to Bryce: 'I fear you will comfort both our Imperialists and the lynchers, for the latter have caste for their stronghold, and it seems to me you justify caste'.[85] In a long review in *Nation*, Garrison regretted that Bryce had thrown 'the weight of his humane authority into the white scale' noting that he 'pointedly omits to recommend abolition of the laws forbidding intermarriage'. In this way, Garrison charged, Bryce was denying African-Americans' equal humanity:

the weight of the statutory prohibition lies in its perpetuating the doctrine of slavery, that the colored man is, when all is said and done, less than a human being. This doctrine has not been eradicated from the white mind in the generation since the war, and it coexists with a logical toleration not only of exceptional punishments for crimes perpetrated by the blacks, but for atrocious cruelty reserved solely for them – the lynchings deplored by Mr Bryce, in which the faggot is ever ready to be applied to the dark skin.[86]

But Bryce continued to insist on the dangers posed to democracies by the influx of 'half-civilized men'. The gift of political power to people who were 'not only ignorant, but in mind children rather than men' was not to confer a boon, but rather to inflict an injury.[87]

The authority of Bryce's assessment of American race relations derived both from his reputation as humanist scholar and liberal statesman and his status as disinterested observer. In the 1890s, the force of his observations about the 'negro problem' was enhanced by his growing standing as a world authority on race relations. As Garrison anticipated, Bryce's arguments would be used to justify the ascendant politics of segregation. *The American Commonwealth* offered validation to this modern doctrine, which was given a legal basis in the same decade by the Supreme Court's 'separate but equal' ruling, in *Plessy v. Ferguson*, which stated

[84] *Nation*, 16 July 1891.
[85] Tulloch, *James Bryce's American Commonwealth*, p.198.
[86] W. P. Garrison, 'The South and the Black Man', *Nation* (31 January 1895).
[87] James Bryce, *Impressions of South Africa* (London, Macmillan, 1897) p.453.

that Louisiana legislation requiring Negroes to travel in separate railway carriages did not violate the 14th Amendment's guarantee of 'equal protection'.

Bryce had commented at length on the 'race repugnance' everywhere evident in the United States. In his dissenting minority decision in *Plessy v. Ferguson*, John Marshall Harlan asked: 'What can more certainly arouse race hate, what more certainly create and perpetuate a feeling of distrust between these races, than state enactments which in fact proceed on the ground that colored citizens are so inferior and degraded that they cannot be allowed to sit in public coaches occupied by white citizens?'[88] Bryce cited 'race repugnance' to justify segregation; Harlan argued that segregation created race hatred.

Bryce's 'scientific' argument that races separated by thousands of years of evolution could not expect to exercise equal rights in a democracy, would be repeated many times in academic and popular literature during the following decades. In *Reconstruction and the Constitution*, Burgess labelled Radical Reconstruction 'the most soul-sickening spectacle Americans have ever been called upon to behold'. Congress did 'a monstrous thing' in enfranchising freed blacks: 'A black skin means membership in a race of men which has never of itself succeeded in subjecting passion to reason, has never, therefore, created any civilisation of any kind'. Burgess applauded the Republicans' imperial turn in the 1890s, for they would again learn by valuable experience 'that there are vast differences in political capacity between the races, and that it is the white man's mission, his duty and his right, to hold the reins of political power in his hands for the civilisation of the world and the welfare of mankind'. With specific reference to the Philippines, Burgess applauded the fact that in 'imposing the sovereignty of the United States upon eight millions of Asiatics', the Republican party had re-assuringly changed its views in regard to the political relations of races.[89]

That Radical Reconstruction had flown in the face of history and science had become orthodoxy. 'One thing is clear', wrote Charles Francis Adams in *Century Magazine*, 'the work done by those who were in political control at the close of our Civil War was done in utter ignorance of ethnologic law and total disregard of unalterable fact'. The negro should have been treated as a dependent:

[88] Quoted in Gunnar Myrdal, 'The National Association for the Advancement of Colored People', in Eric Foner (ed.) *America's Black Past: A Reader in Afro-American History* (New York, Harper and Row, 1970) p.444.

[89] Quoted in Hugh Tulloch, *The Debate on the American Civil War* (Manchester, Manchester University Press, 1999) pp.212–13.

The Negro after emancipation should have been dealt with, not as a political equal, much less forced into a position of superiority; he should have been treated as a ward and dependent – firmly, but in a spirit of kindness and absolute justice. We will in America make small progress towards a solution of our race problem until we approach it in less of a theoretical and humanitarian and more of a scientific spirit.[90]

Sympathy with Southerners became a major theme of political commentary. In *Reconstruction Political and Economic 1865–1877*, W. A. Dunning, Professor of Political Philosophy at Columbia University and student of John Burgess, wrote sympathetically of the 'humiliation' and 'shame' of white Southerners faced with the prospect of 'Negro rule' and quoted at length their views about the 'nefarious design' of the Republicans to 'degrade the Caucasian race as the inferiors of the African negro'.[91] In the *History of the United States from the Compromise of 1850 to the Final Restoration of Home Rule at the South in 1877*, James Ford Rhodes, an industrialist turned historian, described the enfranchisement of freed blacks as an 'effective expedient for enfranchising ignorance and disfranchising intelligence'. 'No such mass of political inexperience, of childish ignorance – no such "terrible inert mass of domesticated barbarism" – was ever before in our country called upon to exercise the suffrage'.[92]

Bryce's judgment about the unfitness of blacks for political rights reverberated in, and was reinforced by, the writings of historians, journalists and the numerous self-styled experts who subsequently published on the 'negro problem'. His views were invoked to justify American imperial ventures in the Caribbean and the Pacific, which denied the capacity of Filipinos, Hawaiians and Puerto Ricans for self-government.[93] Although Bryce doubted the wisdom of American colonising ventures, he did concede that imperial rule offered opportunities for enlightened and disinterested public men. 'Healthy despotism' was required in the Philippines and Cuba, he told Roosevelt in 1898. 'No talk of suffrage or any such constitutional privileges for them; but steady government by the firmest, honestest men you can find, and no interference if possible by Congress when the firm and honest men have been found'.[94]

---

[90] Charles Francis Adams, 'Reflex Light from Africa', quoted in Newby, *Jim Crow's Defense*, pp.78–9.
[91] W. A. Dunning, *Reconstruction Political and Economic 1865–1877* (New York, Harper, 1907) pp.109, 117.
[92] James Ford Rhodes, *History of the United States from the Compromise of 1850 to the Final Restoration of Home Rule at the South in 1877* (New York, Macmillan, 1912) pp.80–2.
[93] Newby, *Jim Crow's Defense*, p.15.
[94] Tulloch, *James Bryce's American Commonwealth*, p.205.

United States and South Africa: white men must rule

Shortly after the publication of the third edition of *The American Commonwealth*, Bryce accepted the invitation from Merriman to visit South Africa to enquire about the complex order of race relations between blacks and whites and Boer republics and British colonies. His enquiry was explicitly framed by his study of American race relations. There were obvious demographic differences: 'In the whole United States the whites are to the blacks as ten to one; in Africa south of the Zambesi it is the blacks who are ten to one to the whites. Or if we compare the four South African colonies and republics with the fifteen old slave States, the blacks are in the former nearly four times as numerous as the whites, and the whites in the latter twice as numerous as the blacks'.[95] Yet there were also strong similarities: 'in both countries we see two races in very different stages of civilisation dwelling side by side, yet not mingling or likely to mingle. In both countries one race rules over another. The stronger despises and dislikes the weaker; the weaker submits patiently to the stronger.'[96]

Bryce also noted the anomaly South Africa presented within the context of the British Empire and he emphasised a distinction that would become increasingly important to white men keen to challenge the common status of imperial subjects. British colonies fell into two groups, said Bryce: 'those which have received the gift of self-government and those which are governed from home through executive officials placed over each of them'. The latter were mostly in the tropics and mostly peopled by coloured races – Negroes, Indians, Malays, Polynesians or Chinese – with a small minority of governing whites. The self-governing colonies, on the other hand, were all within the temperate zone, and, with one exception, chiefly peopled by whites. Bryce then made clear the racial basis for political rights in the British Empire:

It is because they have a European population that they have been deemed fit to govern themselves, just as it is because the tropical colonies have a predominantly coloured population that the supremacy of the Colonial Office and its local representatives is acquiesced in as fit and proper.[97]

The one exception to this division occurred in South Africa, where there were two political systems side by side: 'while democratic as regards one of the races, [it] cannot safely be made democratic as regards the other'. Though this difficulty was new in the British Empire, it was familiar to Americans, advised Bryce, 'and it is instructive to compare the experience of South Africa with that through which the Southern States have passed since the War of Secession'.[98]

---

[95] Bryce, *Impressions*, pp.457–8.　　[96] *Ibid.* p.458.　　[97] *Ibid.* p.435.　　[98] *Ibid.* p.436.

American history lessons offered crucial instruction to contemporary policy-makers in South Africa as in Australia. In South Africa, whites had more reason to feel besieged and Bryce noted that their determination to exclude blacks from the franchise also extended to Indians, regardless of their status as British subjects. He referred to Natal's Franchise Act of 1896, that denied the vote to all the descendants of those not possessed of representative institutions with a parliamentary franchise, and its immigration law of 1897, that permitted the government to exclude all immigrants who could not write an application in a European language. 'I have referred particularly to this matter', Bryce explained, returning to his favourite theme, 'because it illustrates one of the difficulties which arise wherever a higher and a lower, or a stronger and a weaker, race live together under a democratic government'. He again dwelt on the unfitness of certain peoples for political rights:

> To make race or colour or religion a ground of political disability runs counter to what used to be deemed a fundamental principle of democracy and what has been made (by recent Amendments) a doctrine of the American Constitution. To admit to full political rights, in deference to abstract theory, persons, who, whether from deficient education or want of experience as citizens of a free country, are obviously unfit to exercise political power, is, or may be, dangerous to any commonwealth. Some way out of the contradiction has to be found and the democratic southern States of the North American Union and the oligarchical republic of Hawaii, as well as the South African colonies, are all trying to find such a way.

Although Bryce favoured the Mississippi and Cape Colony solution of an education test, which would allow a minority of educated blacks or Indians or natives to achieve political representation, and encourage others to qualify, the outcome of his continued emphasis on the unfitness of non-white races for political rights – and the importance of American history lessons – was to entrench the emergent racial dichotomy between whites and not-whites and the related understanding that democracy was a privilege reserved for white men. The corollary was that white men's countries must exclude, expel or segregate non-whites.

A crisis in the history of the world

Bryce synthesised his conclusions about race relations in the United States and South Africa for his influential, much-quoted Romanes lecture, published as *The Relations of the Advanced and the Backward Races of Mankind*, in 1902. Once again he referred to the 'mistake' of the United States experiment in political equality: 'The moral to be drawn from the case of the Southern States seems to be that you must not, however

excellent your intentions and however admirable your sentiments, legislate in the teeth of the facts. The great bulk of the Negroes were not
fit for the suffrage ... It would therefore have been better to postpone
the bestowal of this dangerous boon'.[99] And as the title of the lecture
suggested, Bryce saw the problems posed by multiracial democracies as
unprecedented world-historic problems.

He thus pointed approvingly to the successful steps taken by 'the Californian and the Australian' to 'avert race contact' through immigration
restriction – 'where the methods have been most stringent, the desired
result is being attained'.[100] Condemnation of such methods was beside
the point, Bryce said, for 'the Californian and the Australian, crudely
selfish as some of their arguments may appear, seem to be right in believing that a large influx of Chinese labour would mean the reduction of
the standard of life, and with that the standard of leisure and mental
cultivation, among the artisan class'.[101]

Once again, Bryce stressed the historical import of recent developments, which were of such significance that they marked, or 'may be
deemed to mark' (the qualification was added in a second draft) 'a crisis in the history of the world'. With new race contact, Bryce declared,
'mankind' had entered 'a new stage in World-history, a stage whose significance has perhaps been as yet scarcely realized either by the thinker
or the man of action'. The 'far closer and more widespread contact' of
'the more advanced and civilized races with the more backward' was 'so
much closer and more widespread than ever in the past that it may be
deemed to mark a crisis in the history of the world, which will profoundly
affect the destiny of all mankind'.

In his earlier essay on 'geography as a basis for history', written ten
years before, Bryce had theorised three forms of population movement:
transference, dispersion and permeation. In the Romanes lecture, he
developed a typology of four possible outcomes of conquest and colonisation or processes of 'unequal race contact': (1) the weaker races would
die out; (2) the weaker race would be absorbed by the stronger; (3) the
races would mix to form something new; and (4) racial difference was so
great that it must result in social separation. 'Aversion to colour', Bryce
advised in Anglo-Saxon mode, 'reaches its maximum among the Teu-
tons': 'Where Americans, Englishmen and Germans rule, there is no
intermarriage with the coloured races and consequently no prospect of
ultimate race fusion'.[102] In such circumstances, segregation and separate
development seemed the only options.

---

[99] Bryce, *The Relations of the Advanced and the Backward Races*, p.39.
[100] *Ibid.* p.33.   [101] *Ibid.*   [102] *Ibid.* pp.19–20.

By 1902, Bryce was an acknowledged expert on race relations in the New World. *The American Commonwealth* had become a compulsory reference work for nation-builders and political science students. Although, following Freeman, he emphasised racial continuity in the English-speaking world, his main achievement had been to draw attention to the challenges posed to democracies by unprecedented racial encounters – 'the crisis in the history of the world' – following on mass migration and black emancipation and enfranchisement.

Bryce's lectures and writing drew a dichotomy between peoples deemed fit for self-government and those not yet capable, or perhaps not ever. His message was the impossibility of multi-racial democracy. His writing gave legitimacy to policies of segregation in the United States and South Africa and authority to Australian nation-builders, who resolved that their new Commonwealth must learn from the mistakes of the American commonwealth and become the very model of a modern white man's country.

3 'The day will come': Charles Pearson's disturbing prophecy

The white man 'elbowed and hustled' and 'thrust aside'

In 1892, Charles Pearson had finally finished drafting his *magnum opus*. He wrote from Melbourne to his friend, James Bryce, in England for advice about a publisher, reassuring him that the book was not solely about Australia: 'The book would probably have some sale here but our purchasing public is not very large I think. It is to some extent the result of my political experience out here: but the Australian side is not much insisted on'.[1] Bryce put him in touch with his own publishing company, Macmillan, whose books reached a trans-Atlantic as well as an imperial market.

National Life and Character: A Forecast was published in London and New York in 1893 and caused a sensation, most particularly because of its startling prophecy. 'The day will come', Pearson wrote, in words that echoed the Chinese Remonstrance to the Victorian parliament and would, in turn, be much quoted:

and perhaps is not far distant, when the European observer will look round to see the globe girdled with a continuous zone of the black and yellow races, no longer too weak for aggression or under tutelage, but independent, or practically so, in government, monopolising the trade of their own regions, and circumscribing the industry of the Europeans . . . represented by fleets in the European seas, invited to international conferences and welcomed as allies in the quarrels of the civilized world . . . We shall wake to find ourselves elbowed and hustled, and perhaps even thrust aside by peoples whom we looked down upon as servile and thought of as bound always to minister to our needs. The solitary consolation will be that the changes have been inevitable.[2]

Pearson's book, written thousands of miles from Europe, from the vantage point of a British colony in the South Pacific, forecast the emergence of a

---

[1] Pearson to Bryce, 21 March 1892, microfilm H 62, Bryce papers, Bodleian library, Oxford.

[2] Charles Pearson, *National Life and Character: A Forecast* (London and New York, Macmillan, 1893) pp.84–5.

post-colonial world and the parallel decline of the white man. Colonised and coloured peoples – industrious, energetic and fertile – would take their place as dynamic historical agents, forming independent states, controlling their own trade and commerce, building their own navies and respected as equal powers in international relations.

Pearson's forecast went completely against the grain of imperial opinion. Its predictions represented a sharp rebuke to, and break from, the Anglo-Saxon triumphalism of Charles Dilke's *Greater Britain*, first published in 1868 and reprinted numerous times during the following decades, and J. R. Seeley's *The Expansion of England*, two courses of lectures, published in 1883 and re-reprinted thereafter. For two years, in 1866 and 1867, Dilke had 'followed England round the world', a voyage to America, India and Australia, that convinced him of 'the grandeur of the English race, already girdling the earth, which it is destined, perhaps, eventually to overspread'.[3] The major barrier to complete victory was the challenge posed by what he called the 'cheap races': blacks, Chinese, Indians and Irish. Arriving in the American state of Virginia, at the close of the Civil War, Dilke commented on the presence of Negroes working on the wharf, but 'not a white man to be seen'. In nearby Norfolk, there were 'hundreds of Negroes' working, building, repairing roads, but 'again not a white man to be seen'.[4] In a neighbourhood bar, however, he came upon 'a crowd of swaggering whites'.[5]

In a slave country, Dilke concluded, labour was degrading to the white man. 'Everywhere we have found that the difficulties which impede the progress to universal Dominion of the English peoples lie in the conflict with cheaper races.'[6] But he was confident that the 'dear' races would hold their own in the struggle. There would be no diminution of strength through 'miscegenation', because 'pride of race, strong in the English everywhere' created 'an absolute bar to intermarriage' and because the Anglo-Saxon spirit of conquest would ensure that the dearer races would destroy the cheaper and 'Saxondom will rise triumphant from the doubtful struggle'.[7]

National Life and Character challenged this prediction of Anglo-Saxon triumph. White men were not destined to rule the world forever. China would become a great power. India would become a self-governing state. Africans everywhere would follow Haiti in establishing independent black republics. Chinese and Indians were migrating to and settling in every land. Meanwhile, the decline in the European birth rate and English

---

[3] Charles Dilke, *Greater Britain: A Record of Travel in English-Speaking Countries* (London, Macmillan, 1868, reprinted 1907; Preface to first original edition).
[4] *Ibid.* pp.4–5.   [5] *Ibid.* p.5.   [6] *Ibid.* p.864.   [7] *Ibid.* pp.85, 564.

people's democratic embrace of state socialism – as exemplified in the progressive colony of Victoria – meant that a sedentary life in 'the stationary state' was the white man's inevitable fate. Whereas Dilke's tone was triumphant, Pearson's was elegiac. The best years of the 'higher races' were behind them: the future would see less enthusiasm, less hope, more resignation; the sky above would be more grey.

Pearson's 'epoch-making book' (as Harvard man Lothrop Stoddard referred to it twenty years later in *The Rising Tide of Color*) provided a discursive framework in which changing world forces would be discussed, welcomed and, more often, resisted during the next decades.[8] As Akira Iriye has noted, Pearson's forecast of 'the awakening of Asia' provided 'the point of departure for many writers, European and American'.[9] Importantly, Pearson had insisted that changing race relations should be understood in a global and historical frame, and warned that non-white races expected equal rights of mobility, residence and respect. Some welcomed his prophecy, for example the African nationalist, Seetsele Molema, who wrote of how it had encouraged hopes of black freedom, but for white men the world over, the book became a call to arms.[10]

National Life and Character prompted claims that territory in the 'Temperate Zone' – in South Africa, North America and Australasia – should be preserved as 'white man's country' – even if that meant, in the words of one critical commentator, penning up 'within the limits of Asia something like half the whole number of mankind'.[11] Pearson was quoted to justify immigration restriction in South Africa, North America and Australasia (citing a passage that largely reproduced his speech in the 1881 Victorian parliament):

The fear of Chinese immigration which the Australian democracy cherishes, and which Englishmen at home find it hard to understand, is, in fact, the instinct of self-preservation quickened by experience. We know that coloured and white labour cannot exist side by side; we are well aware that China can swamp us with a single year's surplus population; and we know that if national existence is sacrificed to the working of a few mines and sugar plantations, it is not the Englishman in Australia alone, but the whole civilised world that will be the losers.[12]

---

[8] See Lothrop Stoddard, *The Rising Tide of Color: Against White World-Supremacy* (New York, Scribner's, 1923) p.29; also L. E. Neame, *The Asiatic Danger in the Colonies* (London, Routledge, 1907) and Viator, 'Asia Contra Mundum', *Fortnightly Review* (1 February 1908).

[9] Akira Iriye, *Pacific Estrangement: Japanese and American Expansion, 1897–1911* (Cambridge, Harvard University Press, 1972) p.29.

[10] Seetsele Molema, *The Bantu: Past and Present: An Ethnographical and Historical Study of the Native Races of South Africa* (Edinburgh, W. Green and Son, 1920) p.346.

[11] Viator, 'Asia Contra Mundum', p.196.   [12] Pearson, *National Life and Character*, p.16.

His book prompted Englishman L. E. Neame to warn in *The Asiatic Danger in the Colonies* that, 'the real Asiatic Peril is the acquisition, by commercial pressure and trade treaties, of the right of entry to lands now closed... The enormous areas suitable for white colonization in Africa, Australia and North America', Neame insisted, 'should be closed to the Asiatic nations, whether British subjects or not.'[13]

Central to Pearson's prophecy had been his sudden realisation, in 1868, that the 'vacant earth' (Carlyle's phrase) on which 'white men' could live was, in fact, limited in extent. Constrained by climate, white men would soon be elbowed and thrust aside as the countries of Africa, the Americas, South East Asia and the Pacific Islands were settled by the more industrious and prolific Chinese, Japanese, Indians and Africans. Pearson's Australian vantage point enabled him to see these migrations from a new perspective. 'Twenty years' residence under the Southern Cross', he wrote in 1893, had forced him to consider 'a new side of this particular question: whether the capacity of European races to form new homes for themselves [was] not narrowly limited by climate, and by the circumstances of prior population'. European expansionists had not given much thought to prior population, but in any case Pearson shared the widespread view that in many places, including Australia, the first inhabitants – 'evanescent races' – were doomed to extinction.[14]

Australia was deemed doubly blessed historically and geographically. The natives had 'died out' as Europeans 'approached' and settlers enjoyed a magnificent temperate climate, in the southern colonies at least. But if coloured labour was introduced, Pearson warned, the northern part of the continent would become another Natal and the southern portion another Cape Colony, where 'the whites [were] indeed a masterful minority but still only as one in four'. With continued coloured immigration, Australia would soon resemble South Africa in the composition of its population. But there was more at stake than the national future. Australians were guarding the last part of the world, for the higher civilisation. 'We are denying the yellow race nothing but what it can find in the home of its birth, or in countries like the Indian Archipeligo, where the white man can never live except as an exotic'.[15]

The first chapter of *National Life and Character*, elaborating his earlier *Contemporary Review* article, offered a detailed consideration of settlement patterns across Africa, Asia, Australasia and the Americas, pointing both to the limits of the 'Temperate Zone' in which Europeans could live and work, and the great expanse of territory being settled by Africans,

---

[13] Neame, *The Asiatic Danger*, pp.x, 2.
[14] Pearson, *National Life and Character*, p.34.   [15] *Ibid.* p.16.

Chinese and Indians, whose migration patterns were as remarkable as those of Europeans. The advent of the census as an instrument of state surveillance provided evidence for a new global history, that tracked 'the great movements of races and their territorial aggregation', in the words of Melbourne journalist, A. M. Topp.[16]

Whereas some native peoples such as the Aborigines, Melanesians, Native Americans and Maoris, seemed destined to disappear, there was no doubting that other coloured peoples such as the Chinese and Indians were industrious, persistent and strong. Ongoing Chinese expansion was an inevitability: 'there is surely a strong presumption that so great a people as the Chinese, and possessed of such enormous natural resources, will sooner or later overflow their borders and spread over new territory, and submerge weaker races'.[17]

The history of Singapore, immediately to the north of Australia, demonstrated the trend. Pearson quoted Baron von Hübner's book, *Through the British Empire*, which used census figures to substantiate his impression that in the late nineteenth century Singapore had quite suddenly become a Chinese settler colony:

On my first visit to Singapore in 1871, the population consisted of 100 white families, of 20,000 Malays, and of a few thousand Chinese. On my return there, in the beginning of 1884, the population was divided, according to the official census, into 100 whites, 20,000 Malays, and 86,000 Chinese.[18]

For Pearson, 'Chinese colonisation of the Straits Settlements shows what the race is capable of'.[19]

In nearby Java, the resilience of the natives – those who had prior occupation – kept white men in a minority. Whereas the local Javanese population had quadrupled during the nineteenth century to reach 20 million, the Dutch population amounted to just 30,000 – 'nothing more than a garrison, a civil service and a collection of foreign traders'.[20] Meanwhile, islands such as Celebes, Sumatra, New Guinea and Borneo remained under-populated, but the future colonists of these tropical territories would not be white men. Between 1851 and 1875, some 250,000 Chinese had settled in the East Indies.

Pearson also attributed great significance to relative birth rates, emphasising that 'the lower races of men increase faster than the higher'.[21] Like many other commentators on the American South, he looked to census figures to track the relative increase in black and white fertility, finding

[16] A. M. Topp, 'Freeman's *Historical Geography of Europe*', *Melbourne Review* 6 (October 1881) p.399.
[17] Pearson, *National Life and Character*, pp.50–1.   [18] *Ibid.* p.47.
[19] *Ibid.* p.29.   [20] *Ibid.* p.42.   [21] *Ibid.* p.64.

that the black population 'increased not only absolutely but relatively in the seven states that are sometimes known as the Black Belt that stretch from North Carolina to Louisiana'.[22] In South Africa, the trend was even more worrying, for despite English settlers' best hopes, it was clear by the 1890s that Natal was 'already not a white man's colony'.[23] The British 'shield of protection' had, in fact, attracted hundreds of thousands of Africans to migrate there, so that by 1891, 'Natal has only 36,000 Europeans out of 481,000 settlers, the remainder being chiefly Zulus, though partly Hindoos and Chinamen'. 'The lower races', noted Pearson, categorising Africans, Indians and Chinese as one, 'have nearly doubled in proportion since 1863, when one seventh of the population was European'.[24]

South Africa was destined to be black. Even if half a million British immigrants arrived, 'where would they be at the end of a century with the black race increasing faster by births, and recruited by constant accessions from the populous interior of the continent? Can it be supposed that such a state would fare better than Georgia or South Carolina has fared?' The best course for a state so constituted, Pearson opined, 'would be to declare itself independent, as the Boers of the Transvaal have done, and so maintain the supremacy of the white race'.[25] White rule could be institutionalised through self-government, but even so, such a state, utilising black labour, would be bound to deteriorate into a class-divided, caste-based, undemocratic society, 'for we know that coloured and white labour cannot exist side by side'.[26] A fully democratic society, Pearson wrote, following Bryce, had to be racially homogeneous.

Even as the 'lower races' claimed a larger place in the world, many European nations were becoming 'stationary', their low birth rates and democratic enthusiasm for state socialism leading to an increased dependence on government and a loss of racial vigour. This was an argument already advanced by the American writer, James Russell Lowell, whom Pearson had met in 1868, when they compared notes on the relative merits of the manhood of English and American men in a discussion about race degeneracy. Lowell impressed the bookish and frail Pearson with stories about 'the Maine lumbermen, whose delight it was to drift over the rapids seated astride on pieces of timber, in constant peril of death, for the mere excitement of a plunge'.[27]

Lowell felt obliged to defend democracy against English criticism. In his lecture to the Birmingham and Midland Institute, published in

---

[22] *Ibid.* p.60.   [23] *Ibid.* p.29.   [24] *Ibid.* p.37.   [25] *Ibid.* p.39.   [26] *Ibid.* p.16.
[27] William Stebbing (ed.) *Charles Henry Pearson Memorials by Himself, His Wife and His Friends* (London, Longmans Green and Co., 1900) p.133.

Democracy and Other Addresses, in 1887, he offered a vigorous defence to the charge that Americans were 'infecting the Old World with what seems to be thought the entirely new disease of Democracy'.[28] On the whole, the experiment had been successful, he averred, but its trial would have been less severe, 'could it have been made to a people homogeneous in race, language and traditions', whereas the United States had been called upon to 'assimilate enormous masses of foreign population, heterogeneous in all these respects'. Lowell was a convinced Anglo-Saxonist, but he also worried about the rise of racism: 'The effect of Darwinism as a disintegration of humanitarianism is . . . yet to be reckoned with.' He praised socialist philosophy as 'the practical application of Christianity to life', but state socialism, he feared, 'would cut off the very roots in personal character – self-help, forethought, and frugality – which nourish and sustain the trunk and branches of every vigorous Commonwealth'.[29] This was an argument that Pearson would endorse.

Pearson believed that the political experiments in self-governing British colonies, such as Victoria, where he served as Minister for Public Instruction, pointed the way of the future: 'the State builds railways, founds and maintains schools, tries to regulate the wages and hours of labour, protects native industry, settles the population on the land, and is beginning to organise systems of State insurance'. The power of capitalists, landlords, patriarchal families and the church had all been eroded by state intervention. As a former Liberal member of parliament, Pearson thought that most of the 'liberal changes of the century' had been 'acts of justice', but still he had misgivings. Some of the outcomes were mixed blessings and, echoing Lowell, he thought the results of state socialism were not 'altogether desirable' for the development of national or individual character, such as the loss of creativity, initiative and vigour.[30]

Some reviewers of *National Life and Character* accused Pearson, the radical liberal, of helping to bring about that which he now condemned. His whole book, said the conservative *Saturday Review,* was:

a laboured, and to a great extent a successful, attempt to prove that the substitution of the State for the Church, the decay of the family, the equalisation of rights and privileges, the dominance of industrial organisations, the great increase of population and so forth, will destroy character, weaken the interest of life, kill genius, favour only the lower races and individuals, obliterate by degrees all that is noblest, most precious, rarest, best worth living for; yet he is imperturbably sure that it was quite the right thing to enlarge the suffrage, to allow a legal status, and practically a free hand to Trade Unions, to impair the authority of husband

---

[28] James Russell Lowell, *Democracy and Other Addresses* (London, Macmillan, 1887) p.10.
[29] Lowell, *Democracy,* pp.20, 26, 40.   [30] Pearson, *National Life and Character,* pp.12–18.

and fathers, to abolish class distinctions, to vulgarise education. His paradox is quite different from the old one; he abhors the end, but delights in the means. He views with horror the roof about to fall in, but he feels a glow of honest joy and pride when he thinks how he helped to pull down the pillars.[31]

Believing such reforms to be necessary and just, even as they produced a duller and more conformist state, Pearson maintained that the only course for civilised men was manly, stoical, acquiescence.

Pearson the liberal reformer

Pearson had, indeed, shown a lifetime commitment to liberal reform. He was raised in a family with strong connections to evangelical circles. His grandfather, a medical doctor, belonged to the Clapham Sect, was one of the founders of the Bible Society, and was 'intimate with Wilberforce, Zachary Macaulay, and the whole connection of Stephens, Venns, Thorntons and Babingtons'. His father, the Reverend John Norman Pearson, was a scholar at Trinity, but was disappointed in his academic ambitions. Pearson, the sensitive son, noted the effect of his father's worldly failure and that he had to rest content with what he called ordinary clerical work, serving for example as Principal of the Church Missionary College in Islington.[32]

Pearson's formal education began in 1843 at Rugby, a school whose self-conscious moralism ('always feeling their moral muscles') would earn his censure, and continued at King's College, London, which he liked, especially for the teaching of Christian socialist, F. D. Maurice.[33] He was subsequently offered a place at Oriel College, through his Babington connection but, disturbed by the general spirit of idleness, shifted to Exeter, where he obtained a scholarship, an important consideration for a boy from a family of modest circumstances.

Like many of his generation of radical liberals, Pearson found his voice in the Oxford Union debates. He soon acquired a reputation for 'extreme Liberal opinions', in the words of Lord Robert Cecil, the future Prime Minister, Lord Salisbury. The *Saturday Review* similarly recalled Pearson's reputation as a speaker in the Liberal cause, when reviewing his major work, *National Life and Character: A Forecast*, forty years later, reminding its readers that Pearson was:

One of the most distinguished of those University Liberals whose youth coincided with the first University Commissions, and who were born early enough to share

---

[31] *Saturday Review*, 25 February 1893.
[32] Charles Henry Pearson, 'The Story of My Life', in Stebbing (ed.) *Memorials*, pp.10–11.
[33] *Ibid.* p.17.

the confidence of Liberals of the middle of this century that abolition of tests, weakening of the power of the Church, and general adjustment of all things to the standard of a doctrinaire Liberalism would do, they did not exactly know what, but would, at any rate be worth doing.[34]

Pearson counted the friends he made at Oxford as its most valuable legacy. He secured a Classical First in 1852, but it was the Essay Society he helped form the same year – with George Goschen, Arthur Butler, George Brodrick and M. E. Grant Duff – who met once a month over wine to listen to and dissect an essay from one of their number, that gave him most pleasure.

During his time at Oxford, Pearson began travelling to Europe and learning more of its languages – he added German, Czech, Swedish and Italian to his French. He combined travel with journalism and, in 1863, with the help of Grant Duff, now at the Foreign Office, travelled to Poland to report on the insurrection, noting in an article for the *Spectator*, 'the abominations which the crime of unjust Dominion inevitably entails'.[35] His reports from Poland also registered the importance of 'race' to his understanding of class and national distinctions.

I left Poland sympathising deeply with the heroic efforts of the people, and thoroughly charmed by the manners and tone of the upper class ... Yet I am bound to confess my general impression was and is that the Poles are inferior to the Russians as a race, and in particular that the Polish peasant is a much more stolid and degraded animal than the Russian *moujik*. Every one must wish that Poland proper should regain the right of self-government ... [but] if Austria really becomes a federation of free states, the best future for Russian Poland would be to form a member of the union.[36]

Pearson referred to the Polish boast that they were a 'pure Slavonic race', but doubted if that were true: 'The existence of the large Polish nobility must surely have been based on a distinction of race, and there seems to me a marked difference of type between peasant and noble, the latter being Aryan, the former Mongolian'.[37]

Shortly after his return from Poland, Pearson suddenly decided, in 1864, to emigrate to the colonies. His health was poor and having been passed over for the Chichele Chair in History at Oxford (even though, as he indignantly noted, he was the only candidate to have published a book), his professional prospects were uncertain. The colonies might provide an 'opening' for an insecure but ambitious Englishman. His first attempt at farming was defeated, however, by an 'unparalleled drought'

---

[34] *Saturday Review*, 25 February 1893.
[35] John Tregenza, *Professor of Democracy: The Life of Charles Henry Pearson 1830–1894: Oxford Don and Australian Radical* (Melbourne, Melbourne University Press, 1968) p.31.
[36] *Ibid.* p.116.   [37] *Ibid.* p.117.

and he returned to England, taking a leisurely voyage via India, where he was confronted by his ambivalent feelings about colonialism and caste: disgust with the way in which the British treated the natives, but also revulsion at the natives themselves. Pearson's visit to India was disturbing in many ways, but it also served to dissipate his regrets at not taking an appointment in the Civil Service: he could not have endured the oppressive climate or the inanimate routine of office work. More importantly, he found that he 'could never have sympathised properly with the natives':

As it was, I left the country revolted by the brutality with which Europeans treated them, and yet feeling towards them myself as the Northerners in America are accused of feeling towards the blacks.[38]

It was an important moment of self-recognition.

On his return to England, Pearson completed the revision and extension of his book on England during the early and middle ages and his contribution to *Essays on Reform*. He then accepted an offer from feminist friends, including Anne Clough, to provide lectures for the North of England Council for Promoting the Higher Education of Women, and to write a pioneering essay in women's history: 'Historical Aspects of Family Life', for J. E. Butler's volume, *Woman's Work and Woman's Culture*, published by Macmillan in 1869.

Through his work for the higher education of women, he met Blanche Clough, the widow of a poet, Arthur Hugh Clough, who had lived with his sister Anne in the United States as a child, and since forged strong connections with New England's literary society. In 1868, as we have seen, Pearson travelled to New York and Boston, where he, like Clough and Goldwin Smith before him, formed a friendship with Charles Eliot Norton, who, with James Russell Lowell, was then co-editor of the *North American Review*. Back in England, he was invited by Henry Sidgwick to take up a position as lecturer in Modern History at Cambridge, where he also joined Liberal colleagues, including Henry and Millicent Garrett Fawcett, in forming a republican club, its guiding principle defined as 'hostility to the hereditary principle as exemplified in monarchical and aristocratic institutions and to all social and political privileges depending upon difference of sex'.[39] It was at this time that Sidgwick invited Anne Clough to found what would become Newnham College.

Pearson enjoyed the company of Cambridge colleagues, but found teaching indifferent students hard work. He had also missed out on the Regius Chair in History vacated by Goldwin Smith, thus dashing all hope

---

[38] Pearson, 'The Story of My Life', p.123.   [39] Tregenza, *Professor of Democracy*, p.54.

of securing a Chair in History at Oxford. Frustrated, restless and nostalgic for the Australian bush, Pearson suddenly decided in 1871 to pack up his library and leave England for good. Life on the land had not made him prosperous, he observed in his memoir, but it had made 'a new man' of him.[40] Back on his property in South Australia, wheat farming once again proved unprofitable, however. His circumstances also changed when he met a young woman whom he shortly married. Edith Butler was twenty-two years younger than he: 'My wife is very young', he wrote to Charles Norton, 'but our characters have much in common together with much that is different'.[41]

Feeling in greater need of society, the Pearsons moved to bustling, commercial Melbourne. His first employment was as a lecturer in history at the University, where he also formed a debating club on the model of the Oxford Union, whose membership included future Liberal politicians Alfred Deakin, H. B. Higgins and William Shiels. His next appointment as founding principal of a new secondary school for girls, Presbyterian Ladies' College (PLC), allowed him to work once again in support of his feminist commitment to the higher education of women. Established to prepare young women for university and the professions, PLC was the first Australian school to offer an education for girls equivalent to that provided by the leading boys' schools.[42] The first matriculant was Catherine Deakin, sister of Alfred. Pearson also pursued his interest in secondary schooling as a Royal Commissioner, appointed to enquire into methods of improving public education which, in Victoria, had been free, secular and compulsory since 1872.

Pearson had acquired a taste for practical politics and finally he was able to make it his profession. After one unsuccessful bid to enter parliament, he was elected in 1878 as the Liberal member for Castlemaine in the Legislative Assembly, where he joined campaigns for a progressive land tax, the break-up of big estates, the establishment of technical training schools, Sunday opening of the Melbourne Public Library, Museum and Art Gallery and the exclusion of Chinese immigrants. During the 1880s, he served as a Minister in successive Liberal governments, all the while continuing to write for Victorian and English papers and journals. Pearson was thus both a participant in and close witness of the experiment in 'state socialism'. Victorian governments, elected by manhood suffrage, had built railways and schools, extended protection to manufacturing

---

[40] Pearson, 'The Story of My Life', p.124.
[41] Pearson to Norton, 14 May 1873, Am/5416, Norton papers, Houghton Library.
[42] Tregenza, *Professor of Democracy*, p.75.

industry and regulated the hours and conditions of workers. They passed factory acts and established wages boards. Its 'state experiments' were already attracting world-wide interest. Australia was 'rapidly creating a State Socialism', wrote Pearson in *National Life and Character*, 'which succeeds because it is all-embracing'.[43]

Most importantly, Pearson became convinced during these years that democracy required unity of race. Returning to Australia in 1871, he had stopped in San Francisco where Republicans had joined Democrats in their determination to exclude the Chinese from California. But unlike many fellow Liberals, Pearson believed that all peoples – with the exception of 'evanescent races' – were capable of civilisation and self-government. Hence, coloured peoples would eventually form republics of their own and be received as equal powers at international conferences and as allies in the quarrels of the civilised world. Such changes he considered inevitable.

In an essay in the mid-1880s, Pearson had pointed to the historical significance of Haiti – the first black republic – whose founding in 1804 provided a new dynamic in world history. When Jean-Jacques Dessalines declared the independence of Haiti at the beginning of the nineteenth century, he brought an end to the only successful slave revolution in history, and one that had transformed the colony of Saint-Domingue into the second independent post-colonial state in the Western hemisphere. Pearson's essay on Haiti, occasioned by the publication of Sir Spenser St John's book, *Hayti, or The Black Republic*, in London in 1884, provided an unusually sympathetic account of 'The Black Republic'. The fact that 'a community of slaves and coloured freedmen should have been able to preserve a centralised government and national unity', 'kept itself free' and produce 'exports to the value of two millions a year' had defied the expectations of those who considered that blacks were incapable of self-government. Pearson's assessment was, remarked the *Spectator*, 'a perfect marvel in its absence of prejudice or forgetfulness of truth'. His conclusions were 'far more favourable to the Haytians [*sic*] than English opinion usually is'.[44]

Similarly, *National Life and Character* defied conventional wisdom about the Chinese. Far from being decadent and indolent, as popular English understandings insisted, China was depicted by Pearson as Lowe Kong Meng and his Victorian compatriots had described their country – as a civilised, industrious and expansive empire with a large population

[43] Pearson, *National Life and Character*, pp.17–18.
[44] Review of *Essays*, in *Spectator*, 25 April 1896, newscutting, Pearson papers, MS 7518–9, box 432, State Library of Victoria (SLV).

of more than 400 million people. The Chinese, like the British, were taking advantage of the technologies of modern mobility. The cheapness of steamship and train travel meant that they were engaged in a process of peaceful expansion into South East Asia, Australasia, the Americas and the islands of the Pacific. 'With civilization equally diffused', wrote Pearson, 'the most populous country must ultimately be the most powerful; and the preponderance of China over any rival – even over the United States of America – is likely to be overwhelming'.[45] The future would see China take 'its inevitable position as one of the great powers of the world'.[46]

'Remarkable', 'novel', 'disturbing': the impact of Pearson's book

National Life and Character was an immediate best seller and talking point. It was reprinted several times in 1893 and 1894, and again in 1913. Having returned to live in London, in 1892, Pearson enjoyed his sudden metropolitan fame. He wrote to Deakin, his protégé, describing the book's reception among leading public men, many of whom Deakin had met on his first visit to London for the first Colonial Conference in 1887. The reviews had been 'very good natured and laudatory', Pearson wrote, 'and the *Westminster Budget* has asked for my likeness!' A few weeks later, he elaborated: 'It has been an unexpected but I think real success. Hutton, Huxley, Green, Mahaffy & Simcox have been among the critics: and it has altogether been reviewed in some thirty papers.'[47]

Readers around the world wrote to tell him of their interest, and old friends congratulated him on his new celebrity. Theodore Roosevelt wrote from the United States to tell him of the 'great effect' of *National Life and Character* on 'all our men here in Washington'. They were 'greatly interested in what you said. In fact, I don't suppose that any book recently, unless it is Mahan's 'Influence of Sea Power' has excited anything like as much interest'.[48] Roosevelt's reading circle included Henry Cabot Lodge, Henry and Brooks Adams, and English diplomat Arthur Cecil Spring Rice.

Reviewers acclaimed the book as 'remarkable', 'novel' 'strikingly original', 'disturbing' and 'extremely disquietening'. The *Westminster Review*

---

[45] Pearson, *National Life and Character*, p.30.   [46] *Ibid.* p.49.
[47] Pearson to Deakin, 29 March 1893, Deakin papers, MS 1540/1/193; MS 1540/1/201, National Library of Australia (NLA).
[48] Theodore Roosevelt to Charles Pearson, 11 May 1894, Pearson papers, Bodleian Library, MS English letters, folios 187–191, d.190.

called it a 'remarkable work – well written, for the most part well-argued, abounding in facts and strikingly original':

The popular view that the Saxon, or at any rate 'Aryan' races will gradually absorb the earth's surface and the earth's goods is fallacious: slowly and irresistibly the yellow and the black races, the Chinamen and the negro, will crowd the higher races out and establish their power over all.[49]

'The author entirely dissents from the theory that the higher races of mankind are destined to gain on the lower,' confirmed *St James' Gazette*. 'The Chinaman, the Negro, the Hindoo will spread everywhere, by sheer force of industry and reproductive energy.'[50] English elder statesman W. E. Gladstone advised: 'The book should be carefully read and digested by everyone who has any interest or influence in public affairs'.[51]

In attributing historical agency to the 'black and yellow races', Pearson posed a radical challenge to conventional race thinking and to Social Darwinists, such as Benjamin Kidd, whose *Social Evolution* was published the following year in 1894. A firm believer in the applicability of the principles of 'evolutionary science' to history, Kidd argued that the 'lower races' must remain indefinitely under European 'tutelage' for the sake of 'social efficiency'. In a long footnote, added to his book at the last minute, he responded to Pearson's book, criticising him for paying too much attention to developments beyond Europe. Pearson had made 'the serious mistake', he wrote, 'of estimating the future by watching the course of events outside the temperate regions', rather than attending to 'the progress amongst the Western peoples'. In other words, Pearson had made the mistake of treating the 'black and yellow races' as historical agents capable of changing the world.

Many articles in 1894 compared the two books. J. Llewelyn Davies, writing in the *Guardian*, pointed to the contrast between their views of the 'less civilised' races:

Both these authors have something prophetic to say about the relation of the Western and more civilised races to the less civilised; and their forecasts are in curious contrast to each other. Mr Pearson sees the Chinese, the races of the Indian Peninsula, the Negroes, all increasing round the European races, and threatening to squeeze them into anaemic languor: Mr Kidd sees the Teutonic races, because they surpass other races in reverence and a sense of duty, tending to rule the whole earth. And instead of having fanciful notions as to the equality or equal rights of inferior races, he sets himself to argue us out of any such notions.[52]

[49] *Westminster Review*, March 1893, Pearson papers, SLV.
[50] *St James Gazette*, 2 February 1893, Pearson papers, SLV.
[51] Quoted in *Westminster Gazette*, 1 April 1893, Pearson papers, SLV.
[52] J. Llewelyn Davies, 'Are All Men Equal?', *Guardian*, 13 June 1894.

Unlike Kidd, Pearson asked white readers to think of blacks, Chinese and Indians as their equals – now or in the very near future. Pearson's provocative argument could also be seen as a delayed response to an attack on his work mounted by E. A. Freeman some twenty years before.

Pearson's challenge to Anglo-Saxon triumphalism

Long before *National Life and Character* appeared as a 'meteor' on the literary scene, Pearson had questioned the racial determinism that dominated historical thinking in the nineteenth century.[53] As a historian, he was best known in England and the United States for his bitter clash with Freeman, in a vituperative exchange that 'scandalised' the literary world in the late 1860s.[54] When Pearson published his *History of England During the Early and Middle Ages* in 1867, Freeman, well known for 'his tendency to vehemence in controversy', launched a long and savage attack in the *Fortnightly Review*.[55] Whereas Freeman believed in Anglo-Saxon continuity and racial triumph, Pearson emphasised historical change and world transformation.

In his history of England during the early and middle ages, Pearson had dared to challenged Freeman's 'extravagant Saxonism'.[56] Freeman, in response, charged that Pearson didn't know or enjoy the period and he couldn't write. More seriously, Freeman also took issue with Pearson's idea of the 'science of history': 'I do not know what the "science of history" is, but I suspect that it has very little to do either with the old Teutonic constitution or with the grand personal drama of the men who fought on Assandun and Senlac.'[57]

Pearson wrote an 'astringent' pamphlet in reply, in which he questioned Freeman's racial theory of history:

He is an enthusiast for Saxon institutions, and dates the History of England from Hengist and Horsa; while I follow Sir Francis Palgrave in tracing it back to the Roman occupation ... when Mr Freeman talks of the 'old Teutonic constitution', I confess he is out of my depth, and I think he is out of his own. Nothing is more tempting than to group all events under a symmetrical theory, and to refer every institution and fact to a Saxon or a Roman original. But the life of a great society does not arrange itself in this manner, and even if the Saxons, when they came to England, made a clean sweep of the cities and the inhabitants, as Mr Freeman seems to suppose, they must, from the very circumstances of a new settlement, have made some changes on the 'old Teutonic constitution'.[58]

[53] Stebbing, *Memorials*, p.304.
[54] Review of *Memorials*, 1896, *Spectator*, Pearson papers, SLV.
[55] James Bryce, 'Edward Augustus Freeman', *English Historical Review* 7, 27 (1892) p.509.
[56] Review of *Essays* in *Liverpool Post*, 11 July 1896, newscutting, Pearson papers, SLV.
[57] Quoted in Tregenza, *Professor of Democracy*, p.48.   [58] *Ibid.* p.49.

Pearson was more interested in the forces making for historical adaptation and change – especially arising from new conquests and encounters between foreign peoples – rather than charting racial continuity. One of the bases for social change was inter-marriage. Pearson argued that Romans and Saxons alike must have 'intermarried with the native women of Britain to a much larger extent than was commonly allowed'. His subsequent *Historical Maps of England* also showed, on the basis of detailed topographical research, the impact of historical change by attending to the evidence of landscape, settlement and building, and the growth and decay of towns and villages.

Pearson withdrew his published reply to Freeman's outrageous attack because – so he told Charles Norton – it could have been used to damage Freeman's chances as a Liberal candidate in the post-Reform election. A more sustained response to Freeman's 'extravagant Saxonism' would have to wait. Frustratingly for Pearson, Freeman would never get to read *National Life and Character* or see its impact. He died just one year before its publication while on an archaeological survey in Spain in 1892.

In his travels through the United States, in 1868 and 1871, Pearson, like Dilke and Goldwin Smith before him and Bryce and Freeman later, was struck by the racial diversity of the country, with its fast-growing population of blacks in the south, a declining native population in the mid- and south west, and increasing communities of Chinese in California. He was critical of the effects of the institution of slavery not only on blacks, but also on 'imperious' southern whites, echoing Dilke in his observation that they had become 'licentious and disdainful of patient toil'.[59] In *National Life and Character* he followed Bryce in discussing the proposal to deport blacks *en masse* to Africa, but by the end of the century it seemed impractical: the American Congress ought to have bought up the slaves and expatriated them while were still 'a mere handful'.[60]

Whereas Pearson and Bryce worried about the unprecedented racial encounters in the new world and charted the increasing numbers of Africans and Chinese, for Freeman and Dilke, the experience of Haitians, Chinese, Indians or Javanese simply lay beyond the bounds of history, such peoples inconceivable as historical subjects. World history was contained within European history; the colonies were simply an extension of Greater Britain.

But what of the worlds beyond Europe? In a reply to critics of *National Life and Character* in *Fortnightly Review*, Pearson reminded his readers, in

[59] Pearson, *National Life and Character*, p.124.   [60] *Ibid.* p.9.

an argument again echoing Chinese community leaders in Victoria, that the Chinese had 'attained to a very complete civilisation of their own, in law, in organisation and in ceremonial courtesy; and even now there are four hundred millions to be transformed before all this is exchanged for something better'.[61] British sceptics remained doubtful, with his friend, M. E. Grant Duff, commenting in the *Academy* that if 'the existence of the British race is incompatible with that of other people, it is that of other people which will give way'. The 'English race [would] certainly awake to a sense of its duties, when the time [came], and massacre as many Chinese and Hindoos as [were] found superfluous'.[62] Grant Duff had served as Governor of Madras during the 1880s, a posting whose endless tours of inspection, addresses and deputations he thoroughly enjoyed. Perhaps he was joking about killing the natives, but Pearson was indignant: 'Can you imagine any European power setting itself to massacre 100 millions of Chinamen?' he wrote to Deakin in Melbourne.[63]

The English conviction of racial superiority was hard to dislodge. 'Mr Pearson has seen the Chinese at work in many parts of the world and he speaks from knowledge', sniffed the *Westminster Gazette*. 'But the future must belong to the most inventive and most fertile peoples, which are certainly not the Chinese, nor any other Oriental race'.

Racial anxiety

Clearly, the novelty of Pearson's perspective on world history owed much to his residence in the Australian colonies, twelve thousand miles from Britain, but close to South East Asia. One of the more perceptive reviews of *National Life and Character*, in the London *Athenaeum*, noted the significance of Pearson's 'Australian point of view':

The forecast will take many by surprise, because the view it presents is not only not fashionable, but is fundamentally different from that to which we have been accustomed since 'progress' became a catchword among us ... In another respect, too, he quits the beaten track of anticipation. His view is not purely or mainly European, nor does he regard the inferior races as hopelessly beaten in the struggle with Western civilisation. The reader can indeed discern that Mr Pearson's point of view is not London or Paris, but Melbourne.

---

[61] Charles Pearson, 'The Causes of Pessimism', *Fortnightly Review* (1 October 1893) p.153, Pearson papers, MS 7112, box 432/3, SLV.
[62] *Academy*, 4 March 1893.
[63] Charles Pearson to Alfred Deakin, 29 March 1893, Deakin Papers, MS 1540/1/201, NLA.

He regards the march of affairs from the Australian point of view, and next to Australia what he seems to see most clearly is the growth of Chinese power and of the native populations of Africa. In this forecast, in fact, Europe loses altogether the precedence it has always enjoyed. It appears here as not only the smallest, but as the least important continent.[64]

From Pearson's perspective in the South Pacific, Europe seemed increasingly marginal to major developments in world history.

Race patriots were outraged. Writing in the Australian edition of the leading organ of Anglo-Saxon solidarity, the *Review of Reviews*, a Melbourne writer, W. H. Fitchett, accused Pearson of being a traitor to his race. He mocked the 'dyspeptic melancholy' Englishman, who refused to 'admit the "superiority" of the Anglo-Saxon' but rather attempted 'to prove that in politics the law of the survival of the fittest is inverted'.[65] Having forgotten his 'pride of race', Pearson expected his own people, wrote Fitchett, 'to vanish before a procession of coffee-coloured, yellow-tinted or black-skinned races'.[66]

Pearson enjoyed the controversy caused by his book, but he didn't live to see its long-term impact or engage with those who came after him. Living in London and bitter about the failure of the Victorian government to provide him with employment as Agent-General, he succumbed to a lethal chest infection in 1894. He didn't live to see China defeated the following year by Japan and the subsequent rise of Japan, not China, as the great naval and military force of modern Asia – although, more than a hundred years on, Pearson's forecast of Chinese commercial might and industrial power seems prescient enough.

Pearson had left England in a dejected mood, his eyesight failing, his prospects declining. As he approached forty, he had begun to harbour, in the words of his friend, George Brodrick, 'a certain sense of unrecognised ability and an impatience of his comparative obscurity in London'.[67] Migration to the colonies might revive his ailing health and rescue his fortunes. In the event, Pearson's desire to be noticed would ultimately be gratified beyond measure, when the publication of his *National Life and Character* turned him briefly into a metropolitan celebrity. His migration to Australia had provided him with fresh vision and novel insight.

The most significant legacy of Pearson's 'epoch-making book' was to shape the discursive and psychic frameworks in which much subsequent discussion of changing world forces would take place, in particular the

[64] *Athenaeum*, 4 March 1893.   [65] *Review of Reviews*, 15 August 1900, p.150.
[66] *Ibid.*   [67] George Brodrick, quoted in Stebbing, *Memorials*, p.157.

idea of a coming rivalry between East and West. Thus for one of his read-ers in Washington, American naval authority Alfred Mahan, the question thenceforth became whether 'Eastern or Western civilization is to dom-inate throughout the earth and control its future'.[68] Mahan, like many of his contemporaries, thought that this struggle for world domination – often characterised as a race war – would occur not in the Atlantic, as had previous historic battles, but in the Pacific, the oceanic neighbourhood of the white men's countries of the New World.

Although careful to state that 'lower and higher races' were 'relative terms', with no fixed meaning, Pearson's argument encouraged racist thinking of a kind that his own forecast called into question.[69] Though critical of the view that the 'lower races' were inherently, biologically inferior, Pearson's arguments, like those of Bryce, encouraged a binary mode of racial thought that lay the basis for the division of the world into white and not-white, a dichotomy that would soon dominate the thinking of English-speaking countries and beyond.

Most importantly, Pearson's book drew attention to what was happen-ing in the world beyond Europe and challenged white men's presump-tion. It was 'not only a treatise but an act', wrote the astute commentator, 'Viator', in *Fortnightly Review*, in 1908, with effects on both sides of the emergent colour line:

It shook the self-confidence of the white races and deprived them of the absolute sense of assured superiority which had hitherto helped them to dominate.[70]

By pointing to the insecurity of white men's place in the world, *National Life and Character* prompted anxious thoughts about what Stoddard called 'the rising tide of color' and proprietorial assertions that certain lands were, and must remain, 'white men's countries'. These defensive state-ments of exclusive possession were also claims of racial entitlement. Other races must keep inside their pre-ordained borders or advance only into tropical zones. Moreover, in suggesting that European peoples were afflicted by 'a decay of vital power in the race' and entering a 'stationary state', Pearson's book stirred deeper anxieties that led, most notably in the case of the future American President, Theodore Roosevelt, to strident re-assertions of national vigour.

Among coloured and colonised peoples, on the other hand, the forecast stirred new hopes, as Molema had written, and as 'Viator' also noted:

---

[68] Alfred Mahan, 'A Twentieth-Century Outlook', *Harper's New Monthly Magazine*, quoted in Iriye, *Pacific Estrangement*, p.31.
[69] Pearson, *National Life and Character*, p.74.
[70] Viator, 'Asia Contra Mundum', 1 February 1908, p.185.

To Asiatic students, the mental pioneers of the Eastern renaissance, it revealed what some of them have suspected – that the impassive forehead of the white man was part of a brazen mask, the mind within being full of doubt and trouble, prone to self-dissolving reflection.[71]

Pearson had anticipated a postcolonial order in which the 'black and yellow races', no longer under subjection or tutelage, would take their place as equal states in a new world order, an aspiration that would indeed shape the twentieth century.

In a recent collection of essays, *Decolonization: Perspectives From Then and Now*, Prasenjit Duara has observed:

From a historian's perspective, decolonization was one of the most important political developments of the twentieth century because it turned the world into the stage of history. Until World War 1, historical writing had been the work of the European conquerors that, in the words, of Oswald Spengler, had made the world appear to 'revolve around the pole of this little part-world' that is Europe. With few exceptions, the regions outside Europe were seen to be inhabited by people without the kind of history capable of shaping the world.[72]

Pearson was an exceptional observer, whose 'monumental book on the Decline of the White Man' (as one reader described it) startled his contemporaries.[73] More than twenty years before the first world war and the publication of Oswald Spengler's *Decline of the West*, Pearson's *National Life and Character* represented the world as a stage of history, on which the 'black and yellow races', energetic, industrious and expansive, were assuming leading roles. In 1893, Pearson asked his readers to imagine 'a condition of political society' in which the peoples of 'China, Malaysia, India, Central Africa and Tropical America' were 'teeming with life, developed by industrial enterprise, fairly well administered by native governments, and owning the better part of the carrying trade of the world'.[74] It was a sobering scenario: 'elbowed', 'hustled' and 'thrust aside', the white man faced an uncertain future.

[71] *Ibid.*
[72] Prasenjit Duara (ed.) *Decolonization Perspectives From Then and Now: Rewriting Histories* (New York, Routledge, 2004) p.1.
[73] Obituary, *Morning Leader*, Cutting in Pearson papers, MS 8744, box 976/2 (e), SLV.
[74] Pearson, *National Life and Character*, p.130.

4 Theodore Roosevelt's re-assertion of racial vigour

'One of the most notable books of the end of the century'

When Theodore Roosevelt read Charles Pearson's *National Life and Character*, in early 1894, he was enjoying life. Working for the Civil Service Commission in Washington, he was proud of American progress and confident about the nation's future prospects, lavishly depicted at White City, the great World Exhibition in Chicago, which he had visited just the year before – 'the most beautiful architectural exhibit the world has ever seen', he wrote to his literary friend, James Brander Matthews.[1]

When not at the office, Roosevelt spent time reading, riding, rowing on the river, romping with his children, taking tea, playing tennis and attending dinner parties. He enjoyed a close circle of friends. 'Cabot and I ride together when we get a chance', he wrote to his sister Anna at the beginning of 1893, 'and this morning Willie Phillips joined me in taking the children for a wild scramble'.[2] William Hallett Phillips shared Roosevelt's interest in conservation and was instrumental in the establishment of Yellowstone National Park, while Henry Cabot Lodge, newly elected Republican Senator for Massachusetts, had been Roosevelt's intimate since Harvard College days.

Like Roosevelt, Lodge was a bookish aristocrat, who had taken up boxing, riding and hunting to develop his courage and physique. They shared a love of history informed by admiration of 'Anglo-Saxon' qualities, defined by Lodge in his 1896 speech in support of immigration restriction as 'an unconquerable energy, a very great initiative, an absolute Empire over self'.[3] Lodge had been a student in Harvard's first post-graduate History seminar conducted by Henry Adams, who advised

---

[1] Theodore Roosevelt to James Brander Matthews, 8 June 1893, in Elting E. Morison (ed.) *The Letters of Theodore Roosevelt* (Cambridge, Harvard University Press, 1951) vol.1, p.320.
[2] Theodore Roosevelt to Anna Roosevelt, 14 January 1893, *Ibid.* p.306.
[3] Immigration Restriction League papers, MS Am 2245 (1122), Houghton Library.

his student to 'use the German historical method'.[4] Both Lodge and
Roosevelt would contribute a volume to the series commissioned by leading Anglo-Saxonist E. A. Freeman on historic towns, Lodge writing on
Boston and Roosevelt on his home town of New York. While in Washington, the two spent much time together, dining and wining, walking
and talking, loudly castigating the 'Mugwumps' and 'peace at any price'
men.

In Boston, at the end of 1893, Oliver Wendell Holmes Jr., another
friend from college days, whom Roosevelt would appoint to the United
States Supreme Court, noted Pearson's book in his list of reading for
that year alongside Karl Marx's *Capital*, Jane Austen's *Emma* and Alfred
Mahan's *Sea Power*.[5] In early 1894, Roosevelt wrote to tell Pearson of
the 'great effect' of *National Life and Character* among his friends in the
national capital: 'all our men here in Washington . . . were greatly interested in what you said. In fact, I don't suppose that any book recently,
unless it is Mahan's "Influence of Sea Power" has excited anything like as
much interest or has caused so many men to feel that they had to revise
their mental estimates of facts' – for example the fact that the population
of China had surpassed 400 million.[6] Roosevelt had a sudden realisation:
large families were not simply a source of personal satisfaction, they were
crucial to national greatness.

The birth rate would henceforth become something of an obsession
with him. 'The woman must be the housewife, the helpmeet and the
homemaker, the wise and fearless mother of many healthy children', he
later declared. 'When men fear work or fear righteous war, when women
fear motherhood, they tremble on the brink of doom'.[7] For Roosevelt,
good breeders and good fighters became key agents in the re-invigoration
of national character. Roosevelt gained insight from Pearson, but he found
the Englishman's forecast of the white man's imminent decline somewhat
perplexing. Nevertheless, he took its general message about changing
'world-forces' to heart.

The 'men in Washington' who formed Roosevelt's literary and political circle included the brothers Brooks and Henry Adams, descendants
of the illustrious political dynasty and writers of ethnography and history. One evening at Henry Adams' house, Roosevelt found he had 'stay-
ing with him a delightful Polynesian chief and adopted brother? [*sic*] a

[4] Henry Adams to Henry Cabot Lodge, 2 June 1872, in J. C. Levenson (ed.) *The Letters of Henry Adams* (Cambridge, Belknap Press, 1982).
[5] Oliver Wendell Holmes, *Blackbook of Reading*, Special Collections, MS 4075a, Harvard Law Library.
[6] Theodore Roosevelt to Charles Pearson, 11 May 1894, Pearson papers, Bodleian Library, MS English letters, folios 187–191, d. 190.
[7] Theodore Roosevelt, *The Strenuous Life: Essays and Addresses* (London, Grant Richards, 1902) p.2.

polished gentleman, of easy manners, with an interesting undertone of queer barbarism'.[8] They discussed Pearson's predictions which Adams had found persuasive. 'I am satisfied that Pearson is right', he wrote to C. M. Gaskell in England, 'and the dark races are gaining on us, as they have already done in Haiti, and are doing throughout the West Indies and our Southern States'.[9]

Roosevelt's dinner companions also included William Rockhill, the Orientalist explorer and diplomat, and the writer Rudyard Kipling, about whom Roosevelt felt ambivalent: 'Kipling is an underbred little fellow, with a tendency to criticise America to which I put a stop by giving him a very rough handling, since which he has not repeated the offence; but he is a genius, and is very entertaining. His wife is fearful however'. Roosevelt compared Kipling's writing favourably with that of the 'diseased' Henry James. He blushed to think that James, writing for and about the English upper classes, was ever American and he turned to Kipling with 'the feeling of getting into fresh, healthy out-of-doors life'.[10] He was, nevertheless, irritated by Kipling's tendency to treat Americans as colonials, being extra-sensitive to any suggestion of English condescension.

In late 1886, Roosevelt had travelled to England, where he would marry his second wife, Edith. On the boat, he met Cecil Arthur Spring Rice, whose role as best man at Roosevelt's wedding was the beginning of a lifelong friendship. In London, Roosevelt was careful not to give any impression of deference to the English ruling class. Writing to Lodge, he was pleased to report: 'Edith, thank Heaven, feels as I do, and is even more intensely anti-anglomaniac; and I really think our utter indifference, and our standing sharply on our dignity, have been among the main causes that have procured us so hospitable a reception'.[11] He was surprised, but pleased at the attention of leading public men. 'I have had very good fun here', he wrote to Lodge, 'I have been treated like a prince I have been put down at the Athenaeum and other swell clubs, have been dined and lunched every day and have had countless invitations to go down into the country and hunt or shoot. I have really enjoyed meeting some of the men – as Goschen, Shaw Lefevre, John Morley, Bryce (who wishes to be remembered to you, and was especially complimentary about your Hamilton [Lodge's biography])'.[12] He also met George Trevelyan

---

[8] Theodore Roosevelt to Cecil Arthur Spring Rice, 25 December 1892, in Morison, *Letters*, vol.1, p.303.

[9] Richard Hofstadter, *Social Darwinism in American Thought* (New York, Putnam's Sons, revised edition 1965) p.186.

[10] Theodore Roosevelt to James B. Matthews, 29 June 1894, in Morison, *Letters* vol.1, p.390.

[11] Theodore Roosevelt to Henry Cabot Lodge, 7 March 1887, *Ibid.* p.126.

[12] Theodore Roosevelt to Henry Cabot Lodge, 22 November 1886, *Ibid.* p.116.

and Joseph Chamberlain, who impressed him with his 'keen shrewd intellect and quiet force'.[13] But it was Bryce, the admirer of America, who disarmed him. 'Bryce, the Historian', he told his sister Corinne, was 'a charming man'.[14]

Other literary men with whom Roosevelt corresponded included James Brander Matthews, Professor of Literature at Columbia, Jacob Riis, an immigrant from Denmark, who worked as an investigative journalist on the *Evening Sun* and wrote *How the Other Half Lives* to expose immigrant poverty in New York; and Captain Alfred Mahan, the author of *The Influence of Sea Power Upon History*, published, like Riis' book, in 1890.

Roosevelt was excited by books and devoured them, often at one sitting. He liked to set out his response in long expository reviews. In May 1890, he wrote to tell Captain Mahan how much he liked his book. 'During the last two days I have spent half my time, busy as I am, in reading your book; and that I found it interesting is shown by the fact that having taken it up I have gone straight through and finished it'. He was impressed by its arguments: 'I can say with perfect sincerity that I think it very much the clearest and most instructive general work of the kind with which I am acquainted. It is a *very* good book – admirable; and I am greatly in error if it does not become a naval classic'.[15] Roosevelt reviewed *The Influence of Sea Power Upon History* for the *Atlantic Monthly* and expressed his hope that it would be read in Congress, especially by the opponents of American naval expansion. The subject had long interested him: his own first book on *The Naval War of 1812*, which he had begun writing while a student at Harvard, had been published in 1882.

Roosevelt reviewed *National Life and Character* in the *Sewanee Review*. It was 'one of the most notable books of the end of the century...no one can read this book without feeling his thinking powers greatly stimulated; without being forced to ponder problems of which he was previously wholly ignorant, or which he but half understood; and without realizing that he is dealing with the work of a man of...deep and philosophic insight into the world-forces of the present'.[16] His review was reprinted as a chapter called 'National Life and Character' in a collection of essays titled *American Ideals*, dedicated to Lodge and published in 1897.

---

[13] Theodore Roosevelt to Corinne Roosevelt Robinson, 6 March 1887, *Ibid.* p.124.
[14] Theodore Roosevelt to Corinne Roosevelt Robinson, 27 February 1887, *Ibid.* p.124.
[15] Theodore Roosevelt to Alfred Mahan, 12 May 1890, *Ibid.* pp.221–2.
[16] Theodore Roosevelt, 'National Life and Character', in Theodore Roosevelt, *American Ideals and Other Essays Social and Political* (New York, Putnam's Sons, 1897) p.271.

It was Pearson's account of 'the world-forces of the present' that attracted Roosevelt's attention and in particular his focus on the implications of comparative birth rates. European nations were entering a 'stationary' state while 'the teeming population of China' was rapidly expanding and spreading outwards.[17] With much of the 'competition between the races reducing itself to the warfare of the cradle', Roosevelt noted memorably, 'no race has any chance to win a great place unless it consists of good breeders as well as of good fighters'.[18] He would henceforth become a great champion of 'good breeders', but it was leading sociologist, Edward A. Ross, in his address to the annual meeting of the American Academy of Political and Social Science in 1901, who gave a name to the problem of the declining birth rate: 'race suicide'.[19]

Pearson's book alerted Roosevelt to 'problems of which he was wholly ignorant' – and for that he was grateful – but the ebullient American was puzzled by his pessimism:

At no period of the world's history has life been so full of interest and of possibilities of excitement and enjoyment as for us who live in the latter half of the nineteenth century... Never before in the world's history have there been such opportunities thrown open to men, in the way of building new commonwealths, exploring new countries, conquering kingdoms, and trying to adapt the governmental policy of old nations to new and strange conditions.[20]

Building, exploration and conquest. In Roosevelt's view of the world, mobility, travel and the opportunity to build new commonwealths were central to English-speaking peoples' progress and their future.

Roosevelt applauded *National Life and Character* for challenging readers to revise 'their mental estimate of facts', but the book also sparked an unease and provoked the would-be political leader to an increasingly strident re-assertion of American vigour and virility. He began for the first time to urge the imperative of overseas expansion – and war if need be – as a national and racial challenge. At the same time, Roosevelt condemned those who didn't share his expansive enthusiasms as 'producing a flabby, timid type of character, which eats away the great fighting features of our race'.[21] In their various accounts of Roosevelt's 'imperial turn', American historians generally date it to the mid-1890s, but offer no explanation for his sudden global orientation and anxiety about racial

---

[17] *Ibid.* p.285.   [18] *Ibid.* pp.293–4.
[19] Edward A. Ross, 'The Causes of Race Superiority', *Annals of the American Academy of Political and Social Science* (18 July 1901) p.88.
[20] Roosevelt, 'National Life and Character', p.273.
[21] Theodore Roosevelt to Henry Cabot Lodge, 29 April 1896, in Morison, *Letters* vol.1, p.536.

vigour and national character.[22] Their national frame of analysis misses the importance of Pearson's book to shaping Roosevelt's thinking.

The new and newest worlds: 'a heritage for the white people'

National Life and Character was also unsettling to Roosevelt because it challenged his own racial triumphalism, recently given voice in *The Winning of the West*, a story of national conquest, but also an account of the global triumph of English-speaking peoples. An ardent patriot, Roosevelt dedicated his book to the historian Francis Parkman, 'to whom Americans who feel a pride in the pioneer history of their country are so greatly indebted'.[23] But his history of race warfare on the American frontier acquired its meaning as part of a larger transnational story about the 'Spread of the English Speaking Peoples', which began, following Freeman, with the 'great Teutonic wanderings'.[24]

The national histories of English-speaking peoples, according to Roosevelt, should be understood in the larger context of 'race-history'. 'The winning of the West', he later wrote in 'Manhood and Statehood', 'was the great epic feat in the history of our race'.[25] Roosevelt's mentors in his project of race history included John W. Burgess, who taught him briefly at Columbia University Law School, but the most important intellectual influence on Roosevelt's conception of history was Freeman. As Richard Hofstadter noted long ago, Freeman's ideas about racial continuity and Anglo-Saxon political genius influenced a whole generation of American historians.[26] And Freeman, as we have seen, had given a series of lectures on race history in Boston and Baltimore in the early 1880s.

Following Freeman and his American disciples, Roosevelt emphasised race continuity, but he was especially interested in the progress of English-speaking peoples in the New World: 'The average Englishman, American or Australian of today who wishes to recall the feats of power with which his race should be credited in the shadowy dawn of its history may

---

[22] Gail Bederman, *Manliness and Civilisation: A Cultural History of Gender and Race in the United States, 1880–1917* (Chicago, University of Chicago Press, 1995) p.277, note 62, locates evidence of Roosevelt's imperialist turn in a letter to Cabot Lodge in October 1894, but doesn't see the impact of Pearson's book. See also, for example, Gary Gerstle, *American Crucible Race and Nation in the American Century* (Princeton, Princeton University Press, 2001) ch.1.

[23] Theodore Roosevelt, *The Winning of the West* vol.1 (New York, Putnam's Sons, 1889).

[24] *Ibid.* pp.4–5. Roosevelt preferred the category 'English-speaking peoples' to 'Anglo-Saxons' because some of his ancestors were not of 'Anglo-Saxon' extraction.

[25] Theodore Roosevelt, 'Manhood and Statehood', in Roosevelt, *American Ideals*, p.254.

[26] Hofstadter, *Social Darwinism*, pp.174–5.

go back to the half-mythical glories of Hengist and Horsa.'[27] English-speaking peoples, he believed, were especially gifted as colonisers: 'The kind of colonizing conquest, whereby the people of the United States have extended their borders, has much in common with similar movements in Canada and Australia, all of them standing in sharp contrast to what has gone on in Spanish–American lands'. The Spanish, Roosevelt would later charge, when determining to eject them from Cuba, were fit only to exercise 'medieval tyranny', lacking the manly qualities, such as honour, restraint and virility, necessary to self-government and the government of others.[28]

The winning of the West was but one, if the most glorious, episode in the heroic saga of Anglo-Saxon world expansion. The settlement of Australia and America, Roosevelt argued, were key events in world history: 'When these continents were settled they contained the largest tracts of fertile, temperate, thinly peopled country on the face of the globe. We cannot rate too highly the importance of their acquisition. Their successful settlement was a feat which by comparison utterly dwarfs all the European wars of the last two centuries'.[29] As with Bryce and Pearson, Roosevelt's imagination was captured by historical developments beyond Europe.

He wrote of the settlement of North America and Australia as twin projects: 'Nineteenth century democracy needs no more complete vindication for its existence than the fact that it has kept for the white race the best portions of the new worlds' surface, temperate America and Australia', he wrote in his review of Pearson.[30] British historians, he charged, had for the most part not grasped the importance of Australia, thinking the acquisition of India more important, 'yet, from the standpoint of the ages, the peopling of the great island-continent with men of the English stock is a thousand fold more important than the holding Hindoostan [sic] for a few centuries'.[31]

The progress of English peoples in the New World was a major theme of Roosevelt's rejoinder to Pearson's pessimism: 'Never before have there been so many opportunities for commonwealth builders; new States have been pitched on the banks of the Saskatchewan, the Columbia, the Missouri, and the Colorado, on the seacoast of Australia and in the interior of Central Africa'.[32]

As we have seen, Roosevelt regarded the pleasures and power of mobility as definitive of modern progress. The ordinary man of adventurous

[27] Roosevelt, *The Winning of the West*, pp.5–6.
[28] Roosevelt, *The Strenuous Life*, p.9.
[29] Roosevelt, *The Winning of the West*, p.14.
[30] Roosevelt, 'National Life and Character', p.289.
[31] *Ibid.* p.281.   [32] *Ibid.* p.273.

tastes might now travel around the world, dwell wherever he wanted, explore strange regions, walk in the wilderness, hunt big game and even take part in a campaign, here and there. 'He sees going on before his eyes a great transfer of population and civilization, which is making America north of the Rio Grande, and Australia, English-speaking continents'.[33]

Like Pearson, Roosevelt linked the progress of the new white commonwealths to their democratic insistence on race purity. It was aristocratic societies – such as Great Britain and Spain – that introduced coolie or slave labour, while the new democratic states acted to save the best portions of the earth as a 'heritage for the white people':

Had these regions been under aristocratic governments, Chinese immigration would have been encouraged precisely as the slave trade is encouraged of necessity by any slave-holding oligarchy, and the result would have been even more fatal to the white race; but the democracy, with the clear instinct of race selfishness, saw the race foe, and kept out the dangerous alien. The presence of the negro in our Southern States is a legacy from the time when we were ruled by a trans-oceanic aristocracy.

Again, Roosevelt emphasised the world-historic significance of the advent of white men's countries: 'The whole civilization of the future owes a debt of gratitude greater than can be expressed in words to that democratic policy which has kept the temperate zones of the new and the newest worlds a heritage for the white people'.[34]

Roosevelt was sceptical about Pearson's forecast of the advancement of the 'black and yellow races'. The Chinese might be populous, and industrious, but they lacked fighting qualities; and if they spread south though Asia, they were merely displacing the Malays and Dyaks. India, if ever freed from British rule, would be prey to famine and internecine war and 'sink back to her former place'.[35] Blacks were simply incapable of building up strong governments. The ascendancy of Africans was a remote prospect: 'it is hardly possible to conceive that the peoples of Africa, however ultimately changed, will be anything but negroid in type of body and mind'.[36] Certainly, tropical peoples would 'cast off the yoke of their European conquerors sooner or later, and . . . become independent nations once more; though it is also possible that the modern conditions of easy travel may permit the permanent rule in the tropics of a vigorous northern race, renewed by a complete change every generation'.[37]

Roosevelt found it hard to understand Pearson's apprehension of personal humiliation. 'Mr Pearson fears that when once the tropic races are independent, the white peoples will be humiliated and will lose heart:

---

[33] *Ibid.* pp.274–75.   [34] *Ibid.* p.289.
[35] *Ibid.* p.287.   [36] *Ibid.* pp.282, 288.   [37] *Ibid.* p.283.

but this does not seem inevitable, and indeed seems very improbable'. Why should 'the mere knowledge of the equality of these stocks cow and dispirit the higher races?' asked the self-confident American. 'No American or Australian cares in the least that the tan-colored peoples of Brazil and Ecuador now live under governments of their own instead of being ruled by viceroys from Portugal and Spain; and it is difficult to see why they should be materially affected by a similar change happening in regard to the people along the Ganges or the upper Nile'.[38] As a self-styled 'free citizen of a mighty and glorious republic', Roosevelt found Pearson's apprehension perplexing, forgetting perhaps that Australians, though constantly declaring their status as self-governing communities, were still, in fact, colonial subjects.[39]

In his private letter to Pearson, Roosevelt was more explicit in his reassurances. 'Inferior races' could never hope to challenge the superior position of white men. The experience of the United States made this clear. If ever blacks or Indians threatened white domination, they were ruthlessly suppressed:

What occurs in our own Southern States at the least sign of a race war between the blacks and the whites seems to me to foreshadow what would occur on a much bigger scale if any black or yellow people should really menace the whites. An insurrectionary movement of blacks in any one of our Southern States is always abortive, and rarely takes place at all; but any manifestation of it is apt to be accompanied by some atrocity which at once arouses the whites to a rage of furious anger and terror, and they would put down the revolt absolutely mercilessly. In the same way an Indian outbreak on the frontier would to this day mean something approaching to a war of extermination.[40]

Roosevelt then returned to the crucial question of whether white men were in racial decline and suggested Pearson look to the development of manly virtues in modern frontier occupations, such as those practised by railway men. Whether brakemen, yardmen, switchmen, conductors or superintendents, such men needed qualities such as hardihood, daring, self-reliance, endurance and physical strength: 'It does not seem to me that any mediaeval trade, or indeed any trade practiced [sic] by men advanced beyond the pastoral stage has ever so tended to develop the hardier, manlier, more soldier-like virtues in the way that our railroad business has tended'.[41]

[38] *Ibid.* pp.290–1.
[39] Theodore Roosevelt, 'Brotherhood and the Heroic Virtues', in Roosevelt, *American Ideals*, p.264; see also John Milton Cooper, *The Warrior and the Priest: Woodrow Wilson and Theodore Roosevelt* (Cambridge, Harvard University Press, 1983) pp.149–50.
[40] Roosevelt to Pearson, 11 May 1894, Pearson papers, Bodleian library, MS English letters, d.190.
[41] *Ibid.*

Roosevelt rejected Pearson's pessimism, yet his subsequent crusade on behalf of 'the strenuous life' was surely a response to the predictions of future decline sketched by Pearson and others of the 'pessimistic' school. As Hofstadter noted, Pearson was one of the most influential of 'pessimistic writers' of the age, but another was Brooks Adams, who published *Law of Civilization and Decay, An Essay of History* in 1895. Roosevelt reviewed *Law of Civilization* in *Forum*, using the occasion to worry over 'a certain softness of fibre in civilized nations, which, if it were to prove progressive, might mean the development of a cultured and refined people quite unable to hold its own in those conflicts through which alone any great race can ultimately march to victory'.[42]

Whereas Pearson saw changing 'world-forces' in terms of an inevitable burgeoning of post-colonial independence, that must be accepted, Roosevelt, like his naval friend, Alfred Mahan, saw only intimations of 'race-conflict' and a 'struggle for supremacy' in which the outcome must be either 'victory' or 'defeat' for the white race. Not for the resolute Roosevelt a life of acquiescence. Within a couple of years he had elaborated his credo of virility in *The Strenuous Life*: 'Far better it is to do mighty things, to win glorious triumphs, even though checkered by failure, than to take rank with those poor spirits, who neither enjoy much nor suffer much, because they live in the gray twilight that knows neither victory nor defeat'.[43] Did he have the fatalistic Pearson in mind?

'We cannot sit huddled in our borders'

In Captain Alfred Mahan, Roosevelt found a like-minded promoter of national expansion through sea power. In the future battle for race supremacy, a powerful navy would be central to the outcome. In 'Hawaii and our Future Sea Power', written in 1893, Mahan urged American annexation of the Pacific Islands because of their strategic value as a coaling station: 'Shut out from the Sandwich Islands as a coal base, an enemy is thrown back for supplies of fuel to distances of thirty-five hundred miles'.[44]

Following the Japanese naval victory over China in 1895, Mahan published 'A Twentieth Century Outlook' in which he again pointed to 'the stirring of the East' and in particular 'the astonishing development of Japan'. The question to be settled in the new century had become:

---

[42] Hofstadter, *Social Darwinism*, p.185; see also Thomas Dyer, *Theodore Roosevelt and the Idea of Race* (Baton Rouge and London, Louisiana State University Press, 1980) p.11.
[43] Roosevelt, *The Strenuous Life*, p.5.
[44] Quoted in Thomas J. Osborne, *Annexation Hawaii: Fighting American Imperialism* (Waimanalo, Island Style Press, 1998) p.40.

'whether Eastern or Western civilization is to dominate throughout the earth and . . . control its future'. With the rise of Japan, the site of the struggle for world domination had shifted: 'it is in the Pacific, where the westward course of the Empire again meets the East, that their relations to the future of the world become most apparent'.[45]

When Roosevelt wrote to his brother-in-law, William Cowles, in March 1896, he promoted intervention in Cuba against Spain as an anti-colonial project: 'I think we ought to interfere in Cuba; and indeed I believe it would be well were we sufficiently far-sighted steadily to shape our policy with the view to the ultimate removal of all European powers from the colonies they hold in the Western hemisphere'. Increasingly, however, Roosevelt's project of removing European powers from the Western hemisphere, a goal that shaped his interpretation of the Monroe doctrine, became the occasion for the expansion of the American Empire.[46]

'We cannot sit huddled in our own borders', Roosevelt wrote in *The Strenuous Life*:

> as the nations grow to have ever wider and wider interests, and are brought into closer and closer contact, if we are to hold our own in the struggle for naval and commercial supremacy, we must build up our power without our own borders. We must build the isthmian canal, and we must grasp the points of vantage which will enable us to have our say in deciding the destiny of the oceans of the East and the West.[47]

For Roosevelt, playing a strenuous part in the world's work was the supreme test of what Pearson had called 'national life and character'. Roosevelt returned to the importance of this idea in the essay 'Character and Success': 'Alike for the nation and the individual, the indispensable requisite is character – character that does and dares as well as endures'.[48] At the end of the century, the United States faced multiple tests of character. Urged on by Kipling, who wrote 'The White Man's Burden' for the purpose, Roosevelt demanded that Americans not shrink from the 'responsibilities that confront us in Hawaii, Cuba, Porto Rico and the Philippines'.

In 1898, the United States annexed Hawaii and declared war on Spain, invoking its 'humanitarian' duty to relieve the Cubans from 'despotic tyranny' and recognise that country's aspirations to political independence. As a result of its intervention, the United States also drove the

[45] Alfred Mahan, 'A Twentieth-Century Outlook', *Harper's New Monthly Magazine* 95 (September 1897) p.531.
[46] See, for example, Theodore Roosevelt, 'National Duties', in Roosevelt, *The Strenuous Life*, pp.289–90.
[47] Roosevelt, *The Strenuous Life*, p.9.
[48] Theodore Roosevelt, 'Character and Success', in Roosevelt, *The Strenuous Life*, p.121.

Spanish from Puerto Rico and Guam and engaged in a bloody land war against Filipino independence fighters. It was a development strongly opposed by a powerful lobby of anti-imperialists, who often invoked the same race-based arguments to denounce American expansion.[49] The incorporation into the republic of new mixed race populations, they argued, whether 'Kanakas', 'coolies' or 'Mulattoes', would only exacerbate American political and social problems. 'This Union had enough of the problem of amalgamating races into one brotherhood to last at least for the rest of the century', wrote James Schouler in *The Forum*.[50]

Other liberal critics worried about the Hawaiians' right to self-determination. 'The citizens of Hawaii have a right to consider whether they shall give their country away', said the Boston *Daily Globe*. 'Even the Kanaka has a claim to be heard when the future of the islands of his ancestors is at stake.'[51] And as Noenoe K. Silva has recently shown in her study, *Aloha Betrayed: Native Hawaiian Resistance to American Colonialism*, thousands of Hawaiians protested and petitioned against annexation. 'No darker cloud can hang over a people than the prospect of being blotted out from the list of nations', declared Queen Lili'uokalani. 'No grief can equal that of a sovereign forcibly deprived of her throne.'[52]

Anglo-Saxonism resurgent

Leaders of the Cuban independence struggle initially took heart from United States support, seeing in the American War of Independence a precedent for their own. Jose Marti, born in 1853 of poor Spanish parents in Havana, and now Cuba's revered 'National Hero', took degrees in philosophy and law in Spain and lived in Mexico, Guatemala and Venezuela before settling in New York, where he planned the republican uprising in Cuba. In the United States, where he became a Director of the Cuban Revolutionary Party, he was encouraged by local support for the Cuban anti-colonial struggle, but also concerned by the implications of burgeoning Anglo-Saxon race pride. It made him suspicious of United States support of 'Pan-Americanism'.[53]

Anglo-Saxons, who had 'consumed the native race, fomented and lived off the slavery of another race and reduced or robbed the neighbouring

---

[49] Matthew Frye Jacobson, *Barbarian Virtues: The United States Encounters Foreign Peoples at Home and Abroad 1876–1917* (New York, Hill and Wang, 2001) pp.228–31.

[50] Osborne, *Annexation Hawaii*, pp.35–6.   [51] Osborne, *Annexation Hawaii*, p.36.

[52] Noenoe K. Silva, *Aloha Betrayed: Native Hawaiian Resistance to American Colonialism* (Durham and London, Duke University Press, 2004) p.164.

[53] Jose Marti, 'Mother America', in Deborah Schnookel and Mirta Muniz (eds.) *Jose Marti Reader* (Melbourne, Ocean Press, 2007) pp.109–19.

countries' believed in the invincible superiority of 'the Anglo-Saxon race over the Latin', he warned:

They believe in the inferiority of the Negroes, whom they enslaved yesterday and are criticizing today, and of the Indians, whom they are exterminating. They believe that the Spanish–American peoples consist mainly of Indians and Negroes. As long as the United States knows no more about Spanish America and respects it no more – although, with the numerous incessant, urgent and wise explanations of our people and resources, it could come to respect us – how can that country invite Spanish America to an alliance that would be honest and useful to our Spanish–American nations?[54]

Marti opposed the presumption of Anglo-Saxon superiority with an appeal to 'Our America': Spanish-speaking peoples of mixed European/African/Indian descent. He attacked the very idea of race: 'There can be no racial animosity because there are no races':

The theorists and feeble thinkers string together and warm over the bookshelf races which the well-disposed observer and fair-minded traveller vainly seek in the justice of nature where man's universal identity springs forth from triumphant love and turbulent hunger for life. The soul, equal and eternal, emanates from bodies of various shapes and colors. Whoever foments and spreads antagonism and hate between the races, sins against humanity.[55]

In what would prove to be his last letter, Marti wrote to his 'dearest brother' Manuel Mercado in Mexico to say that he would give his life to prevent Cuban independence from being subverted through annexation to the United States, a country that despised Spanish America. 'I have lived in the monster and I know its entrails', he wrote; 'my sling is David's.'[56] Marti died in battle soon after he returned to Cuba as a part of the liberating force.

The United States intervened in the Cuban struggle in 1898 and claimed victory over Spain soon after. The subsequent Treaty of Paris ignored the part played by Cuban fighters in their decades-long struggle for independence and paved the way for continuing American control over Cuba. The American war against the Filipino nationalists, which cost hundreds of thousands of lives, the vast majority Filipinos, was justified as both vital to the re-invigoration of American manhood and necessary for the Filipinos, who as a non-white race were as yet unfit for

---

[54] Jose Marti, *Jose Marti Replies* (Havana, Jose Marti Publishing House, 1986) p.19.

[55] Jose Marti, 'Editorial', in Jose Marti, *Three Documents* (Havana, Jose Marti Publishing House, 1984) p.41.

[56] Jose Marti, 'Letter to Manuel Mercado, 18 May 1895', in Schnookel and Muniz, *Jose Marti Reader*, p. 253.

self-government.[57] Writing about the necessity of American rule in the Philippines in *The Strenuous Life*, Roosevelt pointed to the composition of the population: 'half-caste and native Christians, warlike Moslems, and wild pagans. Many of their people are utterly unfit for self-government, and show no signs of becoming fit. Others may in time become fit, but at present can only take part in self-government under a wise supervision, at once firm and beneficent. We have driven Spanish tyranny from the islands. If we now let it be replaced by savage anarchy, our work has been for harm and not for good'.[58]

Much American comment on the Spanish–American war applauded it as a bonding, unifying experience for American soldiers: it had brought together north and south, country and city, Republicans and Democrats. President William McKinley, in Atlanta, Georgia, at the end of 1898, praised the patriotism shown by the southern States and declared that the United States, now one nation for evermore, had planted the Stars and Stripes, their indivisible flag, in two hemispheres as the symbol of liberty and law, peace and progress.[59] Much of the fervour over the war-induced fraternalism in Cuba focussed on the composition and role of the Rough Riders, 'skilled in the wild horsemanship of the great plains' and commanded by Roosevelt, whose exploits turned him into a military hero.[60]

The Spanish–American war was also applauded for strengthening bonds between the different branches of the Anglo-Saxon race and, as Thomas Gossett has noted, the war in the Philippines became an Anglo-Saxon crusade.[61] An English Liberal journal, the *Speaker*, eulogised American people as 'speaking the same language, governed by the same spirit of liberty and law, with a kindred civilisation'. A collision between the two great Anglo-Saxon peoples would be 'against the laws of nature'; rather there must be 'a great alliance ... of the whole English-speaking race'.[62] The formation of an Anglo-American Committee

[57] See Kristin L. Hoganson, *Fighting for American Manhood: How Gender Politics Provoked the Spanish–American and Philippine–American Wars* (New York, Yale University Press, 1998) ch. 6.

[58] Roosevelt, *The Strenuous Life*, p.9.   [59] *Age*, 17 December 1898.

[60] Theodore Roosevelt, *An Autobiography* (New York, Macmillan, 1913) p.238. See also Alexander Saxton, *The Rise and Fall of the White Republic: Class Politics and Mass Culture in Nineteenth-Century America* (New York, Verso, 1990) pp.370–7.

[61] Thomas F. Gossett, *Race: The History of an Idea in America* (New York, Oxford University Press, 1963, reprinted 1997) p.314; see also Paul A. Kramer, 'Empires, Exceptions, and Anglo-Saxons: Race and Rule between the British and United States Empires, 1880–1910', *Journal of American History* 88 (May 2002) p.4; Paul A. Kramer, *The Blood of Government: Race, Empire, the United States and the Philippines* (Chapel Hill, University of North Carolina Press, 2006).

[62] Quoted in Merze Tate, 'Hawaii: A Symbol of Anglo-American Rapprochement', *Political Science Quarterly* 79,4 (1964) p.566.

expressed a commitment, in James Bryce's words, to 'constant cordial co-operation'.[63]

The British government, anxious about German and Russian military ambition, saw in the United States a crucial ally in future European conflicts. In a speech to parliament, in mid-1898, Joseph Chamberlain warned of the future possibility of Anglo-Saxon liberty being 'menaced by a great combination of Powers'. Hoping that 'blood would be found thicker than water', he affirmed 'the closer, the more definite, the clearer the alliance between the United States and ourselves, the better it will be for both nations, the better it will be for the civilised world, and the better it will be for all which we have a right to hope'.[64]

Just as British statesmen looked to the United States as a future ally, so Americans looked to British imperialism as a model for a re-invigorated United States manhood. On a visit to Britain in 1895, the previously sceptical Lodge was impressed by the role of imperial government in building English manhood. 'I am more than ever impressed with the vast difference between the Englishman who has travelled and governed abroad and those who have not', he wrote on his return. 'The latter are insular and self-absorbed and stiff as a rule and the former are almost always agreeable and worth meeting'.[65] Imperialism was character-building, for man, nation and race. 'I believe in the expansion of great nations', Roosevelt affirmed to his friend, Spring Rice, in December 1899. India had done a great deal for 'the English character. If we do our work well in the Philippines and the West Indies, it will do a great deal for our character'.[66]

Although officially neutral, following Britain, Australians rushed to support 'their brother Anglo-Saxons' in their war with Spain, besieging their local consulates with offers of support.[67] An official notice had to be posted reminding Australians that the United States was a foreign country and thus it was illegal to enlist in their armed services. Around the country theatres interrupted their programs to play American anthems and crowds gathered outside newspaper offices to catch up on the latest developments.[68] Editorials observed that while American rule of the erstwhile Spanish colonies was problematic for a democracy, there was no alternative, for, as an Australian businessman visiting Manila reported home, the Filipinos were 'not capable of ruling themselves'. If 'Aguinaldo and his gang were to obtain possession', he wrote with reference to the leader of the war of independence, 'the islands would be a hotbed of

[63] *Ibid.* p.572.   [64] *Ibid.* p.574.
[65] Hoganson, *Fighting for American Manhood*, p.147.
[66] Theodore Roosevelt to Cecil Arthur Spring Rice, 2 December 1899, in Morison, *Letters*, p.1104.
[67] *Sydney Morning Herald*, 23 April 1898.   [68] *Age*, 22, 25 April 1898.

faction and civil war, as are some of the smaller South American republics'.[69] Only white men, all agreed, had the capacity for self-government.

Australians knew little of the history of the Cuban and Filipino struggles for independence or the background of their political and military leaders, but they knew that the 'insurgents', as they were routinely called, weren't white men. 'America undertook the present war because she could not tolerate a constant turmoil in front of her own door', advised the Melbourne *Age*. 'It is not at all likely that the anarchy which she would not permit at the hands of Spain she will allow to be brought about by the Cubans themselves. Self-government is not an art which comes by nature and instinct to any people. It requires training and preparation; and the interests of the world's civilisation will demand that neither the Philippines nor Cuba shall be handed over to the unregulated passions of peoples only a few degrees removed from savagery'.[70]

But the newspaper also reflected on the larger challenge posed by 'Aguinaldo and his 40,000 insurgent troops' in the Philippines to a democratic republic founded on the consent of the governed:

Hitherto, as new territories have been acquired, they have been brought under the Government of the United States and invested with the privileges of a free and self-governing people . . .

In the Philippines this cannot be done for some time. The people have not emerged politically above the self-restraints of semi-savages. Therefore, American authority in these islands must be maintained apart from the people, contrary to their will, set over them, and even pressing them down regardless of their protests . . . To subject the Philippines permanently to an alien rule would be oppression; to enfranchise them would be to invite the entrance of anarchy; to keep them in political bondage would be a repudiation by the United States of the principle that all just government must be founded upon the consent of the governed. These are the problems which Aguinaldo and his 40,000 insurgent troops are forcing on the American people.[71]

In *National Life and Character*, Charles Pearson had prophesied a new world order in which the 'black and yellow races' would form independent states and enter international relations as equal powers. Such a future might be de-moralising for white men – whose sense of self was constituted in relations of racial domination – but in Pearson's view these historical developments were historically inevitable. In urging an imperial course for his country and justifying American expansion as an expression of racial vigour, Roosevelt both heeded and resisted Pearson's forecast, by demonstrating the superiority of English-speaking peoples over

[69] *Ibid.* 26 November 1898.   [70] *Ibid.* 25 July 1898.   [71] *Ibid.* 6 December 1898.

others and reiterating the importance of the distinction between races fit for self-government and those not yet, or not ever, fit.

When James Bryce was asked for his opinion on American territorial expansion, he was discouraging. The much-lauded benefits of British civilisation (the rule of law, railways and currency) to 'savage and backward races' were doubtful, he said. American annexation of Spanish colonies would entail 'a needless and heavy burden'. The only British territorial expansion that really worked well, he argued, was 'the establishment of the British stock as colonists in temperate regions, where they are in little or no contact with black or yellow races, and where they can establish self-governing republics, so as to be parts of the English nation enjoying complete home rule'.[72] In white men's countries, the 'black and yellow races' were cast as 'permanently foreign and unassimilable to the nation'.[73]

Roosevelt agreed that the white self-governing communities of Australia represented the exemplary form of British territorial expansion. In a letter to his friend Spring Rice in 1899, prompted by the latter's concerns about the future of the British Empire, Roosevelt pointed to the 'abounding vigor' of Australia:

To you India seems larger than Australia. In the life history of the English-speaking people I think it will show very much smaller. The Australians are building up a giant commonwealth, the very existence of which, like the existence of the United States, means an alteration in the balance of the world and goes a long way towards ensuring the supremacy of the men who speak our tongue and have our ideas of social, political and religious freedom & morality.[74]

Again, in 1901, the year of the inauguration of the Commonwealth of Australia as a federated nation-state, and, as it happened, the year of his own inauguration as United States president following the assassination of McKinley, Roosevelt reiterated his view that Australia represented the future. Writing to re-assure Spring Rice about the destiny of the race, he pointed to the ongoing settlement of North America and Australasia:

I do not wonder that you sometimes feel depressed over the future both of our race & of our civilization. There are many reasons why one should be, although I think there are also many reasons why one should not be ... Still I should be a fool if I did not see grave cause for anxiety in some of the social tendencies of the day: the growth of luxury throughout the English speaking world; & especially the gradual diminishing birth rate ...

[72] *Ibid.* 25 April 1898.
[73] Mae M.Ngai, *Impossible Subjects: Illegal Aliens and the Making of Modern America* (Princeton, Princeton University Press, 2004) p.8.
[74] Theodore Roosevelt to Cecil Arthur Spring Rice, 11 August 1899, in Morison, *Letters*, vol.2, p.1052.

Nevertheless, the settlement of North America and of Australasia goes on and the remaining waste places of the two continents will be practically occupied in our own life time . . .

In spite of all the unhealthy signs in this country, I still see ample evidence of abounding vigor. There is certainly such vigor in Australia.[75]

Roosevelt's preoccupation with racial vigour – and the diminishing birth rate – spoke to the anxiety awakened by Pearson's forecast, even as he dismissed *National Life and Character* as unduly pessimistic. The Spanish–American war had offered an opportunity to demonstrate the vigour of national character and prove his own manhood.

But one national problem seemed insoluble. The presence of over 8 million blacks in the republic – the legacy, as Roosevelt insisted, of aristocratic rule – mocked the United States' claim to be a 'white man's country'. In a letter to Albion Tourgee in 1901, Roosevelt confessed he was at his 'wits' ends' in dealing with 'the black man'. Defending his controversial decision to invite Booker T. Washington to dine at the White House, he wrote:

I have not been able to think out any solution of the terrible problem offered by the presence of the negro on this continent, but of one thing I am sure, and that is that inasmuch as he is here and can neither be killed nor driven away, the only wise and honourable and Christian thing to do is to treat each black man and each white man strictly on his merits as a man, giving him no more and no less than he shows himself worthy to have.[76]

White men should treat black men as individuals, dealing with them man to man, although Roosevelt came to regret his invitation to Washington and despaired of blacks as a group: 'as a race and as a mass they are altogether inferior to the whites'.[77] He no doubt agreed with Pearson that it would have been better had Congress purchased the slaves when they were 'a mere handful' and transported them to Africa. In framing legislation to provide for the expulsion of Pacific Islanders from the new Commonwealth of Australia, in 1901, Australian leaders determined to learn from America's mistakes.

In South Africa, too, white political leaders expected to learn from American experience. When hostilities broke out between the Boers and the British, Roosevelt, although proud of his own Dutch ancestry, was clear that it was in the interests of the world, that the English-speaking

[75] Theodore Roosevelt to Cecil Arthur Spring Rice, 16 March 1901, *Ibid.* vol.3, pp.14–16.
[76] Theodore Roosevelt to Albion Winegar Tourgee, 8 November 1901, *Ibid.*, p.190.
[77] Theodore Roosevelt to Owen Wister, quoted in Gossett, *Race*, p.268.

race should prevail. 'In South Africa', he wrote to Spring Rice, 'I earnestly hope that when the present dreadful muddle is ended, a process of amalgamation may go on which will build up a great English-speaking commonwealth south of the Zambesi'.[78] His prediction of a South African Union proved prescient.

[78] Theodore Roosevelt to Cecil Arthur Spring Rice, 16 March 1901, in Morison, *Letters*, vol.3, p.16.

5   Imperial brotherhood or white? Gandhi in South Africa

Mr Gandhi arrives in Natal and becomes a 'despised being'

In May 1893, Mohandas Karamchand Gandhi arrived in Natal, a British colony in South Africa, described that year by Charles Pearson in *National Life and Character* as 'already not a white man's colony'.[1] Four years later, in *Impressions of South Africa*, James Bryce was more forthright: 'so far as numbers go, the country is a black man's country'.[2] The anxious preoccupation expressed in these assessments would affect Gandhi's experience there in ways he could not have anticipated.

An urbane barrister trained at London's Inner Temple, M. K. Gandhi was twenty-four years old when he journeyed to Natal to work with a client of his Indian law firm. He was the son of a wealthy family of Gujarat merchants, married at eleven years of age and educated in Ahmedabad. Drawn by ambition to study law, he took a ship from Bombay for London in 1888, leaving his wife and first born son in India. As well as attending the regular dinners at the Inner Temple and learning to dress like an English gentleman, Gandhi also sought out some of the two hundred other Indians in London, who were mostly studying law or business, and local theosophists and vegetarians, for whom he wrote articles in their weekly journal. He befriended theosophist Annie Besant, was introduced to Madame Helena Blavatsky on her death bed, read Hindu and Christian scriptures, sat his law exams and matriculated in Latin, French and Science from the University of London.

On the day after Gandhi was admitted to the English bar, he boarded ship for home, but he returned to India with some reluctance, as he confessed to his friends at *The Vegetarian*. He had grown so attached to the city: 'Who would not be? London with its teaching institutions, public galleries, museums, theatres, vast commerce, public parks and

[1] Charles Pearson, *National Life and Character: A Forecast* (London, Macmillan, 1893) p.29.
[2] James Bryce, *Impressions of South Africa* (London, Macmillan and Co., 1897) p.435.

114

vegetarian restaurants, is a fit place for a student and traveller, a trader and a "faddist" – as a Vegetarian would be called by his opponents'. His return home proved frustrating and humiliating in turn. Unable to find work and exasperated by provincial manners and power structures, he was rescued by his brother, who had been told by a friend that the firm of Dada Abdulla and Co. needed a barrister to handle a big case in South Africa. They offered first class passage to and from Natal, with all living expenses for a stay of one year, as well as a fee of £105.[3]

Gandhi arrived with anticipation in the port of Durban, which, according to Bryce in *Impressions of South Africa*, enjoyed 'the reputation of being the best managed and most progressive town in all South Africa', but from the moment the young Indian lawyer stepped ashore, he encountered hostility and soon became a controversial figure. His well-cut English frock-coat attracted curious, disapproving eyes. 'Being a barrister-at-law', he later recalled, 'I was well dressed according to my lights and landed in Durban with a due sense of my importance.'[4] He quickly realised that Indians, who had travelled to the 'garden colony' as contract labour since 1860, were not held in high regard. Even his well-to-do client was sneered at by Europeans, whose contempt was yet met with obsequious deference.

Although Natal had been originally established as a Dutch colony, it had since become British.[5] Whether Dutch or English, the white residents were, as Bryce noted, 'agreed in desiring to exclude Kaffirs and new-comers from India from the electoral franchise' and thus maintain white rule.[6] In his autobiography, written many years later, Gandhi recalled how he was stung by the attitudes of Durban's colonists who meted out most insulting treatment to Indians, who were referred to generically as 'coolies'.[7] The racial insults made a lasting impression and he determined to fight for what he later called 'national self-respect'.[8] Initially uninterested in the condition of indentured labourers, Gandhi gradually came to identify with them only as he redefined his battle for respect as a national struggle.[9]

During the southern winter of 1893, Gandhi learnt what it meant to be an Indian in a place that had, despite its large African majority, determined to become a white man's country. On his appearance in court, he

[3] Stanley Wolpert, *Gandhi's Passion: The Life and Legacy of Mahatma Gandhi* (New York, Oxford University Press, 2001) pp.28–33.
[4] M. K. Gandhi, *Satyagraha in South Africa: the Selected Works*, vol.III (Ahmedabad, Navativan Publishing, 1928; 1968), p.55.
[5] Bryce, *Impressions of South Africa*, p.356.   [6] *Ibid.* p.357.
[7] M. K. Gandhi, *An Autobiography* (London, Penguin Modern Classics, 2001) p.110.
[8] Gandhi, *Autobiography*, p.139.
[9] Radhika Mongia, 'Gender and the Historiography of Gandhian *Satyagraha* in South Africa', *Gender and History* (vol.18, (1) April 2006).

was ordered by the presiding magistrate to remove his turban. He refused and walked out. 'So here too', he wrote, 'there was fighting in store for me'. He wrote to the local papers protesting against the magistrate's decision and a storm of controversy blew up:

The question was very much discussed in the papers which described me as an 'unwelcome visitor'. Thus the incident gave me an unexpected advertisement in South Africa within a few days of my arrival there. Some supported me, while others severely criticised my temerity.[10]

The conflict over the turban presaged trouble to come. After a week in the colony, the young barrister's business took him on a journey by train and coach to Pretoria, the capital of Transvaal, the Boer Republic. Travelling first class, he yet discovered that, come nightfall, he was expected as a 'coloured' man to vacate his seat and sleep in the luggage van. A white passenger, who saw Gandhi sitting in first class, called the conductor, who ordered him to leave. Gandhi refused. A policeman arrived and pushed him off the train, leaving him on the deserted and freezing platform.

His luggage was removed and stored for the night. His overcoat was in his suitcase but, fearing further insult, he didn't attempt to recover it. In the icy darkness he thought about his future. He could either return to India or stay and fight for the rights of his fellow countrymen, working, as he put it, to remove the 'deep disease of colour prejudice'.[11] In the morning, his plight became known to the local business community, who told him that what had happened was not unusual. Any Indian who presumed to travel first or even second class was bound to be harassed by white passengers, or railway officials, or both.

Gandhi caught the next night's train and continued his journey to Charlestown on the Transvaal border, where Johannesburg-bound passengers were required to board stagecoaches. Here, again, Gandhi was in trouble. Despite having a valid ticket, he was informed by the Boer coachman that he couldn't sit inside with the white passengers, but must take one of the seats on either side of the coachbox. 'I knew it was sheer injustice and an insult', he wrote, 'but I thought it better to pocket it'.[12] He realised that if he again protested, he would certainly be left behind.

But the coachman was not finished with him. When he wanted to smoke, he told Gandhi he must move aside and sit at his feet on 'a piece of dirty sack cloth'. The insult, Gandhi recalled, was more than he could bear, so he stayed in his seat while the driver attempted to pull him down. When the other passengers intervened the driver ordered the 'Hottentot servant' to move instead and he took his seat.[13] The experience was traumatic. Chandran Devanesen, in his study of Gandhi's time in South

[10] Gandhi, *Autobiography*, pp.109–11.   [11] *Ibid.* p.114.
[12] *Ibid.* p.115.   [13] *Ibid.* p.95.

Africa, has remarked that the rag on which he was ordered to sit became 'an insulting symbol to which he referred many times during his early days in South Africa'.[14]

Gandhi arrived in Johannesburg the following evening. He found 'a big city' – a cosmopolitan mining town described by Bryce as 'busy, eager, restless, pleasure-seeking, making money fast and spending it lavishly'.[15] It had a 'very mixed population' – Italians, Germans, French, as well as Americans, British, Indians and colonials – but Gandhi found the city far from welcoming and he was refused a room at the Grand National Hotel. He was indignant, but his compatriots laughed. They could put up with the insults because they wanted to make money. 'This country is not for men like you', they said.[16]

Gandhi learnt that conditions for the Indians were very bad in both Boer republics, Transvaal and the Orange Free State – the latter described by Bryce as 'an ideal commonwealth' because all white men enjoyed the suffrage regardless of property or residence qualifications. Legislation robbed Indians, however, of most civil and political rights. In the Transvaal, a poll tax was applied on entry and they had no right to vote. Indians could lease land only in defined locations, had to have a special permit to be out after nine pm and were not permitted to walk on public footpaths. Gandhi himself was pushed off the footpath when he walked past the residence of President Paul Kruger.

He saw that South Africa was 'no country for a self-respecting Indian' and became increasingly preoccupied with the injustice of the treatment of Indian colonists. Perhaps their own behaviour was to blame. At a meeting of the Indian community in Pretoria he delivered his first public speech in which he stressed the importance of Indian honesty in business, because the reputation of millions of their fellow countrymen depended on it.

The young Indian lawyer summed up his impressions of Transvaal and Natal in an open letter to the Natal parliament in December 1894. There was, he declared, no doubt that the Indian was 'a despised being'. But if colour were the issue then there seemed to be no hope. The sooner the Indian left South Africa the better, for no matter what he did he would never have a white skin: 'The man in the street hates him, curses him, spits upon him. The Press cannot find a sufficiently strong word in the English dictionary to damn him with'.[17]

---

[14] Chandran D. S. Devanesen, *The Making of the Mahatma* (Delhi, Orient Longman, 1969) p.235.

[15] Bryce, *Impressions of South Africa*, p.116.   [16] Gandhi, *Autobiography*, p.117.

[17] Gandhi, Open letter, December 1894, *The Collected Works of Mahatma Gandhi*, vol.1, (Delhi, Ministry of Information, 1958) p.159.

An avid researcher, Gandhi collected evidence of racial vilification from the newspapers. Indians were the 'real canker eating into the community', 'parasites', 'wily, wretched semi-barbarous Asiatics', 'chock full of vice', 'squalid coolies with ruthless tongues and artful ways'. Indians were always 'coolies'. They were 'coolie clerks', 'coolie merchants', even 'coolie barristers'. Newspapers never called Indians by their proper names. They were variously 'Ramsamy', 'Mr Sammy', 'Mr Coolie'. The word 'coolie' was used in the courts as though it were the appropriate designation for all Indians. He tried to explain that the term was extremely offensive, but then 'the Indian was a creature without feelings'.[18]

Gandhi was shocked at the repugnance with which whites regarded Indians and the extent of segregation in South Africa:

The train cars are not for Indians. The railway officials may treat the Indians as beasts. No matter how clean, his very sight is such an offence to every white man in the colony that he would object to sit, even for a short time, in the same compartment with the Indian. The hotels shut their doors against them. I know instances of respectable Indians having been denied a night's lodging in an hotel. Even the public baths are not for the Indians, no matter who they are.[19]

Ultimately, however, it was not the company of Indians that white men found most objectionable, it was the humiliating prospect that Indians could potentially rule over them.

In the colonies, racial power was crucial to white men's sense of self and, in 1893, with the grant of responsible government to Natal, local politicians launched, as Jeremy Martens has noted, 'a concerted assault on the rights of Indians'.[20] According to the census of that year, Natal's population comprised 500,000 Africans, 43,742 whites and 41,208 Indians, including those who had arrived to work in South Africa as contract labour, free immigrants and those born there. Nervous white men began to declare they would never submit to Indian rule.

In reality this was a distant prospect, for in the election following the grant of responsible government, there were only 280 coloured voters out of an electorate of 9,300. The property franchise meant that a few coloured men could vote, but many white men found even that small number of votes unacceptable for, as Bryce observed, echoing earlier observations about poor whites in the United States, white men were especially given to plume themselves on their colour when they had little else to plume themselves upon.[21] Local Europeans demanded that

[18] Gandhi, *Collected Works*, vol.1, pp.159–60.   [19] *Ibid.* p.160.
[20] Jeremy Martens, 'A Transnational History of Immigration Restriction: Natal and New South Wales, 1896–97', *Journal of Imperial and Commonwealth History* 34(3) (September 2006) p.325.
[21] Bryce, *Impressions of South Africa*, p.443.

South Africa declare itself 'a white man's country', by which they meant, not that they would form a majority, but rather that white men would rule.

Amendment to the Franchise Act: 'is this to be a white man's country?'

Gandhi's first political campaign was provoked by Natal's amendment to the Franchise Act, which he read about at a farewell party, on the eve of his planned return to India. The Franchise Law Amendment Bill proposed to restrict the franchise to those who enjoyed self-government in their countries of origin – debarring 'natives or descendants in the male line of natives of countries which had not hitherto possessed elective institutions' – thus effectively disenfranchising the Indian community. Recognising the importance of the issue, Gandhi told his hosts: 'It is the first nail in our coffin. It strikes at the root of our self-respect.'[22] He would delay his return to India and join the campaign of opposition. Immediate action and fund-raising were called for, because the bill was already at the second reading stage in the lower house of parliament. 'The farewell party was thus turned into a working committee.'[23]

In moving the second reading of the Bill, the prime minister of Natal, John Robinson, echoed Anglo-Saxonists in Australia and the United States in declaring that the principle and practice of representative government had evolved in countries characterised by 'race unity'. Self-government was the privilege of 'the Anglo-Saxon race'. Robinson then pointed to problems that occurred when the races were 'mixed up with each other' as exemplified by the 'misfortune' of the United States, where 'the white man' confronted the problem of 'the negro'. 'It was a great misfortune that when personal emancipation was ordained there as regards the negro race, no recognition was made of differences in political capacity.' That question, said Robinson, had been one of the most difficult questions that the citizens of the United States had had to deal with.[24]

On 22 May 1894, seventy-six of Natal's leading merchants joined Gandhi in forming an action committee, later formalised as the Natal Indian Congress, inspired by the example of the Indian National Congress, formed ten years earlier. When the offensive legislation passed, Gandhi sent a petition to Lord Ripon, the secretary of state for the colonies in London, pointing out that in England, 'any British subject

---

[22] Gandhi, *Autobiography*, p.138.   [23] *Ibid.* p.139.
[24] *Natal Parliamentary Debates*, 1894, Enclosure, Colonial Office (CO) 179/189 (UK National Archives).

having the proper property qualifications is entitled to vote irrespective of caste, colour or creed'.[25] With regard to the new qualification for voting in Natal, the petition stated that self-government was exercised in Indian village communities long before 'the Anglo-Saxon races first became acquainted with the principles of representation'. In any case, few Indians would be likely to exercise the franchise. Copies of the petition were published in newspapers in England and India.

To Colonial Office officials in London, however, the petition's arguments were 'beside the mark': 'it is not a question whether the Asiatic should be granted franchise privileges in his own country. It is a question whether he should be allowed to exercise a voice which will surely become a controlling voice, in the government of the colony of Natal'. And certainly, they noted sympathetically, 'Whites would never submit to being overruled by the Indian vote'.[26]

In a letter to Governor Sir Walter Hely-Hutchison, Prime Minister Robinson observed that it was more than ever clear that the question at issue was whether the European or the Asiatic would be politically dominant in South Africa. The legislation would protect the country from the 'vital danger which now menaced its political and social prospects'. And he stressed the solidarity of white men across the country. 'There cannot be', he declared, 'and there is not, any difference of opinion amongst the European inhabitants of South Africa in regard to this question.'[27]

The local newspapers gave strength to the Premier's claim. The colonists were united in their determination, said the *Natal Advertiser*, to 'save the voters' roll from being swamped by coolie votes'.[28] 'If the people of South Africa are of one mind on any subject at all it is on this question of the Indian franchise', declared the editor of the *Natal Mercury*, and he dismissed the idea of racial equality as an impractical abstract theory:

they are as determined as men can be that the Indian shall not be placed on an equality with the white man in political affairs. The British subject theory from an abstract point of view may sound all very well, but when it comes to be applied in detail to the extent of trying to effect the impossibility of making the white man admit or believe that the yellow man or the black man is his equal in all things – then the theory breaks down.[29]

The issue at point was a simple one: was the country to be run by white men or was it to be handed over to the 'tender mercies of the black man

[25] Governor of Natal to Colonial Office, Copy of Petition, Enclosure, CO 179/189.
[26] Governor of Natal to Colonial Office, Minute in response to Petition, CO 179/189.
[27] Letter of 18 October 1895, enclosed in dispatch no.108, CO 179/192.
[28] *Natal Advertiser*, 5 September 1895.   [29] *Natal Mercury*, 6 September 1895.

or the yellow man'?[30] The Natal press took comfort from the support received from Johannesburg colleagues in the Transvaal, quoting the *Star* at length and referring to a straight-to-the-point article, which put before the South African Colonies and Republics the fundamental question: 'is this to be a white man's country?' Echoing Southerners in the United States about the harm done by promises of equality, the editor of the *Star* had written:

the utterances of any British statesman who holds out to Asiatics the hope that they may look to be the equal one day of the whites can only work an infinity of harm, and the people of Natal, if they insist – as they surely will? – that there shall be no coolie vote in that colony, will have the support of every man who intends that South Africa shall be governed neither by black nor coffee-coloured people, but by white men.[31]

For Gandhi, however, the legal equality of all British subjects, regardless of colour, was the key imperial promise.

As a young man Gandhi had become a true believer. 'Hardly ever have I known anybody', he confessed in his autobiography, 'to cherish such loyalty as I did to the British Constitution.'[32] In Natal, he was so distressed by the insults to Indians because of his passionate belief in the British Empire and the common law, believing, as he had been told, that racial prejudice had no place in the British legal system. Gandhi took seriously the frequently asserted principle that the common law did not distinguish between different groups in the community, that 'class legislation', as it was called, had no place in British parliaments.

He frequently quoted the text of Queen Victoria's Proclamation of 1858, known as India's Magna Carta, citing it in a letter to the *Natal Advertiser*:

We hold ourselves bound to the natives of our Indian territories by the same obligations of duty which bind us to all our other subjects, and these obligations, by the blessing of Almighty God, we shall faithfully and conscientiously fulfil. It is our further will that, so far as may be, our subjects, of whatever race or creed, be freely and impartially admitted to offices in our service, the duties of which they may be qualified by their education, ability and integrity, duly to discharge.[33]

He wrote to the *Times of Natal*, which had argued that although there were many highly cultivated Indians, there could be no question of giving them equal political power with the white man. Gandhi reminded the editor about Christian precepts:

Sir, may I venture to offer a suggestion? Will you re-read your New Testament? Will you ponder over your attitude towards the coloured population of

[30] *Ibid.*   [31] *Star*, cited in *Natal Witness*, 5 September 1895.
[32] Gandhi, *Autobiography*, p.166.   [33] Gandhi, *Collected Works*, vol.I, p.80.

the colonies? Will you then say you can reconcile it with the Bible teaching or the best British traditions? If you have washed your hands clean of both Christ and British traditions, I can have nothing to say; I gladly withdraw what I have written. Only it will be a sad day for Britain and for India if you have many followers.[34]

Gandhi was a dedicated Britisher. He had learnt 'with careful perseverance' the national anthem – 'God Save the Queen' – and made sure his children could sing it as well. 'Without fuss or ostentation', he testified, he 'vied with Englishmen in loyalty to the throne'.[35]

For their part, however, Colonial Office officials in London thought his identification with England wrong-headed. 'It is idle to argue, as the Petitioners do in one place, from the example of England', they commented. There were only about two hundred Indians living in the whole of London:

The shoe doesn't pinch us; for in the first place each Asiatic in Natal must be multiplied by eight hundred to produce a proportionate effect on the population at home; and secondly this country being already fully populated, a relatively large influx of a foreign element could only be brought about by a corresponding displacement of the native element.[36]

But there was a further problem in Natal: the presence of several hundred thousand 'natives'. Even if a few Indians were to be granted self-government, they could not be trusted to govern blacks. The Colonial Office noted the impossibility of one subject race being governed by another:

In the contingency which this Bill deals with – that of Asiatics becoming the majority in a tiny electorate – a result would appear, which no-one ever contemplated, and which would be most anomalous and perhaps hazardous in itself viz the Government of a subject Race, which itself does not understand and is permanently unfit for representative Government, by another Race which does not understand it either which has no experience of it, and whose capacity to work it must be doubtful . . . representative government is the monopoly of the European Races.[37]

But they also worried about the international implications of offending their Indian subjects. The measure was of the 'gravest character' and 'calculated to create feelings among the Natives of India in India itself of which the political consequences are difficult to forecast'.[38] The Act to amend the law relating to the franchise, which excluded all those who had not hitherto possessed elective representative institutions founded on the parliamentary franchise, was finally passed in 1896.

[34] *Ibid.* vol.1, p.137.   [35] Gandhi, *Autobiography*, p.166.
[36] CO 179/189.   [37] *Ibid.*   [38] *Ibid.*

Always in the back of officials' minds was the possibility that the 'natives of India' might themselves claim the right to self-government. When Natal was granted responsible government, the colony joined the exclusive club of self-governing settler colonies – Canada, Newfoundland, the Australian colonies, New Zealand and the Cape of Good Hope. White men were deemed to have both the capacity and the right to self-government and most white colonies were indeed more democratic than was Britain, which would not introduce full manhood suffrage until after World War 1.

But, as Bryce pointed out, the Colonial Office drew a fundamental distinction between white, self-governing colonies 'deemed fit to govern themselves' and Crown Colonies – 'tropical colonies [with] a predominant coloured population' – in Asia, Africa, the Caribbean and the Pacific. In these latter colonies, 'the supremacy of the Colonial Office and its local representatives is acquiesced in as fit and proper'. As he wrote: 'Everyone perceives that representative assemblies based on a democratic franchise, which are capable of governing Canada or Australia, would not succeed in the West Indies or Ceylon or Fiji.'[39] Or in India.

In 1858, following the dismantling of the East India Company, Crown rule had been instituted through a Government of India (with executive councils in Bengal, Bombay and Madras) firmly subordinated to the British parliament through the Secretary of State. Central and provincial legislatures, constituted as advisory extensions to the executive councils, were augmented in membership to provide for the expression of unofficial views. Indians could sit on local councils which, from 1892, were represented on legislative councils, but not until 1909 was a (very restrictive) electoral franchise introduced for provincial legislatures. And although few legislative measures were overtly discriminatory on a racial basis, Indians were effectively debarred from the higher levels of the army and the Indian Civil Service.

Although white colonies had been granted self-government, however, there were limits to their jurisdiction, especially with regard to race relations. Again the issue of sovereignty arose. While the imperial government insisted on equality of treatment of all British subjects, white settler communities reminded the Colonial Office of their right to self-government. What was at stake in the eyes of many colonists was their status as white men and their equality of status with Englishmen at home.

Almost all settler governments had to deal with racially diverse populations. There were Indigenous peoples in Canada, New Zealand, Australia and South Africa; indentured labourers in Mauritius, the Caribbean,

---

[39] Bryce, *Impressions of South Africa*, p.435.

Fiji, Queensland and Natal; and Asian migrants in British Columbia, New Zealand, South Africa and all the Australian colonies. Imperial race questions had an international dimension resulting from the global movements of people – Indian indentured labour to Mauritius, Natal, Fiji and the Caribbean; Melanesian labour to Queensland and the New Hebrides; Chinese and Japanese migrants to all British colonies around the Pacific. Several millions of Indians travelled to work as indentured labour in various countries in the nineteenth century, some thousands of whom had arrived in Natal to work in the sugar, fruit and other agricultural industries. White employers relied on indentured labour, but there was increasing opposition to the growing number of Indian free immigrants who planned to stay.

The last years of the nineteenth century witnessed a series of conflicts between the self-governing colonies and the Colonial Office over discriminatory legislation relating to immigration, freedom of movement, political and civil rights, land ownership and access to resources. The colonial governments demanded the right to say who could migrate to, reside and work in their countries and to decide the legal status of coloured minorities, whether Indigenous or immigrant. In the process of these struggles they came increasingly to define themselves as 'white men's countries', by which they meant that non-whites must be either excluded or segregated and politically subordinated.

Colonial Office officials dealt with this new and complex situation with a mixture of diplomacy, delay and duplicity. They continued to affirm the principle of non-discriminatory law – and every now and then advised the Crown to disallow an offensive bill – but usually gave way if the colonists were sufficiently determined. Their sense of moral superiority remained intact while their jaundiced view of white settler politicians was confirmed. As a class-based polity, the British had no problem with discrimination based on income or property. But the principle of non-discrimination on the grounds of race and colour received strong support and colonial officials spoke of it with pride.

Powerful pressure groups such as the Anti-Slavery Society and Aborigines Protection Society continued to act as watchdogs, often supported by the great missionary societies. Colonial governors often endorsed liberal views and sometimes attempted to translate their ideas into practice, antagonising colonists and often enough receiving rebukes from London for their zeal.

Time and time again colonists were outraged by interference from Governors and Colonial Office men. It was often said that while stay-at-home Englishmen had a sentimental regard for non-Europeans, they had no experience of colonial realities and were not themselves threatened with racial competition or rule by coloured men. In 1896, white men in Natal determined to act to stem the 'influx' of Indian immigrants, who were increasingly conceptualised racially – as 'Asiatics' – and their political leaders looked to Australia and United States for legislative models that were initially devised to exclude the Chinese.

We must follow New South Wales

In September 1896, the European Protection Association was formed in Durban with the following objectives: (1) the withdrawal of all State aid, assistance or countenance from all bodies of persons connected with Indian or other Asiatic immigration; (2) to press upon parliament the necessity of enacting such rules and regulations so as to compel the Indian communities to leave the colony at the expiration of their term of indenture; (3) to take all steps that may be found advisable for limiting the number of Indians introduced into the colony; and (4) to endeavour to have the Australian laws on immigration made applicable to Natal.

At a meeting of Australian colonial premiers in Sydney, six months earlier in March 1896, it had been agreed that the different colonies would enact new immigration laws to extend earlier restrictions against Chinese to 'all coloured races' – regardless of whether persons were British subjects – and the New South Wales parliament had proceeded to pass such a law.

The Australian measures against Asian immigration were closely followed in South Africa as they had been in California in the 1870s. In October 1896, members of the Natal government sent a telegram to Prime Minister John Robinson, then in England: 'Five hundred free Indians arrived last week. Inrush must be stopped, or all lower branches of trade and farming will pass into Indian hands. Explain to Mr Chamberlain we must follow New South Wales.'[40] Joseph Chamberlain, the new secretary of state in the Colonial Office, was now charged with reconciling the principle of the equality of treatment of British subjects and the demand by self-governing white settler colonies that they be allowed to decide their own immigration policies.

In November, the Colonial Patriotic Union was formed in Durban with the object of preventing 'the further influx of free Asiatics into the country'.[41] Again, the organisation referred to Australasian precedent in

---

[40] Quoted in Natal Legislative Assembly, 25 March 1897, Sessional Papers, Fifth Session, First Parliament, Enclosure, CO 179/198.
[41] *Natal Witness*, 1 April 1897, CO 179/198.

excluding Asian immigrants and sent a petition to the government arguing that: (1) The older and richer British colonies of Australia and New
Zealand have found that this class of immigrant is detrimental to the best
interests of the inhabitants and have passed laws having as to their object
the total exclusion of Asiatics. (2) The disproportion between white and
black races is already so great in this colony that it appears highly inju-
dicious to further increase this disproportion. (3) The continued introduction of Asiatic races is in the highest sense detrimental to the natives
of this colony from the fact that so long as the cheaper labour supply is
available so long will the civilisation of the natives be retarded, their civilisation depending upon their intercourse with the white races. (4) The
low moral tone and unsanitary habits of Asiatics are a constant source of
danger to the progress and health of the European population. The government responded with an assurance that appropriate legislation would
be introduced without delay.

Newspapers also urged the government to 'follow the course resolved
upon by Australia'. The Ministry should 'hold on to the skirts of Australia.
She might pull us through when nothing else might'.[42] Natal agitators
eagerly cited the New South Wales precedent, but that Act directly targetting 'Asiatics' – including Indians whether British subjects or not –
had been reserved by the New South Wales Governor. Chamberlain
advised that he intended to use the occasion of the celebration of the
sixtieth anniversary of Queen Victoria's accession to the throne, in June
1897, when colonial politicians would gather in London, to arrive at
a solution to the immigration question acceptable to all parties in the
Empire.

Meanwhile, rumours circulated in Natal that Gandhi, who had
returned to India, there to publicise the injustice meted out to his fellow
countrymen in South Africa, was returning to Natal with boatloads of free
immigrants. His arrival on the Indian ship, the *Courland*, at the same time
as another ship, the *Naderi*, which together carried some 600 Indian passengers, seemed to confirm white fears of a forthcoming invasion. When
the ships were placed in quarantine in Durban in response to an outbreak
of the 'plague' in Bombay, fears of contagion took on a new urgency. An
overcrowded public meeting in Durban Town Hall demanded that the
government send the passengers back to India in scenes reminiscent of
those in Melbourne and Sydney provoked by the arrival of the steamer
the *Afghan*, carrying Chinese passengers to Australia in 1888. Threats of
violence prompted the government to act quickly.

[42] *Natal Witness*, 19 January 1897, quoted in Martens, 'A Transnational History of Immigration Restriction', p.332.

Prime Minister Robinson communicated the government's 'full sympathy with the consensus of public opinion . . . as regards the desirability of preventing the over-running of the Colony by Asiatics' but suggested the agitators call off the planned demonstration and avoid unconstitutional action. He agreed to meet a committee of twelve at his house: they were 'fairly representative men of a fairly representative community, they were level-headed men, sensible men, men in good positions, with property at stake. They represented the circumstances and the character of the movement and the intensity of the feeling, and I recognised the difficulty they were then in. I saw that the movement was, as it were, getting bigger than they themselves contemplated, and it was gathering strength day by day'.[43]

When the quarantine was lifted in January, the Colonial Patriotic Union organised a demonstration to gather at the docks to prevent the Indians from landing. To explain their purpose, they issued a manifesto to their fellow colonists announcing: 'A grave crisis has been reached in our history. From the time Natal acquired her autonomy, it was hoped that, beyond any of the neighbouring States, she would be a white-man's and for the most part, an English speaking Colony'.[44] While declaring that the Union felt no hostility towards current Indian residents and their locally born children, the members protested against their number 'being further augmented by free Asiatic importations': 'thus far has Asiatic immigration proceeded, and here shall it cease absolutely and for ever'.

The threats of violence were deplored on all sides. The Prime Minister personally assured the passengers of their safety and they were landed in small groups. Gandhi was advised to remain on board the *Courland* until the evening; he was offered police protection but declined it. His wife and two sons, who had returned with him from India, were taken to a safe house. Gandhi came ashore later with a local solicitor, but was observed by some boys who shouted 'Gandhi', 'thrash him', 'surround him', and began throwing stones. A crowd quickly gathered and encircled the two men. Gandhi was separated from his companion and assaulted. His clothes were covered with mud and rotten fish and eggs were thrown at him. His turban was snatched, he was beaten with a riding whip, kicked in the back, cornered against a fence and repeatedly punched.

Fortunately, the wife of the Superintendent of Police, who happened to be passing, was able to rescue him. With umbrella unfurled against the barrage of missiles, she escorted him through the jeering, hostile crowd. Gandhi refused to take action against his assailants, but helped

[43] *Times of Natal*, 26 March 1897, Enclosure, CO 179/198.
[44] *Natal Mercury*, 14 January 1897.

write a thirty-five page 'memorial' to the Colonial Office concerning the 'anti-Indian demonstration' and demanded that the British government 'remove and prevent restrictions on Her Majesty's Indian subjects residing in the Colony of Natal'.[45]

The Natal government, however, confirmed their intention to legislate to prohibit further Indian immigration. New licensing and quarantine laws were also directed at Indians. Colonial Office officials judged the Natal Bills 'objectionable', but unless they imposed exceptional disabilities on Asian subjects they could 'scarcely be disallowed in a responsible government colony'. Chamberlain shared his officials' concerns, observing:

All these Bills are objectionable but in dealing with a self-governing colony we must be very careful not to [intervene] without the most stringent necessity. There is a wave of illiberality in regard to Asiatics which has spread over all our Colonies. We cannot resist it. All we can do is to prevent the exclusion of British subjects.[46]

For the Colonial Office faced a further danger. Self-governing colonies might follow the American example and declare their complete independence. With the 'elephantine memory of imperial elites', as David Armitage has put it, the men at the Colonial Office could not help but have American experience in mind when dealing with colonial confrontations.[47]

On the day of the demonstration in Durban, the Colonial Office sent a telegram to the governor: 'Should it appear necessary to Natal Ministers to place restrictions on immigration, I earnestly trust that the legislation be directed not against race or colour, but against impecunious or ignorant immigrants'.[48] The Colonial Office also wrote to the Indian government enquiring whether they might not use local laws to restrict the outflow of immigrants to South Africa. The alternative, they warned, was likely to be special legislation in Natal directed against 'British Indians as such'. Chamberlain again emphasised he was very much opposed to legislation 'specially directed against persons of a particular race or colour'.[49]

As it happened the Natal government borrowed the device of a literary test from the United States government, which had passed its own

---

[45] Memorial to The Right Honorable Joseph Chamberlain by the British Indians in Natal re Anti-Indian Demonstrations, Enclosure, 15 March 1897, CO 179/198, p.35.
[46] Minute, 27 February 1897, CO 179/197.
[47] David Armitage, 'The Contagion of Sovereignty: Declarations of Independence since 1776', *South African Historical Journal* 52 (2005) p.16.
[48] Draft of telegram dispatched to Governor of Natal, 13 January 1897, CO 179/197.
[49] Draft of telegram, CO 179/197.

Immigration Restriction Act in 1896.[50] In February 1897, the Governor forwarded the Colonial Secretary a copy of the proposed legislation, noting: 'The Bill purports to prevent the introduction into Natal of "undesirable immigrants" and had I understand, been drawn on the lines of the United States legislation on that subject'.[51]

Natal immigration restriction: 'founded on the American Act'

The United States Immigration Restriction Act of 1896 had been passed as a result of a concerted campaign by the Massachusetts-based Immigration Restriction League, founded in 1894, their target being recent European arrivals from countries such as Italy, Hungary and Poland and other allegedly ignorant and illiterate European peoples – 'removed from us in race and blood'.[52] Its instrument was the literacy test and its leading advocates included Anglo-Saxonists Francis Walker, president of the Massachusetts Institute of Technology, Prescott Hall, Nathanuel S. Schaler and Henry Cabot Lodge, who had written articles on the subject for the *North American Review* and would sponsor the 1896 Bill in the Senate.[53] As Matt Jacobson has observed in *Whiteness of a Different Color*, the Immigration Restriction League had crystallised around the issue of a literacy test for incoming aliens and 'race was central to the league's conception of literacy from the beginning'.[54] In his speech in the Senate in support of the literacy test Bill, Lodge provided a Freeman-inspired 'history of our race' and referred to Gustave Le Bon's concept of an Anglo-American race of superior qualities whose 'soul' had to be safeguarded that it might rule the world. Lodge had come across Le Bon's *The Psychology of Peoples* when on holiday in France in 1895 and lent his

---

[50] While the historiography in this field mostly recognises the importance of the Natal formula in implementing immigration restriction legislation without naming the races against whom it was directed, no historians seem to have noted that Natal itself borrowed the formula from the United States.

[51] Governor to CO, 26 February 1897, CO 179/200.

[52] Henry Cabot Lodge, 'Lynch Law and Unrestricted Immigration', *North American Review* 152, no.414 (May 1891) p.611.

[53] Immigration Restriction League papers, Houghton Library, Harvard, Am 2245 (1050), (1122).

[54] Matthew Frye Jacobson, *Whiteness of a Different Color: European Immigrants and the Alchemy of Race* (Cambridge, Harvard University Press, 1999) p.77; see also Barbara Miller Solomon, *Ancestors and Immigrants: A Changing New England Tradition* (New York, John Wiley and Sons, 1956) pp.59–81; and John Higham, *Strangers in the Land Patterns of American Nativism 1860–1925*, second edition (New Brunswick, Rutgers University Press, 1988) pp.141–4.

copy to Theodore Roosevelt, who agreed that 'what Le Bon says of race is very fine and true'.[55]

Literacy was deemed fundamental to the republican citizen's capacity for self-government and only Anglo-Saxons were thought to be blessed with that capacity. In the United States, Connecticut and Massachusetts had enacted literacy requirements for voting in the 1850s. The precedent for using a literacy test specifically to effect racial exclusion was American, as we have seen in the previous chapter. Mississippi led the way in 1890, providing an example that was followed two years later in the Cape Colony. Crucially, the republican model of exclusion need make no exceptions, of course, for British subjects.

Prime Minister Harry Escombe who had replaced an ailing Robinson explained that 'the great Republic of the America has found it necessary to have recourse to that restriction, and I may say generally that the Bill that I now have the honour to submit to this Assembly is founded on the American Act. But it goes one step further'. Whereas the American legislation prescribed that would-be immigrants must be able to read and write in their own or another language, the Natal legislation – 'to meet the requirements of Natal in connection with India' – prescribed that applicants must be able to write out a form in a European language. As the literacy test migrated around the world and its target changed from blacks to Italians to Indians, so the requirements of the test changed. And as its binary logic of dividing the world into categories of white and not-white hardened, so groups as diverse as African-Americans, Chinese, Italians, Hungarians, Indians and Japanese were racialised as not-white.[56]

In moving the second reading of the new Immigration Restriction Bill, the Prime Minister explained the aptness of the example of 'the great Republic of the United States': 'the United States claim for themselves what I venture to claim on behalf of this Colony, and which I am certain – I will not say I am certain, but which I have reason to believe many English Colonies will claim – that they have an absolute right in themselves, if they think fit, to place a restriction on the introduction of immigration into their country of persons who are regarded by the community as undesirable immigrants'.

[55] Gustave Le Bon, *Les Premieres Civilisations* (Paris, 1889); Roosevelt to Lodge, 29 April 1896, in Elting E. Morison (ed.) *The Letters of Theodore Roosevelt* (Cambridge, Harvard University Press, 1951) vol.1, p.535.
[56] See Marilyn Lake, 'From Mississippi to Melbourne via Natal: the Invention of the Literacy Test as a Technology for Racial Exclusion', in Ann Curthoys and Marilyn Lake (eds.) *Connected Worlds: History in Transnational Perspective* (Canberra, Australian National University Press, 2006).

In the event, the American Act of 1896 was vetoed by President Grover Cleveland, who cited American traditions of welcoming peoples fleeing poverty or oppression, and condemned the literacy test as a pretext, but not before it was emulated in Natal. The Colonial Office immediately saw the value of the legislation – specifying an education or literacy qualification for immigration that made no explicit mention of race or colour – as a model for Australia and other British colonies. In a memorandum to the India Office, officials explained:

Some form of legislation in restriction of Indian immigration was inevitable in Natal and the Secretary of State was of the opinion that it was desirable that a law should be passed in that colony in a form which was not open to objection that it persecuted persons of a particular colour.[57]

Chamberlain intended to place the advantages of what came to be called the Natal compromise before the colonial leaders who would gather in London that year for Queen Victoria's Diamond Jubilee.

On 24 June, the premiers from Canada, the Cape Colony, Newfoundland, Natal, New South Wales, Victoria, Queensland, Tasmania, South Australia, Western Australia and New Zealand gathered at the Colonial Office to discuss 'certain Imperial questions'. Chamberlain's speech on that occasion sympathised with the determination of the white residents of the settler colonies to prevent an influx of people 'alien in civilization, alien in religion, alien in customs', while emphasising the importance of India to the Empire. He asked the assembled premiers to bear in mind the 'traditions of the Empire, which make no distinction in favour of, or against, race or colour'. To actually exclude by reason of their colour, or by reason of their race 'all Her Majesty's Indian subjects, or even all Asiatics' would be an act so offensive to those peoples that it would be 'most painful, I am quite certain, to Her Majesty to have to sanction it'. He emphasised that overtly discriminatory legislation would provoke ill-feeling, discontent and irritation in India, where there lived hundreds of thousands of men 'every bit as civilized as those assembled, who are, if that is anything, better born in the sense that they have older traditions and older families'.[58]

In any case such racial discrimination was unnecessary, Chamberlain ventured to suggest, in remarks more attuned to the class snobberies of Englishmen, than the racial sensibilities of colonials:

[57] Quoted in R. A. Huttenback, 'The British Empire as a "White Man's Country" – Racial Attitudes and Immigration Legislation in the Colonies of White Settlement', *The Journal of British Studies* vol.XIII, no.1 (November 1973) p.111.

[58] See Marilyn Lake, 'On Being a White Man, Australia, Circa 1900', in Hsu-Ming Teo and Richard White (eds.) *Cultural History in Australia* (Sydney, Allen and Unwin, 2003) p.106.

It is not because a man is of a different colour from ourselves that he is necessarily an undesirable immigrant, but it is because he is dirty, or he is immoral, or he is a pauper or he has some other objection which can be defined in an Act of Parliament, and by which the exclusion can be managed with regard to all those whom you really desire to exclude.[59]

His speech was conciliatory, but also revealed his lack of understanding of the racial identifications that had become so important to the subjectivities of white men in South Africa, North America and Australasia.

Back in Natal, Gandhi read Chamberlain's speech with incredulity. Affronted by the hypocrisy evident in the whole exercise, he wrote another long letter to influential figures in Britain and India. Chamberlain had praised the Natal legislation for not mentioning race or colour and yet, in the local debates, the anti-Indian purpose of the three contentious bills was openly and loudly proclaimed. 'Mr. Chamberlain', he wrote, 'cannot be unaware of the fact that the Natal Act was passed with the deliberate intention of applying it *almost exclusively* to the Indians'. He felt betrayed: Chamberlain's speech was 'a stab in the dark'. He felt disoriented: 'We do not know now where we are or what we are to do'.[60] But his conclusion was irresistible. Chamberlain had deserted the Indian cause and yielded to the 'anti-Asiatic clamour of the different colonies'. The Colonial Secretary had made it clear that an Indian, as soon as he left his homeland, ceased to be a British subject.

But the imperial status in which Gandhi invested so much – the status of British subject – was fast being eclipsed in the self-governing colonies by the ascendant dichotomy of white and not-white. In making an argument that Natal should follow New South Wales rather than the United States and declare explicitly against the immigration of Asiatics, one member of parliament was moved to observe that colonists should forget about Colonial Office objections on behalf of coloured British subjects, for 'the idea of the British subject was fading more and more every year'.

Not so for the British government. In 1899, following increasing tension with the Transvaal, in part related to the rights of British subjects living in the Boer republics, and mindful of their mineral wealth, Britain embarked on a South African war. The Boers, however, proved a more determined and skilled enemy than expected. The war was drawn out and brutal, with the British army resorting to burning the country and incarcerating women and children in concentration camps to force an end to the fighting. In the broader Empire, reactions were mixed: volunteers

---

[59] Extract from *British Parliamentary Paper*, No.15, vol.2 (1897), quoted in Gandhi, *Collected Works*, pp.354–5.

[60] Mr. Chamberlain's Address to Premiers, open letter, 18 September 1897, cited in Gandhi, *Collected Works*, p.351.

rushed to enlist from the colonies as well as the motherland. But the war also attracted fierce criticism, not least from those who identified with the Boer republics' right to self-determination. Some liberal imperialists, on the other hand, hoped that the defeat of the Boer republics might open the way to securing greater justice for the native population and the coloured community in South Africa.

In the United States, Theodore Roosevelt reflected on the fact that although his Dutch heritage predisposed him to sympathise with the Boer cause, and he greatly admired the persistence of the Boer settlers, he nevertheless felt that it was in 'the interest of civilization that the English-speaking race should be dominant in South Africa, exactly as it is in the interest of civilization that the United States themselves, the greatest branch of the English-speaking race, should be dominant in the Western Hemisphere'.[61] James Bryce, sceptical of British motivations, opposed the war. In Natal, Gandhi, the true believer still, threw in his lot with the British, organising and leading an Indian ambulance corps.

When he left South Africa again, in 1901, Gandhi still declared himself a loyal British subject, committed to the imperial ideal of racial equality. But he had discovered in Natal the importance and the impossibility of being a white man. No matter how well he dressed, how polite his manners, how correct his diction, how well-versed in Christianity, European literature and British law, he could never become a white man.

In his farewell address, delivered to supporters in October, Gandhi declared defiantly that what was wanted in South Africa was 'not a white man's country; not a white brotherhood, but an Imperial brotherhood'.[62] But he was already doubtful and his sense of betrayal would ultimately destroy his faith in British goodness and justice. His disenchantment was slow in coming, but its force eventually turned Gandhi into one of the most determined opponents of the Empire and its favoured white brotherhood.[63]

---

[61] Roosevelt to Henry White, 30 March 1896, in Morison, *Letters of Theodore Roosevelt*, vol.1, p.523.
[62] Gandhi, *Collected Works*, p.206.
[63] Devanesen, *The Making of the Mahatma*, pp.317–19.

Part 3

Transnational solidarities

6   White Australia points the way

Inauguration

In 1901, the Commonwealth of Australia was inaugurated in an act of racial expulsion when the first parliament legislated to expel several thousand Pacific Islanders – or 'Kanakas' – who had been brought to labour in the sugar cane fields of north Queensland during the last decades of the nineteenth century.[1] Further legislation – the Immigration Restriction Act – was passed to ensure that other 'non-whites' would be prevented from coming to settle in Australia any time in the future. 'The two things go hand in hand', advised the Liberal Attorney General and future Prime Minister, Alfred Deakin. They were 'the necessary complement of a single policy – the policy of securing a "White Australia".'[2]

When the first Prime Minister, Edmund Barton, rose to speak in support of the Immigration Restriction Bill, he held in his hand a copy of *National Life and Character: A Forecast* by Charles Pearson – 'one of the most intellectual statesmen who ever lived in this country' – from which he quoted Pearson's now famous warning that 'The day will come' when the European observer will wake to find the black and yellow races no longer under tutelage, but forming independent governments, in control of their own trade and industry, invited to international conferences and welcomed as allies by the civilised world.[3] When that day came, Pearson

---

[1] On Pacific Islander indentured labour in Australia, see Tracey Banivanua-Mar, *Violence and Colonial Dialogue: The Australian –Pacific Indentured Labor Trade* (Honolulu, University of Hawaii Press, 2007).

[2] Alfred Deakin, *Commonwealth Parliamentary Debates*, House of Representatives (12 September 1901) p.4806; on the White Australia policy see Myra Willard, *History of the White Australia Policy*, first edition (Melbourne, Melbourne University Press, 1923; reprinted New York, Augustus M. Kelley, 1968); A. T. Yarwood, *Asian Migration to Australia: The Background to Exclusion 1896–1923* (Melbourne, Melbourne University Press, 1964); Andrew Markus, *Australian Race Relations 1788–1993* (Sydney, Allen and Unwin, 1994).

[3] Charles Pearson, quoted by Edmund Barton, *Commonwealth Parliamentary Debates*, House of Representatives (7 August 1901) p.3503.

had suggested, the white man's 'pride of place' in the world would be 'humiliated'.[4]

Pearson's unsettling prediction had become a talking point in political circles around the world, though the author didn't live to see his book's impact, succumbing to a chest infection, in London, in 1894. In the face of changing world forces, Pearson advocated stoic, manly resignation, but he thought it important that white men's countries protect themselves and thus help defend the higher civilisation.[5] The new Commonwealth of Australia resolved, in the words of Prime Minister Barton, 'to make a legislative declaration of our racial identity'.[6] Thus, at the beginning of the twentieth century, Australians drew a colour line around their continent and declared whiteness to be at the very heart of their national identity.

In response to Pearson's warnings that white men would wake to find themselves 'elbowed and hustled, and perhaps even thrust aside', Australian political leaders framed a constitution and passed legislation to secure the new nation-state as 'a white man's country'. In fashioning a White Australia in the South Pacific, close to the heavily populated countries of South East Asia, political leaders were supremely conscious of the global context. Their policies reflected and would in turn shape new racial solidarities across the world.

Australians learnt from history, as they read it, and in nailing their colours to the mast, they embarked on a social experiment that placed them, so they thought, at the cutting edge of modern history. Across the Pacific, sympathetic Americans urged their fellow countrymen to learn from the Australian example. The Secretary of the Immigration Restriction League, Prescott Hall, obsessive in his advocacy of a literacy test, wrote to the Australian Prime Minister within a month of the passage of the new Commonwealth's Immigration Restriction Act to obtain copies of the Australian legislation that incorporated, as he noted, a 'writing test'. Soon after, a special issue of the *Annals of the American Academy of Political and Social Science* on the issue of immigration restriction included an article by Professor Frank Parsons, on 'Australasian Methods of Dealing with Immigration'.[7]

American history lessons

Americans saw the Australians as exemplars in enacting progressive reforms. Australians in turn considered that American history provided

---

[4] Charles Pearson, *National Life and Character: A Forecast* (London, Macmillan, 1893) p.85.
[5] Pearson, *National Life and Character*, p.16.
[6] Edmund Barton, untitled speech on federation, Barton papers MS 5/977, NLA.
[7] Immigration Restriction League papers, Houghton Library, Ms Am 2245(1111).

crucial lessons about past mistakes. In congratulating the authors of the Australian Constitution, among whom he and Barton had been to the fore, Attorney General Deakin pointed to the significance of section 51 in equipping the new Commonwealth of Australia to deal with the 'race difficulty' in its many guises:

> Our Constitution marks a distinct advance upon and difference from that of the United States, in that it contains within itself the amplest powers to deal with this difficulty in all its aspects. It is not merely a question of invasion from the exterior. It may be a question of difficulties within our borders, already created, or a question of possible contamination of another kind. I doubt if there can be found in the list of powers with which this Parliament, on behalf of the people, is endowed – powers of legislation – a cluster more important and more far reaching in their prospect than the provisions contained in sub-sections (26) to (30) of section 51, in which the bold outline of the authority of the people of Australia for their self-protection is laid down.[8]

In their commentary on Section 51, constitutional authorities John Quick and Robert Garran noted that whereas American legislators dealing with the 'race problem' had to reckon with the 'special inhibitions' of the 14th and 15th Constitutional Amendments, Australian legislators had armed themselves with the constitutional power to make 'special laws' for their self-protection.[9]

Quick and Garran cited the pre-eminent United States theorist of the nation-state, J. W. Burgess, who, as we have seen, specified the obligation of 'self-preservation' and 'ethnical homogeneity' in a long section on 'The Nation' in his 1890 textbook *Political Science and Comparative Constitutional Law*. Burgess had written that national unity was the determining force in the development of the modern nation-states: 'The prime policy, therefore, of each of these states should be to attain proper physical boundaries and to render its population ethnically homogeneous . . . it is the highest duty of the state to preserve, strengthen and develop its national character.'[10]

In explaining the White Australia policy to parliament in 1901, Attorney General Deakin echoed these sentiments: 'We here find ourselves touching the profoundest instinct of individual or nation – the instinct of self-preservation – for it is nothing less than the national manhood, the

[8] Alfred Deakin, *Commonwealth Parliamentary Debates*, House of Representatives (12 September 1901) p.4804.

[9] John Quick and Robert Garran, *The Annotated Constitution of the Australian Commonwealth* (1901; Reprinted, Sydney, Legal Books, 1976) p.623; see also Marilyn Lake, 'White Man's Country: The Trans-National History of a National Project', *Australian Historical Studies* 34, 122 (October 2003).

[10] John W. Burgess, *Political Science and Comparative Constitutional Law: vol.1 Sovereignty and Liberty* (New York, Ginn and Company, 1890) p.42.

national character and the national future that are at stake.'[11] Deakin's speech, like Pearson's book, drew on the prevalent discourse on self-preservation as the basic instinct of nations and, like Pearson, he linked the future of the nation to the condition of its manhood. White Australia would secure the status of white manhood.

Burgess and his younger colleague at Columbia University, William Dunning, rested their arguments, as we have seen, about the imperative of racial homogeneity on the lessons of their national past, the most important of which was that the experiment in multi-racial democracy ushered in by Radical Reconstruction had been a disastrous mistake. Following James Bryce, Dunning wrote that the 'anarchy of Negro rule' represented the supreme historical example of 'reckless statecraft'.[12]

Deakin also pointed to American history lessons when he warned the first federal parliament:

We should be false to the lessons taught us in the great republic of the west; we should be false to the never-to-be-forgotten teachings from the experience of the United States, of difficulties only partially conquered by the blood of their best and bravest; we should be absolutely blind to and unpardonably neglectful of our obligations, if we fail to lay those lessons to heart.[13]

Bryce's *American Commonwealth* and his article on 'The Negro problem' had played a crucial role in imparting those 'lessons' to Australia's federal fathers as they went about their business of nation-building during the decade of the 1890s.

Deakin first met Bryce in 1887, when he attended the first Colonial Conference in London, and impressed the English political establishment with his erudition, good looks and remarkable oratorical gifts. As with the young Theodore Roosevelt, who was visiting London in the same year, Deakin found himself courted by the aristocracy, swamped with invitations to city clubs and country houses and patronised by leading public men and women. There is no record that the two visitors met, but their responses to British patronage were similar, though Deakin, still the colonial, was even more determinedly unimpressed by British pomp and pretension. He denounced the excess and superficiality of London life and pointedly turned down the offer of a knighthood. He also famously

---

[11] Alfred Deakin, *Commonwealth Parliamentary Debates*, House of Representatives (12 September 1901) p.4804.

[12] William Dunning, *Essays on the Civil War and Reconstruction* (1897), quoted in Eric Newby, *Jim Crow's Defence: Anti-Negro Thought in America 1900–1930* (Baton Rouge, Louisiana State University Press, 1965) p.66.

[13] Alfred Deakin, *Commonwealth Parliamentary Debates*, House of Representatives (12 September 1901) p.4806; for other references to American experience by members of parliament, see H. B. Higgins, *Ibid.* p.4659; Sir William McMillan, *Ibid.* p.4627; King O'Malley, *Ibid.* p.4638; H. B. Higgins, *Ibid.* p.6815.

spoke up to the Prime Minister, Lord Salisbury, in defence of Australian interests in the Pacific. The memory of imperial condescension and Colonial Office scorn stayed with Deakin and shaped his determination to achieve Australian independence through federation. In union lay power. On matters touching self-government there had to be absolute 'unity and unanimity' he told the Victorian parliament on his return to Australia in July 1887.[14]

When the first Australian constitutional conference met in Melbourne, in 1890, to consider a draft federal constitution, Deakin was to the fore in recommending Bryce's *American Commonwealth* as a key source of advice and was pleased to report to Bryce that his book had been of the 'greatest possible service'. He was certain it would prove 'equally valuable' at the Constitutional Convention planned for Sydney in the following year:

When the Convention comes I have little doubt but that your volumes will form one of its chief text books & may thus contribute to a degree unsuspected by yourself to the shaping of what may prove to be the last new constitution of any great Anglo-Saxon people.[15]

Deakin suggested to Bryce that he write a sequel about Australia:

I trust that you will regard this proposition as suggested by a desire that my race should be as fitly and as fully studied in the Pacific as in the Atlantic & from a conviction that if you would undertake such a task it would be to the great gain of our young self-governing community.[16]

Deakin wrote of 'my race'. In working to build the new Commonwealth of Australia, he saw his labours as contributing not just to Australian nation-building, but to the greater glory of the larger community of Anglo-Saxon peoples, which, importantly, included the United States.

The Australians liked to send records of their constitutional deliberations to American friends as they followed 'so largely the precedent of the United States'.[17] Deakin sent a copy of the 1890 conference proceedings to Josiah Royce at Harvard, which also served as a letter of introduction to Andrew Inglis Clark, Tasmanian Attorney-General and co-author of the first draft of the Australian constitution. Australian-born Clark was, according to Deakin in his letter of recommendation, 'more American in tastes and feelings than many of your own citizens whom I have met'.[18]

---

[14] Alfred Deakin, *Victorian Parliamentary Debates*, Legislative Assembly (6 July 1887).
[15] Deakin to Bryce, 27 February 1890, Bryce papers, 56, folio 91, Bodleian Library.
[16] *Ibid.*   [17] Deakin to Royce, 14 January 1898, Deakin papers 1540/1/411.
[18] Deakin to Royce, 8 May 1890, Royce papers, incoming correspondence, box 1, HUG 1755-3-3, Harvard Archives; on A. I. Clark's admiration for the United States see Richard Ely (ed.) *A Living Force: Andrew Inglis Clark and the Ideal of Commonwealth* for (Hobart, Tasmanian Historical Studies Centre, 2001).

He formed a friendship with Oliver Wendell Holmes Jr. whom Roosevelt would appoint to the United States Supreme Court in 1902. Clark's son, Conway, who later studied architecture in Boston, took up lodgings in Irvine Street, Cambridge, right next door to Royce.

Deakin also struck acquaintances as American in his tastes and feelings. Royce had described him memorably as 'an admirer of America and of good scenery, a lover of life, of metaphysics and of power'.[19] A journalist from the United States who was visiting Melbourne at the time of the 1890 conference was struck by Deakin's enthusiasm for her country's political traditions. Comparing his oratory with that of the great Charles Sumner and Wendell Phillips, she wrote to him, enclosing a report she had written for an American journal, confessing that it was with 'the memories of these men's lives and truth-charged burning words, fresh in mind that I write to say how great the delight I felt in hearing the Constitution and institutions of my country set before this conference of Australasia in the very hour of the conception of the Nation that is to be'.[20] Deakin was less pleased with her suggestion that in his dark good looks he resembled Phillip II of Spain. As an avowed Anglo-Saxonist, he would not have liked to have been mistaken for a swarthy Mediterranean type.

The Constitutional Convention that followed the Melbourne conference met in Sydney in 1891. Deakin again sent a copy of the proceedings to Royce and confessed: 'While in Sydney attending the Convention I ran up to the Blue Mountains and took my Easter by myself in the same hotel and in the same haunts as those in which we passed hours that were among the pleasantest I have ever spent'.[21] The delegate from New South Wales, Edmund Barton, wrote to Bryce in England, confirming that *The American Commonwealth* was in 'great vogue' among Australian politicians: 'I fancy the Convention adopted the title 'Commonwealth' from your pages'.[22] The choice of the name Commonwealth for the Australian nation-state was significant for its American republican resonances. Royce's history of California had been written for the 'American Commonwealth' series and he now lived in the Commonwealth of Massachusetts.

Bryce's survey of United States institutions in *The American Commonwealth* provided extensive information on the technicalities of building a federal state and judiciary and the distribution of state and federal

[19] *Scribner's Magazine*, IX, no.1 (January 1891) p.78.
[20] Gustafson to Deakin, 6 March 1890, Deakin papers, 1540/11/4.
[21] Deakin to Royce, 8 July 1891, Royce papers, incoming correspondence, box 1, HUG 1755-3-3, Harvard Archives.
[22] Barton to Bryce, 18 June 1891, Bryce papers, folio 27, Bodleian Library.

powers. But it also alerted Australians to the political implications of the 'Negro problem', which had become, Bryce wrote, 'the capital question in national as well as state politics'. Echoing Bryce in the first Australian parliament, H. B. Higgins, the Liberal member for North Melbourne, friend of labour and future president of the Commonwealth Court of Conciliation and Arbitration, said of the race question: 'If Australia has any national question this is it'.[23] The decade of Australia's constitutional conventions – the federal decade of the 1890s – was also the period when the number of lynchings in the United States reached their peak. That country was experiencing 'the greatest racial trouble ever known in the history of the world', Higgins told the parliament. Australians should 'take warning and guard ourselves against similar complications'.[24]

Barring all persons belonging to any coloured race

The Australian Constitutional Convention debate was framed by the motion 'that in order to enlarge the powers of self-government of the people of Australia, it is desirable to create a Federal Government'. Australian politicians never lost an opportunity to intone the mantra of their 'self-government'. It both confirmed their special status as white men in a multi-racial Empire and expressed their masculine will to sovereignty, even as they continued to subject themselves to the sovereign British Queen. From the mid-nineteenth century, Australian insistence on the rights of self-governing communities was usually most emphatic when the issue in question was race. In exercising their powers of self-government to legislate their racial identity, Australians asserted their sovereign rights in the domain that mattered most.[25]

In the 1880s, colonial leaders had objected to the expectation that they adhere to the terms of the 1860 Peking Convention, which guaranteed reciprocal rights of free movement between the British and Chinese Empires, when they had not been party or signatories to the international agreement. They insisted on acknowledgment of their rights as self-governing communities and their objections were duly noted. When

[23] Quoted in John Rickard, *H. B. Higgins: The Rebel as Judge* (Sydney, Allen and Unwin, 1984) p.131.
[24] H. B. Higgins, *Commonwealth Parliamentary Debates*, House of Representatives (6 September 1901) p.4659.
[25] Australia remained constitutionally dependent on Britain and sovereignty remained formally with the monarch, but with effective sovereignty in matters of race, the quest for political independence lost its urgency. Not until 1926, with the Balfour Declaration, did Australia gain full power over foreign relations and the implementation of treaties. In 1931, the Statute of Westminster acknowledged the full statutory independence of the Dominions, but Australia didn't sign until 1942.

Britain negotiated a Treaty of Commerce and Navigation with Japan in 1894, that guaranteed 'full liberty to enter, travel or reside in any part of [the] Dominions and possessions of the other contracting party', article 19 specifically stated that the treaty did not apply to British self-governing Dominions, unless they chose to separately adhere to it within two years. In 1896, the Australian Premiers considered the matter and resolved not to sign the treaty, although Queensland, thinking that it would be to its commercial advantage, later became a contractual party, with a protocol that insisted that the terms of the treaty would not affect Queensland laws relating to immigration.

The other colonies decided not just to refuse the treaty, but to legislate against Japanese migrants. Australian attitudes towards Japan became more fearful, with the state's rise as a military and naval power and decisive defeat of China in 1895. Faced with the arrival in Australia of small numbers of Japanese, Malays, Sikhs, East Indian labourers and Pacific Islanders during the 1890s, especially in the north of the continent, colonial governments resolved to extend the earlier ban on Chinese to people of 'any coloured race' – or in the words of the New South Wales legislation of 1896 – 'all persons belonging to any coloured race inhabiting the Continent of Asia or the Continent of Africa, or any island adjacent thereto, or any island in the Pacific Ocean or Indian Ocean' – regardless of their status as British subjects or allies. The new legislation caused embarrassment to the British government but, as we have seen, produced great interest in Natal, whose parliament initially introduced legislation on the New South Wales model.

The Australian legislation of 1896, in dividing the world's peoples between white and not-white, regardless of their standing as powers or status as British subjects, marked a radical new departure in international relations. But the move was a logical development of the binary thinking that governed British imperial rule – the division between Crown colonies and self-governing Dominions or between 'advanced' and 'backward' races – and United States naturalisation law, that divided the world's peoples into white and not-white. White Australia was produced in a convergence of these binary classification systems with the result that a vast range of diverse nationalities, ethnicities and religious groups – Afghans, Chinese, Japanese, Hindus, Moslems, Negroes, Indians, Malays and Pacific Islanders – were lumped together in the ever-expanding category of 'not-white'. The ideal of a white man's country expressed this fusion of imperial and republican traditions of racial rule. The figure of the white man provided the common identity that underpinned Anglo-American rapprochement at the end of the nineteenth century.

The colonial legislation of 1896 encoded for the first time the division of the world into white and not-white. Because of the discrimination against Britain's new ally, Japan, and against British subjects such as Indians, the New South Wales legislation was reserved by the Governor. The Japanese government lobbied the British government incessantly for the 'abandonment of the language which classed them with others to whom they bore no real similarity and inflicted upon the nation an insult which was not deserved'. Japanese Minister Takaaki Kato, a distinguished graduate in law from Tokyo University and future Foreign Minister, suggested that the Colonial Office should persuade the Australians to adopt the so-called Natal formula, because educated Japanese could pass a literacy test, and in any case would not wish to emigrate. The same outcome 'would even more certainly be obtained with regard to other Asiatic countries where general education is less advanced than in Japan'.[26]

Minister Kato protested strongly to the Foreign Office against the slur on his nation, which was being relegated to the same category as the people of China, whom they had recently subjected to an ignominious defeat. Japan, too, had a deep investment in racial hierarchy, their diplomats regularly demanding recognition of their superiority to other Asian peoples. 'The point which had caused a painful feeling in Japan', he wrote, 'was not that the operation of the prohibition would be such as to exclude a certain number of Japanese from immigrating into Australasia, but that Japan would be spoken of in formal documents, such as the Colonial Acts, as if the Japanese were on the same level of morality and civilization as Chinese or other less advanced populations of Asia'.[27]

Immigration restriction was listed, as we have seen, as one of the main items on the agenda for the meeting of colonial premiers in London, on the occasion of Queen Victoria's Diamond Jubilee, in 1897. It was Joseph Chamberlain's task, as Colonial Secretary, to find a compromise between the imperial principle of the equal treatment of all British subjects and Treaty obligations on the one hand, and the determination of the self-governing colonies to implement race-based immigration restriction to preserve their national and racial character on the other. His trump card was the 'Natal formula' – the use of a literacy or education test – as the perfect method to implement racial discrimination without appearing to do so. And, crucially, he was assured that this strategy was supported by Japanese Minister Kato.[28]

---

[26] Foreign Office to Colonial Office, 7 October 1897, CO 418/10/145.
[27] Colonial Office to Australian Governors, 20 October 1897, CO 418/10/145.
[28] Foreign Office to Colonial Office, 7 October 1897; Colonial Office to Foreign Office, 4 January 1902, CO 418/10/145.

Chamberlain's victory had, however, an unforeseen consequence. As noted in Chapter 5, the final Natal legislation was based on the American Act of 1896, which had subsequently been vetoed by President Grover Cleveland. Natal had looked to the example of the 'great Republic of America', which claimed 'an absolute right... to place a restriction on the introduction of immigration into their country of persons who are regarded by the community as undesirable immigrants'.[29] Americans had pioneered the use of an education or literacy test as an instrument of racial exclusion, notably in Mississippi, in 1890. Crucially, the republic had no use for the imperial category of 'British subject'.

In promoting a literacy test as an instrument to effect racial exclusion in the colonies, Chamberlain thus helped dismantle that which he sought to uphold: the traditions of the Empire and the special status of the British subject. Paradoxically, the implementation of a literacy test framed to avoid all reference to race helped consolidate the new binary divide between the 'white' and 'not-white' races, a purpose made explicit in Australian parliamentary debate and the legislation passed to enact White Australia.

The effect was noticed by the perceptive Sir Charles Lucas in the Colonial Office. 'It is, I think noteworthy', he wrote in his paper 'The Self-Governing Dominions and Coloured Immigration':

That Mr Chamberlain, who was in full sympathy with the self-governing communities, was especially outspoken in protesting against giving offence in the methods of exclusion and against harsh treatment of coloured British subjects, but it will be noted at the same time that the object of avoiding giving offence in methods of exclusion militates against giving any preference to British subjects. The principle of the Natal Act, which Mr Chamberlain accepted and recommended, is not to specify any particular race, but to exclude all who cannot write a European language ie not to distinguish in any way among non-European races those who are and those who are not British subjects.[30]

Hence the outrage of Indian migrants who were British subjects who saw in this subterfuge one more betrayal of the idea of imperial citizenship.

But the lack of distinction drawn between different not-white races also angered Japan which, as a sovereign, civilised, imperial state, considered it the worst insult to be placed in the same category as stateless peoples such as Kanakas and Negroes. As the Japanese Consul in Sydney, H. Eitaki, told the *Daily Telegraph*, Japan was entitled to equal rights and

[29] Colonial Office papers, 1897, *Times of Natal*, 26 March 1897, CO 179/198; *Natal Parliamentary Debates* vol. 2, CO 179; Secret Despatch, CO 179/198, National Archives, UK.
[30] Charles Lucas, 'The Self-Governing Dominions and Coloured Immigration', CO 886/1/1, UK National Archives, pp.52–3.

privileges with Western nations in all matters regulated by international law. Their own regulation of Japanese emigration under passport law was one of those privileges.[31] The Japanese Emigration Act of 1896 specifically provided for the issue of passports as the means to regulate their own people's movement, so they would not have to suffer the ignominy of having them regulated by others.

Outside the pale of civilised tongues

Despite their earlier endorsement of the Natal formulation, Japanese diplomats changed their position in 1901, objecting to the Australian proposal to require all immigrants to pass a dictation test in a 'European' language, because this explicitly discriminated against non-Europeans. Consul Eitaki wrote several notes of protest to the Australian government:

The Japanese belong to an Empire whose standard of civilization is so much higher than that of Kanakas, Negroes, Pacific Islanders, Indians or other Eastern peoples, that to refer to them in the same terms cannot but be regarded in the light of a reproach, which is hardly warranted by the fact of the shade of the national complexion...

Might I suggest, therefore, that your Government formulate some proposal which, being accepted by my Government would allow of the people of Japan being excluded from the operation of any Act which directly or indirectly imposed a tax on immigrants on the ground of colour.[32]

As the offended Japanese began to realise, the literacy test was a subterfuge. The issue was not civilisation, but 'the shade of the national complexion'. Even so, like the Chinese before them, they still tried to change Australian minds by pointing to their high educational standards that copied 'the most approved European methods'. Four months later, on 18 September 1901, as the Immigration Restriction Bill passed through the House of Representatives, Eitaki wrote again to Prime Minister Barton:

In Japanese schools and other educational establishments, the most approved methods are adopted, and the most important works on science, literature, art, politics, law etc which are published in Europe from time to time, are translated into Japanese for the use of students. Thus a Japanese, without being acquainted with any other language than his own, is frequently up to a very high educational standard in the most advanced branches of study, by means of a liberal use of these translations.

[31] *Daily Telegraph*, quoted in E. W. Foxall, *Colorphobia* (Sydney, Publisher, 1903) pp.161–2.
[32] Eitaki to Barton, 3 May 1901, CO 418/10, UK National Archives.

Why could not the Japanese language then be put on the same footing as, say, 'the Turkish, the Russian, the Greek, the Polish, the Norwegian, the Austrian, or the Portuguese, or why, if an immigrant of any of the nationalities... mentioned may be examined *in his own language* (emphasis in original), the same courtesy should not be extended to a Japanese'. The Japanese government requested that their people not be marked out 'to suffer a special disability; or in other words, that they may be examined in Japanese'. This could easily be provided for by 'adding the words "or Japanese" after the word "European" in the legislation'.[33] They protested in vain. Reluctantly they realised that Japanese lay 'outside the pale of civilised tongues'.[34]

Ironically, the initial wording of the Australian legislation had prescribed a dictation test in the 'English language', which would have been more acceptable to the Japanese, because it would have discriminated equally against Europeans and Japanese: 'it paid Japan the courtesy of placing her upon an equal footing with other nations'.[35] Prime Minister Barton had, in fact, sought precisely to avoid making explicit distinctions on the grounds of 'race or colour'. The specification of literacy in one's national language removed the necessity to make 'racial' distinctions: 'The English language is our language', said Barton. 'Ours is the right language to use'.[36] It was the Colonial Office that insisted that 'European language' be substituted for 'English' on the principle of the 'equality between white men'. As the official, Bertram Cox, put it, when rejecting the proposal to pose the literacy test in English: 'Foreign (European) countries will in all probability object strongly to the restriction proposed. It is clearly contrary to the policy of equality between all white men for which the South African war is being fought'.[37]

The White Australia policy was supported by all sides of Australian politics from all states, Labor, Liberal and Conservative, Free Traders and Protectionists. Only two members of parliament – one a leading Free Trader, Bruce Smith – spoke against it. There was considerable division, however, over the preferred method of exclusion. The initial legislation proposed a dictation test in English, but this was opposed by the Colonial Office. Labor members and their supporters, impatient with British hypocrisy and diplomatic equivocation, wanted to drop the

[33] *Ibid.* 18 September 1901.
[34] Governor General to Joseph Chamberlain, 12 November 1901, CO 418/10/373.
[35] Eitaki to Barton, 11 September 1901, CO 418/10.
[36] Edmund Barton, *Commonwealth Parliamentary Debates*, House of Representatives (7 August 1901).
[37] Bertram Cox to Governor General, 23 August 1901, CO 418/10/81.

dictation test altogether and state in a straight-out manly manner their 'desire to see coloured people kept out', as Chris Watson, leader of the Australian Labor Party and Australia's first Labor Prime Minister, put it. Watson supported White Australia for industrial reasons, but also on racial grounds, asking 'whether we would desire that our sisters or our brothers should be married into any of these races to which we object'.[38]

W. M. Hughes, also a future Labor Prime Minister, argued that Australians should fear neither the wounded sensibilities of Japanese nor the possibility of political separation from Britain. Issues of national destiny were involved. Australians had 'an inalienable right', he said:

to work out our national destiny unaffected by that blot referred to by the Attorney-General as affecting America, without the leprous curse that is spreading its way through Queensland unhampered and unhindered, and which threatens to make it a country no longer fit for a white man, because it will shortly be a country where no white man can compete with our cheap, industrious and virtuous, but undesirable Japanese and Chinese friends.[39]

Attorney-General Deakin had politely stated that it was Japanese virtues – their business capacities, inexhaustible energy, their power of application, and their endurance – that made them such formidable competitors.[40] Hughes was impatient with diplomatic talk:

We object to these people because of their vices, and their immorality, and because of a hundred things which we can only hint at, and our objections are not to be met by the declaration that the Imperial Government will be embarrassed by them. We must approach this problem as the Americans did the question of the right to govern themselves – in a calm and deliberate spirit.[41]

Like many of the speakers in this debate, Hughes argued that this was an issue of national sovereignty.

Billy Hughes was a small, truculent, English-born working man of Welsh descent, a trade union leader and a lawyer, demagogue and raconteur, who represented the Australian Labor party in the federal seat of West Sydney. His background and personality made him 'quite one of the most unusual men I know', Secretary to the Department of External Affairs Attlee Hunt remarked to the Colonial Office. 'He is, when in the vein, an extremely amusing person and to hear him tell his experiences as

[38] Ross McMullin, *So Monstrous a Travesty: Chris Watson and the World's First National Government* (Melbourne, Scribe, 2004) pp.61–2.
[39] W. M. Hughes, *Commonwealth Parliamentary Debates*, House of Representatives (12 September 1901) p.4822.
[40] *Ibid.* p.4812.   [41] *Ibid.* p.4823.

umbrella mender, plumber, locksmith, sailor and wharf labourer is really amusing . . . He read up Classics and Law in his spare time'.[42] He and the eloquent, urbane, Melbourne-born Deakin, in many ways unlikely allies, were leading spokesmen of the Liberal–Labor partnership that inaugurated and presided over the enactment of the White Australia policy.[43] Hughes would continue the crusade eighteen years later at the Versailles Peace Conference in Paris.

Despite their pained and persistent protests in 1901, and their suggestion that they constituted a special case, an exception to the rule of racial difference, Japanese diplomats were unable to defeat White Australia's binary racial logic, its division of the world into 'white' and 'not-white', and its allocation of all 'Asiatics' into the category of not-white. By October 1901, a dejected Consul Eitaki had concluded that the 'educational test' was 'racial pure and simple'.[44]

Enshrining the status of white labour

The Immigration Restriction Act was complemented by the Pacific Islands Labourers Act, which provided for the deportation of all Islanders (a generic term for diverse peoples from the numerous islands that now comprise Fiji, New Caledonia, New Guinea, the Solomons and Vanuatu) who had been brought to work in the sugar cane fields of Queensland, regardless of how long they had lived in Australia and whether they had married and raised families. Later amendments rendered the application of the law less severe.

Both Bryce and Pearson had reported contemporary American discussions about 'clearing the country of the Negro' by deporting them to Africa, but with a black population numbering around eight million at the end of the century, the plan did not seem feasible. Pearson had suggested that the proposal should have been implemented earlier, when blacks were 'a mere handful'. In 1901, in introducing legislation to expel Pacific Islanders, Australian political leaders took the opportunity to do that which the United States had left too late.

Speaking on the Pacific Islands Labourers Bill, Prime Minister Barton justified the measure in terms of the radical 'difference' that separated the 'Pacific Islander' from the 'white man':

---

[42] Attlee Hunt to Sir Frances Hopwood, 3 September 1907, Hunt papers, MS 52/791, NLA.
[43] L. F. Fitzhardinge, *William Morris Hughes: A Political Biography* vol.1 (Sydney, Angus and Robertson, 1964) pp.133–8.
[44] Eitaki to Governor-General, 5 October 1901, CO 418/10.

The difference in intellectual level and the difference in knowledge of the ways of the world between the white man and the Pacific Islander, is one which cannot be bridged by acts or regulations about agreements. The level of the one is above that of the other, the difference being one in human mental stature – of character as well of mind – which cannot be put aside by passing 50 laws or 1000 regulations... He cannot be made to understand the condition of his engagement. He may be brought to a state of partial understanding, but it is impossible to say that he can have a degree of contracting capacity equal to that of the man who is dealing with him.[45]

Contractual relations were impossible between the 'white man' and the 'Pacific Islander': 'relations which should subsist between man and man' were in the circumstances an impossibility.[46] This was one of the lessons learnt from the well-meaning, but tragically misguided, experiment of Radical Reconstruction.

H. B. Higgins, Liberal member of parliament, Attorney-General in the first, short-lived Labor government of 1904, and future president of the Commonwealth Court of Conciliation and Arbitration, was a key supporter of the legislation to deport Pacific Islanders: it was 'the most vitally important measure on the programme the government has put before us'.[47] He watched its course with the 'deepest anxiety'. Australia had to learn from the American experience. It was unfortunate that blacks had remained there after emancipation: 'So much the worse for America':

I have seen a little of America and I can say that that country, more especially the Southern States, would have been ten times better off if the Negroes had not been left there.[48]

The Pacific Islands Labourers Bill was so significant because its passage would determine whether 'northern Australia should be peopled by white men or not. I feel convinced that people who are used to a high standard of life – to good wages and good conditions – will not consent to labour alongside men who receive a miserable pittance and who are dealt with very much in the same way as slaves'.[49] Higgins spoke from personal knowledge. His brother-in-law, G. E. Morrison, the future *Times* correspondent in Peking, had exposed the slave-like conditions of Pacific Islanders on trading ships and sugar plantations in a series of articles for the Melbourne *Leader*.[50]

---

[45] Edmund Barton, *Commonwealth Parliamentary Debates*, House of Representatives (3 October 1901), p.5503.
[46] *Ibid.*   [47] *Ibid.* p.6819.   [48] *Ibid.* p.6815.   [49] *Ibid.*
[50] Cyril Pearl, *Morrison of Peking* (Sydney, Angus and Robertson, 1967) pp.19–24.

In the Commonwealth of Australia, white men appropriated the discourse on civilisation for themselves, defining it in terms of wages and
conditions and the standard of living. 'The civilization of the white man',
declared the Liberal member for Melbourne Ports, Samuel Mauger, 'is
a civilization dependent on free white labour'.[51] Mauger was an evangelical social reformer and temperance man, who published his book, *A
White Man's World*, in 1901, in the founding year of the Commonwealth.
Higgins agreed: 'We do not want men beside us who are not as exacting
in their demands on civilization as ourselves'. As president of the Commonwealth Court of Conciliation and Arbitration in 1907, it would be
Higgins's historic responsibility to determine a living wage for Australian
workers, whom he took care to define in his famous Harvester Judgment
as 'civilised beings . . . living in a civilised community'.[52]

The project of White Australia was thus a contest over the meaning of
civilisation itself. Much Labor vitriol was directed at the Japanese demand
to be recognised as a civilised power. The *Westralian Worker* reported the
story of a confrontation between a local Labor man determined to 'take
down' 'a Jap standing outside a laundry', who dressed above his station:

There you are looking like a crow decked out with peacock's feathers thinking, I
suppose, that you represent an up-to-date and enlightened nation. A great Power
you call yourself, with your navy and your army, that you haven't paid for yet,
and your factories and other such western civilised innovations wherein you don't
earn enough in a week to keep a white man in beer and tobacco for the same
period.[53]

The tropical north was considered White Australia's point of vulner-
ability. A thousand miles away from the political capitals of the south,
but close to the Dutch East Indies, Singapore and New Guinea, mixed
race communities, including Aborigines, Chinese, Filipinos, Japanese,
Malays and Pacific Islanders, had prospered in towns ranging from
north Queensland through the Northern Territory to Broome in Western
Australia. Readers in the south were regularly informed about the woe-
ful consequences for 'the white man', as in the following verse on
'The Black North-West', published in the nationalist *Bulletin*, in 1898.
Japanese workers were cast as 'Black labour' introduced through capitalist

---

[51] Samuel Mauger, *Commonwealth Parliamentary Debates*, House of Representatives
(3 October 1901) p.6823.
[52] *Commonwealth Arbitration Reports* vol.11, 1907–8, quoted in Marilyn Lake, 'On Being a
White Man, Australia, circa 1900', in Hsu Ming Teo and Richard White (eds.) *Cultural
History in Australia* (Sydney, Allen and Unwin, 2003) pp.107–9.
[53] *Westralian Worker*, 2 November 1900.

conspiracy. The *Bulletin*, which took pleasure in giving offence, regularly referred to the Japanese as 'niggers':

> The white man came to the black north-west
> For the east and south were want-opprest;
> With a willing heart and a strong right hand
> In search of work in a white man's land.
>
> He humped his drum, for his purse was low,
> And he tramped cross-tracks that the drovers know,
> Till he struck a town in the wild north-west
> Which the dark Malay and the Jap infest.
>
> But his worn heart quailed when he learned, alack,
> That he must be cheap, and he should be black.
> For the master-men in the black north-west
> Love the white man well but the cheap men best.
>
> For a white man owns to a white man's *vice*,
> He must have *meat*, but a Jap eats *rice;*
> So the master-men in the wild north-west
> Love a white man well but the black man best.[54]

In settler democracies, working-class identities were forged in terms of gendered, racial difference, commonly represented, as we have seen, as the difference between beef-eating men and rice-eating men, between real men and coolies.

That Asiatic and black workers, characterised as inherently servile, degraded the status of all labour, had long been a core belief of self-governing white men's countries and liberal theorists. Authorities including Charles Dilke, Goldwin Smith, Bryce and Pearson all insisted that the dignity of labour would be undermined if work in settler societies were performed by coloured races. 'From the moment that a white population will not work in the fields, on the roads, in the mines, or in factories', warned Pearson in a passage quoted by Barton, when speaking on the Pacific Islands Labourers Bill, 'its doom is practically sealed'.

In the new Commonwealth of Australia, Liberal and Labor parties agreed on the necessity of the state protecting the wages and conditions of white working men, an approach given expression in the policy of New Protection, so named because tariff protection would depend on employers paying workers a fair and reasonable wage. Deakin explicitly theorised White Australia as an exercise in social justice: 'it means the

---

[54] *Bulletin*, 2 April 1898, quoted in Henry Reynolds, *North of Capricorn: The Untold Story of Australia's North* (Sydney, Allen and Unwin, 2003) p.135.

maintenance of conditions of life fit for white men and white women; it means equal laws and opportunities for all; it means protection against the underpaid labour of other lands; it means social justice so far as we can establish it, including just trading and the payment of fair wages'.[55]

It never seemed to occur to the architects of New Protection, however, that all workers might enjoy, or desire, high living standards. In *The Chinese Question in Australia*, Lowe Kong Meng, Cheok Hong Cheong and Louis Ah Mouy tried to make this obvious point: 'human nature is human nature all the world over; and the Chinaman is just as fond of money, and just as eager to earn as much as he can, as the most grasping of his competitors'. And of course the longer Chinese settlers stayed in the new country, the more likely they would emulate the local standard of living:

Living among people who have invested thousands of artificial wants, and thousands of means of gratifying them, the expenditure of the Asiatic will soon rise to the European level, because his habits and his mode of living will approximate to those of his neighbours; and, as it is, it cannot have escaped the observation of persons who have been brought much into contact with the Chinese in Victoria, that the diet of such of them as tolerably prosperous becomes more generous and costly in proportion to the improvement of their circumstances, and that those who marry and settle here conform to British methods of housekeeping, and are not less liberal and hospitable than their European fellow-colonists.[56]

But such observations about 'human nature all the world over' counted for nothing against nationalist, racist stereotypes of unmanly, inherently servile coolies.

As one spokesman for White Australia put it, confident in his knowledge of the essential difference between the 'white man' and the 'coloured man' and the latter's 'indifference' to civilised standards: 'Coloured aliens engaging in any occupation subject white men in the same occupation to an utterly unfair and improper competition'. The secret of the coloured man's success was 'his complete indifference' to 'the moral and social standards of his white fellow citizens'. He worked from dawn to dark on seven days a week; he ate little else than rice; he clothed himself in rags; and lived in a hovel. White men through no fault of their own would be driven from employment and production, simply because they adhered to 'the most elementary ideals of civilized society'.[57]

---

[55] Quoted in Frank Parsons, 'Australasian Methods of Dealing with Immigration', *Annals of the American Academy of Political and Social Science* no.431 (July 1904) Immigration Restriction League papers, Houghton Library, Ms Am 2245 (1111).

[56] Lowe Kong Meng, Cheok Hong Cheong and Louis Ah Mouy, *The Chinese in Victoria* (Melbourne, 1879) p.201.

[57] Draft paper, author unknown, Deakin papers, NLA 1540/15/2553.

As a further measure to protect white working men's jobs, the Australian parliament passed an amendment to the Post and Telegraph Act, introduced by Hughes, to permit 'white labour only' on ships carrying Australian mail. In speaking explicitly of their intention to engage in racial discrimination against the British subjects who mostly manned these ships, the government knew that it courted British rejection of the legislation. Threatened with the withholding of Royal Assent, one Senator called on his fellow politicians to assert their 'manhood and vigour' so as to give effect to national sovereignty: 'the wish and will of the people'.[58]

The Japanese government again protested against this proposed 'racial discrimination' to the Australian Governor-General, and the Colonial Office conveyed its censure, but white Australian manhood had its way.[59] Writing anonymously as a correspondent for the *Morning Post*, in London, Attorney-General Deakin described this law as 'surely the high-water mark of racial exclusiveness'.[60]

Legislation to provide for a uniform franchise across all the Australian states also employed racist exclusions. Under the Commonwealth Franchise Act of 1902, full political rights were extended to all white women, some of whom had earlier won the franchise in the colonies of South Australia (1894) and Western Australia (1899). Aboriginal people of both sexes were expressly denied the federal vote in the same 1902 legislation, except in those states where they already enjoyed the franchise under earlier colonial legislation in Victoria, South Australia, New South Wales and Tasmania. The original Bill had not provided for the disfranchisement of Indigenous Australians as it passed through the Senate, but did so in the House of Representatives on the basis of an amendment proposed by Higgins, who argued that it was 'utterly inappropriate' to enfranchise Aborigines.[61]

The Franchise Act thus effectively denied political rights to the great majority of Indigenous people who lived in the north of the country in Queensland, the Northern Territory and Western Australia. It also denied political rights to natives of 'Asia, Africa or the Islands of the Pacific except New Zealand'. In recognition of their political status in New Zealand,

---

[58] *Commonwealth Parliamentary Debates*, Senate, 13 June 1901, p.1050.
[59] Eitaki to Governor-General, 5 October 1901, CO 418/10.
[60] *Morning Post*, 12 November 1901, in J. A. La Nauze (ed.) *Federated Australia Selections of Letters to the Morning Post 1900–1910* (Melbourne, Melbourne University Press, 1968) p.81.
[61] John Chesterman, ' "An Unheard of Piece of Savagery": Indigenous Australians and the Federal Vote', in John Chesterman and David Phillips (eds.) *Selective Democracy: Race, Gender and the Australian Vote* (Melbourne, Circa, 2003).

Maoris were treated in this case as honorary white men, as they were also in the 1903 law on naturalisation, that classified natives from 'Asia, Africa or the Islands of the Pacific, except New Zealand' as ineligible for naturalisation.

Under the federal constitution, the administration and sale of land remained a matter for the state governments and, in some states, legislation was passed to prevent 'Asiatics' from taking out freehold or becoming lessees of Crown lands. Queensland employed the dictation test to achieve its aim of denying non-whites the right to own or lease land. State legislation also barred non-whites from certain employments and professions, sometimes using the device of the dictation test, as in the Queensland Margarine and Sugar Cultivation Acts.

The Australian welfare state was conceptualised and structured in racialised terms. Its racist exclusions were, paradoxically, an expression of its commitment to democratic equality and dignity of labour. Manhood asserted its elevation, as we have noted, in opposition to aristocrats and coolies. The advocates of White Australia often argued in terms of social justice.[62] The Invalid and Old Age Pension of 1908, paid from general revenue, excluded 'Asiatics (except those born in Australia) and Aboriginal natives of Australia, Africa, the Islands of the Pacific, or New Zealand'. Aboriginal natives of Australia came under the jurisdiction of the states, which ran reserves and implemented Protection Acts, under which the removal of 'half-caste' children was a key assimilationist practice. Whereas white 'mothers of the race' were feted and remunerated in the Commonwealth of Australia, Aboriginal women's 'race' was invoked to deny their right to and capacity for motherhood.

The keystone of the White Australia policy was the Harvester judgment on the living wage, handed down by Justice Higgins in the Conciliation and Arbitration Court in 1907, in a case brought under the Excise Act of 1906, that required manufacturers who applied for exemption from excise duties to demonstrate that they paid their workers 'a fair and reasonable wage'. In his radical challenge to the power of business and employers, warmly commended by his friend Felix Frankfurter in the United States, Higgins declared that if employers couldn't afford to pay decent wages to their workers, they had no place in Australia.[63] The desire for profit

---

[62] On a similar theme, see also Avner Offer, ' "Pacific Rim" Societies: Asian Labour and White Nationalism', in J. Eddy and D. Schreuder (eds.) *The Rise of Colonial Nationalism* (Sydney, Allen and Unwin, 1988); and Jonathon Hyslop, 'White Labourism Before World War 1', *Journal of Historical Sociology* vol.12, no.4 (December 1999).

[63] Frankfurter to Oliver Wendell Holmes, 11 November 1915, in Robert Mennell and Christine Compston (eds.) *Holmes and Frankfurter: Their Correspondence, 1912–1934* (Durham, University of New Hampshire Press, 1996).

and productivity had to take second place to the moral imperative that a living wage be paid to (white) working men. In gathering evidence of employees' needs – and listening to the testimony of a number of housewives – Higgins built up a picture of the purchases and pursuits necessary to sustain a civilised standard of living.

Central to the white worker's comfort and self-respect was his ability to maintain a family. One reason 'Asiatics' were regarded as cheap labour was because of their limited needs as single men. In the Harvester judgment, Higgins represented the average man as a breadwinner with a wife and three children and thus institutionalised the husband as breadwinner and the woman as dependent, even though many thousands of women also supported families and many thousands of men supported only themselves. Women were paid, for decades thereafter, just over half the male rate.

White citizen mothers

Just as the white working man was the ideal male citizen, so the ideal woman citizen of the new Commonwealth of Australia was the white mother. White Australian women had won the right to vote and stand for election to the national parliament in 1902 – the first in the world to win these political rights – but political leaders urged them to concentrate their energies on producing larger families. In 1903, in New South Wales, the state government appointed a Royal Commission to enquire into the decline of the birth rate and there was much talk, following American sociologist Edward Ross's warning, of 'race suicide'. The Royal Commission placed the blame for the decline of the birth rate on the selfishness of women.[64] A copy of the report was sent to the United States at the request of the Department of Commerce and Labor.[65] White men's countries shared the preoccupation with race suicide.

Charles Pearson had drawn attention to the implications of fertility decline in National Life and Character, but as often as not, when Australian politicians made speeches about the necessity of an increased birth rate in the new century, they quoted not Pearson, who had died in London ten years before, but one of his most ardent disciples on this issue, Theodore Roosevelt, President of the United States since 1901. In Australia one

[64] Neville Hicks, This Sin and Scandal: Australia's Population Debate 1891–1911 (Canberra, Australian National University Press, 1978).
[65] Department of State to John Gray, Consul General, Sydney, 24 October 1908, Records of Foreign Service Posts, RG 84, Despatches from Secretary of State, Sydney, vol.56w, US National Archives.

of the most fervent populationists of the new century was a New South Wales politician, Dr Richard Arthur, who was in regular correspondence with Roosevelt, whom he quoted in numerous newspaper articles and public speeches in support of increased birth rates and large-scale immigration.[66]

Labor women and non-party feminists attempted to use the rhetoric surrounding motherhood to promote the rights of mothers as citizens. Drawing on eugenicist discourse, they argued for the importance of quality over quantity in reproduction and lobbied for better state services and a living wage for themselves in the form of motherhood endowment that would render them economically independent of men. White women enjoyed full suffrage rights in the new Commonwealth and thus wielded considerable electoral power. Politicians on all sides recognised that women electors were a political force to be reckoned with, a constituency to be wooed. In 1912, the Labor government led by Andrew Fisher was persuaded by women in his party to introduce a maternity allowance, a cash payment of £5 to all white mothers, including unmarried mothers, on the birth of a baby.

In the face of condemnation of this official support for single mothers – those who 'became mothers in a dishonourable way' as a Council of Churches Deputation to the Prime Minister put it – Labor women proudly claimed credit for what they considered to be a political victory for working-class women. At a meeting of the women's committee of the Victorian branch of the Labor party, they passed a resolution expressing their 'utter detestation and resentment at the foul slanders levelled at our class' and congratulated the Prime Minister for his 'noble and wise act' in 'conferring this instalment of the mothers' maternal rights'.[67]

The maternity allowance was radical in offering payments to unmarried mothers, but in keeping with other legislation constituting the Australian welfare state, it explicitly excluded non-white mothers. Conceptions of racial difference were central to conceptions of maternal citizenship, but some non-party feminists were moved to protest against the racial exclusions of the Maternity Allowance Act as an example of 'the White Australia policy gone mad': 'Maternity is maternity, whatever the race', protested Vida Goldstein's *Woman Voter*.[68] The universalist politics of maternalism thus had the potential to be used for anti-racist as

---

[66] Michael Roe, *Nine Australian Progressives: Vitalism in Bourgeois Social Thought, 1890–1960* (St Lucia, University of Queensland Press, 1984) pp.155–84.

[67] Marilyn Lake and Katie Holmes (eds.) *Freedom Bound: 11 Documents on Women in Modern Australia* (Sydney, Allen and Unwin, 1995) pp.6–7.

[68] *Ibid.* p.7.

well as racist purposes and would later be deployed by some feminists to protest against the removal of Aboriginal children from their mothers.[69]

Critics of White Australia

The White Australia policy was widely supported across party and gender lines, but it also provoked spirited and persistent opposition. Challenges came from conservatives and socialists, men and women, white and not-white. In the first federal parliament, the Free Trade Liberals, led by Bruce Smith, denounced 'race prejudice' as a barrier to freedom of movement, commerce and trade and extolled the virtues of Chinese civilisation. Some churches worried about Australia's racial arrogance in denying the Christian doctrine of the equality of souls: the Synod of the Church of England denounced assumptions of white race superiority and conveyed their resolutions to the Prime Minister.[70]

Self-styled cosmopolitans in the socialist movement, inspired by a visiting English leader, Tom Mann, called for racial tolerance and international solidarity with 'no concern for race or frontier'.[71] In 1906, the Victorian Socialist Party established a Cosmopolitan Committee, that encouraged contributions from speakers from non-British backgrounds. Bertha Walker remembered an 'International Night' in Melbourne, attended by about twenty different nationalities and 'huge applause for an African who worked as a bootblack in Bourke Street'.[72] The *Socialist* journal explained how 'racial antipathies' and 'national boundaries' stood in the way of socialism:

No narrow nationalism can satisfy our people. Nothing short of Cosmopolitanism can really satisfy a world citizen. 'The world is my country!' is the declaration of every Socialist. It is our mission then to speed the day when racial antipathies shall be completely obliterated, when national boundaries will exist only as indicating that certain areas were the cradles of certain peoples.[73]

This spirit of socialist cosmopolitanism would later be invoked at a meeting organised by the Women's Political Association to question Prime Minister Hughes' attack on the Japanese racial equality clause at Versailles.

[69] Marilyn Lake, 'Feminism and the Gendered Policis of Antiracism, Australia 1927–57: From Maternal Protectionism to Leftists Assimilationism', *Australian Historical Studies* 110 (April 1998); Fiona Paisley, *Loving Protection? Australian Feminism and Aboriginal Women's Rights 1919–1939* (Melbourne, Melbourne University Press, 2000).
[70] Bishop White to Deakin, 6 September 1905, Deakin papers, NLA, 1540/15/2095.
[71] *Socialist*, 1 September 1906.
[72] David Day, *John Curtin: A Life* (Sydney, Harper Collins, 1999) p.111.
[73] *Socialist*, 1 September 1906.

Protests against the enactment of the White Australia policy were also sent to the Australian government by local Pacific Islander, Chinese, Indian and Japanese communities and their official representatives in Australia and London.[74] The *Tung Wah Times* was established in Sydney and the *Chinese Times* in Melbourne, both preaching the necessity to build a strong China to combat discrimination and humiliation: 'a powerful country makes a race strong'.[75] In 1901, Pacific Islanders gathered 3000 signatures for a petition against their imminent deportation, which they forwarded to the Colonial Office:

Many of us have been continuously resident in Queensland for upwards of twenty years, and during these years our parents and brothers in the islands have died and we are forgotten there; villages have disappeared, and some of our tribes have been exterminated; we love the land in which we live, and all our friends are here.[76]

But they had no official representatives who could seek international redress. With Indians it was different and increasingly an anxious British government recognised that 'the growing resentment in India at the attitude that has been adopted in Australia' – and the outrage to Indian self-respect – threatened the future integrity of the British Empire.[77]

In Victoria, a Chinese community leader, Cheok Hong Cheong, maintained his long protest against racial persecution when he wrote to the press in 1904 to denounce new factories and shops legislation that aimed to further curtail Chinese employment in laundries and cabinet-making. Once again he invoked the ideal of the comity of nations: 'It may be comparatively a small matter how the few Chinese sojourners make their living, but if the sense of injustice be allowed to rankle in their minds, and burn into their very souls, it cannot bode well for the future relations of two vast Empires like Great Britain and China'.[78] A meeting of the Public Questions Committee of the Presbyterian Church also condemned the 'cruel and oppressive' legislation, while Ah Ket published a pamphlet on *The Chinese and the Factories Act* in which he denounced the 'ignorant prejudice against the Chinese', demonstrated their compliance

---

[74] See, for example, India Office to Colonial Office, 7 August 1903, CO 886/1/172; also Robert A. Huttenback, *Racism and Empire* (Ithaca, Cornell University Press, 1976), pp.286–8, 304–6; Margaret Allen '"Innocents Abroad" and "Prohibited Immigrants": Australians in India and Indians in Australia 1890–1910', in Ann Curthoys and Marilyn Lake (eds.) *Connected Worlds: History in Transnational Perspective* (Canberra, Australian National University Press, 2006), pp.122–5.

[75] C. F. Yong, *The New Gold Mountain: The Chinese in Australia 1901–1921* (Adelaide, Raphael Arts, 1977) pp.16–19.

[76] Cited in Banivanua-Mar, *Violence and Colonial Dialogue*, p.117.

[77] Colonial Office to Governor-General, September 1908, and Enclosure, CO 886/1/254.

[78] *Argus*, 22 November 1904.

with existing legislation and industrial awards, and once more invoked 'the reciprocal treaties between Great Britain and China', calling for justice for his people who were either British subjects or legal immigrants. A Chinese Convention met in Melbourne in 1905, but political authorities in Britain and Australia had clearly decided that Chinese protest could be safely ignored. The rights of persons who were unfortunate enough to be born in that 'weak and despised Empire of the Far East', as Cheok Hong Cheong put it, could be trampled on at will.[79]

Two books critical of the White Australia policy, E. W. Foxall's *Colorphobia* and E. W. Cole's *The White Australia Question*, were published in Melbourne in 1903.[80] When F. M. Bladen, the Principal Librarian of the Public Library of New South Wales, sent a copy of his own book, *Peopling Australia* – promoting British immigration to 'the great sunny white man's land' – to Arthur Atlee Hunt, Secretary of External Affairs, Hunt asked Bladen in turn what he thought of Foxall's book. 'The fundamental weakness of the whole book', replied the Principal Librarian, 'is that he does not attempt to show in what possible way the influx of Japanese, Kanakas, Chinese and Negroes would benefit us'. He continued:

Ted generally spoils his case by his intolerance and vehemence ... That part of the book where he threatens us with direful consequences of annoying Japan is rather humorous. I wonder whether he really thinks that the scarecrow of an angry Asiatic is likely to disturb anyone. These gentlemen are more dangerous when they smile.[81]

As secretary to the Japanese Consul-General, Foxall lobbied persistently for reform of the Immigration Restriction Act. At the same time the Government of India sought exemptions for certain classes of British Indian subjects.

In 1904, immigration regulations were amended 'with a view to fostering commercial relations between Australia and the East' to exempt, following the United States example, 'merchants, students and tourist travellers' from taking the dictation test provided they were in possession of passports issued by either the Japanese or Indian governments.[82] The acceptance of a passport issued by the traveller's own government replaced the Certificates for Exemption from the Dictation Test for Indians and Japanese, but not for the hapless Chinese.

---

[79] Yarwood, *Asian Migration to Australia*, p.104.
[80] See also C. H. Chomley, *Australian Pros and Cons* (Melbourne, Fraser and Jenkinson, 1905) pp.136–43.
[81] Bladen to Hunt, 28 July 1903, Atlee Hunt papers, NLA 52/1260.
[82] Immigration Restriction Act Correspondence, Commonwealth Parliamentary Paper, 1905, pp.1–4.

In 1905, an amendment to the Immigration Restriction Act replaced the requirement for a test in a 'European language' with a test in any 'prescribed language', in a further attempt to conciliate Japan. On the other hand, a clause allowing Asian Australians to be joined by their wives was cancelled, causing fresh distress and persistent protest.[83] Secretary of External Affairs Hunt responded impatiently: 'If the Japanese or people of any other race comment on the inhumanity of separating husband and wife, the answer is easy. We have no wish for them to be separated, and in fact would prefer to see them united – but in their own country, not ours'.[84]

Members of the public also wrote to the Prime Minister's office to express their dismay at his seeming heartlessness in administering the White Australia policy and in being complicit in the separation of families.[85] 'As an old schoolmate may I beg of you to kill the "White Australia policy" *as it is now being administered*', wrote James Ingham. 'Depend upon it the curse of God will rest upon us as a country unless we withdraw from an enactment, that is inhuman and cruel and God dishonouring'. He referred to the government's refusal to permit the reunion of a Chinese man, long resident in Australia, and his son, 'a respectable Chinese boy'. He continued:

> In our old days at the Grammar school, if a vote had been taken in favor of the most generous & kind-hearted lad in the school, I unhesitate to say that vote would have been won by yourself & I cannot believe that you have so altered as to be party to separate father from son, simply because the skin of the latter is not white.[86]

Deakin was particularly embarrassed by the publicity accorded the deportation of Pacific Islanders and wrote to the Premier of Queensland asking if there were some who ought to be allowed to remain, for example, 'if by any chance a white woman has been reckless enough to marry a Kanaka we could hardly turn him out'.[87] Hunt was in constant correspondence with the Brisbane Immigration Office in an attempt to prevent disturbances and deprive 'enemies of the government' of occasions for criticism, but he remained a determined advocate of the White Australia policy.[88]

---

[83] Foxall to Hunt, 3 December 1908, Hunt papers, 52/1312, NLA.

[84] Hunt to Foxall, 8 December 1908, Hunt papers, 52/1313a.

[85] Church of England Synod resolutions, Deakin papers, 1540/15/2096, Deakin papers.

[86] Ingham to Deakin, 1 October 1906, Deakin papers, 1540/15/2200.

[87] Deakin to Kidston, 20 February 1906, Deakin papers, 1540/15/2155.

[88] Brenan to Hunt, 3 November 1906, 15 January, 26 January, 29 January 1907; Hunt to Brenan, 4 March, 2 August 1907, Hunt papers, 52/1267–1273.

The need for population

With the Japanese victory over Russia in 1905, Australians suddenly felt more vulnerable in their remote southern outpost. Recognition of the low birth rate prompted a new campaign to attract white immigrants to augment the Australian population. Numerous politicians and publicists recommended that Deakin initiate more co-ordinated action with the states, which controlled land settlement and advertise more aggressively to attract British settlers. Richard Arthur, now president of the Immigration League of Australia, was a tireless advocate of the necessity of a dramatic growth in immigration and deplored people's prejudices – against Jews and Italians – that prevented the flow of immigrants from being as strong as it might have been.

Arthur persuaded President Roosevelt to write in support of his efforts. 'The diminishing birth rate both in America and Australia is a matter which should give serious concern to every thoughtful American or Australian', wrote the American president:

But Australia should also concern herself about the need for immigration. America has plenty; her territory is already pretty well filled and is still rapidly filling, even in Alaska. Australia needs more people. She needs full cradles. She needs to open her gates; and especially to put a premium upon immigration into North Australia.[89]

Arthur also publicised Roosevelt's commendation of Mediterranean peoples as prospective immigrants. Whereas his Anglo-Saxonist friend Cabot Lodge had argued strongly that the category 'white' had been interpreted far too broadly in the United States, allowing millions of migrants from eastern, southern and central Europe, peoples alien in language and culture, to enter the country, Roosevelt lent his support to Arthur's campaign to widen the definition of white to embrace Italians, Spanish and Jews.

But immigration to Australia remained a trickle. Roosevelt grew alarmed and impatient, writing to his friend, the British diplomat Spring Rice, at the end of 1907: 'I very much wish that Australia would either encourage European immigration or would see a higher birth rate among its own citizens. It is not pleasant to realize how slowly the scanty population of that island continent increases'.[90]

---

[89] Theodore Roosevelt to Richard Arthur, 10 February 1906, Arthur papers, 473/3, Mitchell Library.
[90] Roosevelt to Spring Rice, 21 December 1907, in Elting E. Morison (ed.) *The Letters of Theodore Roosevelt* vol.6 (Cambridge, Harvard University Press, 1951) p.869.

'A deep colour line of demarcation'

During the first decade in the life of the Commonwealth of Australia, the government legislated to enshrine the status of white men as workers and white women as mothers, proud of its position in the vanguard of modern social progress. The corollary was the deepening divide between white and non-white subjects of the British Empire. In a long article, written in his capacity as anonymous correspondent for the London *Morning Post*, Deakin reflected on Chamberlain's earlier insistence on the equality of treatment of all imperial subjects. In fact, he noted, this equality was 'only on the surface':

In fact, and in effect, our colourless laws are administered so as to draw a deep colour line of demarcation between Caucasians and all other races. No white men are stopped at our ports . . . On the contrary. They are welcomed . . . On the other hand all coloured men are stopped unless they come merely as visitors.

Deakin commended the recent statement of the New Zealand Prime Minister, Richard Seddon, about the British Empire, in which he invoked the significance of the distinction between 'ruled' and 'ruling races':

though united in the whole, [the Empire] is, nevertheless, divided broadly in to two parts, one occupied wholly or mainly by a white ruling race, the other principally occupied by coloured races who are ruled. Australia and New Zealand are determined to keep their place in the first class.[91]

Their determination to maintain their position in the first class of ruling nations – to maintain 'a place parallel and equal to that of the Mother Country' – led the Australian and New Zealand Prime Ministers to offer sympathy and support to the other self-governing colonies of the Empire, when faced with challenges to white hegemony. They offered support to Natal and the Transvaal in South Africa, when those colonies were confronted with black insurrection and large-scale Chinese immigration and denounced British intervention in the government of these places as improper interference with the constitutional rights of responsible, self-governing communities.

In 1905, the attention of the Australian and New Zealand governments was drawn to British Columbia where, faced with renewed 'Asiatic invasions', the provincial government had been prevented once again by Ottawa from legislating to bring about effective immigration restriction.[92] When news arrived that Canada had disallowed the latest British Columbian law against Japanese immigration on the ground of

[91] *Morning Post*, 28 May 1906; La Nauze, *Federated Australia*, p.184.
[92] Huttenback, *Racism and Empire*, pp.170–5.

incompatibility of imperial interests, Prime Minister Seddon urged a joint expression of solidarity with the people of that Pacific province. The Wellington newspaper, the *Evening Post*, reported indignantly: 'British Columbia is not to be allowed to shape its destiny as a white man's country, because the exigencies of British policy in the Far East demand that the white man and the yellow man shall lie down together on equal terms'.[93]

For Prime Minister Deakin, the growth of Japanese power in the Pacific highlighted the necessity of Australia looking to secure its capacity for self-defence through building up its army and navy: 'Self-respect, self-esteem, self-assertion, whatever name is given to it, a sentiment of the duty of self-defence, strong already, is growing stronger the more we realise our strategically perilous position south of the awakening Asiatic peoples'.[94] He was thus very receptive to Arthur's suggestion, in the following year, that an invitation be extended to the United States government to send its naval fleet, about to embark on a tour of the Pacific, to visit Australia. Such a visit could strengthen the bonds between the kindred peoples of the Republic and the Commonwealth, and provide an object lesson in the imperative of modern naval power to national security in a dangerous world.

The great republic provided both heroic example and timely warning to their admirers building their own Commonwealth in the South Pacific. The 'racial problem' loomed large in historical memory, strengthening Australian resolve to maintain racial purity. 'As we Australians look on and note the awful racial animosities which every now and then degrade the records of the great Republic', an editorial in the *Age* newspaper concluded, 'we shall learn more perfectly the lesson of incurring every sacrifice rather than give up in the least degree our national policy of "a White Australia".'[95]

---

[93] *Evening Post*, 4 May 1905, Deakin papers, NLA 1540/15/2090.
[94] *Morning Post*, 3 October 1906, La Nauze, *Federated Australia*, p.192.
[95] *Age*, 3 August 1908.

7   Defending the Pacific Slope

A victory never anticipated

Japan's spectacular victory over Russia in the war of 1904–05 stunned the world, in part because it was unexpected. Theodore Roosevelt wrote to his friend, English diplomat Cecil Arthur Spring Rice, in June 1904, explaining that he had 'never anticipated in the least a rise as this of Japan'.[1] The implications were global. In a letter to the British politician Lord Roseberry, Goldwin Smith, now settled in Canada, asked:

> How far will Japan go? The East may now repel the West. No more spheres of influence for predatory Powers. What is the ultimate outlook for Australia or even for the British Empire in India?[2]

In London, Valentine Chirol, the foreign editor of *The Times*, observed that Japan's triumph had brought the problems of the relations between all the races of the East and the West 'to our very doors'.[3] The American missionary and Japan expert, S. L. Gulick, agreed, believing that it opened up a new era in the history of the world, promising to halt 'the territorial expansion of the white races and to check their racial pride'.[4] At Oxford, Alfred Zimmern, a young lecturer in ancient history, was greatly impressed by the Japanese victory. He told his class he was setting Greek history aside for the morning, explaining:

> I feel I must speak to you about the most important historical event which has happened, or is likely to happen, in our lifetime, the victory of a non-white people over a white people.[5]

---

[1] Roosevelt to Spring Rice, 13 June 1904, in Stephen Gwynne (ed.), *The Letters and Friendships of Sir Cecil Spring Rice: A Record*, vol.I (London, Constable, 1929) p.416.

[2] Smith to Roseberry, 12 February 1904, in Arnold Haultain (ed.) *Goldwin Smith Reminiscences* (New York, Macmillan, 1910) p.402.

[3] *The Times*, 25 December 1906.

[4] Sidney Gulick, *The White Peril in the Far East: An Interpretation of the Significance of the Russo–Japanese War* (New York, Revell, 1905) p.5.

[5] Alfred Zimmern, *The Third British Empire* (London, Humphrey Milford, 1926) p.82.

The impact of Japan's success was even more pronounced in the non-European world. The American commentator, Sydney Brooks, explained to readers of the *North American Review* that the 'unquestionable and staggering fact' was that Asia had found a leader and that something like a 'thrill of recognition and understanding had passed from Cape Cormorin to Peking'.[6] Harry Johnston, cosmopolitan English explorer and Colonial Governor, noted that the Japanese victory had a profound effect in many countries, being discussed in the souks of Morocco, the mosques of Egypt, the coffee houses of Turkey, Indian bazaars and African mud houses.[7]

There were similar reports from many parts of the world. An African correspondent wrote to Johannesburg's *Rand Daily Mail*, announcing that with the Japanese victory over the Russians, the time had come for full racial equality.[8] Muslim newspapers all over the Middle East celebrated the event as 'the victory of the downtrodden Eastern peoples over the invincible West'.[9] In Aceh, the recently conquered province of the Dutch East Indies, activists hoped Japan's victory would herald the 'speedy expulsion of the Dutch'.[10] In Madagascar, the French Governor General attributed a revolt in the south-east of the island in some measure to the Japanese example.[11] Javanese medical students formed a nationalist organisation, *Boedi Oetomo*, 'as if surprised by the bright light of the victory of Japan'.[12]

In Turkey, the nationalist young Turks looked to Japan, its ascendancy the most influential factor in raising their hopes of modernisation.[13] A Turkish feminist, Halide Edip, reportedly named her son Togo after the victorious Japanese admiral; poets in Egypt, Turkey and Persia wrote odes to the Japanese nation and emperor.[14] The Chinese revolutionary leader, Sun Yat-Sen, passing through the Suez Canal in July 1905, was asked by a local man if he was Japanese, explaining that he had observed 'vast armies of Russian soldiers being shipped back to Russia from the east, a

[6] S. Brooks, 'Some Results of the War', *North American Review*, vol.CLXXXI (1905) pp.592–5.
[7] H. Johnston, 'The Rise of the Native', *Quarterly Review* (1910) pp.134–5.
[8] Donald Denoon, *A Grand Illusion: the Failure of Imperial Policy in the Transvaal Colony during the Period of Reconstruction, 1900–1905* (London, Longmans, 1973) p.107.
[9] S. Esenbel, 'Japan's Global Claim to Asia and the World of Islam', *American Historical Review* 109, No.4 (October 2004) p.1140.
[10] Esenbel, 'Japan's Global Claim', p.1141.
[11] Richard Storry, *Japan and the Decline of the West in Asia, 1894–1943* (London, Macmillan, 1979) p.85.
[12] Mohammad Hatta, *Portrait of a Patriot: Selected Writings* (Hague, Mouton, 1972) p.106.
[13] Feroz Ahmad, *The Young Turks: the Committee of Union and Progress in Turkish Politics, 1908–1914* (Oxford, Clarendon Press, 1969) p.23.
[14] Esenbel, 'Japan's Global Claim', p.1140.

fact which seemed an undeniable sign of Russia's admission of defeat'. 'The joy of this Arab, as a member of the great Asiatic race', wrote Sun Yat-sen, 'seemed to know no bounds.'[15]

Fifteen-year-old Jawaharlal Nehru travelled to Britain in 1905 to begin his first term at Harrow. Japanese victories had stirred up his enthusiasm and he eagerly read the daily papers seeking fresh news from the front. He was 'highly excited', when, on the train from Dover to London, he read of Japan's great naval victory at Tsushima.[16] Even Gandhi, despite his commitment to *satyagraha*, was moved to applaud the Japanese, whose heroes had forced the Russians to 'bite the dust on the battlefield'. When that occurred, he wrote, 'the sun rose in the east': 'The peoples of the East will never, never again submit to insult from the insolent whites.'[17]

Yet humiliated like dogs

Insolent whites still troubled the Japanese despite their martial exploits on both land and sea. Writing on the subject of social intercourse between Japanese and Europeans, Baron Keiroku Tsuzuki commented that there was very often a tendency in the Westerner, when he was in the Orient, to consider himself so 'transcendentally superior' to people he met that social intercourse with the locals was regarded as not worth the trouble. To add insult to injury, such people had the additional shortcoming 'of desiring to advertise their assumed superiority'.[18]

Sidney Gulick came to similar conclusions about the personal interaction between the Japanese and Westerners. While the relations between governments were conducted with correct diplomatic protocol, they could not counter-balance the indignation and wrong suffered by individual Japanese at the hands of white men. Those who have not lived in the Orient, wrote Gulick, could have 'no idea of the personal attitude and conduct of the average white man towards the Asiatic. Neither can he understand the feelings of the insulted Asiatic towards the white man himself.' Examples of personal abuse and discrimination, could be 'indefinitely multiplied'. In the treaty ports of China and Japan, the stories

[15] Marius B. Jansen, *The Japanese and Sun Yat Sen* (Cambridge, Mass., Harvard University Press, 1954) p.17.

[16] Jawaharlal Nehru, *Toward Freedom: the Autobiography of Jawaharlal Nehru* (Boston, Beacon Press, 1967) pp.29–30; Marie Seton, *Panditji: A Portrait of Jawaharlal Nehru* (London, Dobson, 1967) p.24.

[17] M. Gandhi, *Collected Works* vol.VII (27 June 1908) p.324.

[18] Marius B. Huish (ed. and transl.), *Fifty Years of New Japan*, compiled by Shigenobu Okuma, 2 vols., 2nd edition, vol.2 (London, Smith and Elder, 1910) p.488.

of relations between the white men and the locals were sickening. The European, relying on his fists and his gun, stirred the Asians into a fierce desire for revenge.[19] No people and no government felt more deeply the 'humiliation and pain of any discourteous treatment'.[20]

Insults and discrimination experienced by prominent Japanese abroad were widely reported in the local newspapers. High status at home was no protection from insult overseas. In 1906, Baron K. Sutematsu and an unnamed professor from the Imperial University, with doctorates from Leipzig and Oxford, were humiliated by demeaning dinner arrangements they were forced to endure on a German ocean liner.[21] In the same year two distinguished scholars, Professor T. Nakamura and Dr F. Omori, were attacked and abused while visiting California to study the aftermath of the recent earthquake. The American historian, R. L. Buell, observed that while these attacks attracted little attention in San Francisco, they were immediately and widely reported in Japan where they had a 'profoundly irritating effect'.[22]

Travellers returned to Japan with stories of racial discrimination and humiliation. Yone Noguchi of Keio University complained that the Japanese were not given rights commensurate with people from 'a first-class nation of the world'. In fact they were treated 'with humiliation like dogs in a yard'. Great mischief was being done by 'the black visaged sneak, called Racial Prejudice'.[23] The naval officer and author Mizuno Hironori recalled his experiences as a young naval cadet in San Francisco where he saw 'white urchins' harassing Chinese residents, calling them monkeys and pulling their pigtails. At the time he felt 'irrepressible anger as an Oriental'.[24]

Individual affront turned to national anger with news in 1906 of riot and discrimination on the Pacific Slope of North America, in particular in British Columbia and California. In the early stages of the Russo-Japanese war there had been some support for the Asian underdog, but opinion changed dramatically as the news of Japanese victories spread. Baron Kaneko watched with concern the increase in racial prejudice while

[19] Gulick, The White Peril, pp.169–73.
[20] Sidney Gulick, The American Japanese Problem: a Study of the Racial Problems of the East and West (New York, Scribners, 1914) p.65.
[21] The Times, 22 January 1908.
[22] R. L. Buell, 'The Development of Anti-Japanese Agitation in the United States', Political Science Quarterly, vol.37 (1922) p.622.
[23] Japan Times, 2 May 1913.
[24] Soichi Saeki, 'Images of the United States as a Hypothetical Enemy', in Akira Iriye (ed.) Mutual Images: Essays in American Japanese Relations (Cambridge, Mass., Harvard University Press, 1975) p.104.

in North America during the war. Writing to the Tokyo newspaper *Jiyu Tsushin*, he explained that he found that 'bad feeling arising out of racial differences' had been 'growing very rapidly'.[25] In his history of American–East Asian relations, *Across the Pacific*, Akira Iriye observed that the war itself created 'anti-Orientalism'. Attempts to arouse mass emotion by talk of a Japanese yellow peril had not been successful before the war. Iriye referred to the observations of American diplomat and war correspondent Willard Straight, who had himself developed noted and felt hostility to Japan, recording in his diary:

They all hate us, all of them, officers and men. They have been the underdog till now, they have been the scholars, we the masters and now they're going to show us a thing or two if it can be done. They hate us. God knows the feeling is mutual.

In a letter to a friend, Straight wrote that for 'no particular reason' he found himself 'hating the Japanese more than anything else in the world'. It was due, he thought, 'to the constant strain of having to be polite and seek favours from a yellow people'.[26]

The Japanese danger

There were few Japanese in the United States until the last years of the nineteenth century. Contract labourers were attracted to Hawaii in the 1880s and by 1894, when Japan brought the trade to an end, 30,000 had crossed the Pacific, many moving on to California, in search of higher wages and larger opportunities. In 1894, a treaty between Japan and the United States provided in its first article that: 'The citizens or subjects of each [country] shall have full liberty to enter, travel or reside in any part of the territory of the other . . . and shall enjoy full and perfect protection for their persons and property.'[27]

During the 1890s, the Japanese population in California increased from just over 1000 to 10,000, to jump again to 41,000 by 1910, at which time the Japanese diaspora outnumbered Chinese Californians. The 1890s saw the first stirrings of anti-Japanese activism on the part of seasoned campaigners against the Chinese. At this stage, however, as Daniels has observed, it was 'mainly a tail of the Chinese kite'.[28]

---

[25] Reproduced in *Japan Times*, 13 February 1907.
[26] Akira Iriye, *Across the Pacific: An Inner History of American-East Asian Relations* (New York, Harcourt, Brace and World, 1967) pp.103–4.
[27] Lancelot Lawton, *Empires of the Far East: a Study of Japan and her Colonial Possessions* (London, Grant Richards, 1912) pp.353–4.
[28] Roger Daniels, *The Politics of Prejudice: The Anti-Japanese Movement in California and the Struggle for Japanese Exclusion* (Berkeley, University of California Press, 1977) p.21.

San Francisco's powerful trade union movement called the first anti-Japanese mass-meeting in 1900 and was subsequently offered strong support by Stanford professor of economics E. A. Ross, who made a powerful public address in 1900, the same year in which he addressed the Academy of Social Sciences on the problem he named 'race suicide'.[29] The American Federation of Labor (AFL) adopted the anti-Asian cause in 1904, calling for an end to all Korean and Japanese immigration, as being even more dangerous than Chinese immigration. The colonisation of the Pacific coast by Oriental races, declared the AFL, threatened wages and conditions. Race preservation demanded that the provisions of the Chinese Immigration Act be extended to Koreans and Japanese.

The Japanese and Korean Exclusion League was formed in May 1905 in San Francisco, but following the arrival of numbers of Indians, changed its name to the more comprehensive Asiatic Exclusion League. The most influential members of the League were O. A. Tveitmoe and P. H. McCarthy, office bearers of the San Francisco Building Trades Council and recently arrived European immigrants. Both were physically intimidating men. McCarthy was described as an organiser who conducted the simplest negotiation with the 'physical and vocal energy adequate to the management of a twenty-man mule team'.[30] Olaf Tveitmoe, a dark, hulking Scandinavian, 'a gorilla' of a man, was a close friend of the leader of the AFL, Sam Gompers. He was convicted in 1912 – and briefly imprisoned – for involvement in a plot to blow up the offices of the *Los Angeles Times*, a paper that was both anti-union and pro-Japanese.[31]

But the anti-Asian movement always received support from the other side of town. The most persistent and influential proponent of the cause was James Duval Phelan, one of California's leading citizens. He was the wealthy and well-educated son of a San Francisco banker and politician, mayor of his native city between 1897 and 1901, a prominent Democrat and US senator between 1914 and 1920. One of the most significant philanthropists on the west coast, he was also a patron of the arts, a man of taste and learning, described as 'California's most elegant, accomplished gentleman'. Dreaming of re-making the city in the style of Rome – 'sun-splashed, spacious and baroque' – Phelan could see no place in it for non-Europeans. He had taken up the anti-Chinese cause as a young man

---

[29] Edward A. Ross, 'The Causes of Race Superiority', *Annals of the Academy of Social Sciences* (1900) p.88.
[30] *The San Francisco Argonaut*, cited in E. F. Penrose, *Californian Nativism: Organized Opposition to the Japanese, 1890–1913* (San Jose, R & E Associates, 1973) p.16.
[31] Penrose, *Californian Nativism*, pp.26, 39.

in the 1880s and continued to pursue his crusade for a white California until his death in 1930.[32]

The problem of the hour

The first large-scale campaign against the Japanese was launched by the leading conservative paper, the *San Francisco Chronicle*, which on 23 February 1905 carried a front-page story with the strident head-lines: 'The Japanese Invasion: The Problem Of The Hour'. Once the war with Russia was over, the paper warned, 'the brown stream of Japanese immigration would become a raging torrent'. For months similar stories appeared under such headlines as: 'The Yellow Peril – How Japanese Crowd Out The White Race', 'Brown Peril Assumes National Propor-tions' and 'Brown Men Evil In The Public Schools'.[33]

In March 1905, the Californian legislature passed an anti-Japanese resolution which received unanimous support in both houses. The doc-ument made the following points:

• Japanese labourers, by reason of race habits, mode of living, disposition and general characteristics were undesirable settlers;
• Japanese labourers did not evince any inclination to assimilate with our people or become Americans;
• Japanese labourers were mere transients who did not buy land or build or buy houses. They contributed nothing to the growth of the State. They added nothing to its wealth and were a blight on the prosperity of it. They were a great and impending danger to its welfare.
• Not less than five hundred each month landed at the port of San Fran-cisco and Californians could not but regard with the greatest sense of disaster, the prospect that the close of the war would surely bring vast hordes, to be counted only in thousands, of the discharged sol-diers of the Japanese Army, who would crowd the State with immoral, intemperate and quarrelsome men, bound to labour for a pittance and to subsist on food with which a white man could hardly sustain life.[34]

By the end of 1906, the Asiatic Exclusion League claimed a mem-bership of 78,000. Boycotts of Japanese restaurants were organised with picketers accosting patrons and urging them to patronise white estab-lishments. A correspondent for *The Times* in London reported that the Japanese were being 'humiliated in a thousand ways'. They were abused

---

[32] Kevin Starr, *Americans and the California Dream, 1850–1915* (New York, Oxford University Press, 1973) pp.250–3.
[33] Cited in Daniels, *The Politics of Prejudice*, p.25.
[34] *Ibid.* p.27.

and assaulted and there was a growing demand to introduce racial segregation as practised in the southern states against blacks. In every possible way, public sentiment was being 'excited against the Japanese'. The correspondent thought the Californians had 'hypnotised themselves' into believing the Japanese were a menace and doing their best to extend the agitation to other parts of the Pacific Slope.[35]

The Schools Crisis

In 1906, anti-Japanese agitation came to focus on the small number of their children attending the San Francisco public schools. Chinese school children were already segregated in a special school and in October 1905, the Board of Education resolved to extend the discrimination to Japanese, by changing the name of the Chinese School to the Oriental School and requiring all Japanese students to leave the public schools immediately,

for the higher end that our children should not be placed in any position where their youthful impressions may be affected by association with pupils of the Mongolian race.[36]

But unlike the Chinese, forced to live close together in a segregated district, Japanese families were scattered across the urban area. The measure effectively meant that many children could not attend school at all, but the Board's decision was popular with whites and much applauded. The *San Francisco Call* was pleased to observe that the resolution was the result of agitation 'against the intermingling of Asiatic races with the Caucasians'. The School Board had properly responded to public opinion in resolving that the races 'should be kept separate'.[37]

The Board was responding, in part, to pressure from the Asiatic Exclusion League, which had a larger agenda than the segregation of schools. Common education carried the implicit suggestion of eventual assimilation. Speaking to a mass rally in December 1906, Tveitmoe declared: 'Give citizenship to the Japanese', he advised, 'and you give them your daughters, your homes, your country'.[38] Debate about the planned exclusion of Japanese children carried with it frequent vilification of their alleged racial characteristics. Thus the *San Francisco Chronicle* observed editorially:

---

[35] *The Times*, 10 December 1906.
[36] T. A. Bailey, *Theodore Roosevelt and the Japanese-American Crisis* (Gloucester, Mass., Peter Smith, 1964) p.14.
[37] Bailey, *Theodore Roosevelt*, p.29.
[38] *San Francisco Examiner*, 24 December 1966, cited in Penrose, *Californian Nativism*, pp.18–19.

Whatever the status of the Japanese children while still young and uncontaminated, as they grow older they acquire the distinctive character, habits and moral standards of their race, which are abhorrent to our people. We object to them in the familiar intercourse of common school life as we would object to any other moral poison.[39]

James Phelan claimed that Japanese youths posed a particular threat to white girls because 'the moral code of the two races was entirely different'.[40]

A national insult

When reports reached Japan about the planned exclusion of their children from San Francisco schools, there was an initial sense of bewilderment. The United States was widely thought to be the country's closest friend, the Japanese alliance with Britain notwithstanding. Only a few months earlier, Japan had sent $246,000 to San Francisco for relief works following the earthquake and fire. The Tokyo *Asahi* deplored the fact that 'even our most intimate friend America' could not escape the contagion of bias and misunderstanding prevalent among foreign powers.[41] A writer in *Jiji* similarly regretted that talk 'of such a bigoted nature should continue to be heard among a people noted for generous sentiment and gallant feeling'.[42] The *Japan Times* expressed disappointment that 'of all people' the Americans should subscribe to a view subversive of one of the fundamental principles that underlay both their federal and state constitutions.[43]

As the facts of the situation emerged Japanese commentators expressed anger as well as disappointment. There were only ninety-three Japanese students in the public schools among a total school population of 25,000, and twenty-four of them were American-born. Headmasters and school inspectors emphasised that the Japanese pupils were healthy, clean and conscientious. A writer in the Tokyo *Hochi* suggested, indeed, that the Japanese migrants in California were of a higher moral standard than many of the European people flooding into the United States at the same time. The only reason for discrimination was that 'we are a coloured race'.[44] The editor of the *Japan Times* noted that if the 'accident of complexion' be insisted upon as 'a mark of our racial inferiority', the adherents of such a view should be pitied for their innocence. But the paper recognised the serious implications. Racial conflict sprang from 'the claim of

---

[39] Cited in Bailey, *Theodore Roosevelt*, p.36.
[40] Quoted in Lawton, *Empires of the Far East*, p.352.
[41] Cited in *Japan Times*, 20 October 1906.   [42] *Ibid.*
[43] *Ibid.* 11 December 1906.   [44] *Ibid.* 5 February 1907.

superiority on one side and resentment against inferior treatment on the other'.[45]

The American Ambassador to Japan, reporting on the crisis to the Secretary of State in Washington, explained that the news of the segregation of Japanese children had provoked criticism and indignation, first, because it resulted from the deliberate action of responsible government officials and second, because it was taken to indicate racial hostility. He recorded and endorsed a remark made to him by the Minister for Foreign Affairs, Viscount Hayashi, that there was 'especial sensitiveness upon this point'.[46] A week later, he observed that while Japanese political and business leaders and newspaper editors were moderate and patient, he had the impression that 'underneath it all is a current of feeling which shows how nearly the implied racial discrimination has touched home'.[47] The Tokyo correspondent of the Washington *Herald* reported the reactions he observed at a meeting of prominent bankers and businessmen at the Imperial Hotel. He believed that it would be difficult to overestimate the gravity of the situation. Surprise was expressed that the United States government should regard with indifference acts that were 'tantamount to actual war'. Little was said about other issues in contention between the two countries, but the exclusion of their children had, he wrote, 'cut this child-loving nation to the quick'.[48]

For many Japanese, the planned exclusion of Japanese children was a national insult. Acccording to the editor of the *Nichi Nichi*, the affair involved in its principle 'the international rights and honour of our people'. Without a comprehensive solution, there would certainly be a recurrence of such insulting treatment of their compatriots 'at some other time in other places'. Something had to be done.

As it stood Japanese migrants would be left for a long time to come in the status equal to the so-called inferior races, in the two Americas, Australia and all other countries outside the extreme East. Such discrimination against our people will foster in the end a bitter racial and religious bias and can only lead to the disturbance of the peaceful relations of the countries.[49]

Japanese reactions to the Schools Crisis were complicated by the fact that the United States was regarded in Japan as a model and a friend. The prominent intellectual, Inazo Nitobe, observed that 'the very peasants' were aware that England was an ally and America was a friend.[50]

[45] *Ibid.* 27 Dececember 1906.   [46] Bailey, *Theodore Roosevelt*, p.58.
[47] C. E. Neu, *An Uncertain Friendship: Theodore Roosevelt and Japan, 1906–09* (Cambridge, Mass., Harvard University Press, 1967) p.37.
[48] Bailey, *Theodore Roosevelt*, p.54.   [49] Cited in *Japan Times*, 21 November 1906.
[50] Inazo Nitobe, 'The Influence of the West on Japan', in Huish, *Fifty Years of New Japan*, p.460.

Count Hayashi declared fulsomely that Japan regarded America as its benefactor. The Government and people remembered the long friendship with the Republic and were deeply indebted to her for much help and for many improvements.[51] The hurt occasioned by the events in California was therefore all the deeper. A writer in the Tokyo *Kokomin* urged that 'our authorities and people' remain firm in their conviction of the true friendship that existed between Japan and America. The problem lay with 'mischief makers' who sought to 'introduce rupture in the standing harmony between the unwritten allies'.[52]

Many other commentators sought to attribute anti-Japanese agitation to particular locations or specific social groups. The Osaka *Mainich* argued that Asiatic exclusion had always been a favourite outlet for 'low-class labourers' and that it was used by demagogues to capture the labour vote. But it was of only regional significance, because while being 'locally powerful', race prejudice was checked by the 'more comprehensive views and better judgement of American statesmanship'.[53]

The question at the centre of the Schools Crisis in California was whether Japan had the same rights as Western powers to migrate, settle and work in colonial territories. Overseas expansion had become a popular cause in Japan in the 1890s and the young writer Tokutomi Soho was one of its most articulate promoters. He had begun his career as a teacher educated in the Western tradition, and was a passionate advocate of British liberalism, strongly influenced by the works of Charles Pearson, John Seeley and, above all, Charles Dilke's *Problems of Greater Britain*; reading that convinced him of the need for overseas expansion and Japanese colonisation. But what territorial base was his race building overseas, he asked in his journal, *Kokumin no Tomo*. On consideration, he thought it shameful that, unlike China, Japan had almost no international presence beyond a few thousand students in the United States, 'ten thousand workers in Hawaii and a few prostitutes in Hong Kong and Singapore'. To exert influence on the world it was essential for Japan to develop a policy 'to motivate our people to embark on great adventures abroad . . . to encourage their spirit of boldness to seek residence outside the homeland'.[54]

California's hostility to Japanese immigrants shocked Tokutomi, and he initially expected Washington to impose its will on the recalcitrant west coast and thus restore harmony between the two nations. The failure of

---

[51] A. M. Pooley (ed.) *The Secret Memoirs of Count Tadasu Hayashi g.c.v.o.* (London, Eveleigh Nash, 1915) pp.246–7.
[52] Cited in *Japan Times*, 29 October 1906.   [53] *Ibid.* 22 October 1906.
[54] J. D. Pierson, *Tokutomi Soho, 1863–1957* (New Jersey, Princeton University Press, 1980) p.226.

the federal government to grant basic citizenship rights to the Japanese diaspora was profoundly disillusioning. Tokutomi began his transformation from a champion of Western liberalism to its determined and persistent opponent.

The diplomats' compromise

Opinion on the east coast of the United States did not generally sympathise with the strong anti-Japanese feelings aroused in the West. In a Presidential Message, President Theodore Roosevelt had deplored the agitation against Japanese school children as 'a wicked absurdity': 'The overwhelming mass of our people cherish a lively regard and respect for the people of Japan, and in almost every quarter of the Union the stranger from Japan is treated as he deserves; that is he is treated as the stranger from any part of civilised Europe is and deserves to be treated'.[55]

The Californian Schools Crisis was resolved with a diplomatic compromise, the so-called Gentleman's Agreement hammered out between the two nations' diplomats in late 1907. It gave a little to each side. Japanese children were permitted to remain in Californian public schools. The United States banned the entry of Japanese labourers arriving from Hawaii, Canada and Mexico, while Japan agreed to control emigration by restricting the issue of passports to students, merchants and tourists and by closely investigating each applicant's circumstances. The provisions came into immediate effect. Japanese migration into California peaked in 1907 and then began a long decline.[56]

But anti-Asian sentiment in California was neither weakened nor appeased by the diplomats' compromise, nor was Japan's acute awareness of ongoing racial antagonism. Akira Iriye observed that Japanese leaders had been aware of generalised 'talk of the yellow peril' and decided to co-operate with the Western powers to prevent the growth of such fears. But the intrusion of 'something as irrational as race prejudice into foreign policy considerations was a shocking development for Japanese leaders'.[57] And no matter how hard they tried to minimise racial friction, Western prejudice did not seem to abate.[58] The Schools Crisis left behind it a residue 'of dismay, frustration and ultimately anger'.[59]

[55] Lawton, *Empires of the Far East*, p.357.
[56] Bill Ong Hing, *Making and Remaking Asian America through Immigration Policy, 1850–1990* (Stanford, Stanford University Press, 1993) pp.207–12.
[57] Akira Iriye, *Japan and the Wider World* (London, Longmans, 1997) p.28.
[58] Iriye, *Across the Pacific*, p.115.
[59] Akira Iriye, *From Nationalism to Internationalism: US Foreign Policy to 1914* (London, Routledge & Kegan Paul, 1977), p.201.

The race question undermined the long and arduous Japanese crusade to achieve the goal of 'absolute equality with the leading nations of the West', the central national motivation for half a century.[60] Professor Kemuriyama of Waseda University observed that the desire for international equality was 'a great national concern that touches the very foundations of its new civilisation'.[61] Revered elder statesmen, Prince Ito, explained the motivation of his contemporaries' drive for modernisation:

to fortify the nation with the best results and resources of modern civilization, in order to secure for the country prosperity, strength and culture and the consequent recognized status of membership on an equal footing in the family of the most powerful and civilized nations of the world.[62]

Japan had taken the West at its word. It had modernised its institutions, established a legal code, a system of universal education, a parliament, an efficient bureaucracy and a powerful army and navy. It had assumed that the hurdles that had to be negotiated to achieve equality were political, technological and cultural. The Japanese had to become civilised in Western terms. Almost everyone was eventually forced to admit that Japan had been an extraordinarily apt and successful pupil. The victory over Russia was the final test, not just for the skill of its soldiers and sailors, but for the efficiency with which the whole nation mobilised.

But in 1906, the Japanese government came to appreciate that while the nation had gained military power, it was still not accorded the status and respect accorded to white men. Australia had made that clear with the passage of the Immigration Restriction Act in 1901, but discrimination by the United States was more distressing given Japanese admiration for the great republic and their desire for its friendship. Events in California confirmed the message sent by Australians five years earlier, that there was another hurdle in Japan's path that was biological and immutable. Japanese migrants might emulate white men, but they could never become part of the white tribe. Civilisation could be copied and learned, but the achievement of whiteness remained out of reach. This was also the lesson that would be learnt by Japanese migrants to the Canadian province of British Columbia.

'White Canada Forever'

In common with the other white settler societies, British Columbia had enacted a series of measures against Chinese migrants, who had come

---

[60] Tokyo correspondent, *The Times*, 21 June 1913.
[61] K. K. Kawakami, *Japan and World Peace* (New York, Macmillan, 1919) pp.48–50.
[62] Kawakami, *Japan and World Peace*, p.50.

to work in gold mines and then, most importantly, on the Canadian Pacific Railway. But as a result of Colonial Office and Canadian government pressure, Japanese migrants generally received more favourable treatment. When British Columbia passed legislation preventing Japanese from working in coal mines, for example, in 1899, Colonial Secretary Joseph Chamberlain explained that it was not acceptable: 'It is not the practical exclusion of Japanese to which the Mikado objects, but their exclusion *nominatum*, which specifically stamps the whole nation as undesirable persons'.[63] When British Columbia replied that it was not disposed to change its legislation 'in conformity with the wishes of the Japanese government', Chamberlain asked the Governor General to disallow it.[64]

The Chinese were treated with rather less consideration, as they noted in protest.[65] A poll tax of $50 had been imposed on arrivals in 1885, raised to $100 in 1900 and $500 two years later. When the President of the Chinese Board of Trade in Vancouver lodged a protest to the British government about this discrimination, the Secretary of State replied that he regretted that 'the Colonial Office was unable to interfere with the discretion of the Dominion Parliament in this matter'.[66]

In January 1906, Canada became a signatory to the 1894 Treaty of Commerce and Navigation between Britain and Japan, with a special proviso agreed to by the Japanese consul-general in Ottawa that Japan would restrict emigration to Canada through its control over the issue of passports.[67] On the west coast, however, white men remained suspicious. British Columbia, like California, often felt frustrated by the lack of sympathy displayed with its views on immigration by the distant national government. Vancouver was separated by 3,000 miles of prairie and mountain range from the seat of government in Ottawa and local politicians found it difficult to persuade the national government to their point of view.

Altogether twenty-two statutes of the British Colombia legislature directed against the Japanese had been annulled by the federal government, including no fewer than nine statutes between 1897 and 1901 prohibiting the immigration of Japanese. To the white settlers of the western province, Ottawa was very far away and out of touch, whereas Asia was

[63] Chamberlain to Governor General, 19 April 1899, CO 886/1/3.
[64] Chamberlain to Governor General, 25 May 1899, CO 886/1/3.
[65] T. J. Chang to Lord Lansdowne, 21 May 1903, CO 886/1/3; Wang Tahsieh to Elgin, 24 September 1906, CO 886/1/1; see also C. P. Lucas, 'The Self-Governing Dominions and Coloured Immigration', CO 886/1/1, pp.9–10.
[66] President of Chinese Board of Trade to Colonial Office, CO 886/1/1.
[67] Claude MacDonald to Sir Edward Grey, 18 February 1908, Enclosure, CO 886/1/110.

just across the ocean. White settlers wanted to keep the vast, yet-to-be developed territory to themselves, yet large and increasing numbers of Japanese were arriving every year.[68] Whereas only 354 Japanese arrived between July 1904 and June 1905, by 1906 the number had jumped to 2,233 and then during the first ten months of 1907, 8,356 Japanese immigrants reached Canada.

Central to white settlers' aspirations, as W. P. Ward has shown, was the goal of 'White Canada Forever'. As in Australia and the United States, Canadian settlement rested on the dispossession of the original Indigenous owners. Land ownership was crucial to the settlers' vision of the new society, but the lands had to be preserved for whites. As M. E. McInnes wrote from the west coast to the government in Ottawa, 'Our millions of acres of vacant areas, especially in the milder climates of British Columbia, must necessarily appear more and more tempting to Asiatics in the coming years, and it is a forgone conclusion that they will carry on unremitting efforts to possess themselves of the land which should be reserved for our own race and races capable of assimilating with us.'[69] As popular verse expressed it:

> Then let us stand united all
> And show our fathers' might
> That won the home we call our own
> For white man's land we fight
> To oriental grasp and greed
> We'll surrender, no never
> Our watchword be 'God Save the King'
> White Canada Forever[70]

In 1907, leading citizens and the press began to express increasing anxiety about new arrivals from Asia. By then, it was estimated that there were already 25,000 Asiatics in British Columbia, practically all of whom were males, compared with 75,000 white male adults. The editor of the *Daily Province* joined the chorus, urging that the 'outpost of Empire' had to be guarded against all comers. British Columbians did not wish to be 'dominated by Japanese, or Chinese or any colour but their own'.[71]

---

[68] P. Roy, 'British Columbians' Fear of Asians, 1900–1950', *Social History* vol.XIII, no.25 (May 1980) pp.161–2.

[69] W. E. McInnes, Report to Frank Oliver, Minister of the Interior, 2 October 1907, CO 886/1.

[70] Cited in W. P. Ward, *White Canada Forever: Popular Attitudes and Public Policy Towards Orientals in British Columbia* (Montreal, McGill-Queens University Press, 1978) p.xii.

[71] *Daily Province*, 9 September 1907.

There had been some support for Japan in the early months of the Russo–Japanese War. Bartenders in Victoria were said to have given Japanese patrons free drinks when early successes were reported.[72] But the decisive nature of the Japanese victory created concern in British Columbia as in other parts of the Pacific world. With only rudimentary defences, the west coast considered itself specially vulnerable to attack. A local poet expressed community anxieties in *Westward Ho!*:

> Ye Japanese clad with equipments of war
> Whose armies and navies and Juggernaut car
> Would crush, if they dare, and claim as their own,
> What belongs to the white man – the white man alone.[73]

Many of the new Japanese arrivals had come from Hawaii, where plantation owners were driving down wages and news spread of the impending United States prohibition on entry. In those same months over 2,000 Sikhs and 1,300 Chinese also arrived in British Columbia. To fearful white witnesses, it seemed, as it had in Melbourne in 1888, and Durban in 1894, that an alien invasion was imminent. As ever, rumour fanned the flames of hostility; 50,000 Japanese labourers were said to be about to arrive to work on new railway projects.[74]

In August 1907, an Asiatic Exclusion League was formed in Vancouver. It was the first in Canada, but similar to comparable bodies established in the American Pacific states from 1905. The inaugural meeting was large and enthusiastic, representing all classes, community organisations, unions and the major political parties. Its President was A. W. Von Rhein, a delegate of the Bartenders' Union, its treasurer, S. J. Gothard, a printer by trade and business manager for the Amalgamated Trades Unions of Vancouver. Robert McPherson, the federal member for Vancouver, urged everyone present to become 'a missionary to preach this gospel of a white man's country'.[75] Although dominated by working men, it was estimated that at least fifteen per cent of League members were from the mercantile and professional classes.

A month later, a mass march was held and by the time the procession reached the town hall, 8,000 had rallied. As many as possible crowded into the hall to hear, among other speakers, the Rev. Dr Fraser who, the *Vancouver World* reported, spoke with earnestness and enthusiasm, stating that he was with the movement in body and spirit and declaring:

[72] Ken Adachi, *The Enemy that Never Was: a History of the Japanese Canadians* (Toronto, McClelland & Stewart, 1976) p.44.
[73] Cited by Roy, 'British Columbians' Fear of Asians', p.167.
[74] Adachi, *The Enemy that Never Was*, p.70. [75] *Daily Province*, 13 August 1907.

He believed that if something is not done to stop the influx it will go so far as to see the pulpit in the hands of the Japanese or Chinese. It was pure Anglo-Saxon blood that made the Empire and it would never be made with a mixture of Asiatic blood.[76]

Many of the sentiments voiced in the speeches would have been familiar to audiences in the other white settler democracies. W. E. Fowler, the Secretary of Seattle's Asiatic Defence League, referred to action that month in Bellingham, in Washington State, when a European mob forcibly expelled a group of East Indians from the town, who had subsequently sought refuge, as British subjects, in Canada.

Reportedly the 'best received' speaker at the Vancouver meeting was a New Zealander, J. B. Wilson, who explained how the problem of Asian migration had been dealt with in other British colonies, drawing vivid pictures of the 'horrors of the Rand' and the lives of 'the Celestials' in the great Australian cities. 'Let Canada say to England', Wilson cried, 'as Australia had said: "How can you expect us to help you fight the whites if you will not help us fight the blacks?"' After a 'swinging peroration', the New Zealander sat down amid 'a prolonged howl of applause'.[77]

After the meeting, a large crowd moved on to Chinatown, where rioters broke every window within reach. Participants then walked towards the Japanese houses and businesses in 'Little Tokyo'. The police were unable to stop the progress of the march, but on reaching the Japanese quarter, the demonstrators were met with a deluge of stones and bottles thrown from well-prepared positions on the rooftops. A Japanese column shouting 'Banzai' and armed with sticks, clubs, iron bars, knives and bottles attacked the front line of the rioters. According to one account, the mob 'wavered, broke, retreated – some men gashed and bleeding, their lust for conflict quickly dissipated by the unexpected and fiery resistance'.[78]

Tensions remained high in Vancouver for several days. Gun shops sold their entire stock and Chinese workers went on strike. Details of the riot were reported around the world. The government in Ottawa sent officials to Vancouver to assess the situation. Compensation was promptly paid to Chinese and Japanese property owners. A delegation led by the Federal Minister of Labour, Rodolphe Lemieux, travelled to Japan to negotiate what became known as the Canadian Gentleman's Agreement, in three-way talks with Japanese officials and the British Ambassador.

[76] *Vancouver World*, 9 September 1907.
[77] *Daily News Advertiser*, 8 September 1907.
[78] Adachi, *The Enemy that Never Was*, p.74.

The provisions were similar to those in the Gentleman's Agreement negotiated just weeks before by the United States. There would be tight restrictions on the immigration of labourers, unless they had approved contracts with Canadian employers, and agricultural labourers would be permitted 'under [the] same restrictions as those provided for by their arrangements with the United States, namely, from five to ten labourers per 100 acres'.[79] Lemieux received verbal assurances from the Japanese that they would restrict the emigration of all labourers, domestic and agricultural, to 400 a year, through the issue of passports, but the Japanese would not put this in writing for in their view, 'any limiting of treaty rights would mean their defeat, and perhaps lead to serious trouble'. 'Impossible to do better', Lemieux telegrammed his government.[80] 'Japanese Government object to make them public because they consider this a national humiliation. Again I urge acceptance of arrangement'.[81] The Japanese had agreed to restrict emigration of its people to Canada 'within reasonable limits', but in the end this qualification was omitted from the Agreement submitted to the Canadian parliament with Japan's acquiescence.[82]

The Agreement was announced in the federal parliament in January 1908, but because Japanese assurances remained confidential, British Columbian politicians remained suspicious. The provincial government proceeded to pass immigration restriction legislation based on the Natal/Australian model of a literacy test to be applied to all Asian arrivals, but it was again disallowed by the Canadian government.[83] Japanese labourers continued to land in Vancouver in violation of the Agreement.[84]

Meanwhile, the Asiatic Exclusion League, at the suggestion of its President, O. A. Tveitmoe, became a transnational organisation, with an international executive, operating from headquarters in San Francisco, its first conference held in Seattle in February 1908. The following month, however, a secret agent, W. E. McInnes, was pleased to send a confidential report to the Minister of the Interior stating that his underground activities, in driving a wedge between the Americans and the Canadians, had

[79] Telegram from Lemieux, enclosure, Governor General to Secretary of State, received 10 December 1907, Copy to Foreign Office, CO 886/1.
[80] Telegram from Lemieux, enclosed in Governor General to Secretary of State, received 21 December 1907, CO 886/1.
[81] Secret telegram from Lemieux to Wilfred Laurier, 21 December 1907, CO 886/1/66; Sir C. MacDonald to Sir Edward Grey, 20 January 1908, CO 886/1/97.
[82] Tadasu Hayashi to Sir Claude MacDonald, 18 January 1908, Enclosure, CO 886/1/97.
[83] C. J. Woodsworth, *Canada and the Orient* (Toronto, Macmillan, 1941) pp.84–90.
[84] Earl Grey to Claude MacDonald, 3 March 1908, CO 886/1/114.

been successful and thus the main object of his mission to Vancouver had been accomplished.[85]

Transnational identities and interests

The Vancouver riots, the Schools Crisis in San Francisco and the campaigns of Indians in the Transvaal all occurred at much the same time in different white settler democracies, and were seen as having greater than provincial significance, providing focal points for what many contemporaries had come to see as the major global question: the relations between the races in a rapidly shrinking and increasingly interconnected world.

Politicians and officials in Washington, Ottawa and London were often perplexed by the deep passions aroused by Asian immigration, even when the actual numbers migrating didn't seem to warrant such concern. They were disturbed by what they saw as provincial and vulgar excess, but they came to appreciate that this was an issue like no other. It united self-styled white men across geographical distance and deep class divisions, bringing together individuals who otherwise didn't have much in common and whose material interests often clashed.

Above all, metropolitan governments realised that here was an issue capable of mobilising whole communities and creating new transnational ones, of changing voting behaviour and political allegiances. The British Ambassador to the United States, James Bryce, noted 'an identity of feeling and of interests (real or supposed)' between the Canadian inhabitants of the Pacific Coast and their neighbours in the United States.[86] Washington and Ottawa talked about the possible secession of British Columbia, Washington, Oregon and California – 'where the same question is agitating the public mind, and threatens to combine all classes, irrespective of boundaries, in one common cause' – leading to their amalgamation into a new republic.[87] The British government feared that the United States would stand forth as the leader and protector of white men's interests, attracting western Canada – and possibly Australasia – into a new alliance.

Following the Vancouver riot, the Canadian government had sent McInnes to the west coast to assess the degree of American involvement in the anti-Asian agitation and to counteract it. 'There appears to be good reason', wrote the Governor General to the Colonial Office, 'for

[85] McInnes to Frank Oliver, Minister of the Interior, Confidential Report, 14 March 1908, CO 886/1/115.
[86] Bryce to Sir Edward Grey, 5 February 1908, CO 886/1/90.
[87] Lemieux memorandum, 15 November 1907, enclosure in C. MacDonald to Edward Grey, 27 November 1907, CO 886/1/65.

the belief that the Vancouver riots were fomented by agitators coming from the United States.'[88] In his report to the Minister of the Interior, McInnes increased these suspicions, warning that the Americans:

to their own obvious advantage, may egg on and secretly increase the anti-Japanese feeling now becoming rampant in the province till that feeling reached a stage where the British Columbians forget that they are British and look upon their highest interests as identical with those of California, Oregon and Washington.[89]

McInnes remained in Vancouver until the early months of 1908 and worked actively to subvert the political alliances forged by the Asiatic Exclusion League between Canadian and American working men. He suggested that should the United States fleet visit British Columbia, the Governor General should also lend his presence to the occasion. 'It would strengthen and uphold the Imperial spirit of our people and would tend to keep our young fellows from being too much impressed with the might of Washington and the glory of the Stars and Stripes'.[90] McInnes changed his mind about this plan, however and recommended in the strongest terms that the fleet not be invited to Vancouver: 'We are peculiarly open to American influences; already the sentiment is freely expressed among the masses here that it is to the American Fleet that British Columbia must look for protection; that the British Fleet will never return here'.[91]

The British, too, worried about the Empire disintegrating, Britain being marginalised and the United States assuming leadership of a new white men's alliance. In his paper 'Suggestions as to Coloured Immigration into the Self-Governing Dominions', prepared for the Colonial Office, Charles Lucas observed that this was 'a question second to none in difficulty and importance' for the Empire. The British government should endeavour therefore to show some leadership on the question:

There is also to my mind a constant and serious danger that, if we do not take the initiative, the United States may stand out on and through this question as the leaders of the English-speaking peoples in the Pacific as against the coloured races. This is not my own view alone.[92]

Indeed it was a commonly held concern. 'The English speaking peoples in the Pacific are therefore united in the determination to preserve the exploitation of their territories for the white man, and for the white man

[88] Governor General to CO, 24 September 1907, CO 886/1/1.
[89] McInness to Minister of Interior, 2 October 1907, CO 886/1, p.48.
[90] McInnes to Governor General, 13 February 1908, CO 886/1/96.
[91] McInnes to Minister of Interior, enclosure, 13 February 1908, CO 886/1/96.
[92] Charles Lucas, 'Suggestions as to Coloured Immigration into the Self-Governing Dominions', no.2, CO 886/1/1, p.2.

alone', wrote Lancelot Lawton in *Empires of the Far East*. 'If any doubt on this subject is entertained in the Mother country, then, for the sake of the maintenance of the integrity of the Empire, the sooner this doubt is once and for all dispelled, the better.'[93]

A related challenge for imperial leaders in London was the need to assuage the resentment of an increasingly anti-colonialist and nationalist India, while honouring the white Dominions' right of self-government. When the British government suggested that the Indian government follow the Japanese in using passports to prevent Indians migrating to Canada, the Government of India sent a strongly worded telegram advising that it would *not* take steps to prevent Indians from migrating: 'any action in the direction of taking general powers of restriction by legislation will be the subject of severe criticism in present state of feeling in India. We consider legislation of this kind particularly inadvisable'.[94]

In her study of the introduction of passports for Indians in Canada, Radhika Mongia has interpreted the recommmendation as an example (following Partha Chatterjee) of 'the rule of colonial difference' – a British strategy of colonial rule – but her analysis lacks awareness of the larger transnational context of the challenge posed, and precedent set by China and Japan.[95] China had agreed to introduce passports for selected categories of travellers in its renegotiated Treaty with the United States in 1888, and Japan had introduced passports in 1896 to regulate the emigration of its own people to avoid being subject to the kind of demeaning and discriminatory legislation that earlier targeted the Chinese. Japan volunteered the use of the passport as a way of taking the initiative, exercising control and thus saving face.

Confronted with Indian protest about discrimination within the Empire, the Colonial Office suggested that the Indian government might follow Japan in introducing passports to regulate emigration. It also advocated the principle of reciprocity in these arrangements – or at least the 'appearance' of reciprocity as Charles Lucas put it in a 'Very Confidential' memo on the subject of coloured immigration to Australia, Canada, New Zealand and South Africa in July 1908.[96] Reciprocity would give the appearance of equality, but would have differential effects. 'The case

---

[93] Lawton, *Empires of the Far East*, pp.396–7.
[94] Government of India to Canadian Government, telegram, 22 January 1908, CO 886/1.
[95] Radhika Viyas Mongia, 'Race, Nationality, Mobility: A History of the Passport', in Antoinette Burton (ed.) *After the Imperial Turn: Thinking With and Through the Nation* (Durham, Duke University Press, 2003) pp.198–208; see also Partha Chatterjee, *The Nation and its Fragments: Colonial and Postcolonial Histories* (Princeton, Princeton University Press, 1993).
[96] Charles Lucas, 'Suggestions as to Coloured Immigration into the Self-Governing Dominions', no.2, CO 886/1/2, p.8.

of the white Australian workman wanting to go to India', he noted, 'is sufficiently rare to make the requirement of some permit in his case no real hardship'.[97] Not until the conducive conditions of wartime, however, was the principle of reciprocity in passport control finally introduced.

The discrimination against Indians in the Empire rankled. 'We are treated worse than cats and dogs of Englishmen in the British Colonies', wrote Taraknath Das' journal *The Free Hindusthan* in a report on the Vancouver riots. 'The gate of the Commonwealth of Australia, a British colony is barred against the natives of India. We are getting worse treatment in the South African colonies than we used to get from the hands of the Boer republics'. Why were such laws passed? 'Only because we are slaves and do not know how to stand up like men and fight for our rights as men'.[98] *The Free Hindusthan* received financial support from subscribers in Canada and the United States and encouraged a united front of protest.

On 22 March 1908, the 'natives of Hindusthan' held a mass meeting in Vancouver: 'The meeting was largely attended by all classes of people, but no white man was present'.[99] They sent a telegram to John Morley, Secretary of State for India; 'Mass meeting natives of India protest deportation, exclusion from Canada. British subjects claim Government protection throughout the Empire. If our interest is overlooked, brothers in India must necessarily resent your Government's neglect'.[100] Other petitions and protests followed.[101] Just as the race question united white men across the world, it also brought together Indians of conflicting interests and political views. In 1911, an Indian Office official wrote to the Colonial Office, reflecting on events of the previous decade:

The gravity of the friction between Indians and the Dominions lies in this, that on the Colonial question, and on that alone, are united the seditious agitators and the absolutely loyal representatives of moderate Indian opinion.[102]

While Indian opinion became incensed with the race exclusion policies of Transvaal, Natal, Australia, British Columbia and New Zealand, the same shift in attitudes and the growth of militant nationalism occurred among young intellectuals in Japan.

Gandhi and Tokutomi Soho were representative in their disillusionment. As young men, both were influenced by Christianity, although

[97] Lucas 'Suggestions', p.8.
[98] *The Free Hindusthan, An Organ of Freedom, and of Political, Social and Religious Reform,* enclosure, April 1908, CO 886/1/ 117.
[99] *Ibid.*   [100] *Ibid.*   [101] Mongia, 'Race, Nationality, Mobility', pp.204–5.
[102] India Office memo, 'The Dominions – Further Correspondence', 5 April 1911, CO 886/3/2, p.395.

neither converted. Both read English literature and liberal political commentary with enthusiasm and wanted to join the modernisation of their societies. Gandhi had an idealistic view of the British Empire and Tokutomi believed in the principles embodied in the United States constitution. At much the same time, both came to realise that the race question – and the spread of what W. E. B. DuBois called the new religion of whiteness – deeply compromised British and American ideals. When forced to choose sides, Washington and London would come down on the side of the white men in the provinces.

Asia against the world

The prevalence of international racial conflict and the anticipated struggle between East and West were widely discussed in the English-speaking world in the first decade of the twentieth century. One of the cautionary contributions to the debate was an article, 'Asia Contra Mundum', by an author who took the pen-name 'Viator', in London's *Fortnightly Review* in February 1908. It attracted much attention and was read with great interest in Japan.[103] H. J. Wolstenholme, the scholarly friend of J. C. Smuts, wrote to him from Cambridge in March 1908, urging him to read the article because it showed 'more grip' on 'the Asiatic question' than anything else he had seen.[104]

The article opened with a tribute to the presience of Charles Pearson's forecast of 1893. Half a generation had passed since the 'thought of the world' had been 'startled' by his prediction of the inevitable decline of the white man's world. Such was the impact of Pearson's book, wrote Viator, that it could be considered not so much a treatise, 'but an act', which shook white self-confidence and deprived Europeans of the absolute sense of assured superiority which had hitherto helped them to dominate the world. The effect was 'like the first moment when the trainer's glance flinches before the eye of the tiger'.[105]

Recent events must have recalled for many people, observed Viator, 'the strange predictions of that disquieting thinker'. Indeed *National Life and Character* appeared all the more extraordinary in 1908 because of the apparent accuracy of Pearson's predictions. Yet of the 'yellow races' it was Japan, not China, as Pearson had suggested, that had successfully challenged the West. Yet Japan had been rebuffed because of the 'permanent disability' of 'their complexion'.

---

[103] The article was republished in *Japan Times*, 3 July 1913.
[104] Wolstenholme to Smuts, 4 March 1908, in W. K. Hancock and J. Van Der Poel, *Selections from the Smuts Papers*, vol.II (Cambridge, Cambridge University Press, 1966) p.419.
[105] 'Viator', 'Asia Contra Mundum', *Fortnightly Review* (1 February 1908) p.185.

Japanese migrants were excluded by white nations, who yet claimed both the right of migration and the 'Open Door' in Asian nations. The new phase of the colour conflict provoked by the rise of Japan had converted it, in the view of Viator, into one of the 'greatest perils which has yet menaced the future of mankind'. Japanese, together with Chinese and Indians, now found themselves 'shut out of the other Continents because they are Asiatics'.[106]

Denied the 'privilege of free settlement' that white men enjoyed, Asiatics realised at last that the problem was their racial identity. Viator concluded his piece by returning to Pearson's forecast of white decline, but suggested that this might now be brought about in a way utterly unanticipated. Might not the provocations of white men lead to the formation of a new political alliance:

Let Japan be invoked by China as a leader and by India as a liberator; let the black races feel that the white man is likely to be swept back at last, and then indeed the strangest dreams of the eclipse and extinction of Western civilization might come true.[107]

Might not the conceit of whiteness bring about its own demise?

---

[106] *Ibid.* p.195.   [107] *Ibid.* p.200.

8 White ties across the ocean: the Pacific tour of the US fleet

'the white races must stand together'

In February 1908, Sir Edward Grey, the Canadian Governor General, sent a 'Very Secret' note to Lord Elgin, the UK Secretary of State for the Colonies, informing him about a 'sensational speech' made by the United States President, Theodore Roosevelt, at a dinner in Washington, attended by the Deputy Minister of Labor and future Canadian Prime Minister, William Lyon Mackenzie King, recently returned from investigating the Vancouver riots. Roosevelt had invited Mackenzie King to Washington after hearing about the report he had written regarding Asian migration.

According to Mackenzie King's report to the Canadian government, Roosevelt, in speaking at the annual dinner of the Gridiron Club, the Washington-based organisation of newspaper men, had stated that 'the time was approaching when it might be desirable to substitute the "big stick" for politeness in dealing with Japan', and that 'the fleet had been sent round the Pacific for a purpose!' Mackenzie King reported, wrote the Governor General:

> that the President took up the position, with characteristic vehemence, that the brown and white races cannot assimilate, that they must keep to their respective areas and that this is a question on which all the white races must stand together.

Mackenzie King formed the impression that unless Japan acted to restrict the emigration of its people, the United States would legislate to exclude them and that if Japan resorted to hostile measures in response, then the United States was prepared for war. Roosevelt requested Mackenzie King to ask the Canadian Prime Minister, Wilfred Laurier, for Canada's assistance.[1]

Roosevelt was a recent convert to the cause of the white man on the Pacific coast. He had earlier deplored the proposal for segregated

---

[1] Governor General to Secretary of State, 2 February 1908, CO 886/1/85, received 17 February 1908, CO 886/1/86, UK National Archives.

schooling in California as a 'wicked absurdity' and was embarrassed by displays of rudeness in international relations, but increasingly Japan preyed on his mind.[2] 'One practical problem of statesmanship', he wrote to Arthur Balfour in England in March 1908, 'must be to keep on good terms with these same Japanese and their kinsmen on the mainland of Asia, and yet to keep the white man in America and Australia out of home contact with them'.[3] According to Mackenzie King, Roosevelt now agreed with the Californian view that the Japanese had 'political designs on the country' and had offered to support the working men of British Columbia.[4]

In a typically frank conversation with a deputation of British Columbian politicians in Washington, Roosevelt had told them that US and Canadian interests were 'identical' in the matter. 'Gentlemen', he said:

we have got to protect our working men. We have got to build up our western country with our white civilisation, and (very vehemently) we must retain the power to say who shall or who shall not come to our country. Now it may be that Japan will adopt a different attitude, will demand that her people be permitted to go where they think fit, *so I thought it wise to send that fleet around to the Pacific to be ready to maintain our rights.*[5]

Roosevelt had become convinced that the Japanese must be barred from immigration to so-called white men's countries and was sceptical about the effectiveness of the recently negotiated Gentlemen's Agreement. He told Mackenzie King that the United States government had not been able to obtain a satisfactory assurance from Japan with regard to the restriction of immigration, which is why the fleet was sent into the Pacific.

As James Bryce, now British Ambassador to the United States, reported to his government: 'The despatch of the fleet had been, therefore, decided upon partly in order to show Japan that the United States government was determined, while acting with all due courtesy in the matter of forms, to insist on the exclusion of Japanese labourers'.[6] His impression was confirmed in April in a specially commissioned paper by Captain Horace Hood, on the 'Naval Situation in the Pacific', by which time Roosevelt's previously voiced reasons for the fleet's tour of the Pacific were being denied: 'Despite official statements to the contrary,

[2] Roosevelt's Presidential Message, quoted in Lancelot Lawton, *Empires of the Far East* (London, Grant Richards, 1912) p.357.
[3] Roosevelt to Balfour, 5 March 1908, in Elting E. Morison (ed.) *The Letters of Theodore Roosevelt* (Cambridge, Harvard University Press, 1951) p.963.
[4] Bryce to Sir Edward Grey, Governor General, 5 February 1908, CO 886/1/90.
[5] Emphasis in original. Report of Interview with Roosevelt, 10 February 1908, Enclosure, CO 886/1/102.
[6] Bryce, report, 5 February 1908, CO 886/1/89.

there can be little doubt that the Japanese question was the principal cause of the transfer of this formidable fighting force to the Pacific. By the early part of April, there will be ready for sea a force consisting of 17 battleships, 8 armoured cruisers of the largest type, a number of unarmoured cruisers, 12 destroyers, and a number of auxiliaries of various kinds'.[7]

Roosevelt was convinced that Canada and the United States had a common interest in restricting Japanese immigration, but felt that neither the Canadian nor the British government appreciated the urgency of the matter. Thus it would not be surprising, in his view, if the white men on the Pacific Slope moved to form a new republic to safeguard western interests from the results of eastern neglect.[8] Ambassador Bryce reported this possibility back to his government in February 1908: the western states of America and of Canada might secede 'to create a new Republic'.[9] But Roosevelt, having little faith in Bryce's capacity to press the issue – 'a fine old boy' but getting on in years and perhaps 'fonder of books than he is of active politics' – asked if young Mackenzie King would be willing to approach the British government directly which, after consulting Canadian Prime Minister Laurier, he did.[10] Bryce, meanwhile, told Canadian Governor General Grey that he had informed Roosevelt that the British government was very familiar with the issue of Asian migration, because of 'what had happened in Australia and South Africa'. The American President need not worry. Whatever theories might formerly have prevailed, the British would not insist, 'upon compelling or even favouring the admission of Orientals into any Colony which strongly opposed their entrance'.[11]

Roosevelt warmed to the possibility of playing a role in bringing all English-speaking countries together in a 'convention' on Asian immigration. 'What I would like to accomplish', he told Mackenzie King, 'is not merely an understanding for today, but some kind of a convention between the English-speaking peoples, whereby, in regard to this question it would be understood on all sides that the Asiatic peoples were not to come to the English-speaking countries to settle, and that our people were

[7] Horace Hood to Bryce, 17 February 1908, 'Report respecting the Naval Situation in the Pacific', CO 886/1/95.
[8] R. MacGregor Dawson, *William Lyon Mackenzie King: A Political Biography 1874–1923* (London, Methuen, 1958) pp.152–3.
[9] Bryce report, 'Most Confidential', 5 February 1908, CO 886/1/86.
[10] Dawson, *William Lyon Mackenzie King*, p.153; there is considerable dispute in the historiography as to who took the iniative in these consultations. See also Raymond A. Esthus, *Theodore Roosevelt and Japan* (Seattle and London, University of Washington Press, 1966) pp.219–27.
[11] Bryce to Grey, 5 February 1908, CO 886/1/92.

not to go to theirs'.[12] Any possible insult would be mitigated by adopting the principle of reciprocity. The immediate occasion for this remark was his receipt of an invitation from the Australian Prime Minister, Alfred Deakin, for the US naval fleet to extend its tour south to Australia. Roosevelt wondered whether the fleet might also visit Vancouver, but the British government actively discouraged the idea.[13]

In his autobiography, Roosevelt recalled that on some matters he made his own decisions without consulting colleagues. One of those decisions was to send the great armada of sixteen battleships on a tour of the Pacific: 'I had become convinced that for many reasons it was essential that we should have it clearly understood, by our own people especially, but also by other people's, that the Pacific was as much our home waters as the Atlantic . . . I determined on the move without consulting Cabinet'.[14] He was at pains to express his support for Californians in their 'fundamentally sound and proper attitude', but also to insist on the importance of courtesy and respect in dealing with civilised powers. The issue was not Japanese inferiority, he insisted, but their difference: 'In the present state of the world's progress it is highly inadvisable that peoples in wholly different stages of civilisation, or of wholly different types of civilisation even though both equally high, shall be thrown into intimate contact. This is especially understandable when there is a difference of both race and standard of living'.[15]

With the ascendancy of Japan as a naval and military power in the Pacific, Australian political leaders had become increasingly concerned with the imperative of self-defence. The Federation had not ended Australian dependence on Britain, whose government was yet seen as utterly unsympathetic to the Australian sense of isolation and insecurity. The arrangement whereby Australia paid a subsidy to the British Admiralty in return for a commitment of general naval support was unacceptable, especially since the British navy had withdrawn from the Pacific under the terms of the new British–Japanese agreement of 1902. Did Britain expect Australians to rely on Japan for its defence?

Deakin was adamant that Australia should have its own navy under the command of its own government. Impatient with Australian demands, the British yet deplored their gestures of independence. But, as an *Age* editorial put it in a telling analogy, without a navy, white men could suffer the same fate as they had inflicted upon the Aborigines: 'Australia can only be attacked or invaded by sea; hence a navy is our

[12] Dawson, *William Lyon Mackenzie King*, pp.157–8.   [13] *Age*, 4 April 1908.
[14] Theodore Roosevelt, *An Autobiography* (New York, Macmillan, 1913) p.592.
[15] *Ibid.* pp.411–12.

paramount defence requirement . . . Without a navy we should be as help-less to drive off [invaders] as a race of untutored aboriginals armed with spears'.[16]

Deakin issues an invitation

In London for the Colonial Conference in April 1907, Deakin and his Secretary of External Affairs, Arthur Atlee Hunt, found themselves in daily conflict with the men of the Colonial Office, who condescended to the colonials but never consulted them – always the complaint of the powerless. His biographer, J. A. La Nauze, noted that Deakin approached Colonial Conferences as 'battlefields' – his own war of independence dis-placed onto hostilities with British bureaucrats.[17] The Australian Prime Minister argued without success for the abolition of the Colonial Office and its replacement with an imperial Secretariat to mediate between autonomous governments. He reiterated his grievances about lack of consultation over the last twenty years and Britain's resistance to Aus-tralian initiatives in the Pacific, in particular with regard to the govern-ment of the New Hebrides. Rather than realising an independent nation-hood, the Federation had exacerbated the tensions inherent in Australia's continuing condition as a self-governing colony.[18] Hunt was personally affronted by British aloofness, writing to his friend Robert Garran that he could hardly imagine what unimportant people Australians were in the eyes of British officials and that the Australian government wanted to 'remove from the Colonial Office practically all control of the self-governing Colonies'.[19]

The irritation between Deakin and the Colonial Office was mutual. Officials found the Australian Prime Minister 'bitter, parochial, perpet-ual in his talk'.[20] Bertram Cox thought any further effort at negotiation pointless because it was clear that Deakin 'hated' the United Kingdom.[21] His only desire, they concluded, was to give offence. Deakin bruised himself daily in these encounters, but achieved little and by the time he returned home that year, 'there was', in La Nauze's words, 'something

---

[16] *Age*, 7 July 1908.
[17] J. A. La Nauze, *Alfred Deakin: A Biography* vol.1 (Melbourne, Melbourne University Press, 1965) p.500.
[18] On federation as a failure of manhood, see Marilyn Lake 'Monuments of Manhood and Colonial Dependence: The Cult of Anzac as Compensation', in Marilyn Lake (ed.) *Memory, Monuments and Museums: The Past in the Present* (Melbourne, Melbourne University Press, 2006).
[19] Atlee Hunt to Bob Garran, 18 April 1907, Hunt papers, 52/769, NLA.
[20] La Nauze, *Alfred Deakin* vol.2, p.502.   [21] *Ibid.* p.489.

damaged in Deakin and it could not be repaired'.[22] Writing to Richard Jebb in London, Labor politician W. M. Hughes observed that the Prime Minister had had a 'nervous breakdown'.[23]

But, later that year, Deakin prepared to fight back by invoking the fraternity between the Commonwealth and the United States. He acted on a suggestion of a member of the New South Wales legislative assembly and President of the Immigration League of Australia, Richard Arthur, who, on 14 July 1907, recommended that Australia extend an invitation to the United States fleet, then planning its tour of American bases in the Pacific.[24] An alarmist with regard to Japanese ambition, and obsessive about the need for population growth and improved defence forces, Arthur was in regular correspondence with Roosevelt and with United States naval expert Rear Admiral Alfred Mahan, 'the most philosophic present-day student of the destiny of nations', according to Arthur. Mahan was the author of *The Influence of Sea Power in History*, which had been glowingly reviewed by Roosevelt a decade earlier.

Arthur delighted in quoting Mahan's warning about Australia's lack of capacity for self-defence in his articles for the press:

I wonder at the improvidence of Australasia in trusting that laws, though breathing the most popular convictions and purpose, can protect their land from that which threatens. All the naval power of the British Empire cannot suffice ultimately to save a remote community which neither breeds men in plenty, nor imports them freely.[25]

Arthur also quoted Roosevelt on the need for Australia to build a powerful navy: 'as President Roosevelt said some months ago . . . the strength of the navy RESTS PRIMARILY ON ITS BATTLESHIPS [*sic*] and they must be the best of their kind'.[26]

Deakin was enthusiastic about Arthur's suggestion that he invite Roosevelt to detour the American fleet to Australia. He had long admired the great Anglo-Saxon republic, as he called it, declaring to the federal

---

[22] *Ibid.* p.514. See also Neville Meaney, *The Search for Security in the Pacific 1901–1914: A History of Australian Defence and Foreign Policy* (Sydney, Sydney University Press, 1976) chs. 4 and 5.

[23] L. F. Fitzhardinge, *William Morris Hughes: A Political Biography* vol.1 (Sydney, Angus and Robertson, 1964) p.191.

[24] Arthur Atlee Hunt to Richard Arthur, 20 July 1907, Arthur papers, MS 473, item 2c, Mitchell Library; and see report of Arthur's letter to the British press observing: 'No wonder that Australians hail America as a possible supporter in an hour of trial', *Age*, 17 July 1908.

[25] Quoted in Richard Arthur, 'Again the Tocsin', *Bulletin* (30 April 1908).

[26] Capitals in original. Richard Arthur, 'Australian Naval Defence', *Sunday Times* (13 October 1907).

parliament: 'Next to our own nation we place our kindred in America'.[27] But there were constitutional difficulties in issuing an invitation direct to the American president. Despite the extension of self-government through federation, Australia's freedom of action in the world at large was limited. In conducting foreign affairs, Australia was still, in constitutional terms, a colonial dependency, not permitted to enter into negotiations with foreign powers. Yet, increasingly, leading Australians came to believe that an enhanced capacity for national defence was a matter of urgency.

Newspaper editorials contributed to popular anxieties about Asian ambitions, pointing to the growing resentment on the part of 'Asiatic patriots' towards the idea that the 'Kingdom of the earth is for the white skin'.[28] In an article on 'Australia and the South Pacific', in October 1907, that called up Pearson's prophecy of 1893 and Mahan's writings on Asia and the Pacific, the Sydney *Daily Telegraph* agreed that the Pacific was a coming 'storm centre' – indeed the 'true Armageddon of the world': 'Time, not prophecy will unfold whether Caucasian Australia is to hold her own against her next door neighbour – the countless Asiatic. The true Armageddon of the world, in which the tawny and yellow, or both combined, will engage in a life and death struggle with the white for final supremacy, may be fought out in the Pacific south of the Equator'.[29]

Australia needed adequate defence forces of its own so that it might be able to enter into an effective partnership with the United States to hold the Pacific for the white man: 'With an invincible Australian sentinel at the south west, and America at the east', advised the *Daily Telegraph*, 'the Pacific and its innumerable islands of amazing fertility and beauty will be secured to the Caucasian for all succeeding time'.[30] The prospect of a partnership with the great republic strongly appealed to Deakin, who perhaps recalled Josiah Royce's fond prediction that one day Australia and the United States might greet each other as 'sister republics' across the Pacific.

On Christmas Eve 1907, in a provocative gesture of political independence, Deakin wrote a letter to John Bray, the American Consul in Sydney, expressing his interest in inviting the fleet to Australia. The British government didn't learn of this act of defiance for six weeks. He sent a similar 'fulsome' letter of invitation – as Sir Charles Lucas

[27] Quoted in Ruth Megaw, 'Australia and the Great White Fleet, 1908', *Journal of the Royal Australian Historical Society* 56 (1970) p.122.

[28] Amear Ali, judge of the Bengal High Court, quoted in a letter from W. Awrdry, Missionary Bishop in Tokyo, to *The Times*, reprinted in the *Brisbane Courier*, 12 July 1908; Awdry's letter was also reported in the *Age*, 17 July 1908.

[29] *Daily Telegraph*, 30 October 1907.   [30] *Ibid.*

in the Colonial Office described its language – on 7 January to Whitelaw Reid, the American Ambassador in Britain, whom Deakin had met and charmed when in London earlier in the year. Deakin annotated his letter 'This is to be kept confidential', and began, characteristically, by saying how delighted he had been to offer hospitality to some visiting United States scientists: 'Both of them were typically charming Americans, intellectual, efficient, and frankly outspoken'.[31]

He asked Reid if he might persuade the President to accept an invitation to the naval fleet to visit Australia, in advance of a formal invitation to be submitted through the Colonial Office. Deakin spoke of the countries' common interests as 'kinsmen' and 'neighbours' in the Pacific Ocean: 'The appearance in the Pacific of such an Armada is an event in the history not only of the United States, but of the Ocean. We are naturally deeply interested in its significant voyage, and anxious to have some opportunity of expressing our sympathy with our kinsmen in their timely demonstration of naval power in what may be loosely termed our Oceanic neighbourhood'.[32]

'those colonies are white man's country'

In his letter to Reid, Deakin enthused about the similarities of Australia and the United States: 'No other Federation in the world possesses so many features of likeness to the United States as the Commonwealth of Australia and I doubt whether any two peoples could be found who are in nearer touch with each other, or likely to benefit more by anything that tends to knit their relations more closely'. (The official letter of invitation later despatched through the Colonial Office was rather less effusive in tone.) Roosevelt was keen to accept Deakin's invitation, informing the Secretary to the Navy: 'I particularly desire the fleet to visit Australia'. Provocatively, he told a correspondent of the *New York Times* that the visits (New Zealand was added to the itinerary) were intended to 'show England – I cannot say a "renegade" mother-country – that those colonies are white man's country'.[33]

Roosevelt asked his Secretary of State for the Navy whether it was feasible to keep the fleet in the Pacific longer than first planned to accommodate the Australians, even as he refused invitations from Argentina,

---

[31] Deakin to Whitelaw Reid, 7 January 1908, Secretary of State papers, roll 598, 8758/161, US National Archives; Colonial Office 418/60, UK National Archives.

[32] Deakin to Whitelaw Reid, 7 January 1908, Secretary of State papers, roll 598, 8758/161, US National Archives.

[33] Quoted in James R. Reckner, 'The Great White Fleet in New Zealand', *Naval History* vol.5, no.3 (Autumn 1991).

Uruguay and Ecuador.[34] In a note to the Ambassador in Buenos Aires, the Secretary of State, Elihu Root, advised: 'Say to Minister for Foreign Affairs that cruises of American battleships have been determined upon and arranged exclusively in Navy Department, the State Dept not being consulted', and in a letter to the President of Uruguay, he regretted that the fleet could not call on that country because 'visits have ... been limited to coaling ports selected in advance with reference to distances and bunker capacity'.[35]

As the fleet made its way around South America in January 1908, it was given 'a fraternal reception by Peruvians' and a 'more than generous welcome by the Government and people of Brazil'.[36] Newspapers in that country celebrated the friendly relations between 'the two greatest American republics' even as it was also noted that, until recently, Latin America had been treated as the 'sick continent', with 'a lamentable incapacity for government'.[37] In the ascendant dichotomy of white and not-white nations, South Americans' alleged incapacity for self-government and their infamous 'hybridity' confirmed their ineligibility, in the eyes of English-speaking peoples, for membership of the white men's club.

As it steamed on, invitations to the United States fleet were also received from China, Hong Kong, Fiji, Japan and belatedly, the United Kingdom. Baron Kogoro Takahira, in the Japanese Embassy in Washington, let it be known that his government was 'sincerely anxious to be afforded an opportunity to cordially welcome that magnificent fleet and to give an enthusiastic expression to the sentiment of friendship and admiration invariably entertained by the people of Japan towards the people of the United States'. The American government accepted in like fashion: 'It gives this government peculiar pleasure to accept because of the long existing and unbroken friendship' between the two countries.[38] Limited time restricted the visit to one Japanese port, however, and led to refusals to China, Fiji, Hong Kong and the United Kingdom.

Ambassador Reid had been pleased to add his support for an Australian visit when the formal invitation from the British Foreign Office finally arrived in the US. 'Deakin's appeal was so strong and my relations

[34] Roosevelt to Metcalf, 21 February 1908, Secretary of State, 8258/160-2, US National Archives.
[35] Secretary of State to President of Uruguay, 28 February 1908, Secretary of State, 825/159, roll 598, US National Archives.
[36] Irving B. Dudley to Secretary of State, 28 January 1908; Jose Pardo, president of Peru, to Roosevelt, 24 February 1908, State Department, 8258/148–9, 8258/160, Roll 598.
[37] Newsclippings, State department, 8258/163.
[38] Takahira to Roosevelt, 16 March 1908, State Department, 8258/247.

with him so cordial that I feel bound to say, on behalf of his invitation, all I properly can', he wrote.[39] Roosevelt needed no persuading. In his *Autobiography* he recalled: 'It was not originally my intention that the fleet should visit Australia, but the Australian Government sent a most cordial invitation, which I gladly accepted; for I have, as every American ought to have, a hearty admiration for, and fellow feeling with, Australia, and I believe that America should be ready to stand back of Australia in any serious emergency.'[40]

In his anonymous column in the London *Morning Post*, Deakin explained the invitation to the United States in terms of Australia's interest in the 'racial disputes' that had recently erupted on the Pacific Slope:

The invitation, though hospitable, was given in deadly earnest and is being warmly pressed on other grounds that are not mentioned. For Australia the entrance of a fleet under the Stars and Stripes into the Pacific is an incident of the utmost significance. Whatever the immediate cause of its going there may be, the act is popularly associated with the racial disputes which recently became acute in the West of the Dominion and of the great Anglo-Saxon Republic. Nowhere in the Empire and perhaps nowhere outside the Southern States of the Union, is the import of the colour question more keenly realised than in the Commonwealth. The ties of kinship are potent too.[41]

A new idea began to form in the minds of some British observers: perhaps the fulsome fellow feeling and ties of kinship between the commonwealth and the republic might form the basis for a white man's alliance that would bypass Britain altogether.[42]

When the Colonial Office learnt of the diplomatic activity between Australia and the United States, officials were furious – even more so when a premature announcement made the plans public knowledge and when the United States formally declined the British invitation to the fleet to visit 'a port in Great Britain'.[43] Asked to explain his actions, Deakin said that his initial enquiries had been informal and preliminary. Sir Charles Lucas seemed as annoyed at the warm language of Deakin's approach to the United States as at the impropriety of the invitation. He wrote:

[39] Whitelaw Reid to Root, 3 March 1908, Secretary of State 8258/215, roll 598, US National Archives.
[40] Roosevelt, *An Autobiography*, p.598.
[41] A. Deakin, *Morning Post*, 14 April 1908, in J. A. La Nauze (ed.) *Federated Australia: Selections of Letters to the Morning Post 1900–1910* (Melbourne, Melbourne University Press, 1968) p.229.
[42] Charles Lucas, 'The Self-Governing Dominions and Coloured Immigration', CO 886/1/1; Lawton, *Empires of the Far East*, pp.396–7.
[43] Bryce to Root, 2 April 1908, 8258/309; Root to Bryce, 18 April 1908, 8258/324.

As a matter of fact Mr Deakin is, it seems, to be hopelessly in the wrong. A prime minister cannot write, as he wrote, to an American consul general & treat it as unofficial. He did this as far back as 24 December & we heard nothing until 12 February. He ought to have consulted the imperial government before taking any step & I think that the effusive terms of his letters written without having made any attempt to know whether the visit would accord with Imperial policy were premature & unwise.

Lord Elgin remarked that it was 'useless to explain to Mr Deakin', while his Under-Secretary, Winston Churchill, thought the visit should be 'discouraged from every point of view'. Their colleague, Sir Francis Hopwood, suggested 'I should be disposed to ignore Mr Deakin'.[44]

But on this occasion Mr Deakin could not be ignored and he savoured the success of this defiant gesture, in which he had simultaneously pre-empted the Colonial Office and invoked the fraternity of Australians and Americans. No wonder that he trembled with 'ecstatic passion' when he made the news of the visit public, as a Sydney journalist, W. R. Charlton, reported in the New York *Independent*: 'Mr Deakin is an orator, a scholar and an emotional man. In fervid words and trembling with ecstatic passion he broke the news to his audience'.[45]

From South America, the fleet sailed up the coast to San Francisco, scene of the recent agitation against Japanese immigrants and school children. One million people – 'representing practically the whole of the Pacific Coast' – assembled to give the ships a frenzied welcome.[46] The outstanding social event of the incessant round of festivities was said to be a dance given by prominent society women to the sailors of all classes: 'Beautiful girls and women of the Golden Gate were brimful of welcome for the men of the navy, who were men and brothers under the starry flag, and who came home to their charming sisters'.[47] Similar feminine interest would be displayed in the men of the US navy when the fleet reached Australia in August.

White man to white men

Immediately it became known that the American fleet was to visit Australia, the United States Consul in Sydney, John Bray, was inundated with enquiries and offers of goods, services and hospitality. Traders and

[44] CO 418/60, UK National Archives. See also La Nauze, *Alfred Deakin*, vol.2, p.490, and Meaney, *The Search for Security in the Pacific*, pp.164–5.
[45] W. R. Charlton, 'The Australian Welcome to the Fleet', *Independent*, New York, 8 October 1908, vol.LXV, p.813.
[46] *Age*, 8 May 1908.   [47] *Ibid*. 15 June 1908.

suppliers, photographers and printers sent brochures and information.[48] The Australian Art Decorating Association demonstrated their wares with examples of letterhead ('Hail Columbia') and verse:

> Answer then, sons of self-same race,
> And blood of the self-same clan,
> Let us speak with each other, face to face
> And answer as man to man,
> And loyalty love and trust each other as none but free men can.

The Association advised prospective customers that it only engaged leading artists such as Norman and Lionel Lindsay, D. H. Souter and Dattilo Rubbo.[49] The visit of the fleet stimulated a frenzy of business and sales throughout Australia. When Rear Admiral Charles S. Sperry notified the Consul that his men would need eighty tons of potatoes, several quotes came in for 'Prime Tasmanian'. Similarly, suppliers of butter, milk, meat, bread, vinegar, cordials and wine in several states pointed to the superior virtues of their products.

The United States Consul also received numerous invitations for officers to visit private homes and public organisations. The Association of Coach Builders, for example, advised they would hold a smoke night social evening and wondered whether 'the presence of a few officers of the fleet might be obtained, say half-a-dozen'.[50] Correspondents asked for access to the ships and the official parties and women were to the fore in wanting to meet the officers and men. Donald Fraser wrote to the Consul: 'Mrs Fraser and a mutual friend, Mrs Irwin would like very much to visit some one of your mighty ships . . . At least that is what has made Mrs Fraser woman-like keep at me till I either wrote to you or called upon you'.[51] The manager of a stock and station agency asked similarly for a card to enable five ladies, 'constituents of ours', to visit one of the ships.

Americans living in Australia sought to make contact with particular seamen or to play host to their fellow countrymen. Elizabeth Jenkins and Margaret Arnold, who ran the Kindergarten Training College in Sydney, asked for invitations to go aboard Rear Admiral Sperry's flagship, the *Connecticut*. 'I am wondering if it is too late for you to arrange the matter for us', Elizabeth Jenkins, the Principal, write to Bray. 'You may possibly remember Mrs Arnold's and my calling on you two weeks ago, and telling

[48] Miscellaneous correspondence received, 1907–08. John Bray, American Consul General Sydney, vols. 39–41, Records of Foreign Service Posts, State Department records RG 84, US National Archives.
[49] *Ibid.* Charles Tindall to Bray, 3 June 1908.
[50] *Ibid.* A. J. Sage and Co. to Bray, 24 August 1908.
[51] *Ibid.* Donald Fraser to Bray, 13 August 1908.

you something of our work here and of our respective homes in America – Chicago and New York'.[52] Lelia Seton Walker was more direct with the Consul: 'I want you to pick out two nice Southern officers, and give them an invitation from me to dinner Sunday August 30th at 7.30 at Menzies. My cousin and her husband will also be present. I have given you wide latitude, although I would prefer Alabamians . . . I will leave it, however, entirely to your good judgement, only don't have them too young – blond or brunette, married or single it matters not'.[53] Walker had also written to Prime Minister Deakin, who promised her she would be invited to 'some of the Federal entertainments'.[54]

Some local residents saw the arrival of the fleet as an opportunity to secure a passage to the United States. Joseph White wrote to John Bray about his disillusionment with the land of the so-called 'living wage'. White told the American Consul in uncertain English that he wanted 'to become a Amearcan Subject to Presedend Rule and leave King for ever. In this Country Poverty is a crime Low wageses is now the rule + a Labour Platform . . . Labor members only know what a living wage is When it applyes to themselves. I wont to volunteer as soldier. I am 40 years of age.'[55] Americans living in Australia also asked if they could enlist in the navy or work their way home.

Official welcoming committees in Sydney and Melbourne vied with each other in planning illuminations, receptions, sports performances, school children's enactments of the national flags – 'to display the children picturesquely and symbolically' – and myriad other events.[56] The American fleet Reception Committee co-ordinated months of planning in both states. The Victorian Racing Club organised a special race meeting at Flemington, which featured the Squadron Race, the Roosevelt Handicap, the Washington Steeplechase, the America Cup and the Stars and Stripes Handicap. An interstate football match was organised, tours in motor cars to scenic resorts and seats reserved in all city theatres. The Commercial Travellers' Association invited officers to dine at their club, the Mark Foy emporium issued invitations to the men to shop, and the School of Arts publicised the availability of American magazines and newspapers. The more discriminating Melbourne Club offered to entertain captains and admirals.[57]

Similar preparations were underway in Auckland, New Zealand, where a joint local–national committee organised an elaborate schedule of

[52] *Ibid.* Elizabeth Jenkins to Bray, 22 August 1908.
[53] *Ibid.* Lelia Seton Wilder to Bray, 16 August 1908.
[54] *Ibid.* Wilder to Bray, 16 August 1908.   [55] *Ibid.* White to Bray, 14 August 1908.
[56] See for example reports in the *Age*, 13, 22, 27, 28 May; 2, 8, 10, 12, 13, 18 June 1908.
[57] *Age*, 24 June 1908.

entertainments and ceremonies, including the first state banquet ever held in the city and a meeting with Maori chiefs at the opening of the Rotorua thermal baths and a welcome to their meeting house, billed by them as an opportunity to enlighten 'the Government party and American officers'.[58]

The United States fleet steamed into Auckland's Waitemata Harbour on 9 August. It was a quiet Sunday morning in this British outpost, but still 100,000 people – or 10 per cent of New Zealand's population – lined the shores to greet the sixteen battleships. 'At last there it lay, a long white emissary from a great and mighty nation', wrote one rapturous journalist. 'These vast and splendid instruments of war come forging on, each giant a seeming counterpart of each, silent and white and wonderful to behold. A pageant truly fit for gods to marvel at and give applause . . . Look, here they come! . . . We gaze enthralled full into the grand breadth of the noble Connecticut surging on . . . By heaven what a sight!'[59]

Journalists vied with each other in their powers of description, but they were also challenged to reflect on the historical significance of this expression of Anglo-Saxon solidarity:

scattered members of the Anglo-Saxon family welcome the coming of their big brother to these lonesome southern latitudes in which their new homes have been founded, for a yellow spectre has appeared to them, the suddenly uprisen ghost of a race long looked upon as internationally dead. America has seen it, too; so has Europe, and all have marvelled. But the spectre is looking in this direction, looking towards wastelands held in trust here for the posterity of Caucasians. And whatever this may mean, there is no gainsaying that the presence of the big brother, with the power mailed fist, brings a grateful sense of security to the white man in his antipodean isolation.[60]

The *Wellington Post* was more forthright: the United States as 'the champion of white ascendancy in the Pacific' represented 'the ideals of Australia and New Zealand far better than Britain'.[61] Or as another correspondent put it:

> Stars and Stripes, if you please,
> Protect us from the Japanese.[62]

Fifteen years before, Charles Pearson had rung alarm bells about the rise of 'the Black and Yellow races', but the Japanese annihilation of the Russian fleet in 1905 had shocked the world out of its complacency. Isolated in their southern latitudes, New Zealand and Australia cast themselves as nations under siege. Far from seeing Japan as their beneficent

---

[58] *Ibid.* 13 August 1908.   [59] Cited in *Age*, 10 August 1908.   [60] *Ibid.*
[61] Quoted in Reckner, 'The Great White Fleet'.   [62] *Ibid.*

204   Transnational solidarities

ally, as Britain proposed, Australasians saw the newly ascendant Empire as the chief danger to their continued existence.

The New Zealand Prime Minister, Sir Joseph Ward, welcomed the United States fleet, not as representatives of a foreign country, but as 'kith and kin of the Anglo-Saxon race'. One day a military struggle would take place to determine which power would control the Pacific. It was in the interests of Britain to dump the Japanese as allies and enter into an alliance with the United States. As a former British diplomat, Lancelot Lawton, observed in his book on *Empires of the Far East* four years later: 'The striking welcome accorded the American fleet was an unmistakeable indication that the Colonies have an overwhelming preference for the natural alliance that exists among all branches of the Anglo-Saxon race – an alliance recorded in a sentiment far deeper and far stronger than any that can be represented in written words; an alliance without the limitations of time or of the political expediency of the moment'.[63]

In Australia, the United States warships were represented not so much as 'big brother' to the rescue, but rather as an object lesson in the virtues of self-defence. This was the message Deakin wished to convey – to Australians and to the imperial government. As the sixteen battleships entered Sydney Harbour, reporters again competed with each other to capture the grandeur and historical significance of this event 'unmatched in history':

To the thousands of expectant watchers, whose eyes were strained across the rolling seas from the glimmering of dawn, the outlines of the American battleships appeared faintly though the morning haze like the towers and turrets and minarets of some majestic city . . . Sydney had obtained only forty winks or had not slept at all. Torrents of humanity were sweeping through the streets at daybreak, racing for the cliffs upon the outer harbour . . . Everything that went on wheels – trams, cabs, coaches, bicycles, motors – tore along, double weighted with human burdens . . . It was the sparkling harbour that formed the setting for the inspiring panorama of the day – a day whose glories, unmatched in the history of the Australian people, will live long in memory.[64]

The week of high carnival that followed was, to Deakin's mind at least, 'without precedent in the history of Australia'.[65] In his autobiography, Roosevelt wrote that 'the reception accorded the fleet in Australia was wonderful, and it showed the fundamental continuity of feeling between ourselves and the great commonwealth of the South Seas'.[66]

The visit of the American fleet to Australia was indeed a huge popular success, but it was also endowed with momentous geo-political significance. Newspapers around the country competed with each other

[63] Lawton, *Empires of the Far East*, p.374.   [64] *Age*, 21 August 1908.
[65] *Sydney Mail*, 26 August 1908.   [66] Roosevelt, *An Autobiography*, p.598.

in explaining its racial meaning.[67] 'Relations we are – blood relations – we and the Americans', observed the *Age* in Melbourne. 'We are more than cousins. We are brethren in thought, in speech, in aspiration'.[68] In Brisbane, the *Courier Mail* advised: 'The presence of the United States fleet gives the opportunity for the peaceful development of the interests of the white races in the Pacific', while in Adelaide, the *Register* was pleased to note: 'The remoteness of Australia from the Great Powers, the comparative fewness of her population, and the feeling that their nearest neighbours are the teeming millions of Asia . . . are the cogent reasons why any large body of progressive whites would be treated with delight'.[69]

There was also agreement between political parties on the importance of the event. Although a minority of socialist papers opposed the United States as a capitalist danger to Australia, members of the Labor party joined in the effusive greeting of these representatives of the white race. 'An epoch making-event has occurred', wrote a New South Wales politician, Arthur Griffith, 'which goes a long way to neutralise the effect of Tsu-Shima' (where the Russian fleet was destroyed by the Japanese):

A great Anglo-Saxon democracy, Britain's eldest-born daughter and the wealthiest and most advanced nation in the world, the United States of America has leapt full-armed into the gap, and by the transference of the Great White fleet from the Atlantic to the Pacific, has flung down the gauntlet to the Mongol and challenged the naval supremacy of Japan, and by its visit to Australia has given notice to the yellow races that they will have to stop in Asia.[70]

And in Sydney, the Prime Minister's greeting paid tribute to Americans' racial kinship. He bade the sailors thrice welcome: 'as guests . . . as the honoured representatives of a mighty nation [and as] blood relations'.[71]

An earlier version of his speech had expressed admiration for Roosevelt as a man and for his great presidential qualities, but this personal tribute was omitted in favour of more general praise of the officers and men. Admiral Sperry, knowing how to flatter his hosts, returned the compliment, greeting them at a press luncheon in Sydney as a 'white man to white men, and may I add, to very white men'.[72] On numerous occasions, in both Sydney and Melbourne, Deakin took the opportunity to speak of the two nations' 'mutual sense of kinship, sympathy and solidarity' and his desire for 'a perpetual concord of brotherhood'. And he was pleased to quote his personal copy of Josiah Royce's new book *The Philosophy of Loyalty* in support of these ideals.

[67] Megaw, 'Australia and the Great White Fleet'.   [68] *Age*, 17 August 1908.
[69] Megaw, 'Australia and the Great White Fleet', p.127.   [70] *Ibid.* p.129.
[71] Deakin papers, MS 1540/15/3906.   [72] *Age*, 27 August 1908.

When Royce learnt that his country's naval fleet was about to cross the Pacific to visit Australia, he decided to send his friend a copy of this, his most recent book, together with his own personal greeting. 'Our fleet is going to see you soon, as I hear next August', Royce wrote. 'I venture to send in advance of the fleet – vast and noisy as it is – my very tiny and silent book . . . a word of greeting about our common ideals. If you have time to look at it some day – for an hour or two – remember that its author loves you'. Now fifty-two years old, 'an oldish professor' who 'stoop[ed] a little, and carr[ied] too many books about', as Royce described himself, he took the opportunity to once again call up their special time together exactly twenty years ago:

Few memories stand out more clearly and encouragingly, and more pleasingly, in my life, than our meeting in 1888, our days together in the wonderland of your mountains, our talks, and your kindness, and the gracious cheer of all your hospitality. What a place the meeting and your presence and personality, have since occupied in my life, I can hardly tell you.[73]

The arrival of *The Philosophy of Loyalty* prompted Deakin to change the text of the message he was preparing for the American press.

In the first draft, Deakin spoke of the 'object lesson in naval power' afforded by the visit of the fleet and the 'true kinship' and 'fraternal sentiments' that drew Australia and the United States together. He also linked the visit with the issue of immigration restriction, which he justified, as had Roosevelt, by speaking of the difficulties posed to democratic institutions by racial difference:

Self-government with us is based everywhere on principles of equality, which demand that all our citizens shall possess a sufficient similarity in their instincts, dispositions & capacity to blend into one efficient nation.

And, like Roosevelt, Deakin combined his discourse on difference with a diplomatic call for polite dealings with all foreign peoples and mutual agreement: 'The highly intelligent Hindu is a subject of the same Empire, the energetic and patriotic Japanese are our allies, the Chinaman possesses all the potentialities which go to make them a great power in the East . . . The question is one for calm consideration & mutual agreement without giving or taking offence'. Peaceful respectful diplomacy could solve all difficult problems.[74]

When Royce's book arrived, however, Deakin dropped references to immigration from his speech and changed the theme of his message to 'E pluribus unum' – the American motto – In Many are One – as the

[73] Royce to Deakin, 18 April 1908, Deakin papers, 1540/1/1964.
[74] Deakin draft paper, Deakin papers, 1540/15/3898.

basis for a speech on the ideal of unity. There were parallels, he suggested, between the unifying forces of the American and Australian federations and a possible future imperial federation that would be a 'free union of free Dominions'. Referring to 'Prof. Royce of Harvard', Deakin spoke of the ideals of community and unity immanent in the ethic of loyalty. 'It then becomes of world wide application, pointing, through superb vistas of practical progress, towards the crowning heights of human achievement, where for many warring nations and diverse races of mankind attain at last an all embracing unity of a higher type.' Racial barriers would ultimately drop away, but in the meantime:

realising the riches of natural national relationships, we look, instinctively, first and most confidently, to you Americans, nearest to us in blood, in character, and in purpose. It is in this spirit, and in this hope, that Australia welcomes with open hand and heart the coming of your sailors, and of the flag, which, like our own, shelters a new world under the control of its vital union.
     May the present accord between English-speaking peoples beget a perpetual concord of brotherhood between us.[75]

The imperative of unity between white men, rather than discrimination against non-whites, thus became his theme. In this, Deakin departed, however, from the universalist ideals of Royce to follow the racialised vision of Roosevelt. In the 'perpetual concord of brotherhood', Deakin imagined a transnational fraternity of white men as an alternative, both to the hierarchical multi-racial Empire and the cosmopolitan unity of mankind.

Deakin's farewell speech to the American seamen similarly went through a number of drafts. The first version had referred to 'the friend-ship between the Empire and the Republic', but this was deleted in favour of a more exclusive fraternity between Australians and Americans, informed by the 'ardent hope of all our citizens . . . that their friendship, strengthened as it now is among us by many new personal ties, may long endure and flourish on both shores of the Pacific'.[76]

The great success of the visit of the United States fleet to Australia was followed by further provocations to the Colonial Office, when Deakin suggested that the British navy might also pay Australia a visit, and sent a second invitation to President Roosevelt to visit Australia the follow-ing year, on his retirement, in his private capacity as man and citizen. Deakin's high praise of Roosevelt, commending his leadership in dis-charging his responsibilities 'to the lasting benefit of your fellow citizens of the United States and of all self-governing people, especially this new

---

[75] Deakin final draft, Deakin papers, 1540/15/3912; *Age*, 24 August 1908.
[76] Deakin papers, 1540/15/3910; MS 1540/15/3911.

Commonwealth of Australia', further angered the Colonial Office.[77] It was really 'very unworthy' of the Australian government to attempt to play off the United States against the British government, remarked Lucas. The new Colonial Secretary, Lord Crewe, considered both invitations 'a sort of hint to England that Australia had another string to her bow'.[78] 'We must send [the invitation] on', he noted, 'but it is a most objectionable message, & I cannot help thinking meant to be unpalatable to us'.[79]

Not surprisingly, the British government declined to send the Royal Navy to Australia as requested ('Australia does not deserve a visit'), and Roosevelt declined the invitation to make a personal visit, preferring the manly pursuit of big game hunting in the newly popular, but most unlikely 'white man's country' of Kenya in East Africa.[80] Although Roosevelt was gratified by the warm welcome accorded the fleet in Australia, in his autobiographical account he gave special mention to the Japanese reception, marked as it was by exceptional courtesy. Ever the international diplomat, Roosevelt wrote:

The most noteworthy incident of the cruise was the reception given to our fleet in Japan. In courtesy and good breeding, the Japanese can certainly teach much to the nations of the Western world. I had been very sure that the people of Japan would understand aright what the cruise meant, and would accept the visit of our fleet as the signal honor which it was meant to be, a proof of the high regard and friendship I felt, and which I was certain the American people felt, for the great Island Empire. The event even surpassed my expectations. I cannot too strongly express my appreciation of the generous courtesy the Japanese showed the officers and crews of our fleet; and I may add that every man of them came back a friend and admirer of the Japanese.[81]

Roosevelt, nevertheless, adhered to his conviction that Japanese immigration to North America or Australasia was impossible because it raised 'a race question'. Like Prime Minister Deakin, he was convinced that the different races could never assimilate economically, socially or politically and, in private letters at the time, he reiterated his view that the Japanese as a nation must accept that they would never be permitted to settle in white men's countries.

[77] Deakin to Roosevelt, Deakin papers, 1540/15/3909; CO 418/61, UK National Archives.
[78] CO 418/61/130, UK National Archives.
[79] Lucas, note, 18 September 1908, CO 418/61, UK National Archives.
[80] On Roosevelt as great white hunter, see Iain McCalman, 'Teddy Roosevelt's Trophy: History and Nostalgia', in Lake, *Memory, Monuments and Museums*, pp.58–75; Gail Bederman, *Manliness and Whiteness* (Chicago, Chicago University Press, 1995); on Kenya as white man's country, see Dane Kennedy, *Islands of White: Settler Society and Culture in Kenya and Southern Rhodesia, 1890–1939* (Durham, Duke University Press, 1987).
[81] Roosevelt, *An Autobiography*, p.601.

'Our line of policy must be adopted, holding ever in view the fact that this is a race question', he wrote to William Kent in 1909, 'and that race questions stand by themselves. I did not see this clearly at the outset; but for nearly three years I have seen it, and thruout my treatment of the question has shaped my course accordingly'. But it was crucially important to Roosevelt, in terms of international relations, that the principles of mutuality and reciprocity should govern immigration policies. 'The one important point is that the Japanese should, as a race, be excluded from becoming permanent inhabitants of our territory, they in turn excluding us from becoming permanent inhabitants of their territory'.[82]

To prevent bitterness and resentment from taking hold, it was of the utmost importance, he believed, that the Japanese, a sensitive and proud people, be treated with scrupulous courtesy – as they treated others. Roosevelt was also adamant that dealing with foreign nationals was the responsibility of national governments and their diplomatic representatives, not state governments or crazed local agitators, but arguably it was his administration's very responsiveness to west coast agitators that had led to new curbs on immigration and state discriminations in employment and land ownership, aimed at keeping the Pacific Slope a white man's country for all time.

[82] Roosevelt to William Kent, 4 February 1909, in Morison, *The Letters of Theodore Roosevelt* vol.6, p.1503.

9   The Union of South Africa: white men reconcile

The Treaty

It was exactly eight years between the signing of the Treaty of Vereeniging on 31 May 1902, bringing the Boer War to an end, and the inauguration of the Union of South Africa on 31 May 1910. In that time Boer and Briton were reconciled. The Transvaal and the Orange Free State became self-governing British colonies. White power was consolidated at the expense of African, coloured and Indian communities and all the necessary pre-conditions were established for the creation of apartheid. The reconciliation of Boer and Briton and the alienation of the non-European majority were politically linked. As the liberal Cape politician J. X. Merriman observed, the imperial authorities and colonial politicians had managed, quite consciously, 'to reconcile the whites over the body of the blacks'.[1]

'Sacrifice the nigger'

This outcome was not what many expected while the war was being fought. The British government had, after all, been highly critical of the racial policies of the Boer republics, defended a colour-blind franchise in the Cape and had sought to protect the Indian minority from discriminatory legislation. Lord Lansdowne, a leading member of the war-time government in the House of Lords, declared in 1899 that among the many misdeeds of the Transvaal, he did not know that any filled him 'with more indignation' than its treatment of the Indians.[2] Those of progressive opinion expected that the franchise and the legal traditions of the Cape would be applied to the whole of South Africa.

---

[1] Quoted in Nicholas Mansergh, *South Africa, 1906–1961: The Price of Magnanimity* (London, George, Allen & Unwin, 1962) p.69.

[2] Quotted in G. B. Pyrah, *Imperial Policy and South Africa, 1902–10* (Oxford, Clarendon Press, 1955) p.97; see also L. E. Neame, *The Asiatic Danger in the Colonies* (London, Routledge and Sons, 1907) p.59.

Joseph Chamberlain, the Secretary of State for the Colonies, declared that the imperial government could not

consent to purchase peace by leaving the coloured population in the position in which they stood before the war, with not even the ordinary civil rights which the Government of the Cape Colony has long conceded to them.[3]

In South Africa, Cecil Rhodes defined British war aims in terms of maintaining 'Her Majesty's flag in this country' and promoting 'equal rights for all civilized men south of the Zambezi'. Rhodes used the term 'civilized' to cover those non-Europeans who were qualified through education and property ownership to vote in elections at the Cape.[4]

J. A. Hobson, the radical economist, observed in 1900 that many people were genuinely persuaded that 'one motive' which justified and purified the war was that it would 'afford protection and benefit to the native races'.[5] Having spent several months in South Africa, Hobson was doubtful if the imperial authorities could deliver improved conditions for non-whites, despite the power and authority of those promoting them. 'Let no-one deceive himself', he declared. There was a strong and deep-rooted 'sentiment of inequality' in South Africa, which could not be over-ridden by imperial edict. In fact, any attempt to secure equality of rights in South Africa would involve the colonial office 'in hostility with British and Dutch alike'. The two parties, he predicted, would eventually coalesce in opposition to any developments that threatened their continued racial supremacy.[6]

Alfred Milner, the key imperial official in South Africa from 1897 to 1905, had appreciated this problem from early in his sojourn. Writing to his friend, the leading liberal politician Herbert Asquith, in 1897, he confessed: 'I feel that if I fail out here, it will be over the native question. Nothing else is of the same seriousness'. But he knew he did not have a free hand. If he gave too much emphasis to protecting and promoting the rights of Africans and Indians he would unite Dutch and English colonial opinion against him. 'You have only to sacrifice the nigger "absolutely",' he told Asquith, 'and the game is easy ... There is the whole crux of the South African position.'[7]

[3] Pyrah, *Imperial Policy*, p.91.
[4] Quoted by J. Tudhope, 'The Settlement in South Africa', *The Empire Review* No.1 (1901) p.31; see also David Philips, 'Towards "a White Man's Union"', in John Chesterman and David Philips (eds.) *Selective Democracy: Race, Gender and the Australian Vote* (Melbourne, Circa, 2003) p.40.
[5] J. A. Hobson, *The War in South Africa: Its Causes and Effects* (London, Nisbet, 1900, second edition) p.281.
[6] *Ibid.* p.291.
[7] Milner to Asquith, 18 November 1897, in Cecil Headlam (ed.) *The Milner Papers: South Africa, 1899–1905* (London, Cassell, 1933) pp.178–9; see also Philips, 'Towards "a White Man's Union"' p.40.

In 1901, in the middle of the war, Milner wrote to Chamberlain warning him against 'the fatal doctrine' that the imperial Government could 'deal with the native question regardless of colonial sentiment'.[8] The war was dragging on; the Boers were proving determined fighters; British tactics of scorched earth and concentration camps were becoming an acute embarrassment and Milner was keen to secure peace. The sticking point in the negotiations between Boer and Briton was the question of the franchise in the future self-governing colonies: would the political traditions of the Cape or the Transvaal prevail?

The first serious attempt to negotiate a peace settlement followed the Middleburg Proposals of March 1901. The British military commander, Lord Kitchener, offered to his opposite number, General Louis Botha, an enticement that:

As regards the extension of the franchise to the Kaffirs in the Transvaal and Orange River Colony, it is not the intention of HMG to give such franchise before representative government is granted to those Colonies; and if then given it will be so limited as to secure the just predominance of the white race. The legal position of coloured persons, will, however, be similar to that which they hold in the Cape Colony.[9]

When peace negotiations resumed in May 1902 the key figures – Milner and Kitchener on one side, Botha and Jan Smuts on the other – returned to the question of the franchise. Milner began with the assumption that coloured persons would be able to vote in future elections although this would not happen until after the projected introduction of self-government. But in negotiations the wording was changed in critically important ways. Milner's original text seemed to 'prejudge the decision in the Native's favour': 'The Franchise will not be given to Natives until after the Introduction of Self-Government'. As W. K. Hancock observed, the clear implication was that it would be given to them.[10] Smuts rewrote the proposal to read: 'The question of granting the Franchise to Natives will not be decided until after the introduction of self-government'.[11]

This agreed wording, which left it open as to whether the Africans would ever be given voting rights, formed article eight of the Treaty of Vereeniging. The meaning was clear. The existing all-white electorates in the Boer republics would decide the future franchise. In his book *The*

---

[8] Headlam, *The Milner Papers*, p.311.
[9] J. D. Kestell, *Peace Negotiations Between the Governments of the South African Republic and Orange Free State* (London, Richard Clay, 1912) p.212.
[10] W. K. Hancock, *Smuts, Vol.1, The Sanguine Years 1870–1919* (Cambridge, Cambridge University Press, 1962) p.159.
[11] *Ibid.*

Unification of South Africa, 1902–1910, L. M. Thompson observed that Britain undertook not to admit any Africans or Indians to the franchise in the Transvaal and the Orange River Colony, when the government had the power to do so. Milner had persuaded Chamberlain to change his original intentions 'to the detriment of the non-Europeans', with whom Britain had no quarrel, to make the treaty more palatable to the Boers, with whom it had been waging war.[12]

The young general

Charismatic, confident and good-looking in a Teutonic kind of way, Jan Smuts was 32 years old at the time of his decisive intervention in the framing of the Treaty. He came from an old Cape farming family and could trace his South African ancestors back through seven generations to 1692. His biographer, W. K. Hancock, observed that throughout his life he was proud to 'call himself a Boer'.[13] He was educated at Stellenbosch College and Cambridge University, where a brilliant career was capped with a brace of prizes and a double first.

Smuts returned to South Africa in 1895 and became disillusioned with Cecil Rhodes and his involvement in the Jameson Raid. He moved to the Transvaal where, at 28, he became the State Attorney of the Republic and a key adviser to President Kruger. In the latter stages of the war he led his commando of 340 men south into the Cape Colony, where he campaigned with great skill and endurance until the eve of the peace talks. Despite the brutality and bitterness of the war, Smuts was predisposed to reconciliation with the British.

After returning from Cambridge, he had written of the need to fuse or consolidate the 'two Teutonic peoples', who had taken up their position at the southern corner of a vast continent 'peopled by over 100,000,000 barbarians'. Unless the white race closed its ranks, its position would soon become untenable.[14] In January 1902, reflecting on the 'native question', he wrote that:

the war between the white races will run its course and pass away and may, if followed by a statesmanlike settlement, one day only be remembered as a great thunderstorm, which purified the atmosphere of the subcontinent. But the native question will never pass away; it will become more difficult as time goes on, and the day may come when the evils and horrors of this war will appear as nothing in comparison with its after effects produced on the native mind.[15]

[12] L. M. Thompson, *The Unification of South Africa, 1902–1910* (Oxford, Clarendon Press, 1960) p.12.

[13] Hancock, *Smuts, The Sanguine Years*, p.3.   [14] *Ibid.* p.55.   [15] *Ibid.* pp.148–9.

That day might come, but equality between black and white was unthinkable.

Insulting Asiatics as Asiatics

In the Treaty of Vereeniging, Milner secured the things that mattered most to him. Peace and reconciliation had a far higher priority than enfranchising a small minority of non-Europeans, as desirable as that goal might have been. In the event, the question mattered less to the British government than it did to the Boers, who made it clear that both the peace of 1902 and the unification of 1910 were dependent on maintaining their traditional democratic, all-white franchise.

Milner, nevertheless, persisted with his argument that white dominance could just as easily be secured through an education and property franchise of the kind which had been introduced in the Cape, following the Mississippi example, in 1892. Like many liberals, in Britain and South Africa, he repeatedly argued that political rights should depend on 'civilization' rather than 'colour'. Indeed, he thought outspoken colour prejudice somewhat vulgar and ungentlemanly. In an address to municipal officials in Johannesburg in 1903, he initially engaged his audience by ritually denouncing British humanitarian pressure groups and other 'sentimentalists', but then asked what was the point of perpetually shouting that South Africa was 'a white man's country' when the blacks outnumbered the whites by five to one. If any meaning could be applied to the slogan, it was that the 'white man should rule' and if that were their argument then he, Milner, agreed with them. But the right to rule, he insisted, should not be argued on the basis of race, but on the 'firm and inexpungable ground of civilization as against the rotten and indefensible ground of colour'. If civilisation were the key to full citizenship, then natives could aspire to that goal, even if their advancement might be very slow.

Milner found prejudice directed towards Indians harder to accept than that levelled at Africans. 'Is it justifiable', he asked his Johannesburg audience, 'to denounce Indians as Asiatics' and to assert that all of them 'whatever their degree of civilization, must be unwelcome here, or, if they come here, should be treated as pariahs?'[16] And he warned his audience, echoing Charles Pearson's prophecy of ten years earlier: 'The time may come when this Colony and South Africa generally may wish to enter into relations, commercial or otherwise, with the rulers of great Asiatic states – with British rulers in India, for instance, or with the native rulers

[16] Headlam, *The Milner Papers*, pp.468–70.

of the great Empire of Japan and it was thus inadvisable to insult "Asiatics as Asiatics"'.[17]

But the politics of 'whiteness' as the basis of identity had a relentless binary logic, dividing the world into white and not-white. In 1904, Arthur Lawley, Lieutenant Governor of the Transvaal, wrote a long dispatch to Milner explaining that colonists made no distinction between African, coloured or Indian. There was not 'one man in a hundred', he said, who would agree to recognise the coloured man 'as capable of admission to the same social standard as the white'. Lawley did not himself think these sentiments reasonable, but pointed out:

They imbue the mind of every South African, and find expression in the universal cry of 'a white man's country'. The result of any attempt to ignore them would be attended, I feel sure, with most deplorable results.[18]

In May 1904, Milner wrote of his own progressive, but pragmatic, views of race:

I think that to attempt to place coloured people on an equality with white in South Africa is wholly impracticable, and that, moreover, it is in principle wrong. But I also hold that when a coloured man possesses a certain high grade of civilization he ought to obtain what I call 'white privileges' irrespective of his colour.[19]

On the eve of his departure from South Africa, in 1905, Milner realised that whites were growing more militant in their beliefs and in retrospect considered his concession to the Boer negotiators over article eight of the Treaty of Vereeniging had been a tragic mistake. Writing to his successor, he confessed:

If I had known as well as I know now the extravagance on the part of almost all the whites – not the Boers only – against any concession to any coloured man, however civilized, I should never have agreed to so absolute an exclusion, not only of the raw native, but of the whole coloured population, from any rights of citizenship, even in municipal affairs.[20]

But as one of the great imperial enthusiasts, Milner felt obliged to try to reconcile liberal opinion in Britain with the race thinking of the white-settler democracies and in particular to explain their views about immigration.

White colonists, Milner told his English audience on his return, were threatened with a danger of which people of the British Isles had no experience. No one who had lived in the colonies could fail to appreciate the causes of their anxiety, even though they often reacted in so extreme

---

[17] Cited by Neame, *The Asiatic Danger*, p.151.   [18] *Ibid.* p.141.   [19] *Ibid.* p.103.
[20] Alfred Milner, *The Nation and the Empire: a Collection of Speeches and Addresses* (London, Constable, 1913) pp.296–7.

and unreasonable a manner. Indeed, if it were not so serious an issue, one would be tempted

> to smile at the crude ignorance which makes so many of them confound all men of coloured races from the highest class and cultured Asiatic gentleman or noble, to the humblest coolie, in the common category of 'niggers'.[21]

Milner had hoped to secure for 'Asiatics of a superior class a special status' and to treat them 'virtually like Europeans, to avoid, at any rate, the appearance of race legislation'.[22] But confronted with rampant hostility to any concessions, he had given way, agreeing with Lawley, his Lieutenant Governor, that any attempt to place the Indians on a footing of equality with white men would 'be disastrous'. Imperial commitments to impartial justice and equal rights could not be implemented in South Africa, Lawley had said, because in the long term the country might fall to 'the inheritance of the Eastern instead of Western populations'. With that possibility in mind, some imperial promises must be numbered among those 'which it is a greater crime to keep rather than to break'.[23]

The birth of *Satyagraha*

These were the attitudes that Gandhi confronted when he arrived back in South Africa, on his third visit, in December 1902. His supporters had asked him to lead a delegation to meet Joseph Chamberlain, who was then touring post-war South Africa.[24] When presented with a catalogue of complaints, the Colonial Secretary replied that he could do little about laws passed by a self-governing colony. He suggested the Indians should 'try to conciliate public opinion and work with the authorities in the Transvaal'.[25] It was Gandhi's assessment that Chamberlain shared the fear of the colonists that South Africa would be swamped by Indians unless firm measures were taken.

In his address to Chamberlain, Gandhi outlined the legal disabilities suffered by Indians that included being required to have their names entered into a separate register within eight days of their arrival in South Africa; being denied the right to own property except in certain locations; being restricted to the locations for residence and trade; and being confined to their homes after 9pm. Indians could not take out gold

---

[21] Neame, *The Asiatic Danger*, p.102.   [22] *Ibid.*   [23] Quoted in *Ibid.* p.61.
[24] A Short Statement on the Indian Question, 23 February 1903; M. K. Gandhi, *Collected Works*, vol.III, p.281.
[25] Gandhi to D. Naoroji, 30 January 1903, *Ibid.* p.278.

diggers' licenses; could not travel on trains except in third class; were not permitted to drive hired vehicles in Pretoria or Johannesburg; and were not allowed to walk on the footpaths in those cities.[26]

Not only did discriminatory legislation remain in place after the war, but it was being enforced more harshly by a new department, the Asia Office, headed by one of Milner's young, hand-picked assistants, Lionel Curtis, who had a larger agenda than merely applying existing law. When making his farewell speech in Johannesburg in October 1906, Curtis explained that his Office was crucially important for the future of the country, because its activities would 'keep the Transvaal a white man's country' and thus save it from the fate which had overtaken places like Mauritius and Jamaica.[27] Curtis foreshadowed the policy of racial segregation, looking forward in 1906 to the 'gradual separation of the whites and blacks into their respective territories', with the consequence that the African would be forced to 'fix his home in native territory' or find himself an 'uitlander' when he went outside it.[28]

In 1906, there was new cause for outrage on the part of Asians in the Transvaal. The Asiatic Law Amendment Ordinance, the so-called Black Act, required all 'Asiatics' to be registered, photographed and finger printed, thus imposing, according to Gandhi, 'studied humiliation' not only on Indians in South Africa, but on India itself.[29] At a public meeting in September, Gandhi declared:

This is a very serious crisis. If the Ordinance were passed and if we acquiesced in it, it would be imitated all over South Africa. As it seems to me, it is designed to strike at the very root of our existence in South Africa. It is not the last step, but the first step with a view to hound us out of the country. We are therefore responsible for the safety, not only of the ten or fifteen thousand Indians in the Transvaal, but of the entire Indian community in South Africa. Again, if we fully understand all the implications of this legislation, we shall find that India's honour is in our keeping. For the Ordinance seeks to humiliate not only ourselves, but also the motherland.[30]

For Gandhi, the time had come for Indians to defy the 'intolerable and wicked law' and 'suffer imprisonment'.[31] If the government decided to gaol those who refused to register he would be the first to court

---

[26] Address to Mr. Chamberlain, 7 January 1903, *Ibid.* p.271.
[27] Lionel Curtis, *With Milner in South Africa* (Oxford, Blackwell, 1951) p.348.
[28] Paul B. Rich, *Race and Empire in British Politics* (Cambridge, Cambridge University Press, 1986) p.57.
[29] Gandhi, *Collected Works*, vol.V, p.417.   [30] *Ibid.* p.418.
[31] M. K. Gandhi, *Satyagraha in South Africa* (Acmedabad, Navajivan Publishing, [1928] 1968) p.150.

imprisonment. The decision to embark on a campaign of civil disobedience was taken at a public meeting on 11 September, in the Empire Theatre, where hundreds took an oath to refuse to register, thereby inviting arrest, trial and incarceration.

In his memoir of 1928, *Satyagraha in South Africa*, Gandhi recalled that at first no one knew what name to give to the new movement. Believing that 'some new principle had come into being', they called for an Indian name in place of the English term 'passive resistance', because it appeared 'shameful to permit this great struggle to be known only by an English name'.[32] A competition was held and out of it *Satyagraha* emerged, joining two words meaning love and firmness or force. The resistance struggle intensified with the grant of responsible government to the Transvaal in 1906.

An Asiatic alliance?

The smaller Chinese community in the Transvaal was equally outraged by the legal discrimination against Asiatics and was directly involved in the passive resistance movement between 1906 and 1911.[33] It represented an unprecedented period of co-operation between the Chinese and Indians in South Africa. The Chinese joined all of the political activities, holding large public meetings, refusing to register with the authorities, picketing and lobbying for support, and they went to gaol with their Indian colleagues. Gandhi and the Chinese leader, Leung Quinn, were imprisoned together, along with 2,500 of their fellow activists.

Both communities appealed to an international audience. The Chinese sent a delegate to London to address the Colonial Office, they urged the Chinese Embassy to take up their cause and rallied the Chinese Student Association in Europe to speak out against the Transvaal authorities. The two communities based their appeals on different grounds, the Indians demanding their rights as British subjects, the Chinese calling on Britain to honour its treaty obligations and for recognition of the equality of nations under international law. Each community thought they had the stronger case for just treatment. Thus the Chairman of the Chinese Association of the Transvaal complained to the Chinese Minister in London about the new legislation:

[32] Joseph. J. Doke, *M. K. Gandhi: An Indian Patriot in South Africa* (Delhi, Ministry of Information, [1909] 1967) pp.100–2.
[33] K. L. Harris, 'Gandhi, the Chinese and Passive Resistance', in Judith M. Brown and Martin Prozesky, *Gandhi and South Africa: Principles and Politics* (New York, St. Martin's Press, 1996) pp.69–94.

It places Chinese subjects on the same level as British subjects coming from India. While it may be proper for the British Government to treat its Indian subjects as it pleases, your petitioner respectfully submits that subjects of the Chinese Empire should not be treated in a manner derogatory to the dignity of the Empire to which your Excellency's petitioner has the honour to belong, especially in view of the fact that China is a State in alliance with Great Britain, and that the subjects of Great Britain receive the most favoured nation treatment in China.[34]

Gandhi was also mindful of the difference in their position, admitting that he had always sought to draw a distinction between British subjects and foreigners. Indeed in a deputation to Lord Elgin, in 1906, Gandhi went out of his way to state that:

We have no connexion with anybody else, and we have always endeavoured to show that British Indians ought to be treated as British subjects, and ought not to be included with the general body of Asiatics with respect to whom there may be a need for some restrictions which ought not to apply to British Indians as British subjects.[35]

Ironically, however, by classifying all Asiatics as one group, the British and Transvaal governments inadvertently encouraged their political alliance and solidarity.[36] Or as 'Viator' would put it in his article 'Asia Contra Mundum' in *Fortnightly Review* in 1908, an 'identity of interests' between Asian nations on the migration question tended to create 'a solidarity of policy'.[37]

The mutual support of white men

The introduction of large numbers of contracted Chinese labourers to work in the Transvaal goldmines from 1904 also worked to strengthen the solidarity of white men around the world. There was an outcry among political leaders and much international comment about the 'Asiatic Invasion of the Transvaal'.[38] The Australian Prime Minister, Alfred Deakin,

---

[34] Charles Lucas, 'Suggestions as to Coloured Immigration into the Self-Governing Domions', no.2, CO 886/1/2, National Archives, UK, pp.50–1.
[35] Report of deputation, in Neame, *The Asiatic Danger*, p.170.
[36] Gandhi, *Collected Works*, vol.VII, p.111.
[37] Viator, 'Asia Contra Mundum', *Fortnightly Review* (February 1908) p.189.
[38] See, for example, articles in *Fortnightly Review*: Frank Hales, 'The Transvaal Labour Difficulties' (July 1904); J. Saxon Mills, 'Chinese Labour and the Government' (April 1906); M. A. Stobart, 'The Asiatic Invasion of the Transvaal' (February 1907). See also, Herbert Samuel, 'The Chinese Labour Question', *Contemporary Review* (April 1904); William Maitland, 'The Chinaman in California and South Africa: A Comparison', *Contemporary Review* (December 1905); W. Wybergh, 'Imperial Organisation and the Colour Question 1 & 2', *Contemporary Review* (May and June 1907); Anon., 'Empire and Race', *Saturday Review* (May 1904); Anon., 'The South African Situation', *Saturday*

agreed to join the New Zealand Prime Minister, Richard Seddon, in an official protest.[39] The Cape Colony and Newfoundland passed special Chinese Exclusion Acts. Even though the Chinese labourers were brought in under contract on the explicit understanding that they would be returned to their countries of origin on the completion of their terms, the response on the part of white men's countries – and in Britain where the issue helped the Liberal Party to victory in the election of 1906 – was passionate in condemnation. 'Where the Asiatic gains a foothold among a sparse European population', wrote W. Wybergh in a characteristic assessment in *Contemporary Review*, 'experience shows that sooner or later the white man is driven out'.[40]

In the Colonial Office, Charles Lucas also worried about the consequences of this growing transnational conflict for imperial unity. In his paper entitled 'The Self-Governing Dominions and Coloured Immigration', Lucas noted that the introduction of Chinese labour in the Transvaal undoubtedly served to strengthen 'the bias against coloured immigration in the self-governing Dominions'.[41] In Johannesburgh, L. E. Neame responded to the new level of feeling that attended the issue of Asian immigration, both in South Africa and on the Pacific Slope, by writing his book *The Asiatic Danger in the Colonies* (dedicated to the 'Old Folks at Home') to explain colonial feeling to British opinion and urge the imperial government to 'support the Colonies in the ideal of White Man's Country'.[42] A key issue in the debate, he pointed out, was the sovereign right of self-governing colonies to say who could and who could not enter their country. Australians had established this right in the nineteenth century, and although its policy had probably retarded economic development, at least 'Australia deserves praise', wrote Neame, 'for having acted up to the ideal of a White Man's Country'.[43]

The protest against the employment of Chinese labour in the Rand goldmines was spearheaded by labour unions often led by Australian or British officials. As Jonathon Hyslop has argued, the white imperial working class of this period was 'bound together by flows of population

Review (July 1906); Anon., 'Can South Africa Be Saved?', *Saturday Review* (August 1906).

[39] Jonathon Hyslop, 'The Imperial Working Class Makes Itself White', *Journal of Historical Sociology* vol.12, no.4, pp.404–8.

[40] W. Wybergh, 'Imperial Organisation and the Colour Question', *Contemporary Review* (June 1907) p.810.

[41] Charles Lucas, 'The Self-Governing Dominions and Coloured Immigration', CO 886/1/1, p.47.

[42] Neame, *The Asiatic Danger*, p.105.   [43] *Ibid.* p.80.

which traversed the world' as well as an ideology of 'white labourism' that fused a critique of exploitation with racial exclusion to defend their privileged access to the labour market.[44]

Thousands of Australian workers arrived in Transvaal both before and after the Boer war. By 1904 there were over 5,000 Australians in the area of Johannesburg, many of whom were miners and artisans, some of whom played a crucial role in the organisation of white trade unions. Peter Whiteside, the Ballarat-born President of the Witwatersrand Trades and Labour Council, took a lead in opposing the importation of Chinese labour and in subsequently campaigning for the deportation of Chinese miners. An Australian, J. Forrester Brown, was a leading figure in the mine workers' union. The Cornish-born Tom Matthews, the General Secretary of the Miners' Union, who had a background in trade union organising on the west coast of the United States, urged that they must fight for the expulsion of coloured labour, 'just as the Australians ousted the Chinamen and the Kanakas'.[45] The South African Labour Party, which emerged to represent white workers in the first national elections, was led by the Australian, F. H. P. Creswell.

Transnational gestures of racial solidarity were also forthcoming following the Zulu uprising in the 'Bambatha Rebellion' of 1906 in Natal.[46] When the warriors implicated in the murders of a trooper and an inspector were tried by Court Martial and sentenced to death, Colonial Secretary Lord Elgin intervened, ordering a postponement of the executions. When the Premier, G. M. Sutton, resigned in protest against Elgin's interference with the operation of responsible government, he was supported in the resulting constitutional crisis not only by his white fellow countrymen, but by white leaders from around the Empire. In Australia, Prime Minister Deakin sent off a cable to the Colonial Office, protesting against imperial interference with the administration of 'a self-governing colony' and the precedent it set. Later that day it was reported that Elgin had backed down.

Deakin wrote to Premier Sutton, advising him of the Australian initiative in support of his government, because the fact that a cable was sent had been 'withheld from the public'.

[44] Hyslop, 'The Imperial Working Class'; see also Elaine N. Katz, *A Trade Union Aristocracy: A History of White Workers in the Transvaal and the General Strike of 1913* (Johannesburg, African Studies Institue, 1976).

[45] Hyslop, 'The Imperial Working Class', p.409; H. J. and R. E. Simons, *Class and Colour in South Africa, 1850–1950* (Harmondsworth, Penguin, 1969) p.95.

[46] Shula Marks, *Reluctant Rebellion: the 1906–08 Disturbances in Natal* (Oxford, Clarendon Press, 1970).

It has, however, occurred to me that you were entitled to know that you had our practical support and that, unhesitatingly, when it appeared as if aid was necessary. I informed New Zealand and Canada on the step we had taken, but Mr Seddon hesitated until it was known that the British government had receded and Canada had not replied. If the attempt to interfere with your constitutional powers had been persisted in I have no doubt that we should all have been in accord with your protest .[47]

The Australian Prime Minister congratulated Sutton on the 'firmness' with which he faced the crisis and the 'victory' secured. The new Premier, Charles J. Smythe, thanked Deakin for his support, and expressed his hope that 'the people in Downing Street will recognize that Colonies enjoying Responsible Government must be allowed to manage their own affairs'. He added that telegrams subsequently received from the Secretary of State indicated that 'quite a good feeling exists between the Colonial Office authorities and the Natal Government'.[48] Such good feeling was no doubt re-assuring, because the uprising continued, with thousands of rebels joining the insurrection until the situation was reported as critical. Sir Henry Macallum, the governor of Natal added to anxieties by reporting that he had received 'evidence of widespread conspiracy to kill all Europeans in South Africa'.[49] The prospect of native uprisings continued to unnerve the white population, who felt increasingly under siege.

Creating a white man's union

In the Transvaal elections of 1907, the Boer party, *Het Volk*, was returned, with generals Louis Botha taking office as Premier and Jan Smuts as Colonial Secretary. The Asian Registration Act, which had been disallowed by the imperial government, was quickly passed through the new parliament, secure in its new status as a responsible government. The Transvaal parliament also passed an Immigration Restriction Act, which made it clear that the authorities would henceforth totally prohibit the entry of all Asians. Smuts explained to his supporters that the first Act would register Asiatics already in the Transvaal, while the second would 'close the door finally on the others'.[50] As in other white men's countries, a literacy test in a European language was employed to bar the immigration of non-whites, but there were added means of restriction. The legislation, Smuts proudly announced, was the most drastic anti-Asiatic

[47] Alfred Deakin to Sir G. M. Sutton, 4 April 1906, Deakin papers, 1540/15/2178, NLA.
[48] Smythe to Deakin, 8 May 1906, Deakin papers, 1540/15/2181, NLA.
[49] Statement of events in Natal, Deakin papers, 1540/15/2182, NLA.
[50] Cited by Gandhi, *Collected Works*, vol.VIII, p.505.

law that had 'ever been passed in the British Empire'. He reminded his listeners that they belonged to a 'largely black Empire' which was a fact they could not afford to forget. Gandhi had 'referred to Indians being in partnership with the white population of this country'. 'It is a claim,' Smuts thundered, 'which this white population will never allow', a declaration greeted with sustained cheers.[51]

By that time preparations were under way for the creation of the new Union of South Africa, with meetings of a National Constitutional Convention and the drafting of a constitution in preparation for its passage through the imperial parliament. The future national franchise was one of the most contentious questions for the Convention to resolve, with delegates from the Cape urging the national adoption of their colour-blind education and property franchise, while the other three colonies demanded an all-white electorate. By 1909, of a total Cape electorate of 142,000 men, 10 per cent were coloured and nearly 5 per cent African. In the whole of South Africa, whites made up just 21 per cent of the population, while Africans comprised about 70 per cent.[52]

The Boer leader, General C. R. de Wet, told the Convention that providence had 'drawn a line between black and white'. It was essential to make that clear to the natives and 'not instil into their minds false ideas of equality'.[53] In the end, the *status quo* was accepted with the proviso that the national government could not alter the existing colonial arrangements without a two-thirds majority of the Union Parliament. In return for what seemed to be protection for their education and property franchise, Cape leaders accepted that only whites could ever stand for election to the national parliament.

The main principles at issue in the National Convention received their most articulate expression in the correspondence between the leading political figures – Smuts from the Transvaal and J. X. Merriman, the Liberal politician from the Cape. When considering the white electorate, Smuts was the radical democrat advocating full manhood suffrage. Merriman, who described himself as a Whig, appealed to the aristocratic principle of a property franchise, which allowed coloureds, Indians and Africans to vote if they were so qualified. Merriman criticised Smuts' proposals because, like the American Declaration of Independence, they ignored that portion of the country that was coloured.

Merriman nevertheless affirmed that he was not a 'negrophilist' and in fact did not 'like the natives at all'. He wished that there were no black men in South Africa, but there were and the only question was 'how to

---

[51] *Ibid.* p.509.   [52] Philips, 'Towards "a White Man's Union"', pp.39, 42.
[53] E. H. Walton, *The Inner History of the National Convention of South Africa (1912)* (Westport, Connecticut, Negro University Press, 1970) p.138.

shape our course so as to maintain the supremacy of our race, and at the same time do our duty'. Merriman admitted that the Cape policy had its dangers, although he thought it unlikely that the Natives would ever 'swamp the white man'. But the consequences of total disenfranchisement would be worse. 'Does such a state of affairs', he asked,

offer any prospect of permanence? Is it not rather building on a volcano, the suppressed force of which must some day burst forth in a destroying flood, as history warns us it has always done. Our policy you may say is unpleasant, it is derogatory to the pride of the European . . . But it is a safety valve and though it makes some noise and a nasty smell it is the most reasonable guarantee against an explosion.[54]

Smuts was unmoved. While he agreed that all parties should do justice to the natives and take measures to ensure their improvement, they should not be allowed the power of enfranchisement. He did not believe 'in politics for them'.[55]

Africans as true citizens of Empire

Africans had already made it clear through the South African Native Congress that they did expect to play a political role in the new nation. In 1903, the Executive had issued an address to Joseph Chamberlain: 'Questions Affecting the Natives and Coloured People Resident in South Africa'.[56] Like the Indians, the Africans had expected that the British victory in the war would improve their situation. 'We were of the opinion', the statement declared, 'that conditions had undergone a change' and that the Africans would now be received with confidence 'within the political family as true citizens of the Empire' and share with their white brethren the coming prosperity.[57]

The Bantu leaders observed that their communities were 'naturally imperialistic' in their sympathies, owing to the 'high sense of fairness, justice and humanity' displayed by British governors and by the 'untiring zeal and humanitarian sentiment' of English missionaries and organisations such as the Aborigines Protection Society. They were certain that the connection with Britain was the best avenue for receiving justice and that the time was not yet ripe for Britain to divest itself of 'her obligations of Empire'. But they were apprehensive, because talk of

[54] Merriman to Smuts, 4 March 1906, *Selections from the Smuts Papers*, vol.2, pp.239–40.
[55] Hancock, *Smuts: The Sanguine Years*, pp.220–1.
[56] Thomas Karis and Gwendolen M. Carter (eds.) *From Protest to Challenge: A Documentary History of Afrian Politics in South Africa, 1882–1964* vol.1 (Stanford, Hoover Institution Press, 1972), p.40.
[57] *Ibid.* p.41.

reconciliation between Boer and Briton was pervaded with 'antagonism to the Natives'.[58]

In 1906, the South African Native Congress stressed that any conception of unity which was 'founded on the political extinction of the Native element' would be both unwise and unstatesmanlike.[59] Speakers pointed to the example of the United States, where disenfranchisement in the South after 1890 had been accompanied by an increase in lynchings and other forms of racial violence. President Roosevelt himself had said that it was essential that coloured men's aspirations not be frustrated; that they not be 'cut off from all hope of reward'. How the British government would reconcile commitment to South Africa as 'white man's country' with its 'solemn pledges of protection to the weaker races' was the cardinal question for the Africans.[60] If the South African government followed the 'pernicious and retrogressive lines' laid down by Natal and the Transvaal, it would be preferable to be 'taken over by the Crown and be governed from Downing Street'.[61] As the imperial factor was the only moderating influence between the races 'so sharply divided' as they were in South Africa, the refusal of Britain to maintain the power of veto over the colonies was viewed with 'extreme gravity'. In a petition to the King, the Orange River Native Congress called on Britain to retain the administration of native affairs under its direct control until African enfranchisement was accomplished.[62]

A South African Native Convention, with elected delegates from all four colonies and from Bechuanaland, met in Bloemfontein in March 1909. Speakers welcomed the proposal for a Union which, they believed, was essential and inevitable, but also recorded a strong and emphatic protest against the colour bar, calling for a clause in the planned constitution guaranteeing all persons full and equal rights and privileges, 'without distinction of class, colour or creed'. They once more appealed to the imperial government which, they believed, was bound by 'both fundamental and specific obligations' to extend to the Africans and coloured races the same measure of equitable justice as was extended to people of European descent.[63]

The coloured community of the Cape Colony also held protest meetings in Cape Town and sixty other centres, where they passed

---

[58] Resolution of the South African Native Congress, 10 April 1906, *Ibid.* p.28.
[59] *Ibid.* p.21.   [60] *Ibid.* p.21.
[61] *Ibid.* pp.47–8.   [62] *Ibid.* p.48.
[63] Petition to the South African National Convention, March 1909, *Ibid.* p.53; see also Julie Evans, Patricia Grimshaw, David Philips and Shurlee Swain, *Equal Subjects, Unequal Rights: Indigenous Peoples in British Settler Colonies, 1830–1910* (Manchester, Manchester University Press, 2003) p.176.

resolutions criticising the draft constitution. In April 1909, the African Political Organisation held a conference in Cape Town, calling for the extension of the Cape franchise to the rest of South Africa. Delegates called for the 'co-operation of all coloured races in South Africa' and looked forward to united action:

> to protect the rights of all coloured races and secure an extension of civil and political liberty to all qualified men irrespective of race, colour or creed throughout the contemplated Union.[64]

One of the leading spokesmen for the pro-British view that the Cape franchise provided the way of the future was Sol Plaatje, a Tswana man born in the Boer republic of the Orange Free State, who had received a mission education, spoke and read English, German and Afrikaans fluently and secured a clerical position in the Kimberley Post Office.[65]

London sanctions the Union

The debate about the future of South Africa came to a climax in London, in 1909, when the legislation establishing the Union passed through the British parliament in the presence, not only of the new nation's political leaders, but also of delegations from both the Indian and the African and coloured communities, led respectively by Gandhi and W. R. Schreiner, the liberal Cape politician, barrister and brother of novelist Olive Schreiner. Schreiner had worked with the Trinidadian barrister, Henry Sylvester Williams, organiser of the first Pan-African Congress in London in 1900, who had since gone to live and work in Cape Town. One of the main items on the agenda of the Pan-African Congress had been to draw attention to the possible consequences of the Boer War for native Africans and to lobby Colonial Secretary Chamberlain to guarantee their rights. It was Williams who introduced Schreiner to W. E. B. DuBois' *The Souls of Black Folk*, published in 1903, which, according to Schreiner's biographer, inspired his support of the African cause.[66]

By 1909, the British government was prepared to ignore the fate of non-whites in South Africa. It wanted the Union bill to be passed without amendment, because they accepted the right of self-governing Dominions to determine their own affairs and because the South African leaders were adamant that any significant change would endanger the whole venture.

[64] Thompson, *The Unification of South Africa*, p.327.
[65] Evans *et al.*, *Equal Subjects, Unequal Rights*, pp.165–6.
[66] E. A. Walker, *W. P. Schreiner, A South African* (London, Oxford University Press, 1937) pp.272–4.

Indeed, the Union was celebrated as a monument to liberal statecraft – the creation of another self-governing Dominion to join Canada, Australia and New Zealand, which were increasingly seen as a crucial supplement to Britain's strategic strength at a time of growing international tension in Europe.

On the racial question, the South African leaders spoke with the confidence that the great majority of the white electorate stood resolutely behind them. The bill passed both houses of Parliament without amendment with the near unanimous support of the British press. It was an achievement that required the reconciliation of Briton and Boer, an outcome symbolised by the effusive English reception of Louis Botha, the commander of the Boer forces, who was invited to dine with King George V.

Speakers in the parliamentary debate recognised that the issues had larger import than the future constitution of South Africa. Should political power remain the monopoly of the white race? Alfred Lyttleton, the prominent conservative politician, spoke with more experience of South Africa than almost anyone else in the House of Commons and he was especially mindful of the American experiment with multi-racial democracy following the Civil War. Lyttleton had no doubt about the folly of the American Congress which, in extending political equality to 'black races', was 'deceived by the false simplicity of words' such as equality. The result of so 'unprovidentially' granting the franchise to freed blacks had been disastrous. And while he did not approve of the hard line of the Boers, it was better to face reality and acknowledge that the black race was not equal to the white.[67] Historian, writer and Liberal politician, James Bryce, warned his fellow legislators that the abiding problem in South Africa was the reconciliation of white and black. The problem became even greater than in America's southern states, because in South Africa the whites were in a small minority.[68]

Arthur Balfour, the leader of the Conservative Opposition, applauded the creation of the Union, but observed that the relations between the 'races of European descent and the dark races of Africa' and the Asian minorities presented a problem of extraordinary difficulty and complexity. Indeed, said Balfour, echoing Bryce's much-quoted observation in his Romanes lecture on the 'Relations of the Advanced and Backward Races', there was no parallel to it in 'the memory or history of mankind'. Balfour also pointed to American history lessons, the chief one being the absurdity of the idea of racial equality:

[67] House of Commons Debates, 5th Series, vol.IX (1909) Colls.966–7.
[68] Cited by Ronald Hyam, *Elgin and Churchill at the Colonial Office, 1905–1908: the Watershed of the Empire–Commonwealth* (London, Macmillan, 1968) p.371.

I do not believe that any man can approach this question who really thinks that all men are equal in that sense. All men are, from some points of view, equal; but to suppose that the races of Africa are in any sense the equals of men of European descent, so far as government, as society, as the higher interests of civilization are concerned, is really, I think, an absurdity which every man who seriously looks at this most difficult problem must put out of his mind if he is to solve the problem at all.[69]

The Union bill, with its provisions for racial exclusion, passed through the British parliament with a large majority.

Gandhi confronts Smuts

Gandhi was in London between July and November 1909. While accepting the inevitability of the impending Union, he seized the opportunity to publicise the plight of the Indian community, at the moment when the future of South Africa was being decided. He was now less confident about the effectiveness of lobbying English politicians and officials. 'The whites of the colonies', he had concluded, are 'the strong and favoured sons of Empire; Indians the weak and neglected ones'. Under the new constitution it was likely that the Indians would eventually be driven from or extinguished in South Africa.[70] Gandhi did not object to immigration restriction, but to the racial basis of the new Constitution. The principle of legal equality was what mattered.

He engaged in protracted negotiations, through third parties, with the Boer leader, Smuts, who was also in London. The two men circled each other, both offering concessions. Gandhi was willing to accept a limitation on Indian migration so restrictive that only six educated men would be permitted to enter the colony every year. But in doing so the authorities would have to concede the principle of legal equality. Smuts would agree to the entry of six immigrants, but at no point would accept the principle of racial equality. In discussions with the Colonial Secretary, Lord Crewe, Smuts was quite clear. He would not accede to the claim that Asiatics 'should be placed in a position of equality with Europeans in respect of right of entry or otherwise'.[71]

The detailed negotiations between Smuts, Gandhi, Lord Crewe and their go-between, Lord Ampthill, who had served as an official in India, continued without reaching agreement. The Colonial Office was caught between a theoretical commitment to racial equality and the

---

[69] House of Commons Debates, 5th Series, vol.IX (1909) Colls.1001–2.
[70] Gandhi, *Collected Works*, vol.IX, pp.272, 297.
[71] As quoted by Gandhi in Letter to the Press, 5 Nov. 1909, *Ibid.* p.515.

acknowledged right of self-governing colonies – of white men – to determine their own laws. An intra-office memo outlined the dilemma:

We cannot dispute the rightness of [Gandhi's] claim to equality before the law, it is indeed a fundamental principle, we only refuse to press for the recognition of the principle about which we feel, no doubt because we have no power to enforce our views on those who have the settlement of the question in their hands. When a Colony is given responsible Government, the settlement of such questions necessarily passes into the hands of the Colonial Government and Parliament and though the Transvaal Government has shown readiness to meet us on points of detail, they have on the point of principle shown a tenacity (due, no doubt, to the historical abhorrence of equality of white and coloured shown by the Dutch) quite equal to that of the Indians. If they will not accept our principle, the Empire being what it is, we cannot dragoon them.[72]

In a letter to the press, Gandhi agreed that legal equality was at the heart of the matter of immigration restriction, 'even though never a man does enter'. The question was one that Indians were willing to go to gaol and even die for.

It was also a principle that mattered profoundly to the future of the Empire. In explaining his stand to British readers, Gandhi observed that the only possible justification for holding together the different communities of the Empire under the same sovereignty was the fact of 'elemental equality'.[73] Gandhi emphasised the implications for the Empire:

The whole of India is now awakened to a sense of the insult that the Transvaal legislation offers to her, and we feel that the people here at the heart of the Empire cannot remain unmoved by this departure, so unprecedented and so vital, from Imperial traditions.[74]

In the Indian deputation's last letter to Lord Crewe, Gandhi observed that there was nothing for them to do but to place their position before the public and to return empty handed to South Africa. When explaining the situation to his supporters at home, Gandhi declared that Smuts was willing to grant whatever the Indians wanted if only they would concede that 'we are not the equals of whites'. And that betrayed the imperial promise. If the Transvaal could not be coerced, the Empire would cease to have any meaning and Gandhi could no longer feel any sense of loyalty to it.[75]

The discrimination of colour and race

Meanwhile, Schreiner was working with the Africans and coloureds, who had organised protest meetings across South Africa in opposition to the

---

[72] *Ibid.* p.593.   [73] *Ibid.* pp.515–16.   [74] *Ibid.*   [75] *Ibid.*

draft constitution. He was not in favour of mass enfranchisement of non-Europeans, but a restricted franchise of the sort in place at the Cape. He expected whites to remain dominant, but in a free country, where career was open to talent and all 'civilized men', with no discrimination or distinction upon 'such grounds as colour or race'.[76] Schreiner was joined by Dr A. Abdurahman, the leader of the African Political Organization and a member of the Cape Town City Council, and J. T. Jabavu, the editor of the African paper *Imvo*, and together they presented a petition to the House of Commons, arguing that the only practical future for South Africa was to grant equal political rights to qualified men, 'irrespective of race, colour or creed'. They expressed their apprehension about the future, because the racial discrimination embodied in the bill for Union would exacerbate the existing prejudice in the Transvaal, Natal and the Orange River Colony. They feared that the status of coloured people and natives would be lowered still further and that a grave injustice would be done to those who comprised the majority of the people of South Africa.[77]

The African political leaders and the dissident members of the House of Commons were united in their appeal to an ideal of Empire that embodied the promise of racial equality, even-handed justice and fair play. In the Commons, Ellis Griffiths argued that the colour bar was 'contrary to all the proceedings and all the traditions' of the Empire, while his colleague, W. P. Byles, declared that the Union bill contained measures which vitally affected England's honour, character and reputation.[78] British policy had always implied that the civil rights of the subject should not be denied on the grounds of race and colour, whereas the proposed Union would be based on the principle of civil and political rights for white men only. Although the bill had come from 'the most democratic Government which had ever been elected', it was 'a white man's Bill', embodying a 'poisonous principle'.[79]

Harold Cox believed the wording of the legislation was an insult to the whole British Empire, in which coloured men outnumbered whites five to one. It was saying to them that they were unfit to be on a level of equality with us, 'whatever the stage you may have reached in civilization'. Did those who drafted the document imagine that they could 'permanently hold a vast black population in subjection'? By not encouraging individual Africans, Indians and coloureds to become part of the political process they would turn them into enemies, rather than friends. 'The time may come', declared Cox, again echoing Pearson's

---

[76] Walker, *W. P. Schreiner*, p.311.   [77] Karis and Carter, *From Protest to Challenge*, p.56.
[78] *House of Commons Debates*, vol.IX (1909) Coll.998.   [79] *Ibid.* Coll.1028.

prophecy, 'when they would lead a great black revolution against the white race.'[80]

Keir Hardie demanded that the House of Commons not assent to the doctrine that because a man was born with a black skin, he was to be barred from the possibility of ever rising to a position of trust.[81] Charles Dilke pleaded with his colleagues to recognise the enormity of what was occurring. We have, he observed:

stated before the world, and have pressed upon others, and by example have inculcated others who have followed us, the doctrine of no bar of race or colour. We have taught it to South Africa even, and the greater portion of the white people of South Africa have followed it, and, although it was forced on them at first, for fifty years they have followed it voluntarily of themselves . . . But the impression produced by our going back, I am afraid forever, and turning our own back upon our great past is equivalent – personally, I think worse – than it would be if we had turned our back as regards . . . slavery.[82]

While Dilke's commitment to 'no bar of race or colour' was also the official imperial line, leading British officials, including Dilke, made it clear in private that their sympathies were with the white men of the colonies. Indeed perhaps one of the most significant outcomes of the conflict in South Africa was to cause English officials to 'come out' as 'white men'.

In his study of *Elgin and Churchill at the Colonial Office*, Ronald Hyam observed that the key Liberal Ministers and officials such as Lord Elgin, Sir Edward Grey, Lord Crewe, John Morley and Milner were privately dismissive of attempts to apply the 'doctrine of the equality of man' to the affairs of the Empire. Rank and file liberals who spoke out in favour of the principle were referred to pejoratively as 'sentimentalists'.[83] The Secretary for India, John Morley, made it clear that he would never submit to being governed by men of colour, as Austin Chamberlain recalled in his account of a dinner party at Marlborough House, in 1907. Morley confided that he was opposed to promoting Indians to the senior levels of the Indian civil service and Chamberlain agreed, because Britain's position in India rested on the acknowledgement of the English as the ruling race: 'We could not admit equality.' The exchange continued with Chamberlain remarking that 'white men could not and ought not submit to coloured rule', while Morley declared that he 'knew he would not submit to be governed by a man of colour'.[84]

---

[80] *Ibid.* Coll.1568.   [81] *Ibid.* Coll.1575.   [82] *Ibid.* Coll.1566.
[83] Hyam, *Elgin and Churchill*, p.531.
[84] Austen Chamberlain, *Politics from Inside: an Epistolary Chronicle, 1906–1914* (London, Cassell, 1936) pp.59–60.

In Ottawa in 1908, in the wake of the Vancouver riots, Alfred Milner assured his audience there was no question of the black population in South Africa ever becoming a danger to the political supremacy of the white community. Though opposed to discrimination on the grounds of race, he was, he said, a 'British Race Patriot', who had always emphasised 'the importance of the racial bond'. It was 'fundamental'. Just think of what it meant, he enthused, 'for every white man of British birth, that he can be at home in every state of the Empire from the moment he has set foot in it, though his whole previous life may have been passed at the other end of the earth'. Canada was important because Britain needed to keep its best blood within the Empire. The American colonies had been lost and the Empire couldn't suffer a repetition of the process. Left on its own, Milner reflected, Britain could no longer remain a Power of the First Rank.[85]

Elgin set out his private thoughts on race relations in a long letter to Lord Crewe, his successor at the Colonial Office, in 1908. He referred, in particular, to the position of Africans in the impending South African Union. While he had 'a sincere desire to befriend the native', as he put it, he doubted if a recognition of equality for 'all civilized men' in South Africa was practicable or in the Africans' own interest. The Cape franchise, while manageable at present, was fraught with future danger because:

The population figures compel us, if we admit the principle, to contemplate a time when the natives will control the elections. Are we prepared to subordinate the whites to native rule under such circumstances?[86]

The prospect of native rule, whether through political power or insurrection – a 'rising against Europeans' – was a continuing source of anxiety in South Africa. Feelings of insecurity were pervasive.[87] In the House of Commons debate of 1909, A. C. Beck reminded his colleagues that every white man in South Africa and his wife and children lived, 'to a certain degree, in peril'. The threat might not be imminent, but there was 'always that underlying feeling in the heart of the white man'.[88]

The international race question

It was widely recognised that the insecurity and increasing militancy of white settlers posed a serious threat to the unity of the British Empire. It was a subject of special interest to Sir Charles Lucas, head of the

[85] Milner, *The Nation and the Empire*; also Hancock, *Smuts, The Sanguine Years*, p.74.
[86] Hyam, *Elgin and Churchill*, p.377.   [87] *Ibid.* p.538.
[88] *House of Commons Debates*, 5th Series, vol.IX (1909) Coll.1025.

newly formed Dominions Office, who had written at length on the possible consequences in his paper 'The Self-Governing Dominions and Coloured Immigration' in 1908 and again in his book, *Greater Rome and Greater Britain*, in 1912. His analysis rested on the accepted distinction between races deemed fit to rule and those unfit. The 'qualities, character and upbringing of most coloured men', he explained, were not those in demand 'for a ruling race except in rare individual cases.'[89] This was the view of the white Dominions and they had become too important to thwart. As each year passed, their value to Britain rose in much greater proportion than the value of Britain to them. If the United Kingdom were to 'hold her own as a nation, she must keep them with her'. If that meant paying a price, then 'the price must, if possible, be paid'. If Britain were to confront the Dominions over the race question, they might break away and form an alliance with the United States, creating a new political organisation, 'having its roots in race affinity', that would be directly opposed to the idea of imperial citizenship, which took no account of race.[90]

The debate about the future of South Africa raised questions about race relations in the world at large that often recalled, sometimes explicitly, the apprehension with which Charles Pearson had defined these issues in 1893. Neame opened *The Asiatic Danger in the Colonies* by quoting the prophecy from *National Life and Character* – 'The day will come' – and asserting in the preface 'the broad principle' that 'the enormous areas suitable for white colonization in Africa, Australia, and North America should be closed to the Asiatic nations, whether British subjects or not'.[91] Like many of those who followed Pearson, Neame believed that nothing less than the relative power of the East and West was at stake. He quoted Sir Arthur Lawley, Lieutenant-Governor of the Transvaal, to the same effect: 'It is difficult to conceive any question at the present moment more momentous than the struggle between East and West for the inheritance of these semi-vacant territories'.[92]

The South African leader, Smuts, was encouraged to consider the wider implications of the policies of his government by his old friend, the Cambridge scholar, H. J. Wolstenholme, who wrote him a long letter about the issues in May 1909. While believing his friend took no pleasure in cracking down on Indian protestors, he argued that he might give some thought to the wider question of 'the relation between Occident and Orient'. It seemed to Wolstenholme that the policies of the Transvaal and Natal were narrow and parochial and pursued without consideration for

[89] C. P. Lucas, *Greater Rome and Greater Britain* (Oxford, Clarendon Press, 1912) p.97.
[90] *Ibid.* pp.109, 174–5. [91] Neame, *The Asiatic Danger*, pp.ix–x. [92] *Ibid.* p.ii.

the 'international and inter-racial hatreds' aroused as a result. He referred to the Indian nationalist leaders, many of whom had visited England during the previous decade, who resented keenly the unjust and insulting treatment of their people, and more so because it marked them as an inferior race.

This was occurring, wrote Wolstenholme, at a time when 'a perfectly epoch making change' was taking place in the relations between East and West. The balance of global power was shifting. What was required, therefore, were policies of reasonableness, equity and courtesy, 'untinged with racial hauteur or assumption of superiority'. Non-Europeans were proving themselves 'by no means inferior in capacity' and in the long run would achieve equality. It would therefore surely be wise statesmanship, as well as good human fellowship, to concede in time and with a good grace what was sure to be won by struggle.[93] Wolstenholme told Smuts how noteworthy it was that *The Times*, that 'astute spokesman of the worldly-wise possessing and ruling classes of England' had been changing its tone in relation to these matters under the influence of its Foreign Editor, Valentine Chirol. In August 1908, it had published a long editorial on 'The Race Problem':

Asia and Africa have been stirred up into activity, which men of European blood, whether in the Old World, in America, or in Australasia, are finding highly inconvenient, and are probably destined to find troublesome for a long time to come.

The political campaign by Gandhi in the Transvaal indicated, according to Chirol, that a new spirit of 'mutiny and revolt' was arising from among these 'once submissive races'.[94]

Gandhi's manifesto

Gandhi drew a bitter lesson from his failure to exert any influence on events while in London. On his voyage back to South Africa he wrote one of the great classics of anti-imperial literature, *Hind Swaraj* or Indian Home Rule, the 'manifesto of the Gandhi Revolution'.[95] It represented the most decisive step on his journey from loyalist to enemy of the British Empire. The radical message was unmistakable and it was banned as soon

---

[93] H. J. Wolstenholme to J. C. Smuts, 14 May 1909, W. K. Hancock and Jean Van der Poel, *Selections from the Smuts Papers*, vol.11 (Cambridge, Cambridge University Press, 1966) pp.568–73.
[94] *The Times*, 17 August 1908.
[95] Chandran D. S. Devanesen, *The Making of the Mahatma* (Delhi, Orient Longman, 1969) p.364.

as it was published in India. Many sources of the book have been identified, but much of the passionate denunciation of Britain, and Western civilisation in general, can be traced back to his frustration and humiliation experienced at the hands of the white men in South Africa and those who supported them, or at least acquiesced in their demands, in London.[96]

It has often been observed that South Africa shaped the Indian Gandhi – that the white man's country changed him more than he changed it.[97] His brand of dissident politics and restless activism evolved in a society that was repressive, but not tyrannical, when the law, though unjust, still ruled, where lip service was paid to Westminster parliamentary traditions. South Africa turned Gandhi into an Indian nationalist. The common experience of migration provided for Indian and European alike a fund of shared experiences, but the discrimination that targeted all Indians regardless of their education, caste, religion or social standing shaped a nationalist identity. An effective response to disrespect and discrimination demanded the capacity to act together regardless of social or religious differences. Indian diasporic politics and their reverberations in India itself thus helped produce a strong sense of aggrieved nationality. Gandhi observed that in South Africa his compatriots were 'free from certain restrictions from which our people suffer in India. We can, therefore, easily essay an experiment in reaching unity.'[98] Indians in South Africa were forced to achieve the solidarity necessary to challenge the racial camaraderie of self-styled white men, who also united across differences of nationality, class and religion in a passionate crusade.

A complete separation of the blacks and the whites

In the elections of 1910, the Nationalist party, led by Generals Botha, Smuts and Hertzog swept into power. While establishing the basic institutions of the new Union of South Africa, the Nationalists introduced a series of measures discriminating against non-whites. 'When the Union of South Africa was agreed upon and declared', wrote Seetsele Molema, the Bantu, Glasgow-trained doctor, who would return to South Africa

---

[96] See in particular A. J. Parel, 'The Origins of Hind Swaraj', in Brown and Prozesky, *Gandhi and South Africa*, pp.35–55.

[97] J. M. Brown, 'The Making of a Critical Outsider', in *Ibid.* pp.22–7. Dennis Dalton, *Mahatma Gandhi: Non-Violent Power in Action* (New York, Columbia University Press, 1993), pp.13–15.

[98] Cited by A. J. Parel in Brown and Prozesky, *Gandhi and South Africa*, p.46.

to join the African National Congress, 'it was welcomed by white South Africa as the beginning of a new and enlightened era. To the coloured peoples it was a death knell of a long tottering identity':

Those of the latter who were – from sanguine temperament and optimistic nature – in any doubt as to the probable regime of the new Government on the 'native question' were soon eased of their doubts, for scarcely was the Union declared than the Union legislature began its laws, like the Grondwet of Transvaal, by enacting that natives and coloured people will not be allowed to be members of the Dutch Reformed Church.

It was clear, said Molema, that what would follow would be 'a complete separation of the blacks and the whites' along the lines of the South of the United States.[99]

Legislation in 1911 restricted skilled work in mines to white men and further restricted African freedom of movement. In 1913 an Immigration Restriction Act was adopted utilising a dictation test on what had come to be known as the 'Australian model'. But the most decisive move towards segregation was the Native Land Act of 1913, which divided South Africa for purposes of land ownership and usage into two unequal parts, with the Africans being confined to 7 per cent of the area of the Union. Africans would no longer be able to own, lease or even squat on land in areas set aside for whites. It had revolutionary consequences. At the time nearly a million Africans were living on European-owned land as squatters, labour tenants, or farmers paying a percentage of their crop to the landlord. After 1913, their only options were to return to over-crowded homelands or become landless labourers in urban 'locations'. Sol Plaatje, the first secretary general of the African National Congress, wrote: 'Awakening on Friday morning, June 20 1913, the South African Native found himself, not actually a slave, but a pariah in the land of his birth'.[100] Agitation against the legislation led to the passage in 1914 of the Riotous Assemblies Act, which prohibited the distribution of documents judged likely to engender feelings of hostility between whites and non-whites.

Black activists responded by forming a nationwide organisation – the South African Native National Congress (the African National Congress (ANC) from 1923) – at a large conference at Bloemfontein in January 1912. Their first concerted campaign was directed at the Native Land Act, the injustice it embodied and the suffering it was causing. In a petition to the Prime Minister, the Congress declared that practically all

---

[99] S. M. Molema, *The Bantu Past and Present: An Ethnographical and Historical Study of the Native Races of South Africa* (Edinburgh, W. Green and Son, 1920) pp.245, 259.

[100] S. T. Plaatje, *Native Life in South Africa* (Johannesburg, Ravan Press, 1916) p.21.

'well-informed natives of South Africa' felt that under the British flag they had never suffered an act of greater injustice and one which would 'embitter the hearts' of the most loyal native subjects.[101] In 1914 a delegation went to London to petition King George V and appeal to the parliament at Westminster. In their case to the British parliament, the delegation reported their various failed attempts to seek redress in meetings with Prime Minister Botha, the Governor General, Lord Gladstone, and the Secretary of State, Lewis Harcourt. But their faith in British justice had impelled them to come to London and led them to plead with the King as 'their natural protector'.[102]

Central to the African protest was their belief that the key objective of the Native Land Act was the segregation of blacks from whites, 'as if they were so many animals', even though they were the original owners of the land and the white races the invaders. They feared for the future because:

The effect of segregating and separating the natives will be to at once satisfy the natives that the white people intend evil to them, and they (the natives) will deeply resent the treatment and combine against the white people, and the white people will combine against the native, and that inevitable and continual conflict between the two races will be initiated which the natives do not desire.[103]

Smuts also thought about future relations between black and white in his country. Above all he wanted to ensure there would be 'no intermixture of blood between the two colours'. Instead of mixing up black and white in the 'old haphazard way', his government was implementing a scientific policy of separation.[104] It might take a hundred years to work out, but in the end they would see a solution to the native problem in South Africa.

---

[101] Karis and Carter, *From Protest to Challenge*, p.133.   [102] *Ibid.* p.129.
[103] *Ibid.*   [104] Hancock, *Smuts: The Sanguine Years*, p.143.

Part 4

Challenge and consolidation

10 International conferences: cosmopolitan amity or racial enmity?

Race questions

In January 1906, Josiah Royce received a letter from his old friend Felix Adler, writing from the Society for Ethical Culture in New York. Adler wrote with a request: would Royce deliver the address on 'Race Prejudice' in New York, in February, that he had already agreed to present to the Society in Philadelphia, 'the daughter of the New York Society'. 'I trust', wrote Adler in jocular mode, 'that at your age you will not be inclined to take a greater interest in a daughter than a mother.'[1] He proposed an honorarium of $75 plus expenses. The deal was done and the lectures presented. During the following year, Royce gathered these and other addresses into a publication he would name *Race Questions, Provincialism and Other American Problems*.[2]

Royce had been interested in the phenomenon of racial prejudice for years, since his earliest years growing up in Grass Valley on the Californian gold fields, and nearby San Francisco, where as a young, enquiring child he had witnessed the Chinese population segregated into Chinatown, with its exotic temples, gaudy theatres and decorated restaurants. The austere Disciples of Christ church attended by his parents was also segregated – white folks in the front seats and Negroes at the back.[3] Black children had been expelled from the public school but, in 1858, Royce's father had signed a petition to the legislature supporting a law that would allow Negro testimony in court cases involving Caucasians.[4] On issues of race, his parents were Christian liberals and, in *Race Questions*, Royce would condemn American assertions of Negro inferiority as ill-founded and misguided, for self-respect was based on mutual respect.

---

[1] Felix Adler to Josiah Royce, 23 January 1906, incoming correspondence to Josiah Royce, CA 1876–1916, box 1 of 5, HUG 1755.3.3, Royce papers, Harvard University Archives.
[2] Josiah Royce, *Race Questions, Provincialism, and Other American Problems* (New York, Macmillan, 1908).
[3] Robert V. Hine, *Josiah Royce: From Grass Valley to Harvard* (Norman, University of Oklahoma, 1992) pp.23, 38.
[4] Hine, *Josiah Royce*, p.24.

Race questions and prejudices, he noted in his essays, were becoming ever more significant. Like James Bryce, Royce attributed great importance to the unprecedented racial encounters in the Americas and the Pacific. Whether the observer looked at the West Indies or more recently the Pacific Ocean – where Japan's defeat of Russia had changed the future of 'the races of men in the Far East' – diverse peoples confronted each other and pondered the meanings and dangers of racial difference. 'Is it a "yellow peril"', Royce wondered, 'or a "black peril" – or perhaps, after all, is it not rather some form of "white peril" which most threatens the future of humanity in this day of great struggles and complex issues'.[5]

Rather than look to science or ethnology for 'bookshelf races', as Royce's contemporary, Cuban revolutionary Jose Marti had called them, Royce suggested, like Marti, that it would be more fruitful for theorists to get to know real people in the real world. Ignorance was a source of hostility and both conditions caused race problems. The Japanese, for example, once represented in American text books as weird people in a weird land, given to boiling criminals in oil and murdering missionaries – 'whatever Japanese were they were plainly men of the wrong race' – now arrived in the United States as students, unconquerably polite and obstinately reserved, quietly convinced of their own superiority. 'Perhaps the Japanese are not of the right race', Royce observed drily:

But we now admit that so long as we judged them merely by their race, and by mere appearances, we were judging them quite ignorantly and falsely. This, I say, has been to me a most interesting lesson in the fallibility of some of our race judgements.[6]

Perhaps the South was also wrong in its race judgments, in its rush to assert white superiority.

Royce had recently travelled to Jamaica and Trinidad where he found an absence of the race friction that dominated the South, which he explained in terms of the Englishman's habit of reticence. The English coloniser in the West Indies, he thought, had perfected 'a great way of being superior without very often publicly saying that he is superior'. And there were more concessions. Some blacks were permitted to vote and some were employed in the administration of the law – as police for example – which they then came to respect, but the white man remained secure in his domination. 'Superiority is best shown by good deeds and few boasts'. In Jamaica, Royce didn't encounter those painful emotions, those incessant

[5] Royce, *Race Questions*, p.6.
[6] Royce, *Race Questions*, pp.13–16; see too J. H. de Forest, 'The Moral Greatness of the People of Japan', *Independent* (9 July 1908); Matsuzo Nagai, 'Japan and Her Critics', *Independent* (23 July 1908).

complaints and anxieties, that were everywhere evident in the South. Race problems, Royce concluded, were 'caused by our antipathies' – our recoil from the 'hated object'. And they were based on illusions. It was common for people to cherish their illusions, but they should 'not sanctify them by the name of science'. Too often science was invoked to support prejudice. In the contemporary world, 'race' was the name given to the terror of difference.[7]

Race Questions was published in 1908. In the same year, Royce sent a copy of his book, *The Philosophy of Loyalty*, to his old friend Alfred Deakin who, as Prime Minister of the Commonwealth of Australia, was preparing to welcome his fellow white men of the United States Naval fleet. Royce had sent copies of most of his books to Deakin since their cherished time together in the Blue Mountains, but it seems that he didn't send Deakin a copy of *Race Questions*. Did he think it might embarrass him? What might the Australian architect of the 'White Australia policy' have made of it?

In 1888, Deakin had received Royce's endorsement for a nation-building project founded on racial homogeneity, but now the American philosopher was pointing to 'the fallibility of some of our race judgements'.[8] Perhaps Deakin, too, began to entertain doubts. We do know that upon receipt of Royce's book on *Loyalty*, elaborating the theme of unity in diversity, Deakin omitted a section of his proposed welcoming speech to the United States fleet that justified immigration restriction in terms of the racial difference of Chinese, Japanese and Indians in favour of an imagined 'concord of brotherhood' between the Commonwealth and the Republic. Royce made a brief reference to Australia in *Race Questions*, when he discussed the idea that racial difference was probably environmental in origin, rather than genetic. It was easy to show, he said, that the Australian Aboriginal was of a low mental level, but how far was his condition due to the 'inherited and unchanged character of his race', and how far to his endless struggle with the 'dreary desert'? Royce had never been a fan of the arid Australian landscape.

Josiah Royce and Felix Adler were just two of a number of scholars and writers who became convinced during the first decade of the twentieth century that, in order to avert race conflict and armed struggle, it was necessary to promote reasoned dialogue and mutual understanding between peoples of different races, especially between the so-called East and the West. Another influential scholar was a Frenchman, Jean Finot, whose book *Le Préjuge des Races*, providing a 'comprehensive criticism of works that lay stress on the inequality of races', was first published in 1905, and an English version, published by E. P. Dutton in New York,

---

[7] Royce, *Race Questions*, pp.26–66.   [8] *Ibid.* p.15.

in 1906. W. T. Stead prepared an abbreviated version in 1911 called *The Death Agony of the Science of Race* for the Universal Races Congress, Adler's brainchild.[9]

At a meeting of the International Union of Ethical Societies at Eisenbach in 1908, Adler observed that the modern conscience had not kept pace with the racial problems confronting the contemporary world, and that a congress should be convened with a view to finding a way out of the labyrinth of prejudiced opinion in which all races were lost. The spirit of the Hague Conferences on international arbitration would be given new relevance through a congress that explicitly addressed the question of the hour, the increasingly hostile relations between East and West.

A former holder of the Theodore Roosevelt Chair at Berlin University, Adler had recently been appointed Professor of Political and Social Ethics at Columbia University and President of the International Union of Ethical Societies; Gustav Spiller was the Union's Secretary. Together they worked for more than three years, with the aid of a strong international executive council, requesting men and women from around the world to contribute to, and support, a 'universal congress' on race relations.[10] They sought a combination of academic expertise in anthropology, philosophy, sociology and law, official support from governments and direct participation by 'non-European and native interests', as Spiller put it in a letter to Travers Buxton of the Anti-Slavery Society, whose assistance he sought for the ambitious project.[11] Spiller was intent on winning the endorsement of 'the highest functionaries of the diverse peoples of the world ... [to] refute the notion that the most competent and the most responsible persons regard with derision the humane treatment of non-European races and peoples'.[12] Adler became Secretary to the American section of the Congress; he appointed the leading African-American intellectual, W. E. B. DuBois, as American Co-Secretary.

The Pan-African Congress and the problem of the colour line

DuBois had attended an earlier international conference in London, the Pan-African Congress in 1900, the first of its kind, attended by just forty

---

[9] Jean Finot, *Race Prejudice* (New York, E. P. Dutton, 1906).

[10] H. H. Johnston, 'Racial Problems and the Congress of Races', *Contemporary Review* no.2 (1911) pp.149–50; 'Avebury', 'Inter-Racial Problems', *Fortnightly Review* (2 October 1911).

[11] Spiller to Buxton, 1 April 1909, MSS Brit Emp S19, G 441, Box 8, Anti-Slavery Society papers, Rhodes House.

[12] Spiller to Buxton, 30 November 1909, *Ibid*.

men and women from the United States, South Africa, St Kitts, St Lucia, Abyssinia, Liberia, Dominica and Haiti. The advent of such transnational expressions of counter solidarity – African and Asian – was one response to the racial hostilities that now gripped and divided the modern world, and an answer to the emergence of a global politics of whiteness. In his opening address to the Pan-African Congress, Bishop Alexander Walters of Jersey City and president of the National Afro-American Council declared: 'For the first time in the history of the world black men had gathered together from all parts of the globe with the object of discussing and improving the condition of the black race'. In his own country, he advised, the question was simply: 'Was the Negro to be granted equal rights?'[13]

The Pan-African Congress was the brainchild of Henry Sylvester Williams, a 31-year-old Trinidadian barrister trained in Canada and recently established in London. Described by historian David Levering Lewis as 'one of the most visionary colored men of his generation', Williams was cultured, dedicated and inspirational, but practically forgotten when he died aged just forty-two.[14] As honorary secretary of the Pan-African Congress, Williams noted that the meeting was 'the first occasion upon which Black men would assemble in England to speak for themselves and endeavour to influence public opinion in their favour'.[15] He had the calamitous events in South Africa in mind.

There had been a meeting earlier that month of the Aborigines Protection Society, in which participants discussed 'the duty of the English people to the native races', but times had changed. Black men, as Williams said, now wished to 'speak for themselves'.[16] And black women too. Anna J. Cooper and Ada Harris came from Washington DC, Cooper reading a paper on 'The Negro in America' that 'flailed her country for its Christian shortcomings'.[17]

The main question addressed by the Pan-African Congress was 'the position of the black people in South Africa', where war raged between Britain and the Boers and the position of blacks seemed to be in particular jeopardy.[18] Dutch farmers, G. W. Christian told his audience, treated blacks as beasts of burden, inferior to humanity.[19] But Africans, said F. S. R. Johnson, former Attorney-General of Liberia, were 'brave, industrious and manly and only wanted time to develop a capacity for

---

[13] *The Times*, 24 July 1900, p.7.
[14] David Levering Lewis, *W. E. B. DuBois: Biography of a Race* (New York, Henry Holt, 1994) p.248.
[15] *The Times*, 7 July 1900, p.12.   [16] *The Times*, 4 July 1900, p.10.
[17] Lewis, *W. E. B. DuBois*, p.249.   [18] *The Times*, 7 July 1900, p.12; 26 July 1900, p.11.
[19] *The Times*, 26 July 1900, p.11.

self-government'.[20] Williams and others saw the central role of the Pan-African Congress as to lobby the imperial government to take responsibility for the plight of the black population in South Africa. The Colonial Secretary, Joseph Chamberlain, belatedly sent an assurance of the government's intention to take notice of 'natives' rights'. His assurance meant little. Following the conference, Williams tried to make a personal contribution. He went to live in Cape Town, where he became the first black municipal electoral candidate and a friend of Olive Schreiner and colleague of her brother William, who remained neutral in the war, but active in the legal defence of Africans in Cape Town.[21]

The Pan-African Congress has been remembered since for DuBois' 'To the Nations of the World' speech which began portentously: 'In the metropolis of the modern world, in this closing year of the nineteenth century, there has been assembled a congress of men and women of African blood, to deliberate solemnly upon the present situation and outlook of the darker races of mankind.' 'The problem of the twentieth century', he then declared:

is the problem of the color line, the question as to how far differences of race ... are going to be made, hereafter, the basis of denying to over half the world the right of sharing to their utmost ability the opportunities and privileges of modern civilization.

DuBois spoke of Africans' past civilisations and achievements before reminding his audience that:

the modern world must needs remember that in this age ... the millions of black men in Africa, America, and the Islands of the Sea, not to speak of the brown and yellow myriads elsewhere, are bound to have great influence upon the world in future, by reason of sheer numbers and physical contact.[22]

The implications of the unprecedented contact of diverse races that characterised modern times had become a major theme of late nineteenth-century political commentary. In his much-quoted Romanes lectures of 1902, Bryce had written that the contact of 'the more advanced and civilized races with the more backward' was so much more widespread than ever in the past that 'it may be deemed to mark a crisis in the history of the world, which will profoundly affect the destiny of all mankind'. In 1910, *Crisis* magazine was launched by the National Association for the

[20] *The Times*, 25 July 1900, p.15.
[21] Susan D. Pennybacker, 'The Universal Races Congress, London Political Culture, and Imperial Dissent, 1900–1939', *Radical History Review* 92 (Spring 2005), pp.106–7.
[22] Lewis, *W. E. B. DuBois*, p.251.

Advancement of Coloured People in New York, its avowed aim 'to show the danger of race prejudice'.[23]

The magazine was so-named because the editors (one of whom was DuBois) believed 'that this is a critical time in the history of the advancement of man'. One development that made it so, according to DuBois, was the advent of 'whiteness' as a 'new religion', a 'new fanaticism', that was the basis of both personal identity and a global politics. The first issue quoted a letter to the *Baltimore Sun* in which the writer protested 'in the name of white supremacy and white manhood' against the humiliation of living next door to a Negro.[24] In its column 'Along the Color Line', subsequent issues reported on the relentless spread of segregation in the streets, schools, churches and sportsgrounds of the United States.

Whiteness is the ownership of the earth

In 1903, DuBois had published *The Souls of Black Folk* which, according to his biographer, David Levering Lewis, 'redefined the terms of a three hundred-year interaction between black and white people and influenced the cultural and political psychology of peoples of African descent throughout the Western hemisphere, as well as on the continent of Africa'.[25] In 1910, in 'The Souls of White Folk', first published in the New York journal the *Independent*, DuBois wrote about his perception of a sudden change in the world: 'the world in a sudden emotional conversion, has discovered that it is white, and, by that token, wonderful'.[26]

In noting that 'white folk' had suddenly 'become painfully conscious of their whiteness', DuBois was pointing to the emergence of a new mode of identification that crossed national borders, an identification as white men. As a historian, DuBois wanted to emphasise the historical novelty of what he witnessed, especially the emergence of a new 'personal' sense of self:

The discovery of personal whiteness among the world's peoples is a very modern thing – a nineteenth and twentieth century matter, indeed. The ancient world would have laughed at such a distinction. The middle age regarded it with mild curiosity, and even up into the eighteenth century we were hammering our national manikins into one great Universal Man with fine frenzy which ignored color and race as well as birth. Today we have changed all that.

[23] Editorial, *The Crisis: A Record of the Darker Races*, vol.1 (1910) p.10.
[24] *Ibid.*   [25] Lewis, *W. E. B. DuBois*, p.277.
[26] W. E. B. DuBois, 'The Souls of White Folk', *Independent* (18 August 1910) p.339; this essay was re-published in a revised form, in W. E. B. DuBois, *Darkwater: Voices from Within the Veil* (New York, Harcourt, Brace and Howe, 1920).

He also noted the proprietary nature of white men's claims, likening the intermittent outbursts of rage among white folks to the tantrums of possessive children, who refused to share their candy. When applied to the relations between the different races of the world, however, the message seemed rather more ominous: 'whiteness is the ownership of the earth, forever and ever, Amen!' A new global movement was in the ascendancy: 'Wave upon wave, each with increasing virulence, is dashing this new religion of whiteness on the shores of our time'. That nations were coming to believe in it, wrote DuBois, was 'manifest daily'.[27]

In seeking to explain the rise of this 'inexplicable phenomenon', DuBois noted the political claims to equality that were beginning to be made by colonised and coloured peoples around the world: 'Do we sense somnolent writhings in black Africa, or angry groans in India, or triumphant "Banzais" in Japan? "To your tents, O Israel!" these nations are not white. Build warships and heft the "Big Stick".'[28] The US President, Theodore Roosevelt, author of the diplomacy 'Speak Softly and Carry a Big Stick', had sent, as we have seen, the United States naval fleet on its tour of the Pacific in 1908, its ill-concealed intention to intimidate Japan and forge relations of solidarity with the white men's countries of Australia and New Zealand. The exuberant expressions of racial kinship occasioned by the visit of the fleet to Sydney and Melbourne were reported at length in the New York *Independent*, which two years later published DuBois' article on the ascendancy of whiteness.

In seeking to explain the 'new fanaticism' that was taking hold, DuBois insisted on the transnational nature of, and response to, the movement for racial equality: 'when the black man begins to dispute the white man's title to certain alleged bequests of the Father's in wage and position, authority and training; and when his attitude toward charity is sullen anger, rather than humble jollity; when he insists on his human right to swagger and swear and waste – then the spell is suddenly broken and the philanthropist is apt to be ready to believe that negroes are impudent, that the South is right, and that Japan wants to fight us'.[29]

As DuBois recognised, the proprietorial claims of 'white men's countries' were defensive reactions to the geographical mobility and political mobilisations of colonised and coloured peoples. Claim and counterclaim, demands for equal access and racist exclusions, declarations of equality and racist refusals, imperial oppression and colonial rebellion were dynamically inter-related historical processes. In a recent essay, Robert Gregg and Madhavi Kale have suggested that DuBois adopted a

[27] W. E. B. DuBois, 'The Souls of White Folk', p.339.
[28] *Ibid.* p.340.   [29] *Ibid.* p.340.

global perspective on 'the Negro problem' following the Universal Races Congress in 1911: 'The Souls of White Folk' shows that he understood American race relations in a world historical context earlier than this.[30]

Imperialism the enemy

The role of imperialism in economic exploitation and racial oppression was the subject of a 'Nationalities and Subject Races' conference, also held in London, in 1910. 'Imperialism was the enemy', declared the forthright conference chairman, F. C. Mackarness, in his opening address on 28 June at Caxton Hall.[31] Papers were presented about conditions in Finland, Georgia, Poland, Ireland, Morocco and Persia as well as India and Egypt. There was a mix of paternalistic concern about the exploitation and ill-treatment of subject races through forced and indentured labour and angry protest at British hypocrisy and repression in India. This mix of paternalism and protest was evident in the guiding principles of the conference that specified the duty of 'protection' of weaker peoples with the imperative of self-determination. The position of the 'Coloured Races under White Man' (to cite the title of one paper) was a major theme of discussion. National sovereignty was promoted as one answer to the global colour line.

One of the main conference aims was to justify nationalism as a legitimate aspiration for subject colonised peoples. Nationalism was not a denial of cosmopolitanism, but the prerequisite for its full realisation: 'It holds up the ideal of a many-coloured cosmopolitanism of free nations as opposed to a colourless and mechanical cosmopolitanism of big Powers and subject races'.[32]

National freedom, it was also argued, was necessary to manly self-esteem. In a paper on 'The Present Condition of India', lawyer, writer and a leader of the 'extremist' section of the Congress movement, Lala Lajpat Rai, who had first travelled to England with the moderate, Gopal Krishna Gokhale, in 1905, but whose recent agitation in the Punjab had led to his deportation to Burma, repeatedly suggested that British rule in India not only frustrated the desire for national independence, but destroyed Indian men's manhood.[33] The institution of a system of widespread espionage

---

[30] Robert Gregg and Madhavi Kale, 'The Negro and the Dark Princess: Two Legacies of the Universal Races Congress', *Radical History Review* 92 (Spring 2005) p.134.
[31] *Nationalities and Subject Races: Report of Conference: 28–30 June 1910* (London, P. S. King and Son, 1910) p.1.
[32] *Ibid*. p.viii.
[33] Purushottam Nagar, *Lala Lajpat Rai: The Man and his Ideas* (New Delhi, Manohar Book Service, 1977).

'is sapping our manhood, driving virtue out of the land, and making patriotism and public spirit a crime'.[34] The new repressive laws and vindictive
sentences, passed in the wake of Lord Morley's 'reforms' of 1909 – which
saw a modest extension of representative government – made it impossible for the government to tolerate 'the growth of a spirit of manliness
in the people'. Rather, the opposite was the case: 'Unquestioned obe-
dience, unbounded forbearance, and undisturbed quietude, suit them
best.'[35] 'There can be no justification for a policy', Lajpat Rai told his
English audience, 'which by appealing to the baser instincts of human
nature aims at setting up father against son, brother against brother, wife
against husband, friend against friend; and last, but not least, teacher
against pupil.' 'This', he re-iterated, was 'polluting the very fountains of
manhood.' There was only one remedy: 'giving real self-government on
the lines of South Africa'.[36]

In 1906, at the suggestion of the elderly Parsee intellectual Dababhai
Naoroji, the Indian National Congress had adopted 'self-government or
Swaraj like that of the United Kingdom or the Colonies' as its major
goal.[37] In the Commonwealth of Australia, however, self-government
had been used to exclude Asians from migration and citizenship; in the
new Union of South Africa, only the white male minority participated
in self-government. Only white men were believed to possess the requisite qualities of discipline, self-control and reason that qualified them
for 'real self-government'. Yet Indians wanted 'the real thing' too, said
Bipin Chandra Pal, a Congress 'extremist' and advocate of boycott as
a weapon against British rule, in a second paper to the 1910 Conference on the Indian question. Pal was impatient with arguments in favour
of Indians' rights as British subjects: 'not imitations; we do not want
"English reforms" . . . The people of India do not want any legal gifts or
privileges or charters on paper which could be taken away the next day by
another paper. They could not say: "The Lord gave and the Lord taketh
away: blessed be the name of the Lord". That was not what they wanted;
they wanted to be let alone.'[38] Historian S. L. Malhotra has interpreted
Pal's nationalism as seeking ways to reconcile the ideas and achievements
of 'modern civilization with the wisdom of ancient Indians'.[39] Living in
London between 1908 and 1911, after periods of imprisonment in India,
Pal was drawn into the internationalist circle around W. T. Stead, champion of the Hague Peace conference and editor of the *Review of Reviews*,

[34] Lala Lajpat Rai, 'The Present Condition of India', in *Nationalities and Subject Races*,
p.27.
[35] *Ibid.*   [36] *Ibid.* p.40.   [37] Nagar, *Lala Lajpat Rai*, p.37.
[38] B. Chandra Pal, 'Proposed Remedies', in *Nationalities and Subject Races*, p.140.
[39] Quoted in Robert John Holton, 'Cosmopolitanism or Cosmopolitanisms? The Universal
Races Congress of 1911', *Global Networks* 2, 2 (2002) p.163.

who wrote the preface to Pal's *The Soul of India*. Through these networks, he was enticed to join the London organising committee of the more ambitious Universal Races Congress planned for 1911.

To discuss relations between the East and West

The Universal Races Congress aimed to bring together delegates from different peoples and regions of the globe to discuss, 'in the light of science and the modern conscience, the general relations subsisting between the peoples of the West and those of the East, between so-called white and so-called coloured peoples, with a view to encouraging between them a fuller understanding, the most friendly feelings, and a heartier co-operation'. The Congress could carry out its object, advised Secretary Gustav Spiller, through the formation of 'an association designed to promote inter-racial amity'.[40] The 'mutual amity of races should be encouraged', wrote a supporter in *The Times* as 'the only sure basis for the formation of Empires' and to prevent the misunderstanding that was a cause of war.[41] There was strong representation from 'the peoples of the East' – from China, Egypt, India, Japan and Persia for example – although the vast majority of participants and supporters represented 'the peoples of the West' in Europe and the United States.

The President of the Congress was Lord Weardale, a former Liberal politician, committed internationalist and president of the International Parliamentary Union since 1906. He was amply supported by nineteen executive vice-presidents, including the vice-chancellors of fifteen British universities. The Executive Council of the Congress had fifty-two members, while the long list of honorary vice-presidents to the Council included more than ninety members of the second Hague conference and the Court of Arbitration and more than one-hundred Presidents, Ministers of State, Governors and Ambassadors. As the journal, *United Empire*, reported proudly: 'Cabinet Ministers at home, twelve British Governors and eight British Premiers, fifty Presidents of Parliaments, the majority of actual members of the International Hague Court, one hundred and thirty Professors of International Law, have welcomed the proposal and given their names as honorary vice-presidents'.[42] (Australian Prime Minister Deakin was listed as one of the 'British Premiers' to offer their endorsement, but he didn't attend.) In addition, the General Committee, chaired by Felix Adler, had institutional representatives – predominantly from churches and universities – from thirty-three countries. Hundreds of academics from around the world paid to be affiliated.

[40] Gustave Spiller, 'The Problem of Race Equality', *Universal Races Congress Papers* (1911) p.39.
[41] *The Times*, 14 April 1911, p.9.   [42] *United Empire* vol.2, no.5 (May 1911) p.350.

The Congress met at the University of London, over five very hot days during July. Over a thousand delegates, professors and political leaders, representing more than fifty 'races' and nationalities, took their seats in the Imperial Institute on 26 July, to be greeted by 'Odes of Salutation' – Alice Buckton on behalf of Europe, T. Ramakrishna Pillai for the East and DuBois ('A Hymn to the Peoples') speaking for Africa. In his opening address, Lord Weardale observed that in the last ten years, and especially with the 'most remarkable rise of the power of the Empire of Japan, the precursor, it would seem, of a similar revival of the activities and highly developed qualities of the population of the great Empire of China', the power relations of the world had suddenly changed. The time had arrived when 'the vast populations of the East would meet on terms of equality with the nations of the West'. He looked forward to a time when 'colour prejudice will have vanished' and the 'so-called white races and the so-called coloured races' would regard each other 'in truth as brothers and men'.[43]

A letter from the South African writer, Olive Schreiner, was read to the assembled delegates in which she pointed out that the question of the relationship between 'the light and dark races' was not merely of 'abstract intellectual interest' in her country, but rather it was 'the root problem on the solution of which our whole future national life depends'.[44] Other feminist speakers – including theosophists Annie Besant and Sister Nevidita – put the case for women's duty to subvert imperial rule in India.

According to a Frenchman, Baron d'Estournelles de Constant, who had been to the fore in summoning the second Hague conference in 1907, the brutality of imperial rule was not only destructive to the colonised, but rebounded on white men themselves and their 'mother-states':

Where is the white man, however excellent, who can be perfectly certain that in the great wide spaces of our various European colonies he will be able to resist the terribly demoralising effect of unlimited power, conjoined with the influences of solitude and climate? Where is the white man who has not in Africa and Asia felt himself to be more or less *master*, with power to act as he will, with power to oppress? There is . . . a regrettable and retrograde tendency among white men once left to their own devices to cultivate and foster deliberately a brutality whose evil traditions they then bring back with them to their mother-state.[45]

---

[43] Lord Weardale, 'Introduction', in Gustave Spiller (ed.) *Papers on Inter-Racial Problems* (London, P. S. King and Co., 1911) p.viii.
[44] *The Times*, 27 July 1911, p.4.
[45] Quoted in Michael D. Biddiss, 'The Universal Races Congress of 1911', *Race* XIII, 1 (1971) p.40.

The organisers generally tried to avoid such confronting questions about power relations, by inviting scholarly contributions, rather than political viewpoints: 'political issues of the hour will be subordinated, in the firm belief that when once mutual respect is established, difficulties of every type will be sympathetically approached and readily solved'.[46]

The discouragement of political talk extended, wrote one commentator, to a virtual prohibition: 'no discussion will be admissible which seeks to raise political questions or to advocate changes in the boundaries of nations and states'.[47] Yet race questions, as Bryce, Finot, Royce, DuBois and others had noted, were the product of colonial conquest and racial prejudice. For colonised and coloured peoples, solutions to 'race questions' inevitably raised 'political questions' – about discrimination and equality, freedom and independence. The *Fortnightly Review* noted that a 'question of much difficulty' raised in several of the papers was 'the treatment of other races in some of our self-governing Dominions'. Yet self-governing Dominions, it was also noted, had the right to decide the issue for themselves.[48]

The White policy could lead to war

The colour bar instituted by the white democracies was the subject of the paper delivered by Dr Wu Ting-Fang, recently appointed as the Chinese Ambassador to the United States and soon to join fellow revolutionaries in overthrowing the Manchu Empire. Wu Ting-Fang reminded his audience that Chinese civilisation 'may be justly described as the most venerable in existence', 'founded in the remotest period of antiquity and developed under her own peculiar system of ethics, her own social and moral code'.[49] After describing these civilisational codes in some detail, Wu Ting-Fang then took aim at the 'White policy', which was, unfortunately, 'advocated in some influential quarters' and posed the greatest threat to international altruism and friendship:

It is said that some countries should be reserved exclusively for white people, and that no race of another colour should be permitted there . . . If such a doctrine should spread and be generally followed, men would become more narrow-minded than ever, and would not hesitate to take undue advantage of peoples of other colour or race whenever an opportunity occurred . . . Instead of friendly feelings and hearty co-operation existing between Occidental and Oriental peoples, there would be feelings of distrust, ill-will, and animosity towards each other; constant friction and disputes would take place and ultimately lead to war.[50]

[46] *The Times*, 26 October 1909, p.4.   [47] *United Empire* vol.2, no.5 (May 1911) p.350.
[48] 'Avebury', 'Inter-Racial Problems', p.588.
[49] Wu Ting-Fang, 'China', *Universal Races Congress Papers*, p.122.   [50] *Ibid.* p.131.

Wu Ting-Fang then referred, as had many of his countrymen before him, to the fact that white settlers had themselves displaced Aboriginal peoples, engaging in actions that brought into question their very claims to be civilised:

I have noticed that this cry of a 'White Policy' has been raised, not by the aborigines, who might have some excuse, but by the descendants or settlers who had conquered and, in many cases, killed the aborigines of the country, which they now want to keep for themselves, and by politicians who recently migrated to that country. Is this fair or just? To those who advocate such a policy, and who no doubt call themselves highly civilised people, I would remark that I prefer Chinese civilisation.[51]

Confucian doctrine taught that all who lived within the four seas should be treated as brothers and sisters; and adding a Christian gloss, the Chinese delegate added that what one didn't want done to oneself, one should not do unto others.

Wu Ting-Fang's life exemplified the modern mobility that shaped the political consciousness of the 'globally oriented elite' of African, African– American and Asian professionals, intellectuals and political activists identified as 'new cosmopolitans' by John Holton.[52] Born in Singapore in 1842, Wu Ting-Fang returned to Canton at the age of four and was later enrolled at St Paul's College in Hong Kong. After working for a time as an interpreter in the Supreme Court, Wu Ting-Fang decided to study law in London. Called to the bar at Lincoln's Inn in 1877, he then returned to Hong Kong, where he was admitted to practise as a barrister. Wu Ting-Fang was the first Chinese to be called to the English bar and to be admitted to practice at the Supreme Court in Hong Kong. Like his contemporaries in Melbourne and San Francisco, he was active in building philanthropy and welfare services for his people. In 1878, he was the first Chinese to be appointed a Justice of the Peace in Hong Kong.

During the next decade, Wu Ting-Fang's life changed direction when he headed north to become legal adviser and foreign interpreter to Li Hung-Chang, the Governor General of the capital province of Zhili, whom he assisted in drafting the Treaty of Shimonoseki in 1895, which ended the Sino–Japanese war. In 1897, he was appointed Chinese Minister to the United States, Spain and Peru and five years later, back in China, he played an important role in reforming Chinese law and assisting the country's transition into a modern state. Like many of his contemporaries, Wu Ting-Fang had witnessed at first hand the contempt in which his ancient civilisation was held in Western countries.

---

[51] *Ibid.* p.132.   [52] Holton, 'Cosmopolitanism or cosmopolitanisms?', p.160.

In his paper to the Universal Races Congress, Wu Ting-Fang acknowledged that although China was 'physically unable to resist' ill-treatment by white men's countries, such treatment was clearly inconsistent with 'the laudable object of the Congress – to encourage good understanding and friendly feelings between Occidental and Oriental peoples'.[53] Like many leading revolutionaries, including Sun Yat-Sen, who had grown up in Hawaii, Wu Ting-Fang was convinced that in order to take its proper place in the world, and to be treated with respect, China needed to become a modern democratic republic. Following the Congress in London, he returned to China, where he joined with others returning from Japan, Europe and the United States in the successful insurrection against the Qing Dynasty. Late in 1911, they formed a Provisional Government with Sun Yat-Sen as president and Wu Ting-Fang as Foreign Minister. Only a strong, modern nation-state, they knew, could rescue China from racial slurs and redeem their country's honour.

That the East would not forever remain 'unresisting' to 'unchecked aggression' and the 'utter disregard of the rights or feelings' of its peoples, was also one of the main messages delivered by Gokhale in his paper to the Universal Races Congress on the 'East and West in India' that was published simultaneously in India in the *Hindustan Review*.[54] Colonised and coloured peoples were mobilising and they expected to be treated as equals:

The victories of Japan over Russia, the entry of Turkey among constitutionally governed countries, the awakening of China, the spread of the national movement in India, Persia and Egypt – all point to the necessity of the West revising her conception of the East, revising also the standards by which she has sought in the past to regulate her relations with the East. East and West may now meet on more equal terms than was hitherto possible, and as a first step towards such meeting the value of the Universal Races Congress can not be over-estimated.[55]

In the case of India, political rights were the crux of the issue. A moderate former president of the Indian National Congress, and representative of non-official members of the Bombay legislature on the Viceroy's Legislative Council, Gokhale emphasised, perhaps with the recent imprisonment of radical nationalist Bal Gangadhar Tilak in mind, the need for immediate political reform of a substantial kind. While noting that there was a class of English thinkers, for whom 'it was axiom that Oriental people have

---

[53] Wu Ting-Fang, 'China', p.131.
[54] G. K. Gokhale, 'East and West in India', *Universal Races Congress Papers*, p.158; Paul B. Rich, *Prospero's Return: Historical Essays on Race, Culture and Society* (London, Hansib, 1994) p.78.
[55] *Ibid.* p.158.

no desire, or at any rate, capacity for representative institutions', Gokhale urged that the time had arrived for a definite pronouncement on the matter of self-government to be made by the highest authority. Without it, resentment would surely increase.[56] Though espousing a new imperialism, Englishmen seemed increasingly reluctant to grant free institutions to Indians, who grew more disaffected and alienated. Meanwhile, new 'thought-currents' in Asia – 'a new pride in the special culture and civilization of the East, a new impatience of Western aggression and Western domination' – began to exercise a profound influence on India, and these tendencies received 'a powerful stimulus when Japan astonished the world with her victories over Russia'.[57]

India demanded 'political equality' in its dealings with Britain and the introduction of 'a representative government on a democratic basis'. No matter what courtesies were adopted in personal relations, 'the fact remains that . . . the humblest Englishman in the country goes about with the prestige of the whole Empire behind him, whereas the proudest and most distinguished Indian cannot shake off from himself a certain sense that he belongs to a subject race'. That sense had been exacerbated by the treatment of Indians in other parts of the Empire: 'The monstrous indignities and ill-treatment to which the people of this country are being subjected in South Africa, have aroused the bitterest resentment throughout the land.'[58]

Gokhale recognised that the Congress organisers might think he placed too much emphasis on political matters, 'but there [was] no getting away from the fact that, as the contact between England and India at present is predominantly political, it is on the attitude of Englishmen towards the political advancement of India that the future of these relations will mainly turn'.[59] With the timely granting of free institutions in India, 'East and West – white and dark and yellow and brown – will all alike have cause to rejoice'.[60]

The Congress program of more than fifty papers, divided between seven sessions, provided a wide range of viewpoints on the 'problem' of race. As the *Times* correspondent put it, there were: 'papers on China, Japan, Turkey, Persia, the Jewish race, India, Egypt, Haiti, the American negro, and Indian, and the negro of West and South Africa'. Most important, *The Times* noted, in every case, 'the paper was written by a member of the particular people or race concerned'. For instance, 'Dr DuBois, an American negro, will read a paper on "The Negro Race in the United States of America"; Pastor Mojola Agbebi, a native of West Africa, will

---

[56] *Ibid.* p.165.   [57] *Ibid.* p.161.   [58] *Ibid.* p.165.   [59] *Ibid.* p.164.   [60] *Ibid.* p.167.

deal with the West African Problem; a paper on "The Jewish Race" will be contributed by Mr Israel Zangwill; and Abdul Baba Abbas, promoter of the Bahai movement in Persia, will present a paper which will deal with that movement'.[61] Baba Abbas praised the Congress as 'the greatest of events': 'It will be for ever to the glory of England that it was established at her Capital.'

The Congress offered DuBois the perfect opportunity to make a case for racial equality on the world stage and he used the occasion to draw attention to the importance of his country's pioneering experiment in multi-racial democracy following the Civil War. DuBois emphasised the achievements of white and Negro leaders during Radical Reconstruction, which included a more democratic form of government, free public schools, land reforms and new social legislation. Before these reforms were secured, however, they were overturned by a deadly combination of 'force and fraud'. Since that time discrimination had become 'persecution, based simply on race prejudice'.[62] His paper provided a comprehensive array of demographic and social statistics on the oppressed condition of the Negro in the United States.

DuBois argued that a republic built on caste could not survive. A solution to the conflict between a regime based on race prejudice and the increasing determination of the Negro to challenge that prejudice was becoming urgent: 'Radical suggestions of wholesale segregation or deportation of the race have now and then been suggested; but the cost in time, effort, money and economic disturbance is too staggering to allow serious consideration.' Americans were faced with the fundamental challenge of racial equality: 'Whether at last the Negro will gain full recognition as a man, or be utterly crushed by prejudice and superior numbers is the present Negro problem of America.'[63]

In South Africa, the number of whites was not the problem, as W. B. Rubusana, an African member of the Cape Colony Assembly, pointed out in his paper, but rather prejudice and discrimination. Whites would never form a majority. 'It would never become a white country, for the native was there and was going to remain.' But his people were becoming demoralised and damaged by white men's vices. He urged that drink not be imported into South Africa. 'If there was a black peril there was equally a white peril.' Blacks simply asked for an end to the colour bar, for equal opportunity and an open door.[64]

---

[61] *The Times*, 24 July 1911.
[62] W. E. B. DuBois, 'The Negro Race in the United States of America', in G. Spiller (ed.) *Inter-Racial Problems* (London, King and Son, 1911) p.353.
[63] *Ibid.* p.364.   [64] *The Times*, 29 July 1911, p.4.

A new cosmopolitanism or intellectual incoherence?

That white and black and yellow and brown could gather as equals in an international conference – as forecast by Charles Pearson in his prophecy of 1893 – was cause for rejoicing. On his return to New York from the Congress, DuBois was effusive:

> The greatest event of the twentieth century so far was the First Universal Races Congress. It was more significant than the Russian–Japanese war, the Hague Conference or the rise of Socialism … [It was] great because it marked the first time in the history of mankind when a world congress dared openly and explicitly to take its stand on the platform of human equality – the essential divinity of man.
>
> For the first time in history the representatives of a majority of all nations of the earth met on a frankly equal footing to discuss their relations to each other, and the ways and means of breaking down the absurd and deadly differences that make men hate and despise each other.[65]

DuBois was especially pleased with 'the infiltration of Negro blood': 'The two Egyptian Feys were evidently negroid, the Portuguese was without doubt a Mulatto, and the Persian was dark enough to have trouble in the South.'[66]

DuBois was also impressed by a Japanese parliamentarian, another from the Cape Colony (its only black member), a Sioux from the United States, the Liberian Secretary of State, Annie Besant from the Theosophical Society, who delivered a fiery critique of the British Empire, and the novelist and Zionist Israel Zangwill, who pressed for the creation of a Jewish state in Palestine. The success of the Congress, DuBois argued, lay in the fact that it brought people of different races to meet and talk as individuals. Forgetting for the moment the presence of women, he explained:

> It was because the men themselves were there. In their absence a terrible indictment against 'lazy' Negroes, 'dishonest' Chinese and 'incompetent' Asiatics could have been framed; but in the face of gentlemen from various human races of all shades and cultures, the fatal exceptions to sweeping rules of fitness continually occurred.[67]

There were also pleasurable social occasions. DuBois' friend, Mary Ovington, remembered him one evening, radiant with happiness, strolling in evening dress though the gardens of the home of the Countess of Warwick, with Mademoiselle Legitime, the beautiful daughter of General Legitime, the former President of Haiti, on his arm, and a wisp from his Benson and Hedges cigarette coiling in the air above them.[68]

---

[65] *Crisis*, September 1911, p.196.   [66] *Ibid*. p.202.
[67] *Ibid*. p.208.   [68] Lewis, *W. E. B. DuBois*, p.442.

General Legitime also presented a paper to the Congress, 'Some General Considerations on the people and the Government of Haiti', in which he proposed that the progress of humanity depended on the fate of the Black Republic, such was its symbolic importance.[69] As C. L. R. James later suggested in *The Black Jacobins* and Paul Gilroy in *The Black Atlantic*, historical memory of the Black Republic of Haiti and its revolution would serve as an ongoing inspiration to subsequent transnational 'movements of resistance'.[70]

The idealistic organisers of the Universal Races Congress were intent on promoting mutual respect between different peoples and enhanced understanding of unfamiliar cultures, since, 'even the lowliest of civilisations have much to teach'. Greater understanding, they believed, would lead to international peace. As it happened, however, there were a number of rather sharp exchanges between some of the academic participants and, inconveniently, Felix von Luschan, Professor of Anthropology at the University of Berlin, argued that race antagonism was a good thing: 'Nations would come and go, but racial and national antagonism would remain. That was well, for mankind would become like a herd of sheep if they were to lose their national ambition and cease to look with pride and delight, not only on their industries and science, but also on their splendid soldiers, their glorious ironclads.'[71] There was embarrassment as interjectors shouted 'No' and the organisers asked him to clarify his meaning.

Not surprisingly, the Congress was beset by intellectual and political tensions. There was considerable ambivalence, for example, about the value of cultural difference. Exhorted to speak of their culture, many delegates from Eastern nations waxed lyrical about the spiritual wisdom and religious devotion that distinguished their civilizations, even as the Western organisers urged the virtue of modern, rational, scientific enquiry. *The Times* correspondent made fun of the intellectual incoherence and the indiscriminate enthusiasm that greeted 'quite irreconcilable propositions':

At one moment stern-visaged anthropologists stand before us, discussing hard unforgiving facts; next, the President touches a button, and a smile-wreathed delegate in turban or fez is bowing from the platform, breathing peace and brotherhood in broken English or very slightly chipped French. And, unfortunately, the

[69] General Legitime, 'Some General Considerations on the People and the Government of Haiti', *Universal Races Congress Papers*, p.184.
[70] C. L. R. James, *The Black Jacobins: Toussaint L'Ouverture and the San Domingo Revolution* (New York, Vintage Books, 1963); Paul Gilroy, *The Black Atlantic: Modernity and Double Consciousness* (Cambridge, Harvard University Press, 1993).
[71] *The Times*, 27 July 1911, p.4.

logical connection between these successive growlings and cooings is very hard to trace ... Everything is covered up by the applause that we, the members, give to everything, quite indiscriminately; we show our approval of quite irreconcilable propositions with equal enthusiasm, as long as they have the right ring about them. If one speaker says that what we must do above all things is to regard other nations as our equals in every way, and leave them respectfully alone to work out their own national ideals, we applaud him warmly. If next he says that the purdah system and infant marriage are degrading institutions, and we must crush them at any cost, we applaud no less.

In more recent historical assessments, this plurality and incoherence has been hailed as an example of the 'new cosmopolitanism': the Universal Races Congress, Robert Holton has written, 'represented an intercultural encounter and site of conflict between multiple forms of the new cosmopolitanism'.[72] Holton, drawing on Paul Gilroy's account of the *Black Atlantic*, argues that the advent of the Universal Races Congress depended less on 'some kind of internal evolution within the liberal imagination', as Paul Rich had suggested in *Prospero's Return*, than the impact of 'an emergent cosmopolitanism among thinkers and activists from non-European peoples'.[73]

Historical assessment of the Universal Races Congress has, however, remained largely Eurocentric in focus.[74] Writers have examined the liberal humanitarianism of the organisers, the importance of the Hague Peace conferences as forerunners and the growth of the ethical culture movement. Ironically, these historical analyses have often echoed the Eurocentric assumptions of the Congress organisers, noted, for example, by Michael Biddiss with reference to the photographic exhibition mounted by the anthropologist Dr A. C. Haddon, described by *The Times* as follows: 'Some of the photographs are faded, most of them are conventional and inartistic, but, taken together, they illustrate the extent to which our European civilization has been adapted by aboriginal Americans, Asiatics and Africans. The chief interest of the gallery is undoubtedly in such groups as the African Bishops in lawn sleeves, the negro students and Professors in cap and gown, the black lady doctors, the highly educated Sioux and Apache, and the Westernized Japanese'.[75]

A global frame of historical analysis enables us to see these cosmopolitan encounters in a new light. As Wu Ting-Fang, Gokhale and DuBois

---

[72] Holton, 'Cosmopolitanism or cosmopolitanisms?', p.159.

[73] *Ibid.* p.162.

[74] See, for example, Rich, *Prospero's Return*; the recent forum in *Radical History Review* 92 (Spring 2005) has no discussion of the contribution of Chinese, Japanese or Indian participants.

[75] *The Times*, 26 July 1911, p.6; Biddiss, 'The Universal Races Congress', p.43.

all recognised, it was the conflict between white and not-white, played out in the lands beyond Europe, in South Africa, Asia, the Americas and Australasia, and particularly the ascendancy of Japan, that formed the historical context and gave urgency to the Congress. In 1894, Benjamin Kidd, writing in *Social Evolution*, had faulted Charles Pearson for making 'the serious mistake of estimating the future by watching the course of events outside the temperate regions, rather than by following the development of Western peoples'. But Japan's unexpected victory over Russia had shaken Western complacency and helped usher in new global apprehensions. One of the journals speaking for the new order was *The African Times and Orient Review*, founded in July 1912 by anti-imperialist Duse Mohammad Ali, an actor of 'Oriental' appearance, who organised the Congress' programme of entertainments. Duse was a passionate advocate of Pan-Africanist, Pan-Asiatic and Pan-Islamist platforms as well as of Egyptian nationalism.[76]

Stirring up racial animosity

The specific aim of the organisers of the Universal Races Congress had been to bring harmony to the relations between East and West, but even as they planned for mutual understanding and reconciliation, a number of Japanese, Indian and Chinese political activists were plotting a different path of Pan-Asiatic resistance to white arrogance with the proclaimed goal of 'Asia for the Asiatics': 'a free India and Asia purged of the white man's power and presence'.[77] British intelligence services identified networks, organisations and publications animated by 'the sinister object of stirring up racial animosity between the nations of the East and those of the West', feelings which seemed to become more hostile every year.[78] The Pan-Asia movement drew on critiques of British imperialism, such as those offered at the Conference on Nationalities and Subject Races and the Universal Races Congress, to strengthen calls for new race-based solidarities joined in combat with 'the white as a common enemy'.[79]

'The Russo-Japanese war undoubtedly did much to inflate the innate vanity of the Japanese', wrote D. Petrie of the Indian Criminal Intelligence

---

[76] Mansour Bonakdarian, 'Negotiating Universal Values and Cultural and National Parameters at the First Universal Races Congress', *Radical History Review* 92 (Spring 2005) p.126.

[77] D. Petrie, 'The Pan-Asiatic Movement', Paper D 237, Foreign Office to Under Secretary of State for India, 24 January 1919, 'Japan Policy in the Far East', Political and Secret Department, India Office, Singapore National Archives; see too Memorandum on Japanese Pan-Asiaticism and Siberia, 16 September 1918, Political Intelligence Department, Foreign Office, Wiseman Papers, 666/1/6, Yale University Library.

[78] G. J. Davidson, 'Pan-Asiatic Movement', *Ibid.* p.7.

[79] Memorandum on Japanese Pan-Asiaticism and Siberia, Wiseman Papers, p.6.

Department, 'and to lead them to regard themselves as the first Power in the East':

There can be no doubt that the result of the war had a decidedly unsettling effect on the mind of India, and ever since there have not been lacking Indians who have hailed Japan as the defender and champion of Asia – a position which her success and arrogance had already led her to assign herself.[80]

One of these Indians was Lajpat Rai, who had addressed the Nationalities and Subject Races conference in London in 1910. Banned from returning to India, he had travelled to the United States and Japan, where his writings were enthusiastically received and translated, inspiring his friend Shimei Okawa to write his own book, *The Nationalist Movement in India*. Okawa longed for a re-invigorated Japanese nationalism that would arouse his own people to 'great and glorious deeds'. G. J. Davidson, the British Consul in Yokohama, seemed perplexed that although Okawa attacked 'what he terms the racial prejudice shown by the British as well as by Europeans and Americans . . . towards Asiatic nations, the views expressed by him . . . show that he himself is swayed by an even bitterer racial prejudice towards the white races'.[81]

Despite Spiller's call at the Universal Races Congress for inter-racial amity and cooperation, it was clear that what DuBois called the 'new religion of whiteness', and Wu Ting-Fang the 'White Policy', had provoked counter formations of Black and Pan-Asian political identities in hostile movements of resistance. Subsequent developments in California and the expressed determination of citizens there to maintain the Pacific Slope as white man's country would, however, consolidate the colour line and serve to re-constitute the divide between white and not-white.

[80] Petrie, 'The Pan-Asiatic Movement', p.9.   [81] Davidson, 'Pan-Asiatic Movement'.

11   Japanese alienation and imperial ambition

Japanese settlers in California: 'incapable of assimilation'

In 1913, Yamato Ichihasi, a lecturer in history at Stanford University, published a study entitled *Japanese Immigration: Its Status in California*. It provided a comprehensive summary of information about the local Japanese community, culled from the United States census, State government reports and statistics collected by Japanese organisations. In doing so, he sought to counter the torrent of negative propaganda unleashed by local politicians and newspapers. Ichihasi was a path-breaking Japanese scholar in the United States. He had migrated to California in 1894, at the age of sixteen, attended public school in San Francisco, graduated with Bachelor's and Master's degrees from Stanford and enrolled for a PhD degree in Economics at Harvard, where he wrote his dissertation on Japanese immigration.

He opened his study with reference to the Gentleman's Agreement of 1907, which had followed the Schools' Crisis. Ichihasi observed that while the administration of the agreement had been 'most effective', agitation against the Japanese had not ceased. It was 'vigorous as ever, if not more so than it was before the restriction was put in place'.[1]

Japanese migration had peaked in 1907, with over 10,000 arrivals, but rapidly fell away with the application of passport controls, declining to 2,700 in 1910. In fact, more Japanese departed the Californian ports than arrived each year between 1909 and 1913. At the 1910 census, there were 55,000 *Issei*, or first-generation Japanese Californians, who comprised only 2 per cent of the population of the large cities, but in some farming districts their numbers had grown to between 5 and 9 per cent of the community.[2] Ichihasi was able to establish that Japanese migrants had higher literacy rates than most newcomers from central

---

[1] Yamato Ichihasi, *Japanese Immigration: Its Status in California* (second edition, San Francisco, The Marshall Press, 1915) p.1.
[2] *Ibid.* pp.5–6.

and southern Europe. They arrived with more capital than many other migrant groups and learnt English more rapidly. They had very low rates of crime or pauperism and, contrary to the barrage of misinformation, did not receive lower wages than European migrants. He explained to his readers that in most occupations the Japanese were earning just as much as anybody else similarly engaged – 'if not more'. In spite of a 'persistent allegation by anti-Japanese agitators', Japanese migrants did not 'sell their labour at cheap prices'.[3]

By 1913, the Japanese community was undergoing rapid change with a new commitment to permanent settlement promoted by local leaders, who hoped that their people, by adopting Western dress and education, would escape the fate of the despised Chinese. The most prominent immigrant spokesman, Kyutaro Abiko, publisher of *Nichibei Shimbun* and a wealthy labour contractor and landowner, urged his countrymen to become settlers, rather than sojourners and to take up land, marry and raise families.[4] One who followed his advice was Takao Ozawa, who had also emigrated to California as a child in 1894, graduating from high school in Berkeley and enrolling at the University of California. In 1906, he had moved to Honolulu where he married and had two children, whom he sent to an American church and school. Ozawa worked for an American company and spoke English fluently.

Yamato Ichihasi's statistical profile traced the changing face of the Japanese diaspora. In 1904, women made up just over 6 per cent of arrivals, but this had risen to 69 per cent in 1911. Whereas there were 5581 married women in the community in 1910, ten years later there were over 22,000. The same rapid increase could be seen in the number of American-born children, or *Nisei*. From 269 in 1900, their number had risen to 29,000 by 1920.[5]

The other telling statistic concerned the increasing Japanese involvement in agriculture. At the census of 1910, more than half the adult men worked on the land, 20,000 as labourers, 4,500 as farmers. The typical path to farm ownership was to begin as a labourer and then move into some form of leasehold agreement with a European landlord, when he might save sufficient for a down payment on a small property of his own. Japanese farmers owned only just over 2,000 acres in 1905, but by 1913 their holdings had increased to 26,000 acres. Leased farmland increased fourfold in the same period from just under 60,000 to 235,000 acres.

[3] *Ibid.* pp.9–14.
[4] Yuji Ichiska, *The Issei: The World of the First Generation Japanese Immigrants* (New York, Macmillan, 1988) pp.146–7; see too Mai M. Ngai, *Impossible Subjects: Illegal Aliens and the Making of Modern America* (Princeton, Princeton University Press, 2004) pp.38–39.
[5] Ichihasi, *Japanese Immigration*, pp. 9–11; Ichiska, *The Issei*, pp.164, 172.

By that time, Japanese producers dominated production of berries, sugar beet and cut flowers.[6]

Whites in California had been critical of Japanese arrivals, even while they appeared as birds of passage, but their concern turned to alarm when the new settlers established themselves as successful farmers in settled communities. As Yamato Ichihasi observed, agitation in parliament and the press continued unabated. By 1913, it concentrated on the question of ownership and control of land. The claim to be a white man's country was fundamentally a proprietorial assertion. Senator J. D. Phelan, who had become the most powerful figure in the state Democratic Party machine, set out his case for forcing the Japanese from the farming districts in an article published in the New York journal, the *Independent*, the same journal, ironically, that had published W. E. B. DuBois' 'Souls of White Folk' on the claims of whiteness to the ownership of the earth forever and ever.

Phelan wrote that he had no faith in the Gentleman's Agreement, claiming that Japanese migrants continued to arrive illegally from Mexico and Canada and migrants' families also arrived in large numbers. He placed the problem in a larger transnational context: all the 'white man's countries fronting the Pacific' faced the same challenge and had attempted different solutions. The Japanese were skilled farmers and had 'exterminated the white settler' in many districts:

In the place of a sturdy white population – assimilable and homogeneous – we have an alien, incapable of assimilation, loyal to his home government, and hence composing a permanent foreign element in our midst. In other words, we have created a race question, against which all history has warned us: where two races are endeavouring to live side by side, one must take the inferior place, or an irrepressible conflict is precipitated.[7]

According to Phelan, alien races were incapable of assimilation and race conflict was thus inevitable. Lacking jurisdiction over immigration law and prevented by constitutional amendment from passing state laws that discriminated on the grounds of race, California found in naturalisation law the instrument with which its citizens might achieve their desired goal of maintaining California as a white man's country.

Citizenship and land

The Alien Land Law, passed by the Californian legislature in 1913, prevented aliens ineligible for citizenship – notably Chinese, Koreans and

---

[6] Ichihasi, *Japanese Immigration*, p.21; Ichiska, *The Issei*, p.150; Ngai, *Impossible Subjects*, p.39.
[7] 'The Japanese Question from the Californian Standpoint', *Independent* 74 (1913) p.1439.

Japanese – from acquiring land and limited their right to lease it. As had happened with the 1850s laws directed against the Chinese, the critical issue related to who could or couldn't acquire citizenship, a race-based status under United States law since 1790, when the original Naturalisation Act restricted citizenship to 'free white persons'. This had been reaffirmed in the Nationality Act of 1870, which extended the right of naturalisation to 'persons of African nativity or descent'. (The bold bid by Charles Sumner to delete all reference to race was defeated). The racial prerequisite for citizenship continued in the 1906 Naturalisation Law.

As Mai Ngai has argued in *Impossible Subjects*, United States citizenship was defined in terms of a binary that effectively required applicants for citizenship to be categorised as white or not-white. European migrants, despite attracting considerable hostility on the east coast from Anglo-Saxonists such as Henry Cabot Lodge, who considered that many southern and central Europeans were, in fact, not quite white enough, were nevertheless readily admitted to citizenship: between 1907 and 1924, nearly 1.5 million immigrants, nearly all from European countries, became American citizens.[8] The Chinese Exclusion Act of 1882 had included a provision that rendered Chinese ineligible for citizenship, but for groups such as Armenians, Japanese, Indians and Syrians, their eligibility for citizenship was unclear. In the struggles between these groups and the American courts, the legal boundaries between those deemed 'white' and 'not-white', and the very constitution of those categories, clarified and hardened.[9]

Between 1887 and 1923, the federal courts heard twenty-five cases in which the legal status of immigrants seeking citizenship was contested, culminating in the two Supreme Court decisions of *Takao Ozawa v. US* in 1922 and *US v. Bhagat Singh Thind* in 1923. Takao Ozawa, as we have seen, had migrated to California in 1894, but then moved to Hawaii as a young man, where he worked for an American company and raised a family, living a totally assimilated life. He applied for naturalisation to the District Court of Hawaii in 1914, but his application was rejected. He then took his case to the Circuit Court of Appeals and ultimately to the Supreme Court, which ruled that it was irrelevant how well he had personally assimilated; the law posed a racial, not an individual test. And in popular understanding, white meant Caucasian. Indeed the racial prerequisite to citizenship was 'part of our history'.[10] Between 1894 and 1910, federal courts ruled on four successive occasions that Japanese were

[8] Ngai, *Impossible Subjects*, p.38.   [9] *Ibid.*
[10] *Ibid.* p.44; Matthew Frye Jacobson, *Whiteness of a Different Colour: European Immigrants and the Alchemy of Race* (Cambridge, Harvard University Press, 1998) pp.234–5.

not white. Cases in 1909 and 1912 also ruled that people who were half or even one quarter Japanese in descent were also not white.

The Californian legislature was confident, then, that the law of racial citizenship was on their side, and other states followed suit: seven more states prohibited or restricted aliens ineligible for citizenship from taking or holding real estate: Arizona, Idaho, Kansas, Louisiana, Montana, New Mexico and Oregon.[11]

The horror of miscegenation

The motive for the land legislation was obvious to everyone. Long-term Californian Attorney-General Ulysses S. Webb, also a leading eugenicist, observed that the fundamental basis for the Act in question was 'race undesirability'.[12] This had a physical as well as proprietorial aspect. One example of the threat posed by the Japanese was provided by a farmer called Ralph Newman, of Elk Grove, whose evidence acquired legendary status in public memory. Newman declared:

Near my home is an eighty-acre tract of as fine land as there is in California. On that land lives a Japanese. With that Japanese lives a white woman. In that woman's arms is a baby. What is that baby? It isn't a Japanese. It isn't white. I'll tell you what that baby is. It is a germ of the mightiest problem ever faced in this State; a problem that will make the black problem of the South look white.

All about us the Asiatics are gaining a foothold. They are setting up Asiatic standards. From whole communities, the whites are moving out. Already the blood is intermingling.[13]

His testimony was influential, because it called up the linked fears of interracial sex and the birth of mixed-race children, which had already found legislative expression in Californian statutes of 1880 and 1901 prohibiting interracial marriage between whites and negroes, mulattoes and Mongolians. In 1909, the law was amended and extended to prohibit marriage between white Californians and Japanese.

The increasing popularity of eugenics in the early twentieth century coincided with the rise of Japan as a world power and the consequent fear of racial competition. In his book *Across the Pacific*, Akira Iriye argued that with the international success of Japan, racial segregation found new American promoters. Condemnation of mixed marriages, particularly between 'the white and yellow races', was heard more and more often in

[11] Ngai, *Impossible Subjects*, p.286.   [12] Ichihasi, *Japanese Immigration*, p.58.
[13] *Elk Grove Citizen*, 10 April 1913, cited by E. F. Penrose, *Californian Nativism: Organized Opposition to the Japanese, 1890–1913* (San Francisco, R & E Associates, 1973) p.93.

these years.[14] And although it became increasingly difficult to assert that Japanese were racially inferior, the emphasis shifted to the impossibility of successful assimilation and the pressing need to keep the races separate. Rudyard Kipling's famous lines – 'East is East and West is West And never the twain shall meet' – were cited repeatedly in contemporary literature.

In his book of 1912, *Empires of the Far East*, Lancelot Lawton noted that Kipling's lines were quoted 'a thousand times' in support of the view that mingling of the 'races of East and West and a fusion of their blood is neither possible nor desirable'.[15] J. F. Steiner declared in 1917 in *The Japanese Invasion* (originally a doctoral thesis at the University of Chicago) that the fundamental difference between the two peoples was that of colour and physical characteristics:

so marked that the Japanese cannot merge themselves unnoticed into American life. This makes inevitable the establishment of a colour line between the East and the West, no less real than between the White and the Black.[16]

The San Francisco correspondent for London's *Morning Post* reported that Californians believed that it was impossible to assimilate the Japanese because the two races had nothing in common. While Englishmen might know of individual cases of racial intermarriage by hearsay, it did not touch them as a practical question, but Americans, with their experience of slavery and reconstruction had 'a horror of miscegenation'.[17]

American scholars who investigated popular attitudes on the west coast confirmed this judgement. Sidney Gulick, Church of Christ Minister, educator, writer and third-generation missionary, had a lifelong commitment to improving Japanese–American relations. A Japanese-speaking scholar, Gulick taught theology at the Imperial University in Tokyo, before returning to the United States for health reasons in 1913, where he was appalled to find antagonism towards Japanese Americans intensifying. After conducting many interviews on the question of Japanese assimilation, he found that the strongest cause of white hostility was the fear of racial intermarriage and the production of 'mongrel offspring'. Any thought of miscegenation was 'utterly obnoxious'. In discussion with those interviewed, the clinching argument was invariably

[14] Akira Iriye, *Across the Pacific: An Inner History of American-East Asian Relations* (New York, Harcourt, Brace and World, 1967), p.134.
[15] L. Lawton, *Empires of the Far East*, 2 vols. (London, Grant Richards, 1912) vol.11, p.748.
[16] J. F. Steiner, *The Japanese Invasion: a Study in the Psychology of Inter-racial Contacts* (Chicago, McClurg and Co., 1917) p.v.
[17] Cited in *Japan Times*, 13 May 1915.

the rhetorical question: 'Would you let your daughter marry a Jap?' This, Gulick observed, was the 'storm-centre of our problem'.[18]

H. A. Millis, Professor of Economics from the University of Kansas, carried out a similar survey in California at much the same time as Gulick. In both public discussions and private meetings, he found that the principal objection to the Japanese was the conviction that they could never assimilate. There was also much anxiety about the undesirable results of race mixture. It was virtually impossible to have any discussion about assimilation without also raising the question of 'race amalgamation'.[19]

During the early years of the twentieth century, these fears spread beyond the west coast and its organised working class. Akira Iriye pointed to the views of A. C. Coolidge, an influential and well-connected Harvard scholar and one of America's foremost authorities on international relations.[20] His widely read book, *The United States as a World Power*, was the product of a series of lectures delivered at the Sorbonne in Paris. In a chapter on 'Race Questions' he outlined the peculiar difficulties of the American situation. Of all countries, the United States was afflicted with the 'most complicated race problems'. The various non-European elements in the population numbered about 18 million people and while the groups concerned were widely different, their relations with the whites had common characteristics. To begin with, there was the belief of the white man in his superiority. It was something that went deeper than ordinary national pride and seemed, indeed, to be a matter of instinct as much as reason. The success of Japan had given a rude blow to the complacent assumption that Europeans and Americans were 'called upon to rule the world', but this had simply increased the determination of Californians and Australians to keep their lands as a 'white man's country'.

Coolidge then turned to the question of intermarriage, observing that 'the man of European blood' might welcome the Asiatic as an honoured guest in his university and even his home and might admire him personally, but he would 'reject with indignation' the suggestion that a man of another race might marry a member of his family. 'How many of the countless Englishmen and Americans', he asked, 'who sympathised enthusiastically with the Japanese in the late war would prefer Japanese to Russians as husbands for their daughters or sisters'? It was true that the Japanese had proven themselves so adept at European civilisation that

[18] S. L. Gulick, *The American Japanese Problem: a Study of the Racial Relations of the East and West* (New York, Scribners, 1914) p.118.
[19] H. A. Millis, *The Japanese Problem in the United States* (New York, Macmillan, 1915) pp.251–2.
[20] Iriye, *Across the Pacific*, p.134.

they could be regarded as 'virtually one of the white peoples', but the 'instinct of aversion' was always there.

Even if it were admitted that all such antipathies were based on prejudice and should vanish with increasing enlightenment and human brotherhood, there was still good reason, according to Coolidge, why society should hesitate before approving mixed marriages. This scholar of international relations was:

> by no means sure that the offspring of parents racially far apart are likely to be satisfactory. Among English-speaking peoples especially there is a strong conviction to the contrary; and this conviction cannot be dismissed contemptuously as mere prejudice, for there is sound evidence to support it. At all events, the popular saying that children of mixed blood have the vices of both sides and the virtues of neither corresponds with a widespread belief. Granting that many an individual mulatto or Eurasian may be in every respect of a fine type of humanity, does it necessarily follow that a large population of the sort would be a good addition to mankind?

The issue was about radical difference. Dogs, he observed, could be profitably crossed if they belonged to species not too far apart. But if dogs too alien to one another were bred together the product was a worthless mongrel. 'May not something of the same sort hold true of human beings?' he asked his French audience and American readers. Such beliefs, he acknowledged, lacked rigorous scientific backing, but one thing was certain, Americans were overwhelmingly opposed to intermarriage with Asiatics and Africans. Indeed, on the west coast, people would go 'to any extreme' before they would allow their states to become 'the domain of the yellow race or of any but the white'. Californians felt confident, moreover, that they were supported by a more general feeling that the United States must remain 'a white man's country'.[21]

Woodrow Wilson's dilemma

The introduction of the Alien Land Bill into the California legislature created one of the first problems to confront the fledgling administration of Woodrow Wilson, which had been inaugurated just a few days earlier. California was a key state in Wilson's recent victory, as the Democrats had lost heavily in the eastern states. The Californian Democrats, led by Phelan, had insisted that the local presidential campaign include a strong anti-Asian component, something absent from the national platform. A card designed by Phelan was printed in large quantities and distributed all over the state. On one side there was a declaration that

---

[21] A. C. Coolidge, *The United States as a World Power*, pp.64–6, 76–7.

Theodore Roosevelt, one of Wilson's two opponents, and now an Independent Republican, was in favour of granting the Japanese citizenship rights. On the other side of the card a statement headed 'Wilson and the Japanese' explained that 'Woodrow Wilson is for excluding the Japanese from the United States'. Indeed he was quoted as stating:

In the matter of Chinese and Japanese coolie immigration I stand for the national policy of exclusion. The whole question is one of assimilation of diverse races. We cannot make a homogeneous population out of a people who do not blend with the Caucasian race. Their lower standard of living as labourers will crowd out the white agriculturist and is, in other fields, a most serious industrial menace . . . Oriental cooleism will give us another race problem to solve and surely we have had our lesson.[22]

Embarrassed by the probable diplomatic consequences of the passage of the Alien Land Bill, Wilson sent his Secretary of State, W. J. Bryan, to California to negotiate with the state politicians, who showed, however, little desire to compromise, despite pleas that the President be given time to arrange a diplomatic solution to Japanese immigration. Wilson advised against the use in the legislation of 'any language that would offend any people' and in particular asked Californians to delete the phrase 'ineligible for citizenship' from the Bill, with its implication of racial inferiority.[23] Bryan returned to Washington empty handed. The Alien Land Bill passed through both houses of the California Legislature in April with massive majorities. Unlike Roosevelt six years earlier, Wilson had been unable to defuse the issue with a Gentleman's Agreement.

'We coloured people must combine and crush Albinocracy'

The Japanese lodged an immediate protest. In his first official note to Secretary of State Bryan, Japan's Ambassador, Viscount Chinda, expressed 'painful disappointment' over the contentious legislation, which was both 'unfair and discriminatory'. It was, he observed, impossible to ignore the fact that it was primarily directed against the Japanese and was antagonistic to the principles of amity and understanding on which the good relations between the two countries depended. Chinda explained that the Californian statute was 'mortifying' to both his government and the people of Japan, because the racial discrimination 'inferable from these

---

[22] F. Hichborn, *Story of the Session of the California Legislature of 1913* (San Francisco, J. H. Barry, 1913) pp.213–14.
[23] Roy Watson Curry, *Woodrow Wilson and Far Eastern Policy, 1913–1921* (New York, Octagon Books, 1918) p.53.

provisions' was hurtful to their 'just national sensibilities'.[24] Japan's Foreign Minister, Baron Makino, advised that he was unwilling to 'acquiesce in the unjust and obnoxious discrimination'.[25]

Foreign observers in Japan noted how deeply the Californian legislation offended national sensibilities. The Tokyo-based correspondent for *The Times* in London reported that the Japanese were deeply resentful of 'the implications of racial inferiority'. The issue was one 'the significance of which every Japanese feels keenly'. The man in the street 'went straight to the root of the question' and knew that the conflict affected 'the position of his race in the world'. The Californians had created a situation in which the Japanese 'claim of equality with Occidentals' was publicly refuted. The cause had become one of national honour and feelings were running high.[26]

An American scholar, Francis Peabody, who was visiting Japan when news of the Alien Land Law was received, reported that there was 'a general sense of bewilderment', because many people still considered the United States a friendly nation. He observed that a statue of Commodore Perry, paid for by the Emperor, had recently been unveiled on the southern shore of Tokyo Bay.[27] When the United States government failed to impose its will on California, disillusionment grew. The normally cautious, semi-official, *Japan Times* initially suggested that the legislation would be rescinded but, by August 1913, had concluded that the United States government was supporting and encouraging the 'idea of white hegemony in all disregard of humanity and international justice'. Those Japanese who had relied on the American spirit of justice and humanity had 'built a castle of idealism in America, and it collapsed'.[28] The Japanese Nationalist writer, Tokutomi Soho, declared that the many Japanese appeals to American goodwill, sympathy and a sense of justice had all been pointless.[29]

Japanese newspapers kept their readers informed about the debate in California, reproducing transcripts of speeches and articles from American journals. An essay in the San Francisco *Argonaut* provoked particular anger, with the editor of *Japan Times* declaring that in all the country's foreign intercourse during the last fifty years, the Japanese 'as a race' had never been subjected to 'so gross, unreasoning and savage an insult' as offered there. It was 'a trumpet call for a war for a white hegemony' and a challenge to all 'down-trodden Asiatics'. The most offensive passages in

---

[24] Chinda to Bryan, 9 May 1913, cited in Kiyo Sue Inui, 'The Unsolved Problem of the Pacific', *Japan Times* (1925) p.517.
[25] Cited by Inui, 'The Unsolved Problem', p.517.   [26] *The Times*, 21 May, 21 June 1913.
[27] F. G. Peabody, 'Nagging the Japanese', *North American Review* 198 (1913) p.332.
[28] *Japan Times*, 7, 23 August 1913.   [29] *Ibid.* 6 August 1913.

the paper referred to the reasons Americans could not accept the Japanese upon 'even and equal terms'. First, there was the 'instinctive sense of physical repugnance on the part of white people towards the Japanese race'. Nobody entering a street car, observed the reporter, would take a seat beside 'a Jap' and many people avoided the cars normally used by them. It was not so much a matter of cleanliness but an:

instinctive, an inherent feeling based on sensibilities which have little relation to individual habits. The feeling is precisely that which leads the white race everywhere to avoid association with black men.[30]

Japanese intellectuals and political leaders responded to these insults with their own outburst of *jinshuron* or 'racial discourse'.

At a public demonstration in Kyoto, protesting against the Californian legislation, Dr Sanjiro Ichimura of the Imperial University listed what he thought were the principal characteristics of the white races. They considered they alone were human beings and that the coloured races belonged to a 'lower order of civilization'. They were extremely selfish, insisting on their own interests, while ignoring those of all those whom they regarded as inferior. They were full of racial pride and conceit. If any concessions were made to them, they demanded and took more.[31]

In an article in the monthly review *Shin-Nihon*, Dr Ryotaro Ngai of Waseda University, echoing 'Viator' in *Fortnightly Review* and DuBois in 'The Souls of White Folk', noted that the 'whites enjoy possession of half the world' and confined 'the yellows to a corner of Asia', all the while preaching universal peace.[32] The former and future Prime Minister, Count Shigenobu Okuma, added his authority to the attack on Europeans and North Americans, telling an audience at Waseda University in May 1913 that:

The white races regard the world as their property and all other races are greatly their inferiors. They presume to think that the role of the whites in the universe is to govern the world as they please. The Japanese were a people who suffered by this policy, and wrongfully, for the Japanese were not inferior to the white races, but fully their equals.[33]

The white claim to ownership of the whole earth, he said, had to be resisted.

The most dramatic response to the Californian question came from Tokutomi Soho, who used his newspaper, *Kokumin Shimbun*, to launch a campaign against what he called *Hoku Batsu* or 'white snobbery'.[34]

---

[30] *Ibid.* 6, 7 August 1913.
[31] Cited by A. M. Pooley, *Japan's Foreign Policies* (London, Allen & Unwin, 1920) p.16.
[32] *Ibid.* p.18.   [33] *Ibid.* p.17.   [34] *Japan Times*, 3 June 1913.

By now, Tokutomi Soho, an erstwhile admirer of Western liberalism and critic of the Meiji had emerged as a leading promoter of a military state and an imperialist Japan. He had a genius, said the Tokyo correspondent of *The Times*, for expressing what the man in the street 'feels and wants'.[35] Tokutomi Soho declared that it had been by the 'gospel of strength' that Japan had attained its present position and by that alone it would make good its claim to equality with white men. No one should hope to get on in the world, he observed, by always begging mercy of others. It was force alone that counted. White men considered the world was created for their sole delectation. They thought they were the Elect of God and called all other people heathen. It was not religion, however, that determined one's place in the world, but colour. To be 'yellow' was 'not much better than to be black'. In a rallying call for the unity of the not-whites, he wrote: 'We coloured people must combine and crush Albinocracy. We must make the whites realize that there are others as strong as they'.[36]

Tokutomi Soho's call for solidarity with other non-Europeans re-invigorated a debate, decades old, between the competing objectives of pan-Asianism or *Ajia Shugi*, on the one hand, and alliance with the West – *Datsuaron* – or 'escape Asia', on the other. The debate was renewed in mid-1913, on the occasion of a pan-Asian meeting in Tokyo, which brought together political activists from India, Turkey and Malaya. Reporting the meeting, the *Osaka Mainichi* expressed the hope that at a time when the 'white man's domination was at its height' and the 'white peril was growing more and more imminent', Asian leaders would not content themselves with merely giving vent to their resentment, but would join together to start 'a more united movement on a big scale'.[37] The Osaka paper returned to the question two months later, observing that while the country had no global ambitions at present, the racial prejudice of whites might cause the Japanese 'to find their level among the coloured peoples'.[38]

But still some Japanese voices called on their fellow countrymen to persist in dialogue with the West. The idea of providing a cultural bridge between East and West continued to attract many intellectual and political leaders, with the editor of *Japan Times* insisting that the country's distinctive mission in the world was to bring about better understanding between East and West.[39] The *Japan Weekly Mail* still had faith that Japan might educate Europe into the knowledge that a coloured race was capable of matching the achievements of white races. Once that goal

---

[35] *The Times*, 21 June 1913.   [36] Pooley, *Japan's Foreign Policies*, p.16.
[37] Cited in *Japan Times*, 5 June 1913.
[38] Cited in *Japan Weekly Mail*, 23 August 1913.   [39] *Japan Times*, 4 June 1913.

was realised then racial conflict would cease.[40] Prime Minister Count Shigenobu Okuma continued to promote the idea of international mediation. Throughout much of his long political career, he displayed, as Akira Iriye noted, 'a fascination with the idea of cross-culture bridge building'.[41] In an essay in 1914, when he resumed office as Prime Minister, Shigenobu Okuma declared that it was Japan's task to harmonise Eastern and Western civilisations in order to bring about 'the unification of the world'. The Japanese stood at the meeting point between the two civilisations of East and West and could thus serve as interpreters of the Orient to the Occidentals. To brand the Japanese as inferior because their skin was coloured was bigotry, a prejudice that had to be combatted in pursuit of the national mission.[42]

A grave international issue

By the middle of 1913, it was clear that the Japanese demand for equality of status with Western powers had created a far-reaching international disturbance. The local conflict over Californian land law had suddenly emerged as 'a world question', as *The Times* of London put it, in a long editorial on 'Japan's Place in the World'.[43] *Collier's Weekly* called it 'The World's Most Menacing Problem', involving that most confronting issue, 'the riddle of the intermingling of races'.[44] London's *United Service Gazette* observed that Western nations' opposition to the entry of 'the yellow race into their own sphere of influence' had its genesis on the Pacific Slope and in Britain's southern Dominions and would surely result in military struggle.[45]

Visiting New York, Australia's former Labor Prime Minister, Andrew Fisher, declared that California was doing the right thing in trying to exclude Japanese migrants: it was 'a fundamental mistake ... to allow Orientals into a land reserved for Westerners'.[46] The Australian High Commissioner in London, Sir George Reid, speculated like many about the possibility of a race war arising from Japanese assertiveness.[47] The Premier of Victoria, W. A. Watt, also in London at the time, expressed his sympathy with the Californians and his pride that Australia had shown the way with policies to 'keep its skin white and its blood pure'.[48]

[40] *Japan Weekly Mail*, 27 September 1913.
[41] Akira Iriye, *Japan and the Wider World* (London, Longmans, 1997), p.35.
[42] Shigenobu Okuma, 'Mission of the New Japan', in N. Masaoka (ed.) *Japan to America* (New York, Putman, 1915) p.2.
[43] Cited in *Japan Times*, 2 August 1913.   [44] *Ibid.* 20 July 1913.
[45] *Ibid.* 26 August 1913.   [46] Cited in *Japan Weekly Mail*, 23 August 1913.
[47] Cited in *Japan Times*, 2 August 1913.   [48] *Ibid.*

Between May and July 1913, the challenge posed by Japan was the subject of a lengthy debate between Valentine Chirol, the recently retired foreign editor of *The Times*, and Admiral A. T. Mahan, the celebrated American naval historian, political commentator and friend of Theodore Roosevelt. Chirol fired the opening shot in the discursive war with a long article in *The Times* headed: 'Japan Among The Nations. The Bar Of Race. A Grave International Issue'. He made the case that despite the dramatic changes during the previous fifty years, no event could compare with the rise of Japan. 'All the world over' Japan had 'shaken the fatalistic acquiescence of other races in the white man's claim to pre-eminent domination'. The Californian question threatened to force to definitive issue a question which diplomacy had been at pains to avoid. The ultimate issue was whether Japan, which had made good its title to be treated on a footing of complete equality as one of the great powers, was not entitled to rank among the civilised nations, whose citizens the Americans should accept on a basis of equality. Chirol dismissed many of the arguments used in California to discredit Japanese migrants, emphasising the role played by racial prejudice. The question which Japan raised with absolute propriety was whether Asiatic descent should permanently disqualify nations from the enjoyment of the rights fully accorded to one another by the great nations of the world.[49]

Responding to Chirol, Mahan argued that given the overwhelming popular opposition to Asian migration, in both the United States and Canada, there was little room for manoeuvre, because democratic governments rested on the popular will. Then there was the issue of the capacity of the Japanese to assimilate. The cultural traditions of Europe and Asia were profoundly different and deeply entrenched; they were found in the 'moulding of character, national and individual through sixty-odd generations'. While Mahan recognised the 'great superiority of the Japanese, as of the white, over the negro', he thought it perfectly reasonable for Americans to dread the introduction of another race problem, which would see the establishment of a 'homogeneous foreign mass', which would successfully withstand assimilation.[50] In Mahan's defence of white exclusiveness, the Japanese were charged with both an incapacity to assimilate and a lack of desire to really do so.

Across the Pacific, some Japanese leaders shared their American counterparts' anxiety about the prospect of a race war. By 1914, Marshall Yamagata Aritomo, the 'most important military and most influential figure in modern Japan', according to historian R. F. Hackett, had become convinced that the greatest danger to the future of the world was a

[49] *The Times*, 19 May 1913.   [50] *Ibid.* 26 June 1913.

world-wide struggle between the white and coloured races.[51] His conversation and letters written at the time also reflected his fear of an impending alliance of the Western countries 'to subjugate the world of the coloured people'. Yamagata believed that recent events such as 'the exclusion of Japanese in the state of California' and the 'discrimination against Indians in British South Africa' pointed to the likelihood of an eventual clash of world-wide dimensions. But whatever transpired, 'inferiority must end'. It was Japan's intention 'to gain equality'.[52]

Viscount Kentaro Kaneko, one of Japan's most respected elder statesmen, also reflected on the race question. He had been a leading politician, a distinguished jurist with a doctorate from Harvard, a friend of Theodore Roosevelt and long-time President of the Japanese–American Friends' Society. In an essay written in 1915 for an American audience, he noted that racial conflict presented one of the greatest problems in the world, arising in Australia and America and extending 'almost everywhere on the surface of the globe'. The true cause of the current problem, however, was Japan itself and its rapid rise in power and international status. Had Japan remained 'a China or a Korea in its progress', the race problem would not have been raised to 'so high a pitch'. As it was, Japan had 'imposed respectful consideration' on the leading Western powers, thereby challenging 'their traditional assumption that the white race is essentially superior to the yellow'. In a passage recalling Pearson's apprehensions in *National Life and Character*, he observed that:

Japan was allowed a membership in the council of nations, which position had been long denied her. Not all the older members liked to admit her, but she demanded such admission from them on the strength of her achievement and was given it. For scores of years they had been revelling among themselves with self-congratulations on white-superiority; but now, much to their disillusionment, they found yellow Japan squeezing herself in.

Japan expected to associate with the Western powers on equal terms, but was disparaged as 'a yellow race'. This physical difference seemed to loom very large in the eyes of the white countries, which were dismayed by the appearance of a 'little stranger'. If there were anything that Japan could teach the West, it was that mankind was a 'one and indivisible

---

[51] Roger F. Hackett, *Yamagata Aritomo in the Rise of Modern Japan, 1838–1922* (Cambridge, Harvard University Press, 1971) p.343.

[52] Cited by P. G. Lauren, 'Human Rights in History: Diplomacy and Racial Equality at the Paris Peace Conference', in M. L. Krenn, *Race and US Foreign Policy from 1900 through World War II* (New York, Garland, 1998) p.260; Hackett, *Yamagata Aritomo*, pp.270–1; R. F. Hackett, 'The Meiji Leaders and Modernization: The Case of Yamagata Aritomo', in M. B. Jansen (ed.) *Changing Attitudes Towards Modernization* (Vermont, Tuttle Rutland, 1965) p.249; F. R. Dickinson, *War and National Reinvention: Japan in the Great War, 1914–19* (Cambridge, Harvard University Press, 1999) pp.81, 249–51.

whole' and that the yellow race was not 'inferior to the white'.[53] Kentaro Kaneko hoped in vain. The essential 'oneness of humanity' was a lesson that white men's countries were not likely to embrace any time in the near future.

In the United States, agitation continued for the introduction of a more effective regime of immigration restriction. As Japanese newspapers noted, the American anti-Japanese movement was extending from the organised labour movement to include educational and social leaders, and it was moving from the west to the east coast.[54] Indeed, these years saw a convergence of west coast anti-Asiatic agitation and the lobbying of the east coast-based Immigration Restriction League. Since the 1890s, Congress had passed legislation on numerous occasions incorporating a literacy test as a method to curtail immigration from southern and eastern Europe, but Presidents Grover Cleveland, William Taft and Wilson had all vetoed the measure. In 1917 the proposal finally became law, when Congress overrode Wilson's second veto. The Immigration Act also specified a 'barred Asiatic zone' that excluded all the native inhabitants of an area that ran from Afghanistan to the Pacific, with the exception of the Japanese, who still enjoyed the special arrangement of the Gentlemen's Agreement.

A new world order?

During the war, Japanese leaders were encouraged, as were other coloured and/or colonised peoples, by Wilson's talk of a new post-war order based on international equality. The well-known commentator on Japanese–American relations, the elegant and urbane K. K. Kawakami, noted that all the president's addresses were translated and published in the local press. 'Every utterance' that fell from the President's lips, 'every sentence proceeding from his pen', was read and studied by millions of Japanese. Of all his 'noble utterances', there was one in particular that went 'most forcibly to the Japanese mind'. It was a passage from a speech of 2 April 1917, which Kawakami reproduced in his book *Japan and World Peace*:

Only a peace between equals can last. Only a peace the very principles of which are equality and a common participation in a common benefit. The right state of mind, the right feeling between nations, is as necessary for a lasting peace, as is the just settlement of vexed questions of territory or of racial and national allegiance. The equality of nations upon which peace must be founded, if it is to last, must be an equality of rights; the guarantees exchanged must neither

---

[53] Kentaro Kaneko, 'What Japan Has to Teach America', in Masaoka, *Japan to America*, pp.7–8.
[54] *Japan Times*, 13 February 1915.

recognise nor imply a difference between big nations and small, between those that are powerful and those that are weak... Equality of territory or of resources there, of course, cannot be; nor any other sort of equality not gained in the ordinary peaceful and legitimate development of the peoples themselves. But no one asks or expects anything more than an equality of rights.[55]

Historians have noted that Wilson's idealistic promises appealed to oppressed peoples around the world, whose representatives would make their way to the Paris Peace conference to state their case for national independence and self-determination. Japanese leaders were encouraged to believe that the post-war world would recognise the right to racial equality; Chinese and Korean delegates also hoped to secure their liberation from Japanese imperial domination. The Korean nation, like the Chinese, Egyptians and Indians, would seek 'self-determination' in Paris, petitioning Wilson for the reconstitution of Korea as an independent state.[56]

Japan's status as an imperial power constituted, however, one of the bases of its claim to equal status in the world and shaped its expectations of the post-war order. It had occupied Taiwan following the defeat of China in 1895; fifteen years later, Korea and the Liaotung Peninsula, including Port Arthur, were formally annexed as a result of the Japanese victory over Russia. In August 1914, within a few weeks of Germany's declaration of war on Russia and France, Japan declared war on Germany and demanded its complete withdrawal from its possessions in the Pacific. Before the end of the year, the Japanese navy, with the assistance of a small British force, captured Tsingtao and Japan replaced Germany as the colonial power in the province of Shantung. Seeking to allay international concerns about its territorial ambitions, Prime Minister Count Shigenobu Okuma telegraphed a message to the New York *Independent* saying in part that Japan 'had no ulterior motive, no desire to secure more territory, no thought of depriving China or other peoples of anything which they now possess'.[57]

The following year, however, the Japanese government moved to consolidate its control over the unstable new Republic of China, by serving Twenty-One Demands on President Yuan Shih-kai, their basic aims being to succeed Germany in Shantung, to consolidate the Manchurian

[55] K. K. Kawakami, *Japan and World Peace* (New York, Macmillan, 1919) pp.48–50. See also Immigration Restriction League papers, Houghton Library, Ms Am 2245 (1121). The League collected all of Kawakami's books. Advertising material described this latest volume as 'even more eloquent and brilliant, more interesting and informative, than in his previous works'.
[56] Erez Manela, 'Imagining Woodrow Wilson in Asia: Dreams of East-West Harmony and the Revolt against Empire in 1919', *American Historical Review* 111, 5 (December 2006).
[57] *Independent*, 24 August 1914.

territory won in the war with Russia and add to it a part of Mongolia, to gain a controlling share in China's iron output, to secure the military safety of Japan by rendering impossible the further lease of any of China's coastal ports and finally, to enter into such close economic, military and political relations with China as to make it virtually a tributary state. Japan expected to assume leadership of post-war Asia and talk spread of an 'Asiatic Monroe Doctrine'. Some nervous critics suggested that calls for racial equality were simply the latest expression of Japan's pan-Asian ambitions.

Asia for the Asiatics

In his new book, *The Rising Generation in the Taisho Era and the Future of the Japanese Empire*, Tokutomi Soho represented Japanese aims in terms of a colour line drawn to exclude whites:

> What we want is simply that we become independent of the whites . . . The Asiatic Monroe Doctrine is the principle of Eastern autonomy, that is, of Orientals dealing with Eastern questions . . . It is clear as light that the above theory will be received by the whites with anything but favour, but world affairs cannot always be settled to the advantage of the whites, nor were we born to serve the whites.[58]

And in *Modern Review*, Shumei Okawa confirmed:

> It is our firm conviction that the mission of the Japanese Empire consists in carrying out the Asiatic Monroe Doctrine in the most complete manner. By this Asiatic Monroe Doctrine we mean the principle that Asiatic affairs should be dealt with by the Asiatics.[59]

British intelligence reported on their writings and the activities of the semi-secret and ultra-nationalist Black Dragon Society and its publication, *The General Outlook in Asia*, which advocated 'an uncompromisingly hostile attitude towards the white races and [asserted] the moral superiority of the Eastern races and more especially of the Japanese race over those of the West'. It presented Japan, in the words of the British Consul in Yokohama, G. J. Davidson, as 'the heaven-sent liberator of the Eastern races from the domination of the white races'.[60]

---

[58] D. Petrie, 'The Pan-Asiatic Movement', Memorandum, p.14, Enclosure, Foreign and Political department, India to J. Shuckburg, Secretary, India Office, 26 September 1918, Singapore National Archives; see, too, 'Memorandum on Japanese Pan-Asiaticism and Siberia', in William Wiseman papers, 666/1/6, Manuscripts and Archives, Yale University Library.

[59] Petrie memorandum, *Ibid.*

[60] G. J. Davidson, 'Japan Pan-Asiatic Movement', Secret Political Department, 24 January 1919, India Office, Singapore National Archives.

In a 'Confidential Memo' between the United Kingdom and the United States, it was noted that although 'Pan-Asiaticism' could not, for obvious reasons, be openly adopted by the Japanese government, 'it occasionally seems to lie in the mental background... of individual Ministers'.[61] It influenced the view that the European war was 'a war of the white peoples' and that after the war, Japan, as a first-class power, would demand entry to Australia, the annexation of the South Sea Islands, a Protectorate over China and 'whichever way the [European] war may be terminated', an active role in settling the disposal of the Ottoman Empire.[62] At any future Peace Conference, wrote Dr Hosuke Nagasa, in *Shin Nippon*, 'Japan will be the sole representative of the Asiatic race, and in my opinion it is the duty devolving on this country to speak on behalf of the Turk on that occasion, if not to claim the emancipation of the whole Asiatic race'.[63]

Another British intelligence report suggested that these views were probably shared at the highest level in Japan. Speaking to some visiting Indian students in 1916, Prime Minister Count Shigenobu Okuma reportedly stated that he knew that Indians were dissatisfied with British rule and were anxious to be free; that Japan was deeply interested in Indian affairs and that a body of influential and educated men was considering the question of aiding India in accomplishing political reforms. A number of Indian nationalists, including Taraknath Das and Lala Lajpat Rai, had visited Japan before and during the war. Rai's book, *Young India*, was circulating widely, and Das, who before the war had edited the *Free Hindusthan* in Vancouver, now predicted that out of the war would arise a free India and Asia purged of 'the white man's power and presence'. Count Okuma remarked that 'a general hatred for Europeans was growing in Japan everyday'.[64]

The search for solutions

The United States and the British government, conferring before the end of the war, anticipated that Japan would present the Peace Conference with a series of demands in return for its role as a wartime ally. These would include sovereignty over the Shantung Peninsula, occupation of the German islands in the Pacific and possibly the right of immigration to the British Dominions. In a memo to the British government, Sir William Wiseman, the Head of British Intelligence in the United States during the war, wrote that 'there was reason to believe that in the general

[61] Memorandum on Japanese Pan-Asiaticism and Siberia, Wiseman Papers, 666/1/6, Manuscripts and Archives Yale University Library, p.1.
[62] *Ibid.* pp.3–4. [63] *Ibid.* p.5. [64] Petrie memorandum, pp.9–13.

settlement the Japanese will press for the free right of entry into Canada, New Zealand and Australia on the same footing as Europeans'.[65] Wiseman advised that the Japanese claim could be dealt with by the precedent established at the Imperial Conference with regard to Indian immigration, that is, that immigration restriction should be seen as reciprocal. Just as Indians had no right to live in any other part of the British Empire, so the white residents of Australia or Canada had no right to live in India. 'Japan can then be told that within the British Dominions the matter has been settled on a footing of absolutely equal reciprocity . . . This will mean that the Japanese have no right to acquire domicile in Australia and the Australians have no right to acquire domicile in Japan'. Visiting rights could be regulated with passports 'while still in vogue' as a result of war. The United States could also come into the arrangement and if this were done the most dangerous source of friction between America and Japan would be removed.[66]

Japan, meanwhile, was working on a different strategy to address this most dangerous source of friction: an international declaration in support of the principle of racial equality. Woodrow Wilson's high-sounding talk about a new world order based on justice and equality evoked, as we have seen, great enthusiasm in Japan. The editor of the Tokyo *Yorozu* noted that the President was committed to a policy of 'universal brotherhood' and perhaps he would level the wall of racial discrimination as well.[67] His colleague, writing in *Nichi-Nichi*, wondered how far Wilson would go in implementing his professed ideals, but was confident that at the end of the war the allied powers would deal in a just manner with the problem of racial discrimination. After all, the experience of the war had helped 'wipe out or at least mitigate prejudices and antipathies between different races of mankind'.[68]

The war had disrupted conventional ideas of racial solidarity, K. Takahashi observed in the *Japan Times*. On the one hand, the white races were at war with each other. On the other, the British were bringing Indians to fight in Europe and the French were recruiting Africans, South East Asians and Pacific Islanders. Japan was allied to Britain, while Turkey fought alongside Germany and Austria. Nothing fostered mutual trust and regard as much as shared perils and the hardships of military campaigning. The spirit of comradeship thus engendered could not fail to influence those involved. Racial prejudice, Takahashi believed, was a product of misinformation and would die out as inter-racial

[65] William Wiseman, 'Memorandum on Asiatic Migration', William Wiseman papers, Manuscripts and Archives, 666/1/6, Yale University Library.
[66] Wiseman, 'Memorandum on Asiatic Migration'.
[67] Cited in *Japan Times*, 3 December 1918.   [68] *Ibid.*, 8 December 1918.

communication and understanding increased. Indeed, perhaps the war had 'shed a new ray of hope on this extremely difficult problem showing how it might solve itself'.[69] In any case, despite what Kipling had pronounced, the unalterable fact was that 'the West has gone to the East, and the East has come to the West', wrote K. K. Kawakami, and the future peace of the world, he warned, depended on racial reconciliation.[70]

[69] *Ibid.*, 7 January 1915.
[70] Immigration Restriction League papers, Ms Am 2245 (1111), Houghton Library.

12   Racial equality? The Paris Peace Conference, 1919

Fleets in European seas

Japan played a minor, albeit advantageous role, in the First World War, over-running the German colonies in the Pacific Islands and the Concession on China's Shantung Peninsula. The navy patrolled the Pacific and Indian Oceans and, after much persuasion from the allies, extended its sway into the Mediterranean. Ironically, given Australian attitudes towards Japan, it was the Japanese fleet that protected the troopships conveying the Australian and New Zealand armies to the Middle East. The demands of war greatly stimulated Japanese industry and available markets expanded with the temporary eclipse of British and German competitors.

When the world's nations gathered to formalise the peace treaty and create a League of Nations, Japan was accorded the status of one of the great powers alongside the United States, Great Britain, France and Italy, each with two representatives on the Committee. Still virtually invisible to Charles Pearson in 1893, Japan had yet, in a quarter of a century, seemed to fulfil his prophesy about the challenge to the West posed by the rise of the 'yellow races'. The Japanese Empire had been invited into alliances with European powers, was 'represented by fleets in European seas', 'circumscribing the industry of Europeans' and invited to participate as an equal in international conferences.

Japanese race discourse

The long crusade to achieve equality with the Western powers appeared to have been finally successful. But there was still the unresolved question of race. *Jinshuron*, or 'race discourse', had been a feature of public life since the early twentieth century, intensified by well-publicised examples of discrimination by California and the British Dominions. Local interpreters of Western intellectual life were well aware of the salience of race in America and Australasia. Japanese officials could thus never be sure whether they were accepted as equals or if their status was forever diminished by being deemed 'not-white'. While internationally minded commentators welcomed the prospect of a new world order based on a league of equal nations, others feared that it could perpetuate the dominant position of the Anglo-Saxon countries.

In an article in November 1918, in Tokutomi Soho's *Kokumin*, the main object of the projected League of Nations was defined as the 'equalization of the races of the world'. But its role in the world could not be fully realised 'so long as Japanese and other coloured races are differentially treated in white communities'.[1] In his recent study, *Japan, Race and Equality*, Naoko Shimazu observed that the question of racial equality dominated domestic debate in Japan from November 1918 until May 1919, because of its symbolic importance as an expression of Japan's fears and expectations of the new international order.[2]

Advising the delegation

The appointment of Marquis Saionji, Viscount Chinda and Baron Makino in late November to lead the Japanese delegation to France, and the departure of the main party in December, called forth considerable comment and advice from their countrymen. The editor of *Asahi* put his thoughts in an article 'What Japan Should Demand at Versailles'. After referring to the common expectation that Japan would take over the German possessions in China and the Pacific Ocean, he argued that above all else the delegation must persuade the conference to relinquish the policy of racial discrimination, which, if not curbed, would continue to menace the future peace of the world. 'Fairness and equality', the editor declared confidently, 'must be secured for the coloured races who form sixty two per cent of the whole of mankind'.[3]

As the Japanese leaders departed for France they were farewelled with a united chorus of newspaper commentary. The *Kokumin* hoped the delegation would not betray the trust placed in it by the country. The elimination of racial discrimination was as important an objective as the formation of a League of Nations.[4] *Asahi* agreed. No other question was

---

[1] Cited by Naoko Shimazu, *Japan, Race and Equality: The Racial Equality Proposal of 1919* (London, Routledge, 2002) p.55.
[2] *Ibid.* p.51.   [3] Cited in *Japan Times*, 15 January 1919.   [4] *Ibid.* 11 December 1918.

so inseparably and materially interwoven with the permanency of the world's peace as that of unfair and unjust treatment of a large majority of the world's population.

And Japan could not have set forth her views with greater propriety and juster contention than in vindication of the wrong suffered by other races than the white.[5]

The racial discrimination question must be fought to the last, declared the editor of *Yamato*. The elimination of that 'unjust practice' was the 'greatest of Japan's missions'. Discrimination meant the 'usurpation of rights and interests on the part of the white race'. If Japan did not rise to curb them, who would be there to 'check the unbridled selfishness and domination of the white people?'[6] The editor of *Nichi Nichi* expressed hope that the allies would deal with the question of racial equality with 'sincerity and justice'.[7] Referring to US President Woodrow Wilson's talk of universal brotherhood, the *Yorozu* thought it 'unimaginable' that he would retreat from his cherished ideals.[8]

Sixty million souls

In the early months of 1919, public opinion in Japan was mobilised by numerous pressure groups. The Japan–American Association, the Association for Publicists of Peace Issues, the League for People's Diplomacy and the Sun and Stars Association all held public meetings and pressed on government the importance of racial equality. The League to Abolish Racial Discrimination brought together representatives from the major political parties, the bureaucracy, the armed services and thirty-seven other public associations. Following a mass meeting in Tokyo, in February 1919, the League cabled the French President, Georges Clemenceau, expressing its expectation that the Peace Conference would abolish all forms of racial discrimination. At a second mass meeting in March, it was resolved to oppose the establishment of a League of Nations if it were not based on the abolition of racial discrimination.[9] Commenting on the public ferment, the Japanese–American scholar K. K. Kawakami observed that the racial equality question was forced on the government by 'the masses of Japan'. It was 'the proposal of sixty million souls of the Mikado's Empire'.[10]

---

[5] *Ibid.* 31 January 1919.   [6] *Ibid.* 27 March 1919.
[7] *Ibid.* 3 December 1918.   [8] *Ibid.*
[9] *Ibid.* 9 February, 11 March 1919; Ian Nish, *Alliance in Decline: a Study of Anglo-Japanese Relations, 1908–1923* (London, Athlone Press, 1972) p.269; Shimazu, *Japan, Race and Equality*, pp.51–3.
[10] K. K. Kawakami, *Japan and World Peace* (New York, Macmillan, 1919) p.46.

Whose equality?

Officials in the Japanese Foreign Ministry and members of the prestigious Advisory Council on Foreign Affairs were, however, concerned that racial prejudice might jeopardise Japan's position at the projected League of Nations. Draft guidelines prepared by the Japanese Foreign Office for the delegation in Paris urged that plans for such an organisation be shelved 'in view of the racial prejudices which have not yet entirely been banished from among the nations' and which would produce results 'gravely detrimental to Japan'. If, however, the League became a *fait accompli* Japan could not afford to remain on the outside and the delegates should make efforts to secure suitable guarantees against disadvantage arising from racial prejudice. Only then could Japan be confident that the Western powers would not use the new body to 'freeze the status quo'.[11]

The instructions of both the Cabinet and the Advisory Council were clear that the country's participation in the new international organisation depended on the inclusion of a racial equality clause either in the body or the preface of the planned covenant of the League of Nations. As Naoko Shimazu has noted, the Japanese government was principally concerned with attaining equality with the Western powers, but their focus was on the discrimination suffered by its nationals in other countries. Their demand was a 'highly particularistic and nationalistic' expression of Japan's desire to prevent its nationals, and thereby itself, from suffering the 'humiliation of racial prejudice in the League of Nations'.[12]

But once publicised, the idea of racial equality ceased to be merely a national concern. In the heady, idealistic moment at the end of the war – the Wilsonian moment – Japan's cause became a universal one.[13] Supporters and opponents alike came to see the proposal for an end to racial discrimination as a universal crusade. In his recent study of the Indian and Chinese response to Wilson's promise of self-determination, Erez Manela has rightly criticised existing scholarship on the Paris Peace Conference for remaining 'rather single-mindedly focussed on Europe', but his focus is on the appeal of 'self-determination' to colonised peoples, such as Indians and Chinese, rather than the campaign for racial

[11] N. Kawamura, 'Wilsonian Idealism and Japanese Claims at the Paris Peace Conference', *Pacific Historical Review*, vol.66, no.4 (1997) p.515; Lesley Connors, *The Emperor's Advisor: Saionji Kinmochi and Pre-war Japanese Politics* (London, Croom Helm, 1987) pp.70, 233.

[12] Shimazu, *Japan, Race and Equality*, pp.113–15.

[13] For the most recent invocation of the optimism unleashed by the 'Wilsonian moment', see Erez Manela, 'Imagining Woodrow Wilson in Asia: Dreams of East-West Harmony and the Revolt against Empire in 1919', *American Historical Review* 111, 5 (December 2006).

equality and the principle of non-discrimination waged by the Japanese Empire.[14]

Dissent in the delegation

Saionji, the leader of the delegation, and his two lieutenants were pro-Western, cosmopolitan thinkers, committed to the creation of a League of Nations and Japan's participation in it. But this determination was not shared by the whole delegation. Prince Konoe Fumimaro, a twenty-seven-year-old aristocrat, wrote an article called 'Reject the Anglo-American-Centred Peace' in the leading nationalist journal *Nihon Oyobi Nihonjin*, which appeared in December 1918, five days after the delegation left for Paris. Konoe took his stand on the 'sense of equality' among men, which he believed was the 'fundamental moral doctrine for the human community'. In his view, Japanese leaders were so enthralled by the 'spectacular pronouncements' of Anglo-American politicians that they failed to see that behind the rhetoric was a large measure of self interest. The proposed peace treaty would maintain the *status quo*, which preserved the dominance of the leading Western nations and their control of the world's resources through shutting out foreigners from their 'colonial areas'. Konoe demanded that the minimum condition for joining the League should be the eradication of economic imperialism and the 'discriminatory treatment of Asian peoples by Caucasians'. 'We must require', Konoe declared:

all powers to open the doors of their colonies to others, so that all nations will have equal access to the markets and natural resources of the colonial areas. It is also imperative that Japan insist on the eradication of racial discrimination. At the coming peace conference we must demand this in the name of justice and humanity. Indeed the peace conference will provide the opportunity to determine whether or not the human race is capable of reforming the world on those principles.[15]

The initial approach

Aware of likely difficulties with their proposal for a declaration of racial equality, the Japanese delegates Makino and Chinda made preliminary approaches to the Americans, talking in particular to President Wilson's trusted adviser, Colonel Edward Mandell House. Having received an

---

[14] Manela, 'Imagining Woodrow Wilson', pp.1328–9.
[15] Yoshitake Oka, *Konoe Fumimaro: A Political Biography*, Shumpei Okamoto and Patricia Murray (trans.) (Tokyo, University of Tokyo Press, 1972, 1983 edition translated by S. Okamoto) pp.11–13.

unexpectedly favourable response, they presented the Americans with a tentative draft text to be incorporated in the Covenant of the League of Nations, which read:

The equality of nations being a basic principle of the League of Nations, the High Contracting Parties agree that concerning the treatment and rights to be accorded to aliens in their territories, they will not discriminate, either in law or in fact, against any person or persons on account of his or their race or nationality.[16]

House rejected the proposal, but accepted a second one, which added the proviso that the nations in question would accord aliens equality, 'as far as it lies in their legitimate powers'.[17] House and Wilson operated as a team. Both were Southern gentlemen, members of the Democratic Party and dedicated Anglo-Saxonists. But whereas House was small, dapper and accommodating, Wilson was tall, lanky and proud. House specialised in the political diplomacy necessary to give effect to Wilson's self-righteous idealism. The American president never ceased to champion the virtue of his New World democratic republic against the decadence and despotism of Old World European monarchies. The United States government, he insisted, was 'contending for nothing less high and sacred than the rights of humanity'.[18]

Colonel House was not a military man: his title was bestowed by the governor of Texas in recognition of his work for the Democratic Party. As a reformer, House was an admirer of Australian democracy. In his earlier political campaigns and through his novel *Philip Dru*, he had enunciated a set of progressive policies that borrowed heavily on the Australian example: the 'Australian ballot', land title reform, old age pensions, industrial arbitration and women's suffrage.[19] His support of the Australian position at Versailles would be crucial in the defeat of the Japanese bid for racial equality.

Before the war, House had devoted much effort in trying to bring about an Anglo-Saxon alliance of Britain, Germany and the United States that would, in his view, prevent the outbreak of military conflict. At talks in Germany, the Kaiser, who had been strongly influenced by Charles Pearson's *National Life and Character*, 'ranted on about the demographic strength of Asia': it was he who coined the phrase 'yellow peril' after

---

[16] Morinosuke Kajima, *The Diplomacy of Japan, 1894–1922, Vol. III, First World War, Paris Peace Conference, Washington Conference* (Tokyo, Kajima Institute of International Peace, 1980) p.396.

[17] *Ibid.* p.396.

[18] Godfrey Hodgson, *Woodrow Wilson's Right Hand, The Life of Colonel Edward M. House* (New Haven, Yale University Press, 2006) p.112.

[19] *Ibid.* pp.49–51.

reading Pearson's book. He spoke of the necessity of Anglo-Saxons standing together and the impossibility of forming alliances with Latins (the
French) or Slavs (the Russians).[20]

But when the First World War started in August 1914 it was not
between the East and West, as so many had predicted, but a conflagration
that threw Europeans against other Europeans. With the onset of hostilities, House engaged, with the President's approval, in an extensive round
of shuttle diplomacy, crossing dangerous submarine-infested seas, in an
attempt to bring about a negotiated peace. He became close to key British
advisers, especially their chief intelligence agent, Sir William Wiseman,
and Foreign Secretary, Sir Edward Grey, and was ably assisted by his son-
in-law, Gordon Auchincloss, whose law partner was David Hunter Miller,
an author of an early American draft of a constitution of the League of
Nations.

House prided himself on his diplomatic skill, which was nowhere more
evident than in his negotiations with the Japanese and the British over the
proposed racial equality clause. He intimated to the Japanese that Wilson supported the amended proposal. The British delegates, the Conservative politicians Lord Robert Cecil and Arthur Balfour of the Foreign
Office, also gave them some encouragement. But this was not to last. The
white Dominions, which had been accorded separate representation at
Versailles while simultaneously comprising part of the British delegation,
refused to entertain the proposal at all. Its most vociferous opponent was
the 'obstreperous' Australian Prime Minister, W. M. Hughes.[21] House
noted in his diary on 9 February:

I had a good many callers today, including Viscount Chinda and Baron Makino,
who came again upon the inevitable race question. I have placed them 'on the
backs' of the British, for every solution which the Japanese and I have proposed,
Hughes of the British delegation objects to.[22]

Before the Commission

The Japanese decided to take their proposal to the League of Nations'
Commission, where discussions on the draft Covenant were nearing completion. Makino proposed to add the declaration regarding racial equality
to Article 21 of the Covenant, which guaranteed religious freedom. In his
speech in support, he observed that racial discrimination still existed in

---

[20] *Ibid.* pp.96–98; Richard Thompson, quoted in David Walker, *Anxious Nation Australia and the Rise of Asia 1850–1939* (St Lucia, University of Queensland Press, 1999) p.3.

[21] Hodgson, *Woodrow Wilson's Right Hand*, p.207.

[22] Charles Seymour (ed.) *The Intimate Papers of Colonel House*, 4 vols. (London, Ernest Benn, 1928) vol. 4, p.324.

law and in fact and while he was aware of the difficult circumstances which stood in the way of acting on the principle embodied in the clause, they were not insurmountable if sufficient importance were attached to the matter. He argued that the basic principles of collective action embodied in the Covenant could only be effective if all people felt they were on an equal footing with other nations. He reiterated the ideas commonly expressed in Japan during the war:

> In this war, to attain the common cause, different races have fought together on the battlefield, in the trenches, on the high seas, and they have helped each other and brought succour to the disabled, and have saved the lives of their fellow men irrespective of racial differences, and a common bond of sympathy and gratitude has been established to an extent never before experienced. I think it only just that after this common suffering and deliverance the principle at least of equality among men should be admitted and be made the basis of the future intercourse.[23]

But Makino's appeal to shared wartime experience failed to carry the Commission. Instead, a decision was made to delete the whole of Article 21 along with the Japanese amendment.

Public opinion in Japan was inflamed by the failure to achieve the desired amendment to the Covenant and so remove the 'badge of shame' imposed on Asians and Africans by the white race.[24] Japanese commentators considered they were leading an idealistic crusade; the editor of *Asahi* compared the activity of Makino and Chinda with Britain's insistence in 1815 that the delegates at the Treaty of Vienna condemn the slave trade. Racial discrimination, the newspaper declared, occupied precisely the position in the contemporary world that slavery did one hundred years before. Being the leading coloured power, Japan had the responsibility to fight for the cause of two-thirds of the world's population and the country could not fight for a 'nobler cause'.[25]

In Paris, initial frustration notwithstanding, the Japanese delegation persisted with the cause, spending a considerable amount of time in a series of meetings with the Americans, the British and Dominion politicians and officials. They continued to meet with obfuscation and opposition from a variety of sources. While discussing Japan's draft proposal with Colonel House, British Foreign Secretary Balfour announced that while he sympathised with the Japanese, he could not accept the principle of racial equality. This old Enlightenment idea was now 'outmoded',

---

[23] Kajima, *The Diplomacy of Japan*, pp.399–400.
[24] P. G. Lauren, 'Human Rights in History: Diplomacy and Racial Equality at the Paris Peace Conference', in M. L. Krenn, *Race and US Foreign Policy from 1900 Through World War II* (New York, Garland Publishing, 1998) p.265.
[25] Cited by Lauren, 'Human Rights in History', p.266.

he said. While all men of a particular nation might be considered to be born free and equal, he was far from convinced that an African 'could be regarded as the equal of a European or an American'.[26]

Wilson's ambivalence

While Colonel House spent many hours talking with the Japanese and always appeared supportive, the United States position was much more complicated than Wilson's public pronouncements had suggested. The President was born and raised in the South and there is little doubt he remained a Southerner in his attitude to race relations, despite his term as President of Princeton University and Governorship of New Jersey. He was opposed to social relations between the black and white races and barred Afro-Americans from enrolling at Princeton while President.[27] He was a Democrat who was dependent on the southern and western states and their senators to guide his legislation through Congress. Wilson's administration introduced a greater degree of segregation in the federal government than had been seen since the Civil War. Even the accommodating Booker T. Washington was moved to remark, in August 1913, that he had never seen 'the coloured people so discouraged and bitter as they are at the present time'.[28] In 1915, the D. W. Griffith film, 'Birth of the Nation', celebrating the Ku Klux Klan, was given a special screening at the White House, where the President endorsed it as 'all so terribly true'.[29]

It was Wilson's political dependence on California, however, that was more directly relevant to events at Versailles. The west coast states had been of major importance in securing Wilson's presidential victories in 1912 and 1916, when his supporters had distributed electoral material emphasising his opposition to Asian immigration. In the 1918 mid-term Congressional elections Wilson's political enemies inflicted a crushing defeat and long-term anti-immigrationist, Henry Cabot Lodge, became Senate Majority Leader and Chair of the Foreign Relations Committee. So even as they dealt with international challenges in Paris, the leaders of the American delegation remained sensitive to the sensibilities of the voters at home. Colonel House sent a copy of Japan's racial equality

---

[26] S. Bonsal, *Unfinished Business* (London, Michael Joseph, 1944) p.38.

[27] Arthur Stanley Link, *Woodrow Wilson: The Road to the White House* (Princeton, Princeton University Press, 1947) p.502.

[28] Arthur Stanley Link, *Woodrow Wilson and the Progressive Era, 1910–1917* (New York, Harper, 1954) p.249.

[29] Ibid. p. 65; David Levering Lewis, *W. E. B. DuBois: Biography of a Race 1868–1919*, vol. 1 (New York, Henry Holt and Co., 1993) p.506.

clause to Senator Elihu Root, formerly Theodore Roosevelt's Secretary of State, asking for his comment. Root, a supporter of the Immigration Restriction League, replied with an emphatic: 'Don't let it in, it will breed trouble'. It would be difficult enough for Wilson to gain support for the League of Nations, but with the racial equality clause attached, he would 'get nowhere in the Senate'. On the Pacific coast, they would certainly think there lurked behind it 'a plan for unlimited yellow immigration'.[30] American ambivalence about the League of Nations also flowed from their attachment to the Monroe Doctrine – the principle of American sovereignty in the Americas – and hostility to European interference in American affairs.

When news of the Japanese proposal reached California, opposition was indeed immediate and vociferous. J. D. Phelan, now a United States Senator, launched a powerful propaganda campaign and besieged the delegation in Paris with angry telegrams. Any declaration on the subject of race equality, 'or just treatment', he warned, could be construed as giving jurisdiction to an international body over immigration, naturalisation, the franchise, land ownership and marriage. Western senators would oppose any measure by which 'Oriental people' would gain equality with the white race in the United States. It was, he declared, in a now familiar vein, 'a vital question of self-preservation'.[31] Thomas F. Millard, in a report from Paris, explained that the Japanese stand in favour of racial equality was simply a pretext, useful to the 'Pan-Asian propaganda which for a number of years Japan has been carrying on in all Asiatic countries' whose current expression was 'race equality'.[32]

Democrats confront aristocrats

But if the white men on the American west coast sought to curtail Wilson's freedom of movement, their counterparts in the British Dominions – Australia, New Zealand, Canada and South Africa – exercised an equally great influence on the British delegation. From the moment he became aware of the Japanese proposal, in February 1919, until its final defeat in April, Australia's W. M. Hughes refused to consider any compromise. He was implacable and vociferous in his opposition. An American official, Colonel Stephen Bonsal, recorded in his diary on 16 March 1919 how Hughes:

[30] Chitoshi Yanaga, *Japan Since Perry* (New York, McGraw-Hill, 1949) p.21.
[31] Cited by Shimazu, *Japan, Race and Equality*, p.138.
[32] Thomas F. Millard, 'Japan, "race equality" and the League of Nations', 6 April 1919, Immigration Restriction League papers, Ms Am 2245 (1069), Houghton Library.

morning, noon and night bellows at poor Lloyd George that if race equality is recognized in the preamble or any of the articles of the Covenant, he and his people will leave the Conference bag and baggage.[33]

When pressed by House to accept a compromise, Hughes scribbled a message in reply saying that he would sooner 'walk into the Seine – or the Folies Bergeres with my clothes off'.[34] His graphic threat was inspired by recent experience. Hughes had visited that famous Parisian landmark with some Australian colleagues and friends on his very first night in Paris, keen, like most of those who travelled to Paris that spring, to see the tourist sights.

Other Australians in the delegation shared Hughes' anxiety about the Japanese. John Latham, writing to his wife, Ella, told her of the attempt to get 'something' into the Covenant about racial equality. He observed that Hughes was fully aware of the fact that 'no government could live for a day if it tampered with a White Australia'.[35]

As with the United States delegation, the Australians in Paris were inundated with resolutions from home. The Deputy Prime Minister, W. A. Watt, sent a telegram to Hughes on 4 April, following a Cabinet meeting in Melbourne, reaffirming the view of the Government that 'neither people nor Parliament of Australia could agree to principles of racial equality'.[36] Concern to maintain White Australia had also motivated Hughes' attempt to annex the German colony of New Guinea in defiance of Wilson's protestations against perpetuating the spirit of Old World imperialism. Watt urged him to persist, arguing that any 'mandate' should 'specify publicly and definitely' that Australia must control immigration into New Guinea. Surely, Watt urged:

America must sympathize with a people isolated and adjacent to unnumbered coloured millions, but resolutely facing its duty to keep this fertile continent and its intimately associated island for selected white races.

Hughes cabled back, expressing his doubts as to the outcome, because there was no guarantee of upholding 'our policy of excluding Asiatics'.[37] In the event, however, the creation of the Class C Mandate was designed

---

[33] S. Bonsal, *Suitors and Supplicants: The Little Nations at Versailles* (New York, Kennikat Press, 1946) p.229.

[34] Margaret McMillan, *Peacemakers: Six Months That Changed the World* (London, John Murray, 2001) p.328.

[35] Papers of Sir John Latham, MSS. 1009, Series 21, folder 22, National Library of Australia.

[36] Watt to Hughes, 4 April 1919, Series CD 290/3, Box 1, no.16, National Archives of Australia.

[37] Watt to Hughes, 1 February 1919, Hughes to Watt, 13 February 1919, C. P. 290/3, *Ibid.*

precisely to meet the concerns of Hughes in the Pacific and Jan Smuts in South West Africa.

Hughes's opposition to the Japanese proposal for a racial equality clause was driven by his certainty that their real objective was to enable their nationals to migrate to any land of their choosing. He feared that the prevailing spirit of internationalism in Paris – the exotic atmosphere of 'the polyglot Conference' as he remembered it in his memoir – might persuade the majority to support a cosmopolitan approach to world affairs. At such a world gathering, he wrote, the representatives of Australia seemed to be 'almost isolated, a tiny patch of white in a great sea of colour'. But despite the unsympathetic attitude of the majority at the Conference, in which were represented 'nearly 1,000 millions of people – 800 million of which were coloured' – the policy of White Australia triumphed.[38]

Born in London, but of Welsh descent, Hughes decided as a young man to try 'the possibilities of adventure' offered by a steamship voyage to the Australian colonies in 1884.[39] Only twenty-two years old when he disembarked in Brisbane, his work experience in Britain had been confined to a short stint as a teacher. Hughes was formed by the advanced democracy of the New World, working as a bush labourer before being elected to office in New South Wales by manhood suffrage, and to the federal parliament by universal suffrage. While his irreverent, larrikin style was seen as being quintessentially Australian, he would have also felt at home in Auckland, Vancouver, San Francisco or Johannesburg. Hughes rapidly became a champion of the white man and, in the manner of the most contemporary policy-makers, declared that his hostility to Asian migration was not motivated by racial superiority, but by Asiatic difference. When one of his most able officials, Major E. L. Piesse, suggested, in a memo written in preparation for the Peace Conference, that when considering the 'greater part of the Japanese nation', there was little reason for applying discrimination which was not thought necessary in regard to the 'less advanced European nations', Hughes crossed the comments out and scrawled 'Rot' in the margin.[40]

The Australian Prime Minister's rude manner, which served him well in trade union affairs and Australian labour politics, evoked both surprise and antagonism in the polite ambience of the Peace Conference. Frederick Eggleston, a young intellectual attached to the Australian

[38] W. M. Hughes, *The Splendid Adventure: a Review of Empire Relations Within and Without the Commonwealth of Britannic Nations* (London, Ernest Benn, 1929) pp.107–8.

[39] L. F. Fitzhardinge, *William Morris Hughes: A Political Biography: That Fiery Particle, 1862–1914* vol.1 (Sydney, Angus and Robertson, 1964) p.12.

[40] J. R. Poynter, 'The Yo-yo Variations', *Historical Studies*, vol.14, no.54, April 1970, p.240; E. L. Piesse Papers, MSS. 882/2/42, 118, NLA.

delegation, described Hughes as 'a typical battler' with neither reserve nor reticence. He knew little of European history nor of international diplomacy.[41] The elegant British newspaper correspondent Lord Riddell had tea with Hughes and was bemused when he put his unlit cigarette behind his ear, 'creating a curious contrast to his regal surroundings'.[42] His forthright manner – and class origins – antagonised many people. The British Foreign Secretary, the aristocratic Arthur Balfour, was heard to murmur to a companion 'Que je le déteste' as Hughes rose to speak.[43]

Two American lawyers, David Miller and Gordon Auchincloss (House's secretary and son-in-law), were, on the other hand, interested in learning more about industrial regulation in Australia and the role played by the High Court in striking down the Excise Tariff Act in 1908. 'This was a case that David Miller had used in connection with the argument of the Cotton Futures case that we had several years ago in New York', wrote Auchincloss in his diary. Hughes told him that he had been an Attorney for the government concerned with this case. 'This was quite interesting', wrote Auchincloss, 'I had no idea that Hughes had been in the case'.[44]

For Hughes, the Australian democrat, the niceties and courtesies of aristocratic diplomacy smacked of insincerity and hypocrisy. He wrote of Baron Makino entering his office, 'literally wreathed in smiles, and beslobbering me with genuflexions and obsequious deference'.[45] The Australian official, Eggleston, noted that Hughes 'hated these interviews' with Makino and Chinda, whom he referred to as 'two little fat Japanese noblemen in frock coats and silk hats, neither much more than five feet high'.[46] The aristocratic Japanese delegation found these encounters equally unpleasant. In their report to the Foreign Office in Tokyo, they explained that the fact that they had 'such a person' as Hughes as their adversary had been a great inconvenience. His character was 'completely that of a labour leader' and he lacked the temperament to look at situations as a statesman.[47] Ian Nish, historian of Japanese diplomacy, observed that the leaders of the delegation regarded Hughes as 'a peasant'. That he was a leading politician was 'scarcely comprehensible' to

[41] F. W. Eggleston Papers, MSS. 423/6/23, 423/6/70, 423/6/84, NLA.

[42] Lord Riddell, *Lord Riddell's Intimate Diary of the Peace Conference and After, 1918–23* (London, Victor Gollancz, 1933) p.17.

[43] L. F. Fitzhardinge, *William Morris Hughes: A Political Biography: The Little Digger, 1914–1952* vol.2 (Sydney, Angus and Robertson, 1979) p.414.

[44] Gordon Auchincloss, Diary, 2 May 1919, Auchincloss Papers, Series 1, box 3, Yale University Archives.

[45] W. M. Hughes, *Policies and Potentates* (Sydney, Angus and Robertson, 1950) p.245.

[46] Eggleston Papers, 423/6/23, p.4, NLA.

[47] Fitzhardinge, *William Morris Hughes: The Little Digger*, p.414.

them and it came 'as a staggering revelation' that Britain had not been able to discipline its Dominions or lay down a common policy for them.[48] But, as David Miller observed, 'Australia had more influence with London than did Tokyo'.[49]

Negotiations continued

Having been initially rebuffed in February, the Japanese delegation returned to their task in late March fortified by fresh instructions from Tokyo and news of growing public anger over the question of racial discrimination. Over a four-week period, Makino and Chinda had more meetings with the Americans, the British and the Dominion leaders, including Smuts from South Africa, Sir Robert Borden from Canada and William F. Massey from New Zealand. In an attempt to win wider support, the Japanese drafted a new proposal which read:

Equality of nations being a basic principle of the League of Nations, the High Contracting Powers agree to endorse the principle of equal and just treatment to be accorded to all alien nationals of State members of the League.[50]

On 23 March, Makino and Chinda called on the leading British delegate, Sir Robert Cecil, seeking his support. Cecil explained that while he personally favoured the proposal he could not make a definite reply because the question was 'after all an Australian one'.[51] At a meeting the following day, Cecil indicated that Hughes and the other Dominion leaders were maintaining an attitude of absolute opposition and that direct negotiations with them were necessary.

A meeting was arranged on 25 March at Borden's quarters. The Japanese explained that they were under great pressure from the public at home but sought to allay fears about immigration to the Dominions. The Dominion leaders expressed their concern about the difficulties that would be created for them if the provision were applied to the Chinese and the Indians and that they could not agree to it unless the word 'equal' was deleted. The Japanese refused to budge. Borden worked out a compromise proposal which would recognise 'the principle of equality between nations and just treatment of their nationals'. Hughes alone opposed it. Massey was willing to go along with the compromise, but only if Hughes concurred. Hughes declared that as the representative of Australian public opinion, he had no choice but to oppose it absolutely. What mattered was not the wording of the proposal, but the 'underlying idea

---

[48] Nish, *Alliance in Decline*, p.271.   [49] Hodgson, *Woodrow Wilson's Right Hand*, p.210.
[50] Kajima, *The Diplomacy of Japan*, pp.403–4.   [51] *Ibid.* p.404.

itself which ninety-five out of a hundred Australians rejected'. Pressed by
his colleagues to find a compromise, Hughes walked out of the meeting.[52]

Negotiations were resumed with Smuts, the former Boer general promoted to field marshal in the British Army, playing a key role as mediator. A favourite with both the United States and British delegations,
and much sought after as a dinner guest in Paris, Smuts brought to the
negotiations his newly acquired prestige as a war hero and author of the
original British draft of a proposal for a League of Nations. He had fought
alongside Botha in the conquest of South West Africa and then led the
allied forces against the Germans in East Africa in a campaign of dash
and daring. When he arrived in London in March 1917, he was show-
ered with honours and invitations from the most fashionable hostesses
in the capital. Combining the characteristics of the intellectual and man
of action, he was called the 'most romantic figure' in Britain, charming
men and women in equal measure.[53]

Smuts became a key figure in the war effort and post-war planning – a
member of the War Cabinet, a diplomatic emissary and the organiser of
the nascent Air Force. He became friends with many of the leading liberal intellectuals in Britain, including economists J. A. Hobson and J. M.
Keynes, journalist and lobbyist E. D. Morel and imperial scholar Gilbert
Murray, all of whom were engaged in intense debate about the need for
a new world order.[54] When asked by the government to prepare a paper
on Britain's post-war options, Smuts produced a blueprint for a League
of Nations and a system of 'mandates' to be applied to the territories
appropriated from the German and Turkish Empires. It was published
as a pamphlet, *The League of Nations: A Practical Suggestion*, in 1918
and became a bestseller. In London, for the joint United States/British
meeting prior to the Paris conference, in December 1918, the Americans
were impressed with Smuts' draft document. 'It is a remarkable one',
wrote Auchincloss, '. . . & adopts many principles we have been contending for'.[55]

The Wilson entourage was quite smitten by the handsome, manly,
South African statesman. They thought he should be the next British
Ambassador to the United States, because he 'thinks along the same lines
as the President does and it would be a very popular appointment'.[56]

[52] Henry Borden (ed.) *Robert Laird Borden: His Memoirs* (London, Macmillan, 1938)
pp.927–8.
[53] W. K. Hancock, *Smuts, Vol.1, The Sanguine Years 1870–1919* (Cambridge, Cambridge
University Press, 1962) p.437.
[54] *Ibid.* p.462; see also H. R. Winkler, *The League of Nations Movement in Great Britain
1914–1919* (New Jersey, Scarecrow Reprint, 1967).
[55] Auchincloss Papers, 5801, series 1, box 2, Yale University Archives.
[56] *Ibid.* Diary, 24 January 1919.

In the negotiations between the Japanese, the British and the Americans, Smuts played the role of go-between, explaining that the British couldn't support the proposal because Hughes of Australia had threatened to make a public attack on the whole League of Nations should a clause be inserted in the preamble recognising racial equality.[57] Colonel House warned Makino that if Hughes spoke out against the Japanese proposal, President Wilson would be forced to side with him, because of his concern for public opinion on the west coast of the United States.[58] Makino replied that Japan could not tolerate a situation in which the strong opposition of Hughes alone defeated their proposal.[59] Further discussions between Makino, House, Border and Smuts failed to resolve the matter, so the Japanese decided to put their proposal to the final meeting of the Commission.

Top dogs triumph

Makino presented an eloquent and moving speech in his last bid to have a racial equality clause included in the preamble of the Covenant of the League of Nations. He explained that the subject of racial equality was a matter of great moment and concern for a considerable part of mankind. The idealism which shaped the League had 'quickened the common feelings' of people all over the world and had given birth to hopes and aspirations and strengthened the sense of unmet, but legitimate claims. In close connection with the grievances of oppressed nationalities, there existed the 'wrongs of racial discrimination', which were the subject of 'deep resentment on the part of a large portion of the human race':

The feeling of being slighted has long been a standing grievance with certain peoples. And the announcement of the principle of justice for peoples and nationalities as the basis of future international relationships has so heightened their legitimate aspirations, that they consider it their right that this wrong should be redressed.

Makino observed that if the reasonable and just claim embodied in the Japanese proposal were to be denied, it would, in the eyes of many people in the world, cast a lasting reflection on their status. Such a contingency had to be borne in mind, 'for pride is one of the most forceful and sometimes uncontrollable causes of human action'.[60]

David Miller thought the Japanese presentation very admirably done and secured the sympathy of almost everyone present.[61] Writing to Lloyd

[57] *Ibid.* Diary, 29 March 1919.   [58] Kajima, *The Diplomacy of Japan*, p.407.
[59] *Ibid.* pp.411–12.   [60] *Ibid.* p.412.
[61] D. H. Miller, *The Drafting of the Convention*, 2 vols. (New York, Putman, 1928), vol.1 p.461.

George a few days later, Cecil observed that the Japanese had made speeches of great moderation and he, too, thought that practically every member of the Commission supported them.[62] In the ensuing debate they were backed by some of the most prominent personalities at the Conference – Orlando of Italy, Bourgeois of France, Venizolos of Greece and even Wellington Koo of China, who was in conflict with Japan over the future of the German concession in Shantung. Cecil, nevertheless, refused to accept the amendment acting, as he said, under instructions from his government. House's secretary, Auchincloss, reported on the vote in a telegram on 13 April to the US Under-Secretary of State, Frank Polk:

> League of Nations draft of Covenant completed this morning at one o'clock... The Japanese offered amendment to preamble recognising equality of nations and just treatment of their nationals. Their proposals which were ably presented by Baron Makino and Viscount Chinda, were discussed without any bitterness whatever. They received support from more than the majority of the members of the Commission. Lord Robert Cecil on behalf of Great Britain flatly opposed them, and the President made a very conciliatory speech, urging that the matter not be pressed on account of the bitter discussion which might arise at the plenary session... Inasmuch as the inclusion of a clause in the draft covenant required the unanimous consent of the members of the Commission, the Japanese proposal was rejected. Lord Robert Cecil's flat objection made it unnecessary for us to vote on the question.[63]

Observing this scene, Miller thought that Cecil behaved as though he were performing a difficult and disagreeable task. After making his statement, he sat with his eyes fixed on the table and took no further part in the debate.[64]

Cecil had been Under-Secretary for Foreign Affairs under Grey and now under Balfour. Described as 'tall and thin, with the manner of a highly intellectual monk (he was a committed Anglican layman)',[65] Cecil was the son of the Conservative Prime Minister, the Marquis of Salisbury, who had dressed down Alfred Deakin in 1887, at the first colonial conference in London, for his impertinence in speaking out of turn about the role of the French in the Pacific. Cecil's discomfort in Paris was an indication of how the imperial balance of power had shifted over twenty years in favour of the white Dominions.

In 1897, at the conference on the occasion of the Queen's Jubilee, which brought together the leaders of the self-governing colonies,

---

[62] Cecil to Lloyd George, 15 April 1919, Lloyd George Papers, House of Lords, F6/6.
[63] Auchincloss Papers, diary, telegram, No. 80, 13 April 1919.
[64] Miller, *The Drafting of the Convention*, 1, p.461.
[65] Hodgson, *Woodrow Wilson's Right Hand*, p.200.

Colonial Secretary Joseph Chamberlain had been able to impose his will in relation to immigration restriction by persuading the colonial premiers to adopt an educational test, to preserve at least the appearance of the equality of imperial subjects. In Paris in 1919, the Dominion leaders, and more particularly Hughes, had been able to impose their will on the British government. Rather than take a stand on the question of racial equality, Cecil told the Japanese it was an Australian matter and not an issue of fundamental importance for the Empire as a whole. The tables had been turned in favour of the white men of the English-speaking New World. Eggleston noted, with satisfaction, that at meetings of imperial leaders in Paris, the Dominions were 'top dogs'.[66]

Lifting the load of responsibility

The Americans, it seemed, were happy to let the British, and in particular Hughes, take responsibility for the defeat of the racial equality clause. Though a majority of the Commission supported the Japanese proposal, Wilson, as chairman, declared that a unanimous vote was required (although on an earlier occasion he had permitted a mere majority vote prevail). He observed that none of those present wished to deny the principles of the equality of nations or the just treatment of nationals. But the discussion had already lit 'burning flames of prejudice' which it would be very unwise to allow to flare in public view. He may have been responding to Colonel House's note handed to him as discussion proceeded, which read: 'The trouble is that if this Commission should pass it, it would surely raise the race issue throughout the world'.[67]

In his study of Anglo-American relations in Paris, Seth Tillman concluded that Wilson, fearing an outburst of hostile opinion in the western states, submitted to the threats of Hughes, rather than stand up for his principles.[68] But what were his principles? Clearly his commitment to Anglo-Saxon solidarity and white supremacy were all important, but so were his national political interests. His personal physician, Dr Grayson, observed in his diary that concealed in the apparently simple Japanese request was the nucleus of serious trouble in the United States, in as much as it would allow Asians to demand the repeal of discriminatory laws in California and other western states.[69] The Californian politicians

[66] Eggleston Papers, 423/6/68, p.11, NLA.
[67] Miller, *The Drafting of the Convention*, pp. 461, 3.
[68] S. Tillman, *Anglo-American Relations at the Paris Peace Conference of 1919* (Princeton, Princeton University Press, 1961) p.304.
[69] Arthur Stanley Link (ed.) *The Papers of Woodrow Wilson*, vol.57 (Princeton, Princeton University Press, 1981) p. 239.

and newspapers had made their opposition to the Japanese proposals absolutely clear.

In his memoir, *Policies and Potentates*, published in 1950, Hughes claimed that on the night before the vote was taken, he met American reporters from the western states and urged them to protest against 'this evil, this wicked clause', which would bring disaster to the people of the Pacific Slope and gravely imperil those in adjoining states.[70] In a subsequent meeting with the Japanese press in Paris, Hughes pointed to the role of the United States in defeating racial equality. Australia had no vote at the Commission and the Japanese shouldn't take at face value Wilson's avowed support for their position. Alarmed at the prospect of growing anti-American feeling in Japan, House responded to Hughes' press conference by immediately sending a cable to the United States Ambassador in Japan, asking him to make an appropriate reply in the Japanese press.[71]

In her recent study *Peacemakers*, Margaret Macmillan has questioned the sincerity of American support for the Japanese position. While Makino and Chinda repeatedly appealed to House, she suggests that they were looking in the wrong quarter. Wilson was not prepared to fight for a policy that he did not support and which was unpopular in the United States. Privately, he was delighted that the British were forced by Hughes to oppose the racial equality clause. 'It has', wrote Wilson's right hand man, 'taken considerable finesse to lift the load from our shoulders and place it upon the British, but happily it has been done'.[72] Dr Grayson made a similar note in his diary:

However, it was not necessary for the US openly to oppose the suggested amendment because Australia and New Zealand, through the British representatives, had taken the position of positive opposition.[73]

Smuts, too, benefitted from Hughes' truculence, because it enabled him to play the suave international statesman, all the while certain that the proposal for racial equality – a principle he had opposed throughout his political career – would be defeated. He, too, was able to deftly place the blame on Hughes and the White Australia policy. But when the Dominion leaders met again at the Imperial Conference in London in 1921, it was Smuts alone who stood out against the policy of granting equal rights to Indian immigrant communities across the Empire.[74]

---

[70] Hughes, *Policies and Potentates*, p.247.
[71] Auchincloss Papers, series 1, box 3, folder 3.
[72] McMillan, *Peacemakers*, pp.328–9.
[73] Link, *The Papers of Woodrow Wilson*, vol. 57, p.239.
[74] W. K. Hancock, *Smuts, vol. 2, The Field of Force* (Cambridge, Cambridge University Press, 1962–68) p.149.

National shame

Events in Paris were followed closely in Japan. The defeat of the racial equality clause was a profound disappointment, the import of which was thought to be not 'properly understood in the West'.[75] Liberal, internationally minded Japanese were dismayed. They had played the game and had shown themselves ready to participate in the international community on its terms. The rebuff was an important factor in turning the country towards more aggressive nationalist policies at home.[76] To Tokutomi in the *Kokumin*, failure in Paris was a 'disgrace to the country' and disproved Japan's confidence that it had been accepted as a great power. Even more humiliating, Japan had been betrayed by its own wartime allies.[77] The Anglo-American delegates had defied humanity in the 'most outrageous manner to go down in history' and thus invited the ill feeling of one billion coloured people all over the world.[78] The editor of the *Yorozu* remarked that the nation's attention was centred on the failure of the racial equality proposal, which made a mockery of President Wilson's 'contentions for humanity'.[79] *Nichi Nichi* believed that the spirit of the League Covenant was dead due to 'Anglo-Saxon dominance in defiance of racial equality'. The defeat was due to the prejudices of America, England, Canada and Australia, and the paper could not 'suppress its anger' at the Anglo-Saxons, who thought they could control the wealth of the world and subjugate all other races.[80]

Perhaps the most significant comments were made in a long editorial in *Japan Times*. The failure of Japan to achieve the acceptance of racial equality had caused the 'sorest disappointment'. When the motion had been detached from any reference to immigration, the government had been attacked by the nationalists, but moderate thinkers were convinced that there would be no difficulty in having accepted 'a purely academic principle'. The paper observed:

A most careful and comprehensive survey of the feelings of typical and leading thinkers shows that they learnt of the fact with the profoundest regret. All agree in feeling that rejection of a demand formally made by a nation is tantamount to a snub and humiliation.

But some observers, the editor suggested, felt that the Japanese failure had served the purpose of exposing and placing on record the real truth concerning the attitude of whites towards non-whites. The vote in

---

[75] P. J. Treat, *Japan and the United States 1853–1921* (second edition, Stanford, Stanford University Press, 1928) p.242.
[76] McMillan, *Peacemakers*, p.329.   [77] Cited in *Japan Times*, 16 April 1919.
[78] *Ibid.* 20 April 1919.   [79] *Ibid.*   [80] *Ibid.* 26 April 1919.

the Commission would probably result in erecting a perpetual barrier between two groups of people, 'irreconcilable in their respective aspirations'. Japan's admission into the group of the Five Great Powers had been merely a matter of convenience for the allies. The present situation was:

exactly that of a Negro preacher asked to speak in a church because of his oratorical power. To speak from the pulpit is by no means to be identified with an admission of equality from a racial standpoint on the part of the white congregation. It is well for Japan to remember this point.[81]

Japanese commentators continued to discuss the racial equality question after the Peace Conference concluded. In an essay 'My Impressions of the Paris Peace Conference', Konoe Fumimaro argued that he was fully justified in believing that power alone determined the course of international affairs. The racial equality proposal had been defeated because Japan, a lesser power, had proposed it. As a result the hope to reform the world upon principles of justice and equality had been dashed.[82] In 1921, Tokutomi Soho published a book on *Japanese American Relations* (translated in 1922), which sold 300,000 copies and went through twelve editions in a few months. It stressed the disappointment and disillusionment felt by Japan about American racial hostility, that seemed now to be universal in that country. Japan had yet to win the equal treatment that was accorded the human race in general.[83]

But the most authoritative commentary was provided by the eighty-three-year-old former Prime Minister, Marquis Okuma, in an article in *Asian Review*, entitled 'Illusions of the White Race'. Okuma argued that if the Japanese were to see racial equality prevail in the world, the nation must devote itself to the cause with unswerving determination. 'The whites', he observed, 'were obsessed with the mistaken theory that they are superior to all other races'. Such a belief was based neither on science nor evidence of any kind. It was 'mere superstition, backed by historical prejudices', but it was the most serious obstacle in the way of the realisation of racial equality. Some whites, Okuma declared, regarded the development of Japan as an unjustifiable encroachment upon their own rights and aimed to organise a 'league of white nations to perpetuate white supremacy in the world'. Most Asian nations were

---

[81] *Ibid.* 19 April 1919.   [82] Yoshitake Oka, *Konoe Fumimaro*, pp.14–15.
[83] I. Tokutomi [Soho], *Japanese-American Relations*, S. Yanagiwara (trans.) (New York, Macmillan, 1922) pp.138, 154.

fully peers of European nations, yet they are discriminated against because of the colour of their skin. The root of it lies in the perverted feeling of racial superiority entertained by the whites. If things are allowed to proceed in the present way, there is every likelihood that the peace of the world will be endangered.[84]

All well-wishers of mankind, he urged, should do everything possible to remove the gross injustice of racial inequality without delay.

Global disillusion

The struggle for the racial equality clause was closely watched in other parts of the non-European world. The Chinese delegate, Wellington Koo, told the American foreign correspondent, Patrick Gallagher, that he had received letters and telegrams of support from Chinese in all parts of the world including the major American cities, Java, South Africa and Australia.[85] Koo and his fellow Chinese delegate, C. T. Wang, were American-educated cosmopolitans, who published a pamphlet in Paris to put the Chinese case for 'a new order of things which would ensure universal peace'.[86] When the conference decided in late April, in an attempt to assuage Japanese humiliation, to award the former German concession in Shantung to Japan, Chinese disillusionment with the peace conference was complete. Their sense of betrayal fuelled the 4 May protests, that galvanised a larger political and social movement, marking a defining moment in the history of the modern Chinese nation, leading to the downfall of the Chinese liberal republic and its replacement by a Leninist party state.[87]

The Bantu doctor and African National Congress activist S. M. Molema also commented on the outcome of Versailles in his book on the deteriorating position of blacks in South Africa, published in 1920. He pointed to the seething discontent in many parts of the world and his belief that Western liberalism and morality were hollow promises and egregious tricks. Western liberalism was:

an astounding platitude. Its hollowness must have surprised the outside thinking world recently when after four years of hard struggle side by side, after four years of suffering, mutual exchanges of sympathy and help, mutual protestation

[84] Cited in K. K. Kawakami (ed.) *What Japan Thinks* (New York, Macmillan, 1921) pp. 6–7, 161, 170.
[85] P. Gallagher, *America's Aims and Asia's Aspirations* (New York, The Century Co., 1920) p.322.
[86] Manela, 'Imagining Woodrow Wilson' p.1348.
[87] John Fitzgerald, *Big White Lie: Chinese Australians in White Australia* (Sydney, University of New South Wales Press, 2007) p.230.

of friendship, formations and renewals of alliances, after all this and victory, the Western world went to the Peace Table at Versailles with professions of 'Morality', 'Liberalism', 'Justice', 'Making the World Free for Democracy' and so forth, and there at the Peace Table, the Western World made a blot which will go down into history as a fine example of Western Liberalism and Altruism and their idea of 'Brotherhood of Nations'. This was done by making a pointed distinction between the East and the West, and that in spite of all that Baron Makino – Japan's delegate – might say about this being a race question and one that may become acute if not seen to.[88]

W. E. B. DuBois also deplored the refusal to adopt the race equality amendment, but it simply confirmed his view of the arrogance of whiteness and underlined the need for a world congress in which black and white and yellow would sit and speak to curb the 'selfish nations of white civilization'.[89] DuBois elaborated this view in the essays in *Darkwater*, also published in 1920, which included the revised but still prescient 'Souls of White Folk', first published in 1910. The recent war, he declared, a white civil war in Europe, was nothing to compare with the fight for freedom which the 'black and brown and yellow men must make and will make unless their oppression and humiliation and insult at the hands of the White World ceases'.[90]

DuBois had arrived in Paris with accreditation as a newspaper correspondent to cover the peace talks and the formation of the League of Nations. He undertook this journey, he told readers of *Crisis*, because 'the destiny of mankind' was being decided in the French capital.[91] He relished the atmosphere of Paris, with its relaxed attitudes to race and where, he reported, seven Africans sat in the Chamber of Deputies. He looked to the creation of the League of Nations with great hope: it was 'absolutely necessary to the salvation of the Negro race'. He believed 'the organised Public Opinion of the World' would exert an overwhelming influence to counter the doctrine of racial inferiority and antagonism.[92]

DuBois' greatest achievement in Paris was to convene a second Pan-African Congress. He had attempted to win support for this event from Woodrow Wilson, but only got as far as the president's gate-keeper, House, who gave him a 'sympathetic but non-committal hearing', which was more, however, than other activists and nationalists received. The young Vietnamese, Ho Chi Minh, a kitchen hand at the Ritz, sent a

[88] S. M. Molema, *The Bantu* (Edinburgh, W. Green, 1920), p.352.
[89] W. E. B. DuBois, 'The League of Nations', *Crisis*, May 1919.
[90] W. E. B. DuBois, *Darkwater: Voices from Within the Veil* (New York, Harcourt, Brace and Howe, 1920) pp. 49–50, 60.
[91] *Crisis*, May 1919.   [92] *Ibid.*

petition seeking Vietnamese independence from France, but he was 'too obscure' to even receive an answer.[93] DuBois' cause was greatly enhanced by the support of Blaise Diagne, a Deputy from Senegal, and grandly titled 'High Commissioner for the Republic with Special Authority for French West Africa', who sought and received permission for the meeting from Clemenceau, after a wait of two discouraging months.[94] He was assisted in organisation and publicity by the suffragist and widow of a well-known publisher, Madame Calman-Levy, and Ida Hunt, a well-connected and Oberlin-educated American friend, who would serve as assistant secretary to the Congress.[95]

The Pan-African Congress brought together fifty seven delegates from the United States, the Caribbean and Africa on 22 February 1919. With both Britain and the United States denying prospective participants passports, it had been difficult to gather together even that small number. According to the New York *Evening Globe*, there were 'negroes in trim uniforms of American Army officers', other American coloured men in 'frock coats or business suits' and polished French negroes who held public office, including the Senegalese who sat in the Chamber of Deputies.[96] The Congress called on the League of Nations to ensure that all Africans received education, adequate medical care and protection of the rights to traditional lands. There was a demand as well for the abolition of slavery and corporal punishment and the right to participate in government and administration, 'to the end that, in time, Africa be ruled by the consent of the Africans'.[97] The final clause of the manifesto, signed by DuBois and Diagne, declared:

Whenever it is proven that African natives are not receiving just treatment at the hands of any State or that any State deliberately excludes its civilized citizens from its body politic and cultural, it shall be the duty of the League of Nations to bring the matter to the attention of the civilized world.[98]

But, as DuBois reiterated in *Darkwater* in 1920, at that moment in world history, the 'new religion' of whiteness showed no signs of losing its sway. Indeed, in the United States, what became known as the 'Red Summer' of 1919 saw an upsurge of racial hostility – as a tidal wave of arson, murder, riot and rape swept across the country. The murderers and rioters really feared that 'the Negro is breaking his shell', declared *Whip*, a

[93] McMillan, *Peacemakers*, p.67.
[94] W. E. B. DuBois, *The World and Africa* (New York, International Publishers, [1946] 1978) p.8.
[95] Lewis, *W. E. B. DuBois*, pp.568–9.   [96] DuBois, *The World and Africa*, p.9.
[97] *Ibid.* pp.11–12.   [98] *Crisis*, April 1919.

militant Chicago paper, and 'beginning to bask in the sunlight of real manhood'.[99]

In Australia, Prime Minister Hughes, one of the leading proselytisers of whiteness, was basking in his triumph. Returning home as a self-proclaimed national saviour, he celebrated his political victory in Paris. At Fremantle, his first landfall, the local branch of the Returned Servicemen's League congratulated him on the 'brilliant fight' he had put up for Australia, particularly in regard to the White Australia policy.[100] 'May you long be successful', declared the returned soldiers, 'in keeping Australia white'. In his address to the federal parliament, Hughes was pleased to announce:

White Australia is yours. You may do with it what you please; but, at any rate, the soldiers have achieved the victory, and my colleagues and I have brought that great principle back to you from the Conference. Here it is, at least as safe as it was on the day when it was first adopted by this Parliament.[101]

In similar vein, in the United States Congress, Senator Phelan declared that he was 'very glad' that the President, 'standing with representatives of Australia and New Zealand', had stemmed the 'insidious movements of the Japanese' to establish the principle of race equality, 'under which they would have flooded this land'.[102]

The humiliating diplomatic defeat was not easily forgotten in Japan. Naoko Shimazu has concluded that it had deeper psychological effects than has generally been understood. It indicated that the Western powers were unwilling to acknowledge the country as an equal and left an indelible mark on its foreign policy.[103] In 1946, following the Second World War, the Emperor set down his thoughts on 'The Background Causes to the Greater East Asia War'. As a preamble to the document he declared:

If we ask the reason for this war, it lies in the contents of the peace treaty signed at the end of the First World War. The racial equality proposal demanded by Japan was not accepted by the powers. The discriminatory sentiment between the white and yellow remains as always. And the rejections of immigrants in California. These were enough to anger the Japanese people.[104]

[99] Lewis, *W. E. B. DuBois*, p.579.
[100] Hughes Papers, MSS. 1538, Series 16/3, Folder 18, NLA.
[101] Commonwealth Parliamentary Debates, House of Representatives, vol.LXXXIX (1919) p.12175.
[102] Phelan speech in the Senate, 20 February 1920, p.181, cited by Rubin F. Weston, *Racism in US Imperialism: the Influence of Racial Assumptions on American Foreign Policy, 1893–1946* (Columbia, University of South Carolina Press, 1972) p.33.
[103] Shimazu, *Japan, Race and Equality*, p.181.   [104] *Ibid.*

Although the racial equality proposal began its life as a means to achieve equal treatment of Japanese nationals overseas, it came to represent a human rights initiative of global significance. Memory of its defeat weighed heavily on many of those who gathered at San Francisco, in 1945, to draft a Charter for the planned United Nations, with its strong emphasis of human rights for all, regardless of race, nationality, ethnicity, religion or sex.

13   Immigration restriction in the 1920s: 'segregation on a large scale'

Preaching the gospel of whiteness

In February 1924, the sixty-year-old W. M. Hughes sailed from Sydney for a five-month lecture tour of the United States. Now a backbencher, he had lost the leadership of the conservative government after the national elections at the end of 1922, following conflict between the coalition partners. He spoke in major American cities and was invited to leading universities. He had prepared talks on a number of topics – the Versailles Conference, Reparations, the League of Nations and Australia's system of industrial arbitration, but the lectures that attracted most attention were on the future of international relations in the Pacific and the White Australia policy.

It was race that most interested his American audience and Hughes didn't disappoint them, explaining that in Australia, 'we believe in race'.[1] Hughes subscribed to the idea that as Anglo-Saxons, Australians and Americans were 'brother nations by blood' (interestingly, perhaps as a result of the war, Josiah Royce's 'sister republics' were now imagined as masculine in character). Race was responsible, said Hughes, for the energy and the initiative 'of our people'. The greatness of the United States was due to the hitherto purity of stock, which must not be watered down by the mixture of alien races.[2] Australia was of the same select stock and claimed to be 97 per cent Anglo-Saxon.

Australia was 'a world pioneer', Hughes told his audience, holding a great and beautiful land against the hordes of Asia, with whom the Commonwealth had 'no gentleman's agreement or other palavering'. Australia said 'keep out' and they kept out. His countrymen were maintaining a great part of the Earth's surface for white colonisation in future centuries and the destiny of the white race depended upon their success. It was not in the interest of mankind that Australia be submerged in a yellow

---

[1] W. M. Hughes Papers, MSS.1538, file 26, folder 1, draft lecture 'Faith and Works', ANL.
[2] *Ibid.* folder 6, Newspaper report, no date, no place, 'Greatness of America is Due to Purity of Stock'.

sea, which was why the White Australia policy was so important. With every passing year the need for its rigid application grew. Total exclusion was the only remedy. The demographic pressure was so great that the 'smallest trickle' must inevitably become, in a very little time, a steady stream and 'then a rushing foaming cataract'.[3]

Hughes reminded his listeners that Japan had attempted to have the principle of racial equality recognised in the Covenant of the League of Nations and that the European powers had been inclined to support the proposition. 'We were outnumbered', Hughes explained, 'and to all appearances undone'. To Australia and California, this would have meant the abandonment of the policy to which they had hitherto adhered resolutely. If it had not been for Woodrow Wilson's awareness of the strong opposition to racial equality in the western states, the day would have ended 'disastrously for us all'.[4] If the principle of racial equality were ever conceded it would mean the 'end of the White races'. Hughes was 'profoundly convinced' that the East and the West could not meet and live together as one people. It was, he declared:

our thought as it plainly is yours that they must only mingle, if they must, and not blend, for blending inevitably would spell disaster to our race – disaster, grim and irretrievable.

The welfare of mankind could not be promoted by the mixture of races, he said, by 'watering down the bloodstream of race'.[5]

It was for these reasons that Japan posed such a threat to white supremacy in the Pacific. The problem, Hughes confessed to a journalist, had been for years 'his continual study'. He appealed to the people of the United States to provide moral support, and, if necessary, financial and physical assistance to Australia to keep white 'as much of the world as is white today'. You in America, Hughes observed:

seem to be remote from the Far East, but we in Australia are standing as it were at the verge of a great dam, any breach of which would spell our destruction. White Australia is our Protection ... it means we are the garrison of the Western World.[6]

The Commonwealth of Australia was undertaking a great social experiment in which the whole world, and particularly the United States, was interested. It had modelled its constitution on the American one. It followed the same star, but it had learnt from the disastrous experience of

[3] *Ibid.* folders 5 and 6, miscellaneous newspaper clippings.
[4] *Ibid.* folder 4, draft of lecture, 'The Evolution of the White Australia Policy', lecture A.
[5] *Ibid.* cutting from the *Los Angeles Examiner*, 1 June 1924.
[6] *Ibid.* cutting of article by Arthur Brisbane, no place, no date; folder 5, cutting of article, 'Hughes Firm for a White Australia', no place, no date.

the Great Republic with regard to race, the legacy of slavery. Australians felt that in the American people:

we have friends who understand our aspirations, who out of the fund of their own experience subscribe to them, and will if necessary lend support to them.[7]

Resurgent racism

The timing of Hughes' tour was significant. It was surely no accident that it coincided with the introduction of new national immigration restriction legislation – the Johnson Act – aimed primarily at excluding the undesirable races of eastern and south-eastern Europe, who were thought to be 'so alien, so ignorant, and so helpless', sometimes said to have their headquarters in Warsaw, sometimes Constantinople, and increasingly imagined as Jewish.[8] Discourse on undesirable immigration became increasingly anti-Semitic, but there was also the continuing anti-Asiatic crusade on the west coast, with a new law to restrict Japanese land ownership followed by more vociferous demands to put an end to Japanese immigration, which had continued under the Gentlemen's Agreement. 'The state, therefore', wrote Senator James Phelan in a special issue of the *Annals of the American Academy of Political and Social Science*, 'is obliged as a simple matter of self-preservation to prevent the Japanese from absorbing the soil, because the future of the white race, American institutions, and western civilization are put in peril . . . that is what California, Australia and Canada are doing'.[9] The *White American* also pointed to the example of Australia and the other white Dominions:

The Australians are white persons of European birth or descent and they do not believe all persons are good enough to be Australian citizens, so they have declared for a White Australia . . . America, Canada, Australia, South Africa were colonized by the Teutonic and Gaelic races; men who had and still have race pride . . . They have drawn the color line and see the advancement and prominence and population of those countries today. . . [10]

Hughes was gratified that his ideas seemed so much in harmony with the mood of contemporary America. In an article in *North American Review*, in the year of his visit, Phelan demanded that the immigration of 'unassimilable races' be checked immediately to save California for American civilisation, ideals and institutions, otherwise the 'cancerous growth'

---

[7] *Ibid.* folder 4, draft lecture, 'The Evolution of the White Australia Policy', lecture B.

[8] E. A. Ross, 'The Displacement of Higher by Lower Standards of Living', reprint from *American Economic Review* 11, 1 (1912); Immigration Restriction League papers, MS Am 2245 (1129), Houghton Library.

[9] Immigration Restriction League papers, Am 2245 (1111).

[10] *White American*, San Francisco, Immigration Restriction League papers, Am 2245 (1136).

would spread. Assimilation was impossible because intermarriage was unthinkable, 'as tending to mongrelization'. But without marriage there could be no equality, which was the foundation of democracy. Without true assimilation there would be internal racial conflict and strife.[11]

This was the 'flowering time' of eugenics and other forms of 'scientific' racism which dominated so much of political and intellectual life, and the Australian visitor found that his ideas were supported and sanctioned by the leading scholars from the universities he visited – biologists, geneticists, social scientists and anthropologists – many of whom published key works in the early 1920s.[12] To many United States commentators, Australia appeared as a bold pioneer in forging a racially protected homogeneous democracy under the banner of the White Australia policy. It was also leading the way in seeking to establish that the white man – and woman – could live and work in the tropics. Tropical industry did not require black labour or a coolie class.

One of the scholars who met Hughes was the President Emeritus of Chase Western Reserve University in Ohio, Charles Thwing, who had recently visited Australia and published a book, *Human Australasia*, in 1923. One of the many academics who now dominated the national committee of the Immigration Restriction League (others were E. A. Ross, John R. Commons, David Starr Jordan and A. Lawrence Lowell), Thwing believed there was 'a peculiar reason for the adoption of the political and social policy of seclusion' and that Australia's racial experiment would provide the world with valuable knowledge as to the comparative value of 'purity of breed'. How priceless, Thwing declared:

would be the result for human knowledge of the application, for an indefinite period, of the principle of purity of blood of a single tribe or nation, so far as such purity can now be secured.[13]

The decision of Australia and New Zealand to maintain their racial purity was particularly relevant, because of what Thwing considered to be the critical racial situation of the 1920s.

Thwing took his cue from Madison Grant's book *The Passing of the Great Race*, published in 1918, and reprinted in 1921 and 1923.[14] Grant was by then Vice-President of the Immigration Restriction League, and used his trips to the west coast to promote immigration restriction as well as the preservation of the great redwood forests. His book

---

[11] J. D. Phelan, 'Letter to a Japanese Gentleman', *North American Review* (June 1924), in J. E. Johnson (ed.) *Japanese Exclusion, The Reference Shelf*, vol.111, no.4 (1925) pp.128, 131.

[12] J. Higham, *Strangers in the Land* (second edition, New York, Atheneum, 1981) p.271.

[13] C. F. Thwing, *Human Australasia* (New York, Macmillan, 1923) p.247.

[14] Madison Grant, *The Passing of the Great Race* (New York, Arno Press, [1918] 1970).

provided intellectual inspiration for the 'resurgent racism' of the post-war years; his 'thorough-going racial philosophy stirred the imagination of many literate people' including politicians.[15] Grant chaired the Eugenics Sub-Committee of the United States Committee on Selective Immigration that originally recommended an immigration quota of 2 per cent of each group's population based on the United States census of 1890, which would bring about 'a preponderance of immigration of the stock which originally settled this country'.[16] 'It was greatly to be desired', Thwing wrote, that Australia and New Zealand should not be guilty of the 'sin and racial crime which Mr Grant thinks can be charged against the Americans'.[17]

Australia and the other white Dominions were also hailed as heroic pioneers in another influential book, written by Grant's friend, Lothrop Stoddard: *The Rising Tide of Color Against White World Supremacy*, published in 1920. Stoddard became convinced in the early years of the century that the keynote of world politics in the twentieth century would be the coming contest between the primary races of mankind. The campaign against the Japanese was not simply a local issue, but a phase of two larger issues: 'the issue of Asiatic immigration, from whatever source, into the United States; and the even larger issue of colored immigration into lands of white settlement throughout the world'.[18] His global perspective had been influenced by Charles Pearson, whose *National Life and Character* he described as 'epoch-making'. But while Pearson, a liberal and a stoic, had been resigned to the rise of the 'black and yellow races', Stoddard called for decisive action. 'We stand at a crisis', he cried, 'the supreme crisis of the ages'. Nowhere could the white man endure colour competition; everywhere the East could underlive and thus outbid the West. The grim truth of the matter was that:

The whole white race is exposed, immediately and ultimately, to the possibility of social sterilization and final replacement or absorption by the teeming coloured races.[19]

If the world were to avoid the hideous catastrophe of a 'gigantic race war', Asia would have to accept that the white man could not permit

---

[15] Higham, *Strangers in the Land*, p.271; also Matthew Frye Jacobson, *Whiteness of a Different Color: European Immigrants and the Alchemy of Race* (Cambridge, Harvard University Press, 2000) pp.80–3.

[16] Jacobson, *Whiteness of a Different Color*, p.83.   [17] Thwing, *Human Australasia*, p.250.

[18] Lothrop Stoddard, 'Present Day Immigration with Special Reference to the Japanese', *Annals of the American Academy of Political and Social Science* vol.xciii, no.182 (1921), Immigration Restriction League papers, Am 2245 (111).

[19] Lothrop Stoddard, *The Rising Tide of Color Against White World Supremacy* (London, Chapman & Hall, 1920) p.298.

migration to white men's countries or the settlement of the non-Asian tropics. 'Immigration restriction is a species of segregation on a large scale', wrote Stoddard memorably, 'by which inferior stocks can be prevented from both diluting and supplanting good stocks'.[20]

All the white regions of the New World, won by white expansion over the previous four centuries were now menaced, claimed Stoddard, by the 'color migration peril'. On these matters the white man would prefer to 'fight to a finish' rather than ever yield, and he looked to the example of the 'lusty young Anglo-Saxon communities bordering the Pacific' – Australia, New Zealand, British Columbia and California together with South Africa – for guidance and example.[21] They had one and all:

set their faces like flint against the Oriental and have emblazoned across their portals the legend 'All White'. Nothing is more striking than the instinctive and instantaneous solidarity which binds together Australians and Afrikanders, Californians and Canadians, into a 'sacred union' at the mere whisper of Asiatic migration.[22]

Stoddard hailed the emergence of a transnational community of white men with whom Americans should join in solidarity. Subjective racial identification, as much as race thinking, was a key dynamic of white solidarity. The new religion of whiteness had given birth to a celebrated 'sacred union'. The Commonwealth of Australia had declared its racial identity at its inauguration in 1901. White Canada and White New Zealand had followed suit and both countries anticipated the United States in introducing stringent new measures to strengthen their borders though the implementation of harsh new restriction regimes.

A white New Zealand

New Zealand had moved in unison with the Australian colonies in the late nineteenth century, restricting Chinese migration with legislation in 1881, 1888 and 1896, imposing a head tax and limiting the numbers that could be carried in any one ship through tonnage restrictions. In 1907, a dictation test of 100 words in English was added to the armoury of restriction.[23] Successive Prime Ministers had expressed their desire to have 'the purity of our race maintained', while New Zealand, as we have seen, was second to none in its fulsome welcome to the United States fleet in 1908. More stringent immigration controls were being debated in parliament in August 1914, when war broke out and the bill was shelved for the duration of the conflict.

[20] *Ibid.* p.259.   [21] *Ibid.* p.308.   [22] *Ibid.* p.281.
[23] *New Zealand Parliamentary Debates*, vol.142 (1907) pp.838–9, 923.

As in the other white Dominions, a small, post-war increase in the number of Asian immigrants aroused strident demands for tighter controls, especially from trade unions and the Returned Soldiers' Association, which kept up, in P. S. O'Connor's words, 'an almost unremitting scream of horror' about the threat of Asian inundation.[24] An Immigration Restriction Bill was introduced in August 1920. New Zealanders no longer felt constrained to follow the preferred imperial pattern and use an education or literacy test. Prospective non-British migrants were required to make a postal application in advance and the Minister of Customs was given absolute discretion to reject any applicant he considered 'unsuitable'. Any doubt about what constituted unsuitability was removed as the bill passed through parliament. Prime Minister Massey explained that the legislation was the result of a deep-seated sentiment on the part of a huge majority of the people in favour of a white New Zealand. There was little disagreement. The Labor leader, Michael Savage, argued that it was in the interests of both whites and Asians 'that their races should be kept pure'. His colleague, D. G. Sullivan, assured his listeners that the Labor Party was as keen as any party in the country to maintain racial purity in New Zealand. There could be 'no question at all about that'.[25] A commentator in the pro-imperial *Round Table* called the Act 'one of the most arbitrary and reactionary measures ever introduced in a British community'.[26]

Increasingly, opposition to coloured immigration focussed on fears of miscegenation, with one commentator advising in scientific mode that the 'dislike of the inferior races, which is the result of evolutionary forces, is for the purpose of protecting the progressive race against inter-marrying with a backward race'.[27] Also invoking supposed scientific knowledge in the parliamentary debate, J. Q. Young stated that racial amalgamation tended to 'weakness', something which could be seen in 'half-breed races all over the world'. For many New Zealanders, the nearby Pacific Islands provided evidence for all to see. The evil of the mixed breed could be witnessed in Fiji, Samoa and in New Zealand itself, according to E. Kellett and 'it was time we stopped it absolutely'. The only way this could be done was by 'restricting the entry of even one Asiatic'. J. A. Hanan argued similarly that any intermarriage could have but one result and that was a 'sad deterioration of our race'. The French colony of Tahiti was also cited as an object lesson of the evil results of the admixture of races.[28]

[24] P. S. O'Connor, 'Keeping New Zealand White, 1908–1920', *New Zealand Journal of History* vol.2, no.2 (October 1968) p.54.

[25] *New Zealand Parliamentary Debates*, vol.187 (1920) pp.905–24.

[26] 'A White New Zealand and Immigration', *Round Table* (December 1920) p.223.

[27] O'Connor, 'Keeping New Zealand White', p.63.

[28] *New Zealand Parliamentary Debates*, vol.187 (1920) pp.926–37.

A white Canada

Canada followed in New Zealand's wake, appreciating that the southern Dominion had overthrown the Natal compromise, which had been the accepted policy of the Empire since 1897. In 1919, a new law followed the United States in introducing a literacy test, aimed at southern Europeans, but the Dominion went much further in 1923, when the Immigration Restriction Act gave the Minister of Immigration complete discretion to refuse any application for entry, allowing for the virtual prohibition of Asian migration. While moving the second reading of the Bill, A. W. Neill spent half his speech reporting on the New Zealand legislation, quoting extensively from what had been said in the parliament there.[29] While it was New Zealand that provided Canada with a precedent on this occasion, it was British Columbia, like California in the United States, that had played a major role in persuading the national parliament to introduce more stringent legislation.

Immigration had increased during and after the war. The census of 1921 showed that Canada's Asian population grew from 37,000 to 55,000 in ten years. Anti-Asian agitation intensified on the west coast. As in New Zealand, petitions were sent to Ottawa from trade unions and Returned Soldiers' Associations and, during the federal election campaign of 1921, almost every candidate in the province promised to bring Asian immigration to an end. In November 1921, the provincial legislature unanimously passed a resolution asking the Dominion government to amend the Immigration Act so as to totally restrict the immigration of Asiatics, 'keeping in view the wishes of the people of British Columbia that this province be reserved for people of the European race'.[30]

In May 1922, members from British Columbia moved a motion in the House of Commons calling on the government to exclude 'oriental aliens' whose rapid multiplication was becoming 'a serious menace' to living conditions on the Pacific coast and to the future of the country in general. Introducing the proposal, the member for New Westminster, W. G. McQuarrie, posed the question: 'Why should Orientals be excluded?' He provided eight reasons. The first was the fact that they could not be assimilated and would always exist as a foreign element in the nation. The real test of assimilation was intermarriage, yet the differences between the races were so marked as to make this unthinkable. Intermarriage between races so far apart was an unnatural thing and had never produced anything but degradation for both parties. After dealing with problems of cheap labour and economic competition, McQuarrie

---

[29] *Canadian Parliamentary Debates* (1922–3) p.497.   [30] *Ibid.* p.1509.

concluded with the argument that it was desirable that there should be 'a white Canada' and not 'a yellow or a mongrel nation'.[31]

During a long debate, members referred to Australia's successful defence of racial purity, quoted Lothrop Stoddard's *The Rising Tide of Color* and urged the need for racial purity. J. A. Clark declared that it was:

> not a British Columbia question, it is not even a Canadian question, but it is a question which vitally affects the white world today. In my opinion the basic factor in the future of the white race is a racial type. That is the basic factor in the future of the Dominion, and if our race is to be mixed with that of an oriental country, we cannot have a racial type.[32]

The Chinese community mobilised in protest. The Chinese Association of Victoria, in British Columbia, organised public meetings of protest all over Canada. One Chinese observed that his people were being 'treated with disgust and contempt'. They were regarded not as immigrants, who might eventually become Canadian citizens, but as 'aliens who will remain aliens forever':

> Socially, the Canadian homes, clubs and other gathering places are not open to them. They are not invited to dinners and dances. In British Columbia some of the hotels, theatres and restaurants bar them from admission. They are a sort of outcast.[33]

The Act of 1923 had the effect desired by White Canada. It virtually shut the country to new migration until the reforms of the 1940s and 1950s. Between 1925 and 1940, only eight Chinese arrivals were legally permitted to enter the Dominion and, as in Australia, New Zealand and the United States, the Chinese community aged and dwindled.

The power of inheritance

Debates in New Zealand and Canada testified to the new importance of race thinking about inheritance and the dangers of miscegenation. Popular understandings were influenced not only by Grant's and Stoddard's polemical works, but also academic studies which provided intellectual underpinning and moral justification for racial segregation and immigration restriction. One of the most distinguished authors on the racial dangers of miscegenation was a leading social psychologist, William McDougall, who had migrated from Britain to the United States to take

[31] *Ibid.* p.1516.   [32] *Ibid.* pp.1522–3.
[33] Cheng Tien-Fang, *Oriental Immigration in Canada* (Shanghai, Commercial Press, 1931) p.239.

up the chair of psychology at Harvard. His book *An Introduction to Social Psychology*, first published in 1908, went through twenty three editions in the following twenty years.[34]

McDougall was a powerful advocate of racial purity. In *The Group Mind*, published in 1920, he purported to show that the crossing of widely different human stocks produced an inferior race deficient in vitality and fertility, possessing the 'inharmonious combination of physical features, characteristic of the mongrel'. This fact had an important bearing on one of the most urgent problems confronting the world's statesmen as well as the citizens of the British Empire and the United States. It justified abundantly the refusal of the white settler societies to admit immigrants 'of the yellow or negro race to settle among them' as well as the objection to intermarriage which Englishmen had upheld wherever they had settled.[35]

McDougall pursued the same themes in his book *Ethics and Some Modern World Problems* which was published while W. M. Hughes was touring the United States. Like Stoddard, McDougall paid tribute to the prophetic work of Charles Pearson on the rise of Asia, but he was confident that the spirit of nationalism would prevail against the dangers of free immigration, the dilution of the advanced races and the 'immense multiplication of the peoples of the lower cultures'. Australia's absolute restriction on non-European migration was an example worthy of emulation, for it seemed safe to suppose, that if no such barriers had been raised:

North America and Australia and South and East Africa would already have been made the homes of many millions of Asiatics, both yellow and brown.[36]

Race thinking in the 1920s was permeated by reference to the new science of genetics and the contemporaneous spread of intelligence testing. In his book, published in 1923, *Mankind at the Crossroads*, Edward East, also a Professor at Harvard, explained that geneticists had made heredity an exact science to be ranked closely behind physics and chemistry in definiteness of conception.[37] Inheritance was now considered far more important in determining racial possibilities than the environment. Lamarkian theory, popular in the United States and associated with the work of Herbert Spencer, had been superseded, and most biologists now

[34] William McDougall, *An Introduction to Social Psychology* (London, Methuen, 1908).
[35] William McDougall, *The Group Mind: a Sketch of the Principles of Collective Psychology* (Cambridge, Cambridge University Press, 1920) pp.242–4.
[36] William McDougall, *Ethics and Some Modern World Problems* (London, Methuen, 1924) pp.57, 64, 67.
[37] E. M. East, *Mankind at the Crossroads* (New York, Scribner, 1923) p.v.

believed that acquired characteristics were not transmitted to offspring. The implication was clear. Racial traits were passed on, from generation to generation, and could not be changed by environment or social amelioration. The 'innate endowments of races', in the words of S. J. Holmes, constituted a basic factor 'conditioning the nature of every type of civilization and every historic movement'.[38]

Intelligence, too, was conceptualised as an inherited racial trait. The grade of both individuals and races was 'little affected by later influences', asserted H. H. Goddard, and intelligence testing was 'fast becoming an exact science'.[39] The testing of 1.7 million recruits for the American army in 1917 provided a unique data base for racial speculation. Carl Brigham's book *A Study of American Intelligence*, published in 1923, established to his satisfaction the superiority of whites over blacks and of mulattoes over full bloods. It confirmed the fears of Madison Grant about the fate of the Nordic race, swamped by migration and miscegenation. More alarmingly, because of racial admixture, American intelligence seemed to be actually in decline.[40]

Excluding the Japanese

W. M. Hughes was motoring through the western states on his way to California on 1 July 1924 when the new Johnson Immigration Act came into force, introducing a quota system designed to strongly favour migrants from north-western Europe over those from central and southern Europe and the rest of the world – dividing the world's peoples, as Matthew Jacobson has put it, between 'Anglo-Saxons and others'.[41] Hughes would have approved of this development, but he would have been even more pleased by the special provisions which prohibited Japanese migration and effected a unilateral scrapping of the Gentlemen's Agreement initiated by Theodore Roosevelt sixteen years before. Hughes told a reporter that the new Act was implementing policy which Australia had had in place for the past quarter of a century: total exclusion without agreement, apology or 'other palavering'.[42]

The total exclusion of the Japanese was a victory for Californian politicians and activists who had spent decades attempting to impart to the

---

[38] S. J. Holmes, *The Trend of the Race: a Study of the Present Tendencies in the Biological Development of Civilized Mankind* (London, Constable, 1921) pp.1–2.

[39] H. H. Goddard, *Human Efficiency and the Levels of Intelligence* (Princeton, Princeton University Press, 1920) pp.vii, 1.

[40] C. C. Brigham, *A Study of American Intelligence* (Princeton, Princeton University Press, 1923) pp.184, 205, 209, 210.

[41] Jacobson, *Whiteness of a Different Color*, pp.82–90.

[42] Hughes Papers, article in *Los Angeles Examiner*, 1538/26/349.

rest of the republic their own sense of urgency about Asian migration. The years immediately after the war saw an upsurge of anti-Japanese activity initiated by trade unions, war veterans, exclusion leagues and other community groups. The avowed purpose of this revived campaign was to make it 'so uncomfortable' for resident Japanese that they would voluntarily return home.[43]

The decision of Congress by substantial majorities in both chambers to prohibit future Japanese migration was a radical and portentous one. Both the Secretary of State, Charles Hayes, and the President, Calvin Coolidge, attempted to persuade Congress to allow time for them to negotiate a new agreement with Japan. They pointed out that with the Gentlemen's Agreement in place and the application of the quotas which were to apply to Europeans, only 246 Japanese migrants would be allowed entry every year. In a letter to Albert Johnson, the Chairman of the House Committee on Immigration and driving force behind the exclusion cause, Hayes warned that such a statutory exclusion would be deeply resented by the Japanese people. It was idle to pretend that Japanese migrants had not been singled out for exclusion. It was clear that the enactment would be regarded as a deep insult and no amount of argument could 'avail to remove it'.[44]

There was strong opposition to Japanese exclusion from the east coast newspapers, churches and leading intellectuals, including the indefatigable Sidney Gulick, who lobbied hard to have the Japanese treated the same as all other would-be immigrants. The Japanese did not seek an unrestricted opportunity to migrate, he insisted, but rather the recognition of racial equality. Perhaps the most dramatic gesture of protest was the resignation of the American Ambassador to Japan, Cyrus Woods, three days after the legislation was passed by the Congress. Japan, he declared, was bewildered, disappointed, dismayed and indignant. In his judgment, the decision was 'an international disaster of the first magnitude' for American diplomacy, American business and the American churches in Japan.[45] Gulick warned that in passing such discriminatory and humiliating measures, the United States was giving encouragement to the most militarist elements in Japan: 'Japanese militarists could adopt no more astute policy for the attainment of their ends in China and in the whole Far East than secretly to subsidise . . . humiliating, discriminatory

[43] R. L. Buell, 'Again the Yellow Peril', *Foreign Affairs* (15 December 1923), in Johnson, *Japanese Exclusion*, p.41.
[44] Hughes to Johnson, 8 February 1924, in R. L. Buell, *Japanese Immigration*, World Peace Foundation Pamphlets, vol.VII, nos.5–6 (1924) p.355.
[45] Cited by Sydney L. Gulick in 'Re-establishment of Right Relations between America and Japan', in Johnson, *Japanese Exclusion*, p.64.

and drastic legislation'. Anti-Japanese agitators 'do not seem to understand the relation of cause and effect in international and inter-racial affairs'. What was needed was not white supremacy or world-wide segregation but 'The New Internationalism'.[46]

In 1925, John Trevor, a New York lawyer, friend of Madison Grant, and close personal advisor to Albert Johnson, wrote a paper for the House Committee on Immigration justifying the policy of Japanese exclusion, which was based, he said, not on theories of relative racial superiority, but on the fundamental principle that colonies of unassimilable people provided the seeds of national dissolution. He found support for his ideas in the fact that the British Dominions throughout the world – Canada, New Zealand, Australia, even 'the far off African Dominions' – all upheld with 'unshakable determination' a ban on the entry of the Japanese. The alternative to separate colonies within a nation was miscegenation, which was unthinkable. Nature itself had determined inhibitions regarding the practice, which constituted a perversion of natural law. It was a threat to both the Japanese and the Americans:

Therefore, we may say that miscegenation, while occasionally practised, is an unthinkable solution of the problem, and exclusion of permanent settlers of both people from the country of the other, is inevitable.[47]

As John W. Burgess and William A. Dunning had suggested thirty years before and commentators repeated in the 1920s, the strength of nation-states rested on racial homogeneity. Australians such as Hughes, who had played a key role in applying this lesson in nation-building, were gratified that the world seemed to be following suit.

Japanese outrage, again

Japanese official concern was expressed by Ambassador Hanihara during the week before the final vote in Congress. His letter to the Secretary of State recapitulated many of the complaints voiced during the earlier confrontations over migration in 1907 and 1913. He was disturbed that the public statements of the sponsors and supporters of the new legislation made it clear that its manifest object was to single out the Japanese, 'stigmatizing them as unworthy and undesirable in the eyes of the American people'. 'The important question', Hanihara explained, was:

---

[46] Sidney L. Gulick, 'How Should America Respond?' and 'The New Anti-Japanese Agitation', Immigration Restriction League, Ms Am 2245 (1117), Houghton Library.
[47] J. B. Trevor, 'Japanese Exclusion', House Document no.600 (4 February 1925), in Johnson, *Japanese Exclusion*, pp.125–6.

whether Japan as a nation is or is not entitled to the proper respect and consideration of other nations. In other words, the Japanese Government ask of the United States Government simply for that proper consideration ordinarily given by one nation to the self-respect of another, which after all forms the basis of amicable international intercourse throughout the civilized world.[48]

While the Ambassador's protest echoed earlier complaints, the reaction in Japan itself was unprecedented, as though the sense of outrage had compounded and exploded. Commentators were quick in their judgements. Gulick observed that between January and July 1924, Japan's attitude toward the United States had passed from one of friendship to one of 'deepest disappointment, resentment and indignation'.[49] K. K. Kawakami agreed that Japan had been cut to the quick. What the country was asking was not the right of free immigration, but simply that the American government, whatever it might privately think of Japan, desist from 'humiliating her openly, deliberately and unwarrantedly in the concourse of Great Powers' by flinging Japan into the fold of 'excluded, and impliedly inferior races'.[50] General Kunishige Tanaka, president of the Seiyukai Party, told an American academic that the Japanese could never be assured of Anglo-Saxon friendship until the stigma placed upon their race by the Immigration Act and by similar restrictions in the British Dominions were removed.[51] Returning to New York after an extensive Japanese tour, Helen Pankhurst observed that the Japanese were not so much bitter as humiliated, because Americans had 'belittled them in the eyes of the world'.[52]

On 1 July 1924, when the Immigration Act took effect, both Houses of the Japanese Diet met in special session to pass protest resolutions. An 'Association of Men of the Same Mind Facing America' dedicated itself to securing international intercourse 'on the plain of real equality'. Members decided to observe 1 July as 'American Peril Day'.[53] An editorial in *Japan Times* entitled simply 'July 1' declared that the day was destined to go down in history as the day on which the Japanese people had been subjected to insult and humiliation.[54] The Osaka *Asahi* observed that anti-American sentiment was running high, adding that 'one can almost hear the beating of every citizen's heart with ever increasing indignation against the injustice committed by the prejudiced congress'.[55]

[48] Hanihara to Charles E. Hughes, 10 April 1924, in Buell, *Japanese Immigration*, p.361.
[49] Gulick, 'Re-establishment of Right Relations', p.63.
[50] K. K. Kawakami, 'Japan Looks Across the Pacific', *Contemporary Review*, vol.131 (1927) pp.475–7.
[51] Upton Close (pseudo.) *The Revolt of Asia: The End of the White Man's World Dominance* (Sydney, Cornstalk Publishing, 1927) p.9.
[52] *Japan Times*, 1 July 1924.   [53] *Ibid.* 29 June 1924.
[54] *Ibid.* 1 July 1924.   [55] Cited in *Ibid.* 27 June 1924.

American goods were boycotted; cinemas removed American films; young women eschewed American fashion; one hundred geishas in Kobe threw away American cosmetics; Japanese Christian churches declared that they were cutting all ties with the United States.[56] The Nagoya Ladies Association wrote to the American feminist and peace activist Jane Addams seeking her help in having the legislation rescinded.[57] Tokyo was placarded with signs saying 'Hate Everything American'. Mass prayer meetings were held at Shinto shrines throughout the country.[58] America, the Osaka *Mainichi* declared, had 'spat at Japan in the very face'.[59] The *Yomiuri* said that the country's prestige had been 'crushed to the ground'.[60] Tokyo's *Nichi Nichi* believed that the honour of the country had been 'mercilessly destroyed'.[61]

Peoples of Asia unite

Pro-Western liberal intellectuals were deeply shocked by the immigration legislation, which seriously impaired their influence and standing in national politics. Tokutomi Soho dismissed them as people who had made the fatal error of regarding the United States as their spiritual mother country.[62] The leading writer Inazo Nitobe who had become a Quaker while in America and assumed a role as intellectual mediator between the two countries, swore that he would never again set his feet 'on American soil' as long as the law remained in place. He believed that this was 'the feeling of many intelligent Japanese'.[63]

Viscount Kentaro Kaneko felt similarly betrayed. Harvard educated, friend of Theodore Roosevelt and long-time President of the Japan–American Society, Kaneko had telegraphed President Coolidge urging him to veto the Immigration Act, as numerous presidents had vetoed immigration restriction acts before him. When Coolidge declined to do so, Kaneko was deeply distressed, saying that the Japanese people could 'never forget the injustice and inhumanity' of the Americans as long as the discrimination lasted. He resigned from the Japan–American Society and cut himself off from his American friends. In his letter of resignation he explained that on hearing that the Immigration Act was passed 'in so

---

[56] Buell, *Japanese Immigration*, p.315.
[57] Izumi Hirobe, *Japanese Pride, American Prejudice: Modifying the Exclusion Clause of the 1924 Immigration Act* (Stanford, Stanford University Press, 2001) p.27.
[58] Cited in *Japan Times*, 29 May 1924.   [59] *Ibid.* 1 May 1924.
[60] Cited by Buell, *Japanese Immigration*, p.314.
[61] Cited in *Japan Times*, 5 June 1924.   [62] Hirobe, *Japanese Pride*, p.30.
[63] Cited by Arthur Brown, *Japan in the World of Today* (New York, Revell, 1928) p.226.

drastic a manner' and with such an overwhelming majority, he felt as if the hope of his life was destroyed.[64]

With public anger at its height in Japan, the Indian poet, Rabindranath Tagore, arrived in Nagasaki and declared that the time had surely come for all peoples of Asia to unite.[65] While scarcely a novel idea, it proved newly attractive in the context of the furore over American immigration. Ten days after the new regulations went into operation, two hundred prominent figures met in Tokyo to establish the Pan Asiatic Association, dedicated to the study and research of the Asian region. Other voices claimed that a worldwide war between the white and yellow races would soon eventuate.[66] Shimizu, the leader of the patriotic Great Deeds Association, urged the nation to fight immediately rather than wait ten years and be crushed altogether.[67] Even the cautious *Japan Times* was caught up in the mood of aggressive foreboding, arguing that the United States Congress had virtually challenged Japan to war.[68]

The immigration question also influenced military thinking at the official level. A secret report written by the General Staff Office in April 1924 observed that the American action had humiliated Japan and would have an impact around the world, especially in assisting the consolidation of non-white peoples.[69] In another report on 'Japan–US Relations and the Defence of the Empire', the General Staff Office concluded that it was impossible to expunge the racism represented by the United States legislation and Australia's 'white policy' and that officers should expect that racial war would break out sooner or later.[70] Close observers of the Japanese scene concluded that 1 July 1924 was a portentous moment. French ambassador Paul Claudel considered it a turning point in history, marking the moment when Japan departed from 'the circle of Western powers and joined the Asian powers'.[71]

Contemporary Japanese scholars have confirmed the importance of the immigration question in determining Japanese foreign policy. In his essay on 'Japanese Images of War with the United States', Kimitada Miwa argued that the train of events which culminated in the bombing of Pearl Harbour had been set in motion when Congress passed the Immigration Bill. As Gulick had warned, it marked the beginning of a new era in Japanese–American relations. The conflict that culminated in war between the two countries 'had already begun' in 1924.[72]

[64] *Ibid.* p.226; Hirobe, *Japanese Pride*, pp.29–30.   [65] Cited in *Japan Times*, 19 May 1924.
[66] *Nichi Nichi*, cited in *Ibid.*   [67] *Japan Times*, 2 July 1924.   [68] *Ibid.* 27 May 1924.
[69] Hirobe, *Japanese Pride*, p.40.   [70] *Ibid.* p.41.   [71] *Ibid.* p.39.
[72] Kimitada Miwa, 'Japanese Images of War with the United States', in Akira Iriye (ed.) *Mutual Images: Essays in American-Japanese Relations* (Cambridge, Harvard University Press, 1975) p.115.

South Africa: in the land of the white man

The end of the war also saw the consolidation of white supremacy in South Africa. White racial fears were fuelled anew when the census of 1920 showed African population growth far outstripping that of the European community. Africans and Indians hoped for better times after the war, both because of their wartime co-operation with the Allies and hopes for reform stimulated by Woodrow Wilson's promises and the idealism accompanying the creation of the League of Nations. African political activity had declined during the war years, but in 1919 a delegation took a petition to London and then travelled to Versailles. Discontent with the Botha–Smuts government was summed up by the activist Mesach Pelem in an address to a nationalist conference in Queenstown, in February 1919. He expressed his disappointment with the imperial government which had ignominiously 'surrendered their obligations and rights' to the South African government and had thereby:

taught the people of this country the new doctrine unparalleled in English Consti-tutionalism that 'white' is supremacy and 'black is slavery'. It would be impossible to promulgate a more monstrous doctrine than that which has as its war cry 'Africa is a White Man's Country' with the eventual deprivation of its black inhabitants of every shred of citizen rights, land rights and other liberties and privileges.[73]

The Indian community in South Africa also came under renewed attack with 'frenzied demands for compulsory segregation and compulsory repa-triation'.[74] The Transvaal government introduced legislation which pro-hibited the granting of new trading licences and abolished the various strategies, which had allowed Indians to circumvent legislation prevent-ing non-Europeans from owning fixed property. Looking on from India, Gandhi accused the South Africans of pursuing a policy of 'ruthless exter-mination', all the while professing loyalty to a common Empire.[75]

By this time the question of India's place in the Empire had become critical. The country's massive war effort had made a major impact and the Imperial Conferences of 1917 and 1918 had held out the prospect of future Dominion status, responsible government and the removal of discriminatory legislation in the white Dominions, which had aroused such nationalist anger in India itself. The question of the status of the

---

[73] T. Karis and G. M. Carter (eds.) *From Protest to Challenge: Vol. 1, Protest and Hope, 1882–1934* (Stanford, Hoover Institute, 1972) p.102.

[74] W. K. Hancock, *Survey of British Commonwealth Affairs, Vol. 1, Problems of Nationality, 1918–1936* (London, Oxford University Press, 1937) p.203.

[75] M. K. Gandhi, *The Collected Works of Mahatma Gandhi*, vol.XV (Delhi, Ministry of Information, 1958) p.109.

Indian diaspora came to a crisis at the Imperial Conferences of 1921 and 1923. Australia, New Zealand and Canada, with their small Indian communities, promised to remove offending legislation and grant Indians the franchise, a reform that took place in 1924.

Representing the Union of South Africa, Jan Smuts was isolated. He declared that he was up against a stone wall and could not climb over it. Equal rights for Indians, he declared at the 1921 conference, would lead to the same rights for Africans and that would result in the destruction of white South Africa. His country was not based, he said, on 'a system of equality'. The whole basis of our political system, he declared, 'rests on inequality and recognizing the fundamental differences which exist in the structure of our population ... We have never in our laws recognized any system of equality!'[76] When asked about the Rhodes dictum of equal rights for all civilized men south of the Zambezi, Smuts said that so far South Africa had 'done nothing to approximate to that standpoint'.[77] When addressing a party meeting in South Africa, just before the Imperial Conference of 1923, Smuts reiterated that the 'coloured line' was drawn between white and non-white and that meant that Indians and natives would be treated as one group:

All I can say is that with regard to the franchise, we see no reason to make a distinction between Indians in this country and Natives in this country. There is the coloured line which is in existence today. Right or wrong – I do not argue about that. It is a clearly marked line you can follow, but once you cross that line we see no reason why there should be any distinction between Indians and the Natives.[78]

The binary politics of whiteness drew a 'clearly marked line'.

The Hertzog government, which came to power in 1924, needed no encouragement to maintain Smuts' commitment to segregation on the basis of the clearly marked line of colour. It was already apparent by the 1920s that segregationist policies embodied an inescapable logic which led on to ever tightening repression. Each turn of the screw made retraction more difficult. One of Hertzog's parliamentary supporters declared that his leader would tolerate no injustice to any section of the community, unless he was 'absolutely certain that it is for the good of the white man'.[79] The legislative record bore this out. The 1926 Mines and

---

[76] Minutes of the 1921 Imperial Conference, Hughes Papers, 1538, Series 25/1, Box 124, 531–2, NLA.

[77] *Ibid.*

[78] W. K. Hancock, *Smuts, vol. 2, The Field of Force* (Cambridge, Cambridge University Press, 1962–68) pp.146–7.

[79] Hancock, *Survey of British Commonwealth Affairs Vol.II*, p.47.

Workers Act restricted Africans to unskilled work; the Masters and Servants legislation imposed greater controls on the non-white workforce. The Immorality Act of 1927 declared intercourse between white and non-white to be a criminal offence. The Native Administration Act of the same year allowed the Executive to rule by proclamation and to deport any African, who was judged to be promoting hostility between black and white.

Hertzog sought to create a white man's country within South Africa in the midst of the African majority. Africans would be required to work within the white man's realm, but they would never be allowed to forget they were 'in the land of the White man where the White man shall rule and have the right to live safely and peacefully'. Nobody compelled an African to settle in the white territory, but if he did it was demanded that he should 'respect the White man and obey the laws of the country'. Hertzog declared that the white man would never allow the government of the Union and its people to be 'held by the Native, or would the Native be given authority within or over the government of the country'. He warned Africans, that whoever was so presumptuous as to claim equal authority with the white man would experience the greatest disappointment and failure.[80]

While Hertzog can be characterised as embodying the spirit of the Orange Free State, and more generally of Afrikaners, segregation drew support from across the political spectrum and was applauded as a liberal and progressive policy in both South Africa and Britain. Parallel institutions were, as Smuts' biographer, W. K. Hancock, observed, the orthodoxy 'and not least the liberal orthodoxy of the time'.[81] As John Cell wrote, it was Smuts, rather than Hertzog, who was the principle architect of segregation. At the time when South African racial policies were being consolidated, he had reached the height of his stature as an international statesman and public intellectual, illustrated by his election as President of the British Association for the Advancement of Science in its centenary year of 1931. His most sophisticated justification of segregation had been delivered in his Rhodes Memorial Lectures, in Oxford, two years earlier.

Smuts argued, as both Bryce and DuBois had done a generation before, that the 'contact of colours and civilizations' was the dominant issue of the twentieth century. But contact could not be uncontrolled; a separation between racial types must be maintained. Indeed the separation was

[80] L. E. Neame, *The History of Apartheid: The Story of the Colour War in South Africa* (London, Pall Mall Press, 1962) pp.53–4.

[81] Hancock, *Smuts, vol. 2*, p.121. See also Saul Dubow, *Racial Segregation and the Origins of Apartheid in South Africa 1919–36* (Basingstoke, Macmillan, 1989).

imperative, not only in the interests of the native culture and to prevent Indigenous institutions from being swamped, but also for other important purposes 'such as public health, racial purity and public good order'. The mixing up of two such alien elements 'as white and black' led to unhappy social results including miscegenation, moral deterioration and racial antipathy. Segregation, he assured his audience, was welcomed by the vast majority of Africans, although it was resented by a small educated minority which claimed equal rights with the white man.

Smuts linked his favoured policies with contemporary developments in social anthropology, with the trusteeship principles of the League of Nations and policies of indirect rule favoured by progressive British colonial administrators. While previous policies based on the principle of equal rights may have given the African a 'semblance of equality' with the whites it was of little value to him and destroyed the basis of his native African system, which was 'his highest good'. Nothing could be worse than the policies which would 'de-Africanize the African' and turn him into a pseudo-European. The African 'type' had some wonderful characteristics, even if it had largely remained 'a child type', with 'a child psychology and outlook'.

Smuts' most deft intellectual manoeuvre was to equate equality with a repressive assimilation. If Africa were to be redeemed and make its own contribution to the world, the policy-makers would:

have to proceed on different lines and evolve a policy which will not force [African] institutions into an alien European mould, but which will preserve her unity with her own past, conserve what is precious in her past, and build her future progress and civilization on specifically African foundations.

Such an endeavour was in line with the best traditions of the Empire, which did not promote the assimilation of its people into a common type, but the 'fullest, freest development of its peoples along their own specific line'.[82]

Not everyone was persuaded by Smuts' mask of cosmopolitanism. The veteran newspaper man, Valentine Chirol, doubted whether Smuts realised the responsibility he incurred by persisting in a policy of injustice towards Indian South Africans, which was the original cause of 'Mr Gandhi's anti-British evolution' and had disastrously stimulated the growth of 'racial bitterness and a spirit of revolt against Western ascendancy and against British rule itself all over India'.[83]

Smuts also attracted the attention of W. E. B. DuBois, who wrote of him as the world's 'greatest protagonist of the white race' in an article,

[82] J. C. Smuts, *Africa and Some World Problems* (Oxford, Clarendon Press, 1930) pp.75–95.
[83] *The Times*, 3 November 1923.

'Worlds of Color', in the American journal *Foreign Affairs*, in April 1925. He was fighting to keep India from political and social equality in the Empire, to ensure the 'continued and eternal subordination of black to white in Africa' and to encourage cohesion in Europe, which could then present a united front to the 'yellow, brown and black worlds'. In all this, DuBois declared, Smuts expressed:

> bluntly, and yet not without finesse, what a powerful host of white folk believe but do not plainly say in Melbourne, New Orleans, San Francisco, Hong Kong, Berlin and London.[84]

DuBois reflected on his observation of 1900 that the problem of the twentieth century would be the problem of the colour line. A quarter of a century later, he could see that white men had entrenched the colour line more deeply than ever before. New Zealand, Canada and the United States had each shut their doors against non-European migration following the lead of White Australia. The situation of the small Indian populations in Australia, Canada and New Zealand had improved, but other Asian migrant communities continued to suffer from active discrimination. In South Africa and Britain there was still persuasive talk about settling the African high country from the Union to Ethiopia with white settlers, with Kenya as the preferred model. The Hertzog government had taken over from Smuts in constructing a system of segregation to widespread applause even among liberal observers. Race thinking pervaded the intellectual life of western Europe, North America and the British Dominions.

DuBois believed, however, that the white-man's world was less secure than it appeared to be. Nationalist movements challenged imperial and metropolitan powers all over the world. He referred to 'quickened India', the Congresses in both South and West Africa, the Pan-African movement and the National Association for the Advancement of Coloured People in the United States. While he appreciated there was little coordination between such disparate groups, perhaps they might eventually develop a common conscience. Meanwhile, every great European Empire was haunted by its 'colonial shadow' and he speculated on what might happen if 'Asia and Africa and the islands were cut permanently away'.[85]

African and Asian nationalists were not alone in imagining a different future. The Soviet Union and national Communist parties promoted the anti-colonial cause all over the world. Commentators in western Europe and north America watched the changing global scene with foreboding. The celebrated scholar and internationalist, Gilbert Murray, thought that

---

[84] *Foreign Affairs*, vol.3, no.3 (April 1925) p.437.   [85] *Ibid.* p.423.

'hatred of the existing world order' was more rife than it had been 'for over a thousand years'.[86] White men found that the old ways no longer worked. In his 1928 study of Japan, A. J. Brown observed:

All over Asia the time has gone when the foreigner can with impunity kick a coolie. No longer does the white man face a cringing, helpless Asia, but an alert, resolute, resentful people.[87]

At the same time anthropologists and biologists began to undermine the central concepts of racial thought which had dominated European thought for the last decades. Hereditary intelligence, the perils of miscegenation and ideas about racial inferiority were widely questioned. This new work took on fresh urgency with the consolidation of Nazi power in Germany in the 1930s and the pitiless application of eugenic principles and racial technologies – many of which had been rehearsed under colonial regimes – in the heartland of Europe, the results of which were to finally scarify the conscience of the world.

[86] Cited by Brown, *Japan in the World of Today*, p.15.   [87] *Ibid.* p.13.

Part 5

Towards universal human rights

14 Individual rights without distinction

Minority treaties

There was continuing debate about human rights during the 1920s and 1930s, but it was stimulated less by Japan's failed proposal concerning racial equality, and more by the minority treaties imposed on the new nation states created after the end of the First World War. The first was negotiated with Poland in 1919, and by the early 1930s, twenty-four treaties or other agreements had been ratified.[1] They were drawn up to deal with the problems which arose in Eastern Europe as a consequence of the break up of the Hapsburg and Ottoman Empires and subsequent creation of nation-states from diverse and geographically mixed populations, all of whom could have appealed, with some justice, to Woodrow Wilson's promise of self-determination.

The great powers feared that persecution of minorities and irredentism could spark future international conflict. The treaties provided for the protection of individuals against discrimination by the states in question and a number of group rights, relating to language, education and cultural institutions. Minority rights had little chance of support, however, when pitched against the overpowering idea of national sovereignty. A Swiss delegate observed in 1920 that while a policy based on respect for minorities had the full sympathy of the League of Nations, the 'sovereignty of states' was its fundamental principle.[2]

In 1935, the Permanent Court of International Justice declared that the treaties had two main objectives. The first was to ensure that minority individuals would be 'placed in every respect on a footing of perfect equality with the other nationals of the State'. The second was to ensure that 'minority elements' would have suitable means for the preservation of their 'racial peculiarities, their traditions and their national characteristics'.[3]

[1] W. McKean, *Equality and Discrimination Under International Law* (Oxford, Clarendon Press, 1983) pp.14–15, 22.
[2] M. Motta, Switzerland, 10 December 1920, League of Nations, File No. R1647, 1919–27.
[3] Minority Schools in Albania, 64 *Proceedings of the Court of International Justice*, 1935, p.17.

But the creators of the treaty system had no intention of establishing 'a general jurisprudence wherever racial, linguistic or religious minorities existed'.[4] Rather, treaties were created, in the words of Anthony Eden, to deal 'with a specific problem existing in a given area for a given time'.[5] Clearly, the imperial powers, including Britain, were unwilling to consider specific rights for minorities in their Empires or to countenance what became known as the 'generalisation' of rights. The new-world settler societies were equally opposed to giving recognition to minorities, including Indigenous minorities, the Canadians arguing, for example, that the question was 'a purely European one', for on that continent, there was 'a desire to maintain national characteristics', in direct contrast with the assimilationist policies of the Americans.[6]

The generalisation of rights

Discussion about minority rights and the possibility of their generalisation was a regular feature of League of Nations meetings during the 1920s. It was hard to provide any logical argument against the proposition that if minority rights were important in some countries, they must also be so in others. The so-called treaty states led the campaign for generalisation, the Polish government arguing that 'such a distinction between protected and unprotected minorities conflicts with the sense of equity and justice'.[7] In 1922, Latvia proposed the establishment of a convention on the universal protection of minorities with the support of Finland and Estonia. A compromise drafted by Gilbert Murray expressed the hope that states not bound by any legal obligations would observe in the treatment of their own minorities 'at least as high a standard of justice and tolerance' as required by the formal treaties.[8] The treaty states were not appeased by Murray's declaration, however, and continued to argue for the wider application of the rights regime. In 1925, Lithuania prepared a draft convention on minority rights, arguing that it would confer the same rights upon, and require the same duties of, all members of the League.[9]

---

[4] League of Nations, 'The League of Nations and the Protection of Minorities', Secretariat, Geneva, 1927, p.16.
[5] Cited by McKean, *Equality and Discrimination*, p.23.
[6] Admission of new members to the League of Nations, debate of 10 December 1920, p.6, League of Nations Library, Geneva, Box No. R1647, 1919–1927.
[7] Cited by McKean, *Equality and Discrimination*, p.37.
[8] Motion by G. Murray, 12 September 1921, League of Nations Library, Box 1647.
[9] Statement by Galvan Auskas, League of Nations, *Record of the 6th Assembly* (Geneva, 1925) p.77.

Growing concern about the minorities problem led to the organisation of a special conference in Madrid in June 1929. Among the many submissions one of the most striking was from the Chinese government, which called for international protection for all citizens without distinction:

Under the Minorities Treaties concluded up to the present, only a limited number of signatory States are found to ensure to some extent the protection of minorities. Such protection must, however, from every point of view, be essentially international and world-wide, and the laws of every country must provide for effective and equal protection for all its citizens without distinction of language, race or religion.

The Chinese called for an international convention which would ensure that 'unalienable rights should be rendered universally effective'.[10]

From minority rights to human rights

Calls for the recognition of the rights of individuals, without distinction, gathered pace in the late 1920s. On 28 November 1928, the International Diplomatic Academy attended by distinguished diplomats from seventy-three countries proposed a world convention ensuring the protection of the Rights of Men and Citizens. On 12 October 1929, the Institut De Droit International meeting in New York, drew up a Declaration of the International Rights of Man whose first article read:

It is the duty of every State to recognize the equal right of every individual to life, liberty and property, and to accord to all within its territory the full and entire protection of this right, without distinction as to nationality, sex, race, language, or religion.[11]

The assembled jurists drew inspiration from the American Declaration of Independence and the French Declaration of the Rights of Man, directing particular attention to the 14th Amendment of the American Constitution, and the concomitant judgement of the Supreme Court, that the terms of the Amendment applied to 'every person without distinction of race, colour or nationality'.[12] 'Sex' was added to the grounds on which discrimination was disallowed in the 1929 Declaration following the concerted lobbying of American feminists.

At the peace conference in Paris in 1919, Japan had sought recognition of the equality of nations or races in the tradition of international law. The Declaration of 1929 represented a new departure in that it focussed on

[10] Madrid Meeting on the Protection of Minorities, June 1929, *League of Nations Official Journal* vol.10, Part 2 (1929) p.70.
[11] *American Journal of International Law* vol.35 (1941) p.664.   [12] *Ibid.* p.663.

the international rights of individuals. It was a revolutionary document because it repudiated the classic doctrine that states alone were subjects of international law: 'It marks a new era which is more concerned with the interests and rights of sovereign individuals than with the rights of sovereign states'.[13] It both looked back to the 14th Amendment and pre-figured the Universal Declaration of Human Rights of 1948. The *American Journal of International Law* noted that it was adopted on 12 October, 'the 437th anniversary of the discovery of America' and thus could be considered an expression of homage by the Institut De Droit to the New World for its contributions to the liberal development of international law. Indigenous populations, dispossessed and disregarded as a consequence of the 'discovery' of the New World, might have thought differently about the benefits of the liberal development of international law.

While a private organisation, the Institut De Droit had brought together in New York sixty international lawyers from many parts of the world. Its declaration was considered to be 'of immense importance'.[14] Reviewing the document after the Second World War, the *American Journal of International Law* recognised that the Institut had taken an 'advanced position' in respect to the protection of individual rights 'not yet fully recognized'.[15]

The Declaration of the International Rights of Man was taken up at the 14th Assembly of the League of Nations in 1933, when the Haitian representative, M. Frangulis, called for a shift of emphasis from minority treaties to the protection of the rights of men and of citizens in the French tradition. He suggested that rights be so formulated so as to ensure that every inhabitant of a State should enjoy the same protection of life and liberty, the same civil and political rights, 'without distinction of race, language or religion'. Frangulis believed that his call for universal human rights represented the 'very essence of juridical and moral conscience of the contemporary world'.[16] He drew the attention of his colleagues to the movement in favour of human rights among non-government organisations, including the International Diplomatic Academy and the International Federation of League of Nations' Unions. The latter, presided over by Sir Robert Cecil, called a conference at Montreux in 1933 to discuss the formulation of a Convention on the Rights of Man, whose demand that individual rights be recognised 'without any discrimination, whatsoever' was subsequently endorsed at a

---

[13] *Ibid.* vol.24 (1930) p.127.   [14] McKean, *Equality and Discrimination*, p.39.
[15] *American Journal of International Law* vol. 25 (1951) p.109.
[16] League of Nations, *Records of the 14th Assembly* (6th Committee, September–October 1933) p.3.

Plenary Congress of the International Federation at Folkstone in England in May 1934.[17]

In 1941, the *American Journal of International Law* revisited the 1929 Declaration and reprinted the full text, believing that it had acquired new relevance following President Franklin Roosevelt's 'Four Freedoms' speech of 6 January 1941, which was to apply to all peoples 'everywhere in the world'.[18] The Institut's document became even more relevant when world leaders met in San Francisco in April and May 1945 to plan for a new international organisation to succeed the discredited League of Nations. The war in Europe had been fought against Germany and Italy in the name of democracy and equality; the peace was haunted by the horrific revelations about the Holocaust.

A French jurist, René Cassin, observed that the war had 'taken on the character of a crusade for human rights'. Hitler had begun by asserting the 'inequality of men before attacking their liberties'.[19] International delegates, who gathered in Paris in November 1945 to found the United Nations Educational, Scientific and Cultural Organization (UNESCO), concluded that the war had been made possible by the denial of democratic principles of dignity, equality and mutual respect and by the propagation of the doctrine of 'the inequality of men and races'.[20] The overwhelming nature of Jewish persecution and the extent of mass murder had raised the issue of race 'in a way that nothing else in history had ever done before'.[21]

Racial discrimination revisited

While the European war placed racism 'in a new and harsher light', it was the war with Japan, as Christopher Thorne has argued, that ensured that relations between whites and non-whites, and not anti-Semitism alone, 'became the object of greatly increased attention and passion'.[22] Japan presented its wartime mission as one which would finally liberate Asia

---

[17] McKean, *Equality and Discrimination*, p.34; Marilyn Lake, 'From Self-Determination via Protection to Equality via Non-Discrimination: Defining Women's Rights at the League of Nations and the United Nations', in Patricia Grimshaw, Katie Holmes and Marilyn Lake (eds.) *Women's Rights and Human Rights: International Historical Perspectives* (Basingstoke, Palgrave, 2001) pp.263–4.

[18] *American Journal of International Law* vol.35 (1941) p.663.

[19] Cited by Johannes Morsink, *The Universal Declaration of Human Rights: Origins, Drafting and Intent* (Philadelphia, Pennsylvania University Press, 1999) pp.37–8.

[20] P. G. Lauren, *Power and Prejudice: The Politics and Diplomacy of Racial Discrimination* (Boulder, Westview, 1988) p.136.

[21] *Ibid.* pp.136–7.

[22] C. Thorne, 'Racial Aspects of the Far Eastern War of 1941–1945', *Proceedings of the British Academy* vol.LXVI (1980), p.377.

from the grip of the white men. Allied propaganda answered in kind with crude racial stereotypes of inferior fighters and unworthy enemies. Thorne pointed out that the war in the Pacific was in many respects 'a racial war' and that what often troubled those in power in Washington and London was 'the threat to Western white prestige'.[23] But it was also true that some in the West remembered with shame Japan's failed attempt to have racial discrimination recognised in the Covenant of the League of Nations and knew that European behaviour in Asia and Africa was often arrogant and offensive.

In 1942, a distinguished American novelist, Pearl Buck, urged her readers to recognise the cogency of the Japanese point of view. The white man in the Far East had 'too often behaved without wisdom or justice'. No-one who had seen incidents of casual brutality 'or heard the common contemptuous talk of the white man in any coloured country' could forget the 'fearful bitter hatred in the coloured face and the blaze in the dark eyes'.[24] In Britain the Under-Secretary for Foreign Affairs, R. E. B. Butler, consulted his officials in 1941, about a statement promising a 'relaxation of racial discrimination in the Far East'. He thought it was 'impossible for discrimination to be allowed to exist in the world as it stands today' and suggested there should be some statement 'making it clear the white races and the dark races are not unequal'.[25] A high official in the Dutch colonial service declared that in wartime propaganda the most important message was that, with the peace, there would be an 'abolition of all racial discrimination'.[26]

White prestige collapses in the 'Far East'

The spectacular Japanese victories of 1941–2 had an even greater global impact than their defeat of Russia early in the century. In February 1942, a leading American commentator, Walter Lippman (formerly an adviser to Woodrow Wilson), declared that it was time to put away the 'white man's burden' and for Americans to purge themselves of the taint of an 'obsolete and obviously unworkable white man's imperialism'.[27] Pearl Buck thought that a world based on 'former principles of Empire and imperial behaviour is now impossible'.[28] The deep patience 'of coloured

---

[23] C. Thorne, *Allies of a Kind: The United States, Britain and the War Against Japan, 1941–1945* (London, Hamish Hamilton, 1978) p.7.

[24] Cited by W. White, *A Rising Wind* (New York, Doubleday, 1945).

[25] Foreign Office (FO) 371/27889, UK National Archives.

[26] Thorne, 'Racial Aspects of the Far Eastern War', p.360.

[27] Cited by W. R. Louis, *British Strategy in the Far East, 1919–1939* (Oxford, Clarendon Press, 1971) p.138.

[28] P. S. Buck, *American Unity and Asia* (New York, John Day, 1942) pp.17, 25.

people is at an end', she declared. In London, Duff Cooper warned his Cabinet colleagues in 1942 that the West was now faced by vast populations of industrious, intelligent and brave Asians who were 'unwilling to acknowledge the superiority of Europeans or their right to special privileges in Asia'.[29]

As European power collapsed in East and South-east Asia, so too did the prestige of white men. The American State Department believed that the fall of Singapore would 'lower immeasurably . . . the prestige of the white race'. An Australian diplomat, Frederic Eggleston, who as a younger man had accompanied W. M. Hughes to Versailles, sent a cable back to Australia from Chungking in May 1942, warning that the British Empire had depended on prestige which had been 'completely shattered'.[30] An American diplomat and one-time Under-Secretary for State, Sumner Wells, similarly observed in 1944 that:

the thesis of white supremacy could only exist so long as the white race actually proved to be supreme. The nature of the defeats suffered by the Western nations in 1942 dealt the final blow to any concept of white supremacy which still remained.[31]

It was a view with which later commentators agreed. War historian Michael Howard observed that the 'charisma' on which British rule rested in Asia had been destroyed forever.[32] Thorne argued that the Japanese victories of 1941–2 meant that the position of the white man in Asia – American as well as European – 'could never be the same again'.[33]

A rising wind of protest

On 25 April 1945, delegates from fifty countries and representatives of over forty non-government organisations gathered at the San Francisco Opera House for the opening of a Conference to create a new international organisation. It might have been Versailles all over again. There was immense relief that peace had returned to Europe and was impending in Asia; there was, as in 1919, the euphoria that grew from the sense of sharing in a unique moment when the world could be re-made. As the Conference opened, the delegates were faced with the proposals which had been drafted by the four great powers – now defined as the United States, the Soviet Union, Great Britain and China – at Dumbarton Oakes

[29] Cited by Thorne, 'Racial Aspects of the Far Eastern War', p.361.
[30] *Ibid.* p.345.   [31] Cited by White, *A Rising Wind*, p.149.
[32] Cited by Louis, *British Strategy in the Far East*, p.135.
[33] Thorne, *Allies of a Kind*, p.12.

near Washington, late in 1944. Their emphasis was on the rights and obligations of states and the requirements for international security. But it was generally known that China had unsuccessfully proposed to incorporate a reference to the racial equality of nations in the founding document of the United Nations – that the principle of 'equality of all states and all races' – should be upheld.[34] And there was a keen awareness of the fate of the Japanese proposal in 1919.

The leader of the Chinese delegation at San Francisco was Dr Wellington Koo, who had also represented China at Versailles. The American State Department conducted a study into the circumstances of Japan's failure in 1919 and sent the resulting file on to the British Foreign Office.[35] The by then elderly activist W. E. B. DuBois, representing the National Association for the Advancement of Coloured People, feared that history would be repeated.[36] His colleague and fellow delegate, Walter White, wrote of a 'rising wind' of protest against white domination. The trend of 'such awakening and revolution' was clearly seen in China's demand at Dumbarton Oakes that the allied nations 'unequivocally declare themselves for complete racial equality'.[37]

Once the Conference was under way it was obvious just how strong the pressure was from many of the American non-governmental organisations (NGOs) to address the question of racial inequality, and they were joined by the representatives of many Latin American countries and from India, the Philippines and Haiti. The Uruguayan delegation stated that it was essential to establish that justice was the purpose of the organisation in addition to the maintenance of peace and security. There needed to be a guarantee of respect of essential human rights 'without distinction as to race, sex, faith and social status' and a formal declaration of the rights of man.[38] The Indian representative, Rama Swami Mudaliar, 'speaking as an Asiatic', referred to the fundamental human rights of all beings the world over which were 'incapable of segregation or of isolation'. There was, he said, neither 'border nor breed nor colour nor creed on which those rights can be separated as between beings and beings'.[39] An Afro-American historian, John Hope Franklin, reported that when the delegates spoke in this manner there was a feeling in his

[34] Lauren, *Power and Prejudice*, p.148.
[35] Japan and the Issue of Racial Equality at Paris, 1919; FO 371/35949.
[36] W. E. B. DuBois, *Color and Democracy: Colonies and Peace* (New York, Harcourt Brace, 1945) p.7.
[37] White, *A Rising Wind*, p.148.
[38] Statement of Uruguayan Delegation, 15 June 1945, *Documents on the United Nations Conference on International Organization* vol.1 (San Francisco, 1945) pp.22–3.
[39] Cited by Lauren, *Power and Prejudice*, p.151.

community that they 'voiced the yearnings of under-privileged people everywhere'.[40]

The Canadian jurist, John Humphrey, who was to become the first head of the Human Rights Commission, believed that the agitation from within and outside the Conference in favour of human rights had 'no parallel in the history of international relations'.[41] Responding to the concerted pressure, the great powers amended their Dumbarton Oakes proposals to include the objective of promoting and encouraging respect for fundamental freedoms for all, 'without distinction as to race, language, religion or sex'.[42] This became Article One of the Charter and similar wording was used in several other places. There was no agreement as to what the freedoms were or how they could be asserted against states protected by the Charter from outside interference in matters of domestic jurisdiction.

The determination of a range of groups to promote human rights did not abate after the San Francisco Conference and found further expression at the first session of the United Nations in New York, in November 1946. There the Egyptian delegation proposed a motion:

That it is in the higher interest of humanity to put an immediate end to religious and so-called racial persecution and discrimination, and calls on the governments and responsible authorities to conform both with the letter and to the spirit of the Charter of the United Nations, and to take the most prompt and energetic steps to that end.[43]

There was a unanimous General Assembly vote in favour of the motion.

India challenges South Africa

But there were deep divisions in the Assembly on the question of race notwithstanding the positive vote. They were dramatised in a confrontation between two of the most notable figures at the meeting, the elderly Field Marshall J. C. Smuts of South Africa and Y. L. Pandit, representing the Indian provisional government. In a debate pursued in both the General Assembly and in meetings of the Political and Legal Joint Committee, two worlds, two ideologies and two generations came into collision. The

[40] J. H. Franklin, *From Slavery to Freedom: a History of Negro Americans* (New York, Knopf, 1947) p.583.
[41] John P. Humphrey, *Human Rights and the United Nations: A Great Adventure* (Epping, Bowker, 1984) p.13.
[42] *Documents on the United Nations Conference* vol.1, p.2.
[43] Cited by S. R. Castro, El Salvador, *Journal of the General Assembly* (New York, 1946–7, 2nd Part, p.355.

focal point for dissension was the treatment of Indians in Natal, an issue unresolved after fifty years of repression, dissent and intermittent conflict.

During the late 1930s and early 1940s, whites in Durban had become deeply concerned about the expanding property holdings of an increasingly prosperous Indian community, now 85 per cent native born. 'The Europeans', Smuts observed, had 'become panicky for their future in Natal'.[44] The government responded in April 1943, with the so-called Pegging Act, which temporarily banned Indian purchases of property in hitherto white areas. This was followed up with the Asiatic Land Tenure and Indian Representation Bill which gave Indians token and indirect political representation, but maintained controls on property purchases. An increasingly radical Natal Indian Congress engaged in a campaign of passive resistance leading to mass arrests and violent riots by whites.[45] The Indian government recalled their High Commissioner, applied a boycott to South African goods, and later wrote to the Secretary General of the United Nations seeking a debate on the question.

Smuts humiliated

It was a humiliating situation for the seventy-four-year-old Smuts, then at the height of his power and prestige. He was Prime Minister and Commander in Chief of the South African forces and confidante of and adviser to the world leaders involved at the highest level of allied strategic thinking. Having been one of the architects of the League of Nations, he drafted the preamble to the Charter of the United Nations to give it wider popular approval. He vehemently defended South Africa's right to pursue its own domestic policies free from outside interference, pointing to the principles of state sovereignty guaranteed in the Charter. But his erstwhile ability to keep separate his roles of liberal internationalist on the one hand, and architect of segregation on the other, failed in the new world of post-Second World War politics.

The African-American newspapers 'took delight' in his predicament, explaining to their readers that he had devoted the whole of his life to entrench a 'Nazi-like domination' over non-white South Africans.[46] Smuts noted that the world was 'reeling between two poles of White and Colour'.[47] Writing of his experience at the United Nations in November 1946, he recorded his dismay at the changes occurring around him:

---

[44] W. K. Hancock, *Smuts and the Shift of World Power* (London, School of Oriental and African Studies, 1964) p.465.
[45] S. K. Chatterjee, *Indians in South Africa* (Calcutta, Marawari Association, 1944) pp.18, 27, 44.
[46] Franklin, *From Slavery to Freedom*, pp.583–5.   [47] Hancock, *Smuts*, vol.2, pp.11, 14.

Colour queers my poor pitch everywhere. But South Africans cannot understand. Colour bars are to them part of the divine order of things. But I sometimes wonder what our position in years to come will be when the whole world will be against us.[48]

Reflecting on the shifting balance of world politics evident in South Africa's defeat in the General Assembly, historian Hugh Tinker observed that the transforming change was that white racism could no longer shelter 'in its own particular environment'. It was now exposed 'under the world spotlight'.[49]

Mrs Pandit was a formidable opponent. She was the forty-five-year-old sister of Jawahalal Nehru, an aristocrat by birth, an activist by inclination. A follower of M. K. Gandhi, she had been imprisoned by the British in 1932–3, 1940 and 1942–3. She pointed out that both Smuts and his government were inescapably committed to honour the obligations of both the spirit and letter of the Charter and then turned to attack the abiding South African premise that the presence of Indians in the country was a threat to Western civilisation. The logic of this position was that the defence of the West required segregation 'as part of the world social system'. The ghetto would have to be legalised 'as part of the world's stable organisation'. We must remember, she declared

that in the present case the minds of millions of people in India and other parts of Asia and Africa have been moved to intense indignation at all forms of racial discrimination which stand focused on the problems of South Africa. This is a test case. Shall we fail that test?

It was an issue, she insisted, the discussion of which would make or mar the loyalty and confidence which the common people of the world had placed in the fledgling United Nations.[50]

India received the required two-thirds majority in the General Assembly for the motion calling on South Africa to report back on measures taken to reform the system of segregation. Support came from three main blocks – the Soviet Union and its satellites, Latin American republics and the still small number of Afro–Asian member states – China, Haiti, Liberia, Egypt and Abyssinia. One of Pandit's most forceful supporters was General Carlos Romulo, of the newly independent Philippines, who argued that the victory over fascism could not be considered complete until the concept of racial supremacy had been eliminated from both the

[48] *Ibid.*, p.473.
[49] Hugh Tinker, *Race, Conflict and the International Order: From Empire to United Nations* (London, Macmillan, 1977) p.12.
[50] *Journal of the General Assembly*, 1st Session, New York, 2nd Part, Report of the Joint 1st and 6th Committees (30 November 1946) pp.357–9.

minds of men and their mutual relationships.[51] Echoing the sentiments of the Indian delegation, Wellington Koo observed that the question of racial discrimination deeply affected 'the honour of a whole continent, the pride of half of the human family, the dignity of man himself'.[52]

The twisted contradiction

DuBois watched the confrontation between Smuts and Pandit with great interest. He had met the Indian leader during the international conference in San Francisco. His biographer, David Levering Lewis, observed that she 'captivated' both DuBois and his colleague, Walter White. DuBois wrote enthusiastically to his son, describing a dinner with Pandit and the actress Helen Hays at the most fashionable restaurant in the city, surrounded by diplomats and columnists from around the world.[53] DuBois had observed Smuts from a distance for many years. He puzzled at the contradiction in his behaviour – the foremost exponent of 'the suppression of the Negro' calling for a preamble to the United Nations Charter, which recognised human rights. Nothing, he wrote, so vividly illustrated 'the twisted contradiction of thought in the minds of white men'.[54]

The tension reached far beyond Smuts and South Africa. The Western powers had rallied the world to war with declarations about democracy, equality and human rights. But they all found calls for racial equality troubling. While there was a growing awareness during the war years of the importance of the race question, what stood out in retrospect, as Thorne has noted, was the degree to which ambivalence and ambiguity continued to mark attitudes in the West concerning the capacities of non-white peoples and the future of the white man in Asia.[55] Western support for South Africa was cast in terms of the legality of its domestic jurisdiction. Support was partly due to economic investments, but there was also the 'tacit, implicit acceptance of the right of white people to rule'.[56] Canada, the United States, New Zealand and Australia were all sensitive to international criticism of their policies towards their surviving Indigenous populations. Britain was a strong supporter of human rights in theory, but did not want them applied throughout the Empire. Australia and New Zealand stood beside South Africa and the emphasis on the importance of

[51] *Ibid*. p.362.   [52] *Ibid*. (28 November 1946) p.32.
[53] David Levering Lewis, *W. E. B. DuBois: The Fight for Equality and the American Century 1919–1963* (New York, Henry Holt, 2000) pp.508, 11.
[54] W. E. B. DuBois, *The World and Africa* (New York, International Publishers, [1946] 1975) p.43.
[55] Thorne, 'Racial Aspects', p.362.   [56] Tinker, *Race, Conflict*, p.132.

protecting domestic jurisdiction, fearing, as they had in 1919, that international pressure would force them to accept non-European migration.[57] At the same time, American politicians were acutely aware of the depth of the South's commitment to segregation. DuBois appeared before the Senate Foreign Relations Committee to urge their support of the Charter with its support for the rights of 'Latins and Slavs, and the yellow, brown, and black peoples of America, Asia and Africa'.[58]

The universal declaration

But Western equivocation could not slow the momentum for a full declaration of human rights. Those who negotiated and signed the United Nations Charter, according to P. G. Lauren, opened 'a veritable flood gate to new possibilities of expanding international human rights as never before in the history of the world'.[59] Demands made at the meeting of the General Assembly in 1946, for a formal statement of human rights, were momentarily deflected, but the Human Rights Commission was established with the brief to draft the relevant document.

After innumerable meetings, widespread consultation and insistent haggling over detail, the Universal Declaration of Human Rights was presented to the General Assembly at its meeting in Paris, on 10 December 1948, and was passed by a vote of forty-eight in favour with eight abstentions. It contained thirty articles representing a compendium of political, social and cultural rights. At the time no state, regardless of location, system of government, level of development or culture, could meet its standard of achievement.[60] Many of them fell far short in 1948 and have done so ever since. But as the preamble made clear, the Declaration set a common standard of aspiration 'for all peoples and all nations'. The goal was that 'every individual and every organ of society' should strive by teaching and education to promote respect for the enunciated rights and freedoms, and by progressive measures 'secure their universal and effective recognition and observance' among the member states and among the peoples of territories under their jurisdiction.[61]

[57] S. Brawley, *The White Peril: Foreign Relations and Asian Immigration to Australasia and North America 1919–78* (Sydney, University of New South Wales Press, 1995) pp.205–25.
[58] Lewis, *W. E. B. DuBois*, p.510.
[59] P. G. Lauren, *The Evolution of International Human Rights* (Philadelphia, University of Pennsylvania, 2003) p.199.
[60] Lauren, *The Evolution*, p.232.
[61] *Human Rights: A Compilation of International Instruments* vol.1 (Geneva, United Nations, 1994) p.2.

It was the universal application of the Declaration which was a radical departure from previous human rights documents. Article One declared without equivocation or reservation that 'all human beings' were born 'free and equal in dignity and rights'. Article Two dealt with the critical question of entitlement:

Everyone is entitled to all the rights and freedoms set forth in this Declaration without distinction of any kind, such as race, colour, sex, language, religion, political or other opinion, national or social origin, property, birth or other status

Furthermore, the Article continued, no distinction would be made on the basis of the political, jurisdictional or international status of the country or territory to which a person belonged, whether it be independent, non-self governing or under any other limitation of sovereignty.[62]

The meaning was clear. The first sentence challenged the ubiquitous practice of citing racial difference as justification for the denial of rights. The second declared that the full panoply of human rights applied to those many millions of people, still dependent subjects of the great Empires, regardless of the opinion and policy of statesmen in London, Paris, Durban, Sydney, Washington, The Hague or Brussels.

Race had been toppled from its eminence. The shock waves from its fall reverberated around the world. But race was not the only concept under siege. Much of the discrimination within the Western countries and their Empires was premised on the idea of differential development, of peoples being more or less advanced or backward or being more able to exercise the restraint and discipline considered necessary for successful self-government. Such arguments had been commonly promoted in white men's countries, where it was characteristically argued that discrimination had nothing to do with race or colour, as such, but with capacity for self-government.

Smuts had asserted that Africans needed paternal oversight and separate institutions because they were members of a child race. Governments in Australia, Canada and the United States argued that their Indigenous peoples were backward, in need of care and supervision. The Australian Aborigines, in particular, were referred to as a stone-age race, a uniquely primitive people unable to participate in a modern democracy. None of these arguments, sincerely held in many cases, could any longer be presented to the world as cogent reasons for discrimination and denial of human rights, which were now declared to be the birthright 'of all peoples and all nations'.

---

[62] *Ibid.*

A momentous occasion

The continuing shift in world politics put added pressure on crumbling Empires and increasingly defensive white men's countries. Within one generation, ninety ex-colonial states joined the United Nations. By 1961, African and Asian countries had gained a majority in the General Assembly. Though varying widely in culture, traditions and government, they shared a history of imperial domination and the concomitant, inescapable presumption of white superiority. Their principal focus was on furthering the process of de-colonisation and scrutinising the internal policies of the United States, Canada, Australia and New Zealand. Reflecting on her international experience with the new nations, Eleanor Roosevelt observed that there was an intense feeling among Asians and Africans that:

we, because our skins are white, necessarily look down upon all peoples whose skins are yellow or black or brown. This thought is never out of their minds.

She experienced the weight of history for which the Western nations 'were now being called to account'.[63]

With their majority in the General Assembly, the Afro–Asian countries pushed for further elaboration of their crusade against white racism. In 1963, a Declaration on the Elimination of all forms of Racial Discrimination was accepted in the General Assembly with eighty nine votes in favour, and seventeen abstentions. The delegate for the Philippines, Moreno Salcedo, thought it 'a momentous occasion'. For the first time, the equality of man 'regardless of race and colour' had been unanimously proclaimed.[64] The Declaration, he thought, had shattered the myth that whites were superior to non-whites.

The successful passage of the Declaration through the General Assembly prepared the way for the drafting of the International Convention on the Elimination of All Forms of Racial Discrimination and its formal adoption in 1965. Taking as its starting point the principles of equality and non-discrimination enunciated in the Charter and the Universal Declaration, the convention expressed the conviction that the existence of racial barriers was 'repugnant to the ideals of any human society'. The preamble asserted that any doctrine of superiority based on racial differentiation was:

scientifically false, morally condemnable, socially unjust and dangerous, and that there [was] no justification for racial discrimination, in theory or in practice, anywhere.[65]

---

[63] Lauren, *Power and Prejudice*, pp.226–7.   [64] *Ibid.* p.229.   [65] *Human Rights*, pp.66–7.

Race thinking assailed

As the political currents turned rapidly away from the Western imperial powers, the intellectual structure underpinning racial thinking also
underwent complete transformation. White superiority had been profoundly challenged by Japanese military victories on at least two occasions, decades apart. But the belief in racial hierarchy remained. The
Japanese were as committed to it as any Western peoples, thinking of
themselves as a distinctive nation, equal to Europeans and superior to
other Asians. But their campaign for racial equality at Versailles was both
an inspiration to non-Europeans and a direct challenge to white racial
ideology and concomitant policies. Even more subversive were attacks
on the concept of race itself, which came under increasing pressure from
anthropologists, geneticists, sociologists and historians from the 1930s.

The collapse of faith in race thinking can be illustrated by the career
of a prominent American sociologist and proselytiser for the white man,
E. A. Ross, as outlined in his autobiography of 1936. As a young man
at Stanford University, he had taken part in the Californian agitation
against the Japanese and had written essays opposing immigration from
Eastern Europe – 'beaten members of beaten breeds' – he had called
them.[66] The originator of the term 'race suicide', Ross had published his
bestselling *Foundations of Sociology* in 1905. In a section on the 'Causes
of Race Superiority' he declared that supremacy could not be preserved
without 'pride of blood and an uncompromising attitude towards the
lower races'.[67] But a generation later, he wrote that he had 'shed all his
colour prejudices'. He explained that from a career of study and travel,
he had gained insight and sympathy, until his heart 'overleapt barriers
of race'. 'Far behind me in a ditch', he confessed, 'lies the Nordic myth
which had some fascination for me forty years ago'.[68]

The rise of Hitler and the application of Nazi racial and eugenic policies had created consternation in intellectual circles in western Europe
and North America in the 1930s. A joint meeting of the Anthropology
and Zoology Sections of the British Association for the Advancement of
Science, in 1936, called to discuss the concept of race heard from a distinguished geneticist, H. J. Fleure, who declared that pure races didn't
exist and that it was better not to use the term race at all.[69] Similar views

---

[66] E. A. Ross, *Seventy Years Of It: An Autobiography* (New York, Appleton-Century, 1936)
pp.276–7.
[67] E. A. Ross, *The Foundations of Sociology* (New York, Macmillan, 1905) p.379.
[68] Ross, *Seventy Years Of It*, p.276.
[69] *Report of the British Association for the Advancement of Science* (London and Blackpool,
British Association, 1936) p.459.

were expressed by the leading anthropologist Ashley Montagu at the 1941 meeting of the American Association of Physical Anthropologists, when he declared that the accepted view of race was artificial and it did not agree with the facts. It led to the perpetuation of error and was essentially meaningless. 'Being so weighed down with false meaning', he said, 'it were better that the term were dropped altogether'. It was a dramatic moment. Montagu explained that he had always taken the idea of race for granted and he thought that all his colleagues had done likewise. Indeed, the idea was 'one of *the* most fundamental concepts' with which anthropologists had habitually worked 'and which they had all been intellectually brought up on'. He charged that anthropologists had taken a very crude eighteenth-century notion, offered originally as no more than an arbitrary convenience, to erect a 'tremendous terminology and methodology' with which he, too, had 'deceived himself'.[70]

The post-war assault by the General Assembly on discrimination was paralleled by a concerted attack on racial ideas, co-ordinated by UNESCO, which brought together a group of eminent sociologists and anthropologists who, in 1950, issued a *Statement on Race*. It opened with the declaration that scientists had reached general agreement in recognizing that mankind was one and that all people belonged to the same species. Because there was little connection between cultural traits and biological characteristics, 'it would be better when speaking of human races to drop the term "race" altogether and speak of ethnic groups'. Race, then, was not so much a biological phenomenon as a social myth, which had 'created an enormous amount of damage, taking a heavy toll in human lives causing intolerable suffering'.[71]

A second document, *Statement on the Nature of Race and Race Difference*, compiled by biologists and geneticists, was issued by UNESCO in June 1951. The *rapporteur*, Columbia University zoologist L. C. Dunn, declared that the group had unanimously concluded that there were 'no scientific grounds whatsoever for the belief that there were pure races or a hierarchy of superior and inferior human groups'.[72] Both statements were widely publicised. In a front page story, the *New York Times* announced: 'No Scientific Basis for Race Bias Found by World Panel of Experts'.[73] On the same day, *The Times* in London declared to the world that leading scientists had concluded that race was 'a social myth'.[74]

[70] Ashley Montagu, *Race, Science and Humanity* (Princeton, Van Nostrand, 1963) pp.1–2, 8.
[71] Leo Kuper (ed.) *Race, Science and Society* (Paris, Unesco Press; London, Allen and Unwin, 1975) pp.343–7.
[72] *Ibid.* pp.348–53.   [73] *New York Times*, 18 July 1950.
[74] *The Times*, 18 July 1950.

White men in retreat

White men's countries felt increasing pressure from the 1940s onwards to repeal the array of discriminatory legislation and particularly their immigration restriction laws, which had been built up over the past one hundred years. Internationally, they were attacked by the Soviet Union and its satellites and the Afro–Asian block of new nation-states. China assumed the role previously played by Japan in demanding an end to racial discrimination. The government of Chiang Kai-shek was able to exert the authority previously lacking from Chinese diplomacy and it utilised the relentless Japanese war-time propaganda about white assumptions of racial superiority. Individual nation-states began to bow to the pressure. In 1947, the *chargé d'affaires* of the Republic of China asked the Australian government to clarify its conditions of entry for Chinese, a request that led to the establishment of a new Commonwealth Immigration Advisory Council that same year.

The intellectual and political case for racial exclusion was progressively harder to maintain and in all the countries domestic lobbyists added to international pressure seeking to break down barriers to non-European migration. Australia had pioneered the vision of a white men's country and was one of the most reluctant to change, as the title of Gwenda Tavan's study of the process, *The Long Slow Death of White Australia*, indicates. Frederick Eggleston in Chungking, like other Australian diplomats in Asia, found himself under constant attack and continually urged Canberra to consider reform. In 1954, the High Commissioner to India, Walter Crocker, wrote to the Department of External Affairs about the need for immediate change: 'At the present time nothing costs us so much goodwill as our immigration policy... The extent and depth of resentment can hardly be exaggerated.'[75] In the same year, the Indian High Commissioner to Australia publicly attacked the White Australia Policy, claiming it was driving 400 million Indians and Pakistanis into the arms of communism.[76]

But at home it was considered 'un-Australian' to question the White Australia Policy.[77] Responding to calls for amendment the federal Attorney General, J. T. Beasley, paid tribute to his forebears:

We inherited the White Australia Policy from our fathers and grandfathers... It is our responsibility to see that it is handed down by the great grandchildren of our great grandchildren.[78]

---

[75] Gwenda Tavan, *The Long Slow Death of White Australia* (Melbourne, Scribe, 2005) p.86.
[76] *Ibid.*   [77] Brawley, *The White Peril*, p.193.   [78] *Ibid.*

It was a key part of Australia's heritage. In 1950, the now eighty-six-year-old W. M. Hughes published a book of reminiscences in which he retold the story of what he still saw as his heroic victory, when he helped defeat the Japanese race equality clause at Versailles. Had it not been stifled at its birth, the elderly politician declared, 'it would have meant the end of Australia as we know it'.[79] Some academic authorities still agreed. At a meeting of the Australian Institute of Political Science Summer School in 1954, A. G. Price asserted that 'the White Australia policy must remain inviolate'.[80]

The United States Congress made the first breach in the dykes of exclusion, when it repealed the sixty-year-old Chinese Exclusion Act in 1943 and allowed for a small annual quota of Chinese immigrants. Indians and Filipinos were granted the same rights in 1946. Canada repealed its 1923 immigration legislation in 1947, allowing for the entry of wives and children of resident Chinese. In 1944, New Zealand abolished the poll tax and tonnage restrictions targetting Chinese, which had been in place since the 1880s. In Australia, the conservative government of R. G. Menzies introduced a variety of administrative reforms that enabled the number of Asian immigrants to slowly increase, partly through educational schemes such as the popular Colombo Plan, introduced in 1950, and the admission of Asian spouses and 'specially distinguished' or 'highly qualified' applicants who could most easily assimilate. For the first time resident Asians were able to become naturalised and in 1958 the infamous dictation test was finally abolished. Further administrative reforms were gradually put in place, but the government chose not to publicise them for fear of a public backlash.

The major steps away from discrimination in all countries took place in the 1960s and 1970s. The United States and Canada adopted non-discriminatory legislation in 1965 and 1967, and in 1973, the recently elected Australian Labor government announced that it had 'buried' the White Australia policy and was inaugurating a shift to the policy of 'multiculturalism'. Two years later, the Australian parliament ratified the Convention on the Elimination of All Forms of Racial Discrimination and passed the Racial Discrimination Act.[81]

While the United States, Canada, Australia and New Zealand moved with varying degrees of reluctance and at different speeds away from policies of white exclusion and discrimination, South Africa took the opposite

---

[79] W. M. Hughes, *Policies and Potentates* (Sydney, Angus and Robertson, 1950) p.244.
[80] Tavan, *The Long Slow Death*, p.80.
[81] Mark Lopez, *The Origins of Multiculturalism in Australian Politics 1945–1975* (Melbourne, Melbourne University Press, 2000) pp.220–3; Tavan, *The Long Slow Death*, pp. 198–212.

course. After his defeat in the General Assembly, J. C. Smuts approached Pandit and with courtly paternalism took her hand in both of his saying: 'My child you have gained a hollow victory. This vote will put me out of power in our next election and you will have gained nothing'.[82] His comment was prophetic. At the elections of May 1948, the Nationalists, led by Dr D. F. Malan, swept to power with a minority of votes, but a majority of seats under an electoral system favouring rural electorates. Smuts was defeated in his own East Transvaal electorate that he had represented for so many years. Race was, as ever, at the centre of the contest, the Nationals campaigning under the banner of Apartheid, a more complete and thorough version of the segregation favoured by all major parties for the past generation. During the campaign Malan insisted that only his party could safeguard the future of the white race and wondered whether, in the future, it would:

be able to, but also want to maintain its rule, its purity and its civilisation, or will it float along until it vanishes without honour in the black sea of South Africa's non-European population.[83]

The Nationalist government moved rapidly to purge the public service, the army, police, the judiciary and the non-elected Senate and to appoint Afrikaaners with approved views on race. They introduced laws to complete the machinery of segregation. The Mixed Marriage Act of 1949 banned marriage between whites and non-Europeans, while the Immorality Act of 1950 made any form of sexual relations across the colour line illegal.

However, even in South Africa the ruling binary divide between white and not-white gave way to a recognition of a multitude of racial groupings. In 1950, the Population Registration Act required everyone in South Africa to carry an identity card, which defined their race as African, White, Asian or Coloured. The Group Areas Act allowed any district to be nominated for the use only of one race, while the Illegal Squatters Act of 1951 gave the government power to remove Africans from any chosen area. The Pass laws made it mandatory for Africans and Indians to carry passes at all times. The Suppression of Communism Act in 1950 allowed the government to proceed against anyone who sought to bring about any political, industrial, social or economic change 'by the promotion of disturbance or disorder'.[84]

During the southern winter of 1950, as the Nationalists perfected the machinery of Apartheid, Smuts lay dying on his farm, 'Doornkloof', on

---

[82] Cited by F. Welsh, *A History of South Africa* (second edition, London, Harper Collins, 2000), p.423.
[83] Hancock, *Smuts*, vol.2, p.500.   [84] Welsh, *A History of South Africa*, p.445.

the high velt, north of Johannesburg. The new regime was the work of his long-time political opponents, who had captured the Africaaner electorate. But, enemies notwithstanding, the Nationalists were completing the life work of Smuts, Botha and Hertzog, the three Boer generals who had led South Africa for thirty eight years. Apartheid was the logical extension and intensification of policies and beliefs long in place – the insistence on rule by whites (now including women), separate development, the rejection of racial mixture, the fear of being swamped by a sea of colour.

There was pathos in Smuts' lament in 1946 that the world was reeling between two poles of white and colour. It was, after all, the prescription he had advocated for his homeland – 'a clearly marked line you can follow'. After the Second World War, he found himself trapped and vulnerable on the wrong side of the line, discovering that colour queered his pitch everywhere. By 1948, segregation had been stripped of its progessive gloss, which Smuts had maintained by adding varnish during the inter-war years. It was left to the Nationalists to dramatise to a hostile world the violence and repression long latent in South African politics.

Smuts had built his career as a prophet of racial segregation. He had always been a pragmatic politician, able to stay in touch with the fears and hopes of the white electorate, but political necessity was only part of the story. He did not change his basic views about race despite experience of the world that was so much wider than that of most of his supporters. The Afrikaaner in Smuts always overshadowed the cosmopolitan statesman. And yet his sharp intelligence told him that South Africa was veering into painful isolation, or as his old antagonist, M. K. Gandhi, observed in 1946, he was taking the 'white men of South Africa down the precipice'.[85]

The UNESCO statement on race was released as he lay dying. We cannot know if he read it. By denying the reality of race, by declaring it to be a social myth, the statement undermined the core of his political legacy, the rationale at the heart of a forty-year political career. He had been admonished and warned about his policies by his most able and admired interlocutors. J. X. Merriman saw clearly that rigid segregation held little prospect of a permanent solution, that it was building on a volcano 'the suppressed force' of which would one day 'burst forth in a destroying flood'. His Cambridge mentor, H. J. Wolstenholme, had urged Smuts to understand that it would be wise statesmanship to concede in time and with good grace 'what was sure to be won by struggle'. In 1946, Gandhi lamented that the South African Union of 1910 had not seen

[85] M. K. Gandhi, 'Press Statement', 20 March 1946, in Gandhi, *Collected Works*, vol.LXXXIII, p.285.

the union of all the races in South Africa. 'What a noble tradition', he wrote, 'such a union would have been for the world'.[86] It took fifty years before the 'Rainbow Nation' set out to pursue that vision handicapped and tormented as it was by the legacy of Apartheid.

Smuts was probably the most distinguished of the leaders of white men's countries, the only one who gained sustained international and intellectual recognition. DuBois, who would die in exile in Ghana in 1963, thought Smuts the greatest protagonist of the white race, a man he both 'detested and respected'.[87] DuBois' rival, Marcus Garvey, noted that Smuts stood 'not only for a white South Africa, but a white world'.[88]

South Africa stood out to the end. When the other white men's countries changed direction, albeit reluctantly, and moved with the shifting currents of world opinion, South Africa felt a sense of betrayal. By the 1960s, erstwhile friends and allies had joined the massed choir of condemnation. The country was ostracised, left in isolation trying to maintain policies and principles which had inspired white men in many countries from late in the nineteenth century as they strove to hold back what they believed was a rising tide of colour. They had shared Charles Pearson's apprehension that the lower races were increasing on the higher, but not his stoical acceptance of changes he believed were historically inevitable. Such acquiesence was foreign to the ebullient white men of the New World. Noting changing world forces from the peculiar vantage point offered by Australia, Pearson was convinced that China must become the dominant world power and that South Africa must eventually be governed by Africans. These developments took longer to eventuate than he might have expected. It was exactly one hundred years between Pearson's death in 1894 and the South African elections of 1994, which saw Nelson Mandela and the African National Congress sweep into power and dismantle the last bastion of white supremacy.

---

[86] M. K. Gandhi, 'Memo for the Viceroy', 8 March 1946, in *Ibid.* p.231.
[87] Lewis, W. *E. B. DuBois*, p.112.   [88] *Ibid.* p.70.

Index

357

For EU product safety concerns, contact us at Calle de José Abascal, 56–1°,
28003 Madrid, Spain or eugpsr@cambridge.org.

www.ingramcontent.com/pod-product-compliance
Ingram Content Group UK Ltd.
Pitfield, Milton Keynes, MK11 3LW, UK
UKHW020807190625
459647UK00032B/2270